WILEY **PLUS**
www.wiley**plus**.com

accessible, affordable,
active learning

WileyPLUS is an innovative, research-based, online environment for effective teaching and learning.

WileyPLUS...

...motivates students with confidence-boosting feedback and proof of progress, 24/7.

...supports instructors with reliable resources that reinforce course goals inside and outside of the classroom.

Includes Interactive Textbook & Resources

WileyPLUS... **Learn More.**

www.wiley**plus**.com

www.wileyplus.com

ALL THE HELP, RESOURCES, AND PERSONAL SUPPORT YOU AND YOUR STUDENTS NEED!

www.wileyplus.com/resources

2-Minute Tutorials and all of the resources you & your students need to get started.

Student support from an experienced student user.

Collaborate with your colleagues, find a mentor, attend virtual and live events, and view resources.
www.WhereFacultyConnect.com

Pre-loaded, ready-to-use assignments and presentations. Created by subject matter experts.

Technical Support 24/7 FAQs, online chat, and phone support.
www.wileyplus.com/support

Your *WileyPLUS* Account Manager. Personal training and implementation support.

SIMHA R. MAGAL | **JEFFREY WORD**

Grand Valley State University

SAP AG
Manchester Business School

INTEGRATED BUSINESS PROCESSES
with ERP SYSTEMS

WILEY

JOHN WILEY & SONS, INC.

Vice President & Executive Publisher	Don Fowley
Acquisitions Editor	Beth Lang Golub
Production Manager	Dorothy Sinclair
Senior Production Editor	Anna Melhorn
Marketing Manager	Christopher Ruel
Creative Director	Harry Nolan
Senior Designer	Wendy Lai
Editorial Assistant	Elizabeth Mills
Executive Media Editor	Thomas Kulesa
Cover Photo	©Imre Forgo/iStockphoto

This book was set in 10/12pt Times Ten by MPS Limited, a Macmillan Company, Chennai, India and printed and bound by RRD/Jefferson City. The cover was printed by RRD/Jefferson City.

Founded in 1807, John Wiley & Sons, Inc. has been a valued source of knowledge and understanding for more than 200 years, helping people around the world meet their needs and fulfill their aspirations. Our company is built on a foundation of principles that include responsibility to the communities we serve and where we live and work. In 2008, we launched a Corporate Citizenship Initiative, a global effort to address the environmental, social, economic, and ethical challenges we face in our business. Among the issues we are addressing are carbon impact, paper specifications and procurement, ethical conduct within our business and among our vendors, and community and charitable support. For more information, please visit our website: www.wiley.com/go/citizenship.

Evaluation copies are provided to qualified academics and professionals for review purposes only, for use in their courses during the next academic year. These copies are licensed and may not be sold or transferred to a third party. Upon completion of the review period, please return the evaluation copy to Wiley. Return instructions and a free of charge return shipping label are available at www.wiley.com/go/returnlabel. Outside of the United States, please contact your local representative.

Printed in the United States of America

10 9 8 7 6 5 4 3 2 1

To **Kajal**, **Anushka**, and **Vandana**
—SRM

To **Chelsi**, **Benton**, **Davis** and **Maggie**
—JBW

Contents

*Additional Chapters available on WileyPlus

Preface

As more and more businesses around the world adopt enterprise systems, it becomes increasingly important for students to develop a more process-centric perspective that reflects the realities of the modern business environment in which they will work. Because business operations and enterprise systems are so tightly integrated, we have designed *Integrated Business Processes with ERP Systems* to reflect the ways in which real-world business processes are managed and executed in the world's leading enterprise resource planning (ERP) system, SAP® ERP. Students, regardless of their functional discipline, will be able to apply the real-world concepts discussed in this text immediately upon entering the workforce and will be better prepared to succeed in their careers.

Integrated Business Processes with ERP Systems covers the key processes supported by modern ERP systems. This textbook is designed for use as both a reference guide and a conceptual resource for students taking ERP-focused courses at schools that are members of SAP University Alliances program (http://uac.sap.com). It examines in depth the core concepts applicable to all ERP environments, and it explains how those concepts can be utilized to execute business processes in SAP systems.

● KEY FEATURES

INTEGRATED PROCESS APPROACH

Integrated Business Processes with ERP Systems approaches ERP topics using an integrated process perspective of the firm. Each process is discussed within the context of its execution across functional areas in the company, with special emphasis on the role of data in managing the coordination between activities and groups. Students will gain a deep appreciation for the role of enterprise systems in efficiently managing processes from multiple functional perspectives.

ACTIVE LEARNING

Consistent with the focus on the process perspective of business operations, this book and the accompanying online supplements are designed to actively engage students through multiple learning activities. Students will be required to apply the concepts covered in the text to real-world situations and to the running case study used in their hands-on exercises. In this way, students can experience what the each employee in a process must do, what data they need, and how their actions impact other people in the company.

RUNNING CASE STUDY

Many key examples, demonstrations, and assignments incorporated throughout the book are based on a fictional company, Global Bike, Incorporated (GBI). GBI exists virtually in the GBI ERP system, which is used to provide students with hands-on experience with executing the various processes in SAP ERP. Students will become intimately familiar with GBI's operations and will develop a deep appreciation for the real-world importance of the process concepts in the course.

REAL-WORLD EXAMPLES

In addition to the integrated approach and the GBI case study, *Integrated Business Processes with ERP Systems* includes multiple scenarios from companies in diverse industries that demonstrate how businesses actually utilize ERP capabilities. Real-world experiences associated with enterprise systems—both positive and negative—are integrated throughout the chapters to illustrate the key concepts.

GLOBAL APPROACH

The textbook content, GBI running case study, and real-world examples have all been designed from a global perspective. Differences between U.S. and European business practices are highlighted within the context of process execution to illustrate the global capabilities of ERP systems. In addition, the real-world stories are based on familiar global companies.

● SAP® ERP SOFTWARE

This textbook and its associated demos and exercises were prepared using the most current version of the software, at the time of printing: SAP ERP 6.0, Enhancement Pack 4. The key concepts contained in this textbook are unlikely to change in any significant way. Nevertheless, as SAP continues to innovate and update the core SAP ERP solution, it may become necessary to adjust classroom content in minor ways to better reflect the capabilities of the latest version of the software. Please speak with your SAP University Alliances contact to obtain additional information on utilizing SAP ERP software in your classroom.

● PEDAGOGICAL STRUCTURE

Consistent with this textbook's focus on the integration of business processes with ERP systems, we have divided the book into two key areas. The first area, which consists of Chapters 1–3, focuses on the integrated nature of business processes and the enterprise systems that businesses use to manage them. Chapters 1–2 introduce the foundational concepts, which are subsequently developed in the process chapters in the remainder of the book. Chapter 3 examines the basic concepts in financial and management accounting, which are integrated into the subsequent chapters.

The second part of the book contains the process chapters, which are structured based on a standard template that is comprised of two main parts.

The first part of each chapter discusses the organizational and master data associated with the process, and the second part examines each step of the process in detail. Each chapter concludes with a discussion of the reporting capabilities needed to manage the process efficiently.

Links to online demonstrations and additional online learning materials are embedded throughout each chapter to reinforce and expand on the most important concepts.

WileyPLUS is a research-based, online environment for effective teaching and learning. WileyPLUS is an integral part of the learning experience for this textbook. For this reason we have made it available to students 24/7 from anywhere they connect to the Internet. WileyPLUS contains a wealth of supplemental learning materials designed to enhance students' understanding of the concepts introduced in the course. Plus, instructors can use these materials to customize the course to meet their particular objectives. Students will complete and submit their hands-on assignments and quizzes through the WileyPLUS environment. In addition, the authors have taken full advantage of the rich multimedia learning environment in WileyPLUS to provide demonstrations of each process step discussed in the text. We have also embedded videos of real-world examples that highlight the key concepts in each chapter.

WileyPLUS can complement the printed textbook. Alternatively, students can purchase the full textbook and additional materials digitally through WileyPLUS.

Hands-on Exercises Hands-on assignments are provided to students online. Students will access the assignments via WileyPLUS and complete them in a live SAP system (GBI 2.0). They will then submit the exercises digitally to the instructor for easy grading.

Demonstrations: Recorded demonstrations of each key process activity in every chapter are available on WileyPLUS for both instructors and students. Instructors can use the demonstrations in class discussions to illustrate key aspects of the content. Students can also access the demonstrations on WileyPLUS either while they are reading the chapters, to enhance their comprehension of the material, or when they are completing the hands-on exercises, to refresh their memory of the activity.

INSTRUCTOR'S SUPPLEMENTS

This text is supported by many valuable tools to help instructors prepare and deliver engaging lectures and robust testing for conceptual understanding. Instructor supplements are accessible via WileyPLUS and via the Instructor's Companion Site at www.wiley.com/college/magal. Supplements include the following:

Instructor's Manual: The Instructor's Manual is the distillation of more than a decade of classroom experience in teaching an integrated process approach to ERP systems. It contains in–depth pedagogical materials designed to help instructors prepare their courses and deliver an engaging, multi-modal learning experience.

Classroom Presentation Slides: Each chapter includes detailed classroom presentation slides with key concepts, lecture notes, textbook graphics, and discussion questions.

Test Bank: A detailed test bank for each chapter is provided on the Instructor's Companion Site. Each chapter contains multiple-choice, fill-in-the-blank, and true/false questions with multiple levels of difficulty for each question type.

● FEEDBACK

The authors and publisher invite students and instructors to ask questions, provide comments, and communicate directly with the textbook team on the following Web site: www.extrabandwidth.com/forum

Acknowledgments

"Innovation is a team sport." Tom Kelley, IDEO

Integrated Business Processes with ERP Systems is the final product of thousands of hours of work, including invaluable contributions from a diverse group of people located around the world. The authors wish to acknowledge the following individuals for their assistance in preparing and reviewing the book.

The authors are extremely grateful for the collaboration and technical efforts of Stefan Weidner and his team at the SAP University Competency Center at the Otto-von-Guericke-Universität Magdeburg to bring the GBI 2.0 system to life.

Faculty and students in the ERP program in the Seidman College of Business at Grand Valley State University (http://www.gvsu.edu/business/erp/) were also instrumental in developing the GBI system. In particular, we would like to acknowledge the contributions of the following Seidman students: James Anderson, Philipp Claus, Kevin Coolman, Jacob DeLuca, Morgan Hickman, Corey Holstege, Michael Martin, Steve Merritt, John Morrissey, Brandon Stickel, Alice Yamada, and Sandell Wall. We also appreciate the technical assistance provided by Chris Gillespie. Particularly helpful was Prof. David Cannon, who patiently clarified numerous concepts in accounting.

We are very grateful for the efforts of Robert Weiss, our development editor, who tirelessly reviewed and edited our work and provided invaluable guidance in improving it. We also wish to thank the "super" reviewers and reviewers for their efforts to ensure that this book achieved the high standards we set for it.

"SUPER" REVIEWERS:

- Anthony Pittarese, East Tennessee State University
- Jane Fedorowicz, Bentley University
- Paul Hawking, Victoria University
- Rod Sager, Grand Valley State University
- Robert Szymanski, University of Central Florida

REVIEWERS:

- Donna Everett, Morehead State University
- William Mackinnon, Clarkson University
- Earl McKinney, Bowling Green State University
- Jeff Mullins, University of Arkansas
- Al Pilcher, Algonquin University
- Pamela Schmidt, University of Arkansas
- Felicitas Ju Huang Seah, National University of Singapore
- Venkataramanan Shankararaman, Singapore Management University
- Catherine Usoff, Bentley College
- Bindiganavale Vijayaraman, University of Akron
- William Wagner, Villanova University
- Tom Wilder, California State University, Chico

A very special thanks to Lou Thompson at the University of Texas-Dallas, who helped to create the instructor's manual and supplements, and to Ross Hightower from Texas A&M, who assisted us greatly with the Material Planning chapter.

Finally, we wish to recognize the efforts of Beth Lang Golub, Mike Berlin, Elizabeth Mills, and their colleagues at Wiley for keeping us moving and getting this book completed.

Writing a book can be stressful at times, especially for the authors' families. Their patience and encouragement throughout this long and arduous process have been invaluable. They have our deepest gratitude and appreciation.

We are very grateful to Don Bulmer and Bob Lobue for their executive support for this book at SAP, with an extra special thanks to Charla Pachucki from SAP Education for ensuring that we stayed true to the SAP material.

The authors and publisher gratefully acknowledge SAP's kind permission to use its trademarks in this publication.

Author Biographies

Simha R. Magal, Ph.D., is professor of management (MIS) and director, ERP initiative, in the Seidman College of Business at Grand Valley State University. He received his doctorate from the University of Georgia. His primary research interests include e-business and enterprise systems. Dr. Magal's articles have appeared in such publications as *MIS Quarterly, Journal of MIS*, and *Information and Management*, among others, and he has served on the editorial boards of several journals. He also served as co-chair of the inaugural conference of the Midwest Association for Information Systems (MWAIS) in 2006 and as president of MWAIS during 2008–2009.

Dr. Magal has taught courses related to business processes and enterprise systems that utilize SAP for more than a decade. He is an SAP-certified associate consultant and a TERP10 academy instructor.

Jeffrey Word, Ph.D., is vice president of product strategy at SAP AG. He is responsible for defining SAP's future product strategy and for fostering product innovation within SAP. Dr. Word has worked for several Global 1000 companies in the high-tech industry for nearly 20 years, specializing in business consulting and IT strategy. At SAP, he has driven the evolution of the company's enterprise technology strategy, with a special focus on corporate process improvement initiatives and services-based IT architecture design.

Dr. Word earned his Ph.D. in information systems at Manchester Business School in England. His research focused on event-driven process design and next-generation enterprise architecture. He previously earned an MBA in international management from the Thunderbird School of Global Management and a BA in European studies and Spanish from the University of Oklahoma.

Other books by these authors:

Magal, S. and Word, J. (2009). *Essentials of Business Processes and Information Systems*. John Wiley & Sons. Hoboken, NJ.

Word, J (ed.) (2009). *Business Network Transformation: Strategies to Reconfigure Your Business Relationships for Competitive Advantage*. Jossey-Bass (Wiley), San Francisco, CA.

Woods, D., and Word, J. (2004). *SAP NetWeaver for Dummies*. Wiley Publishing Inc., Indianapolis, IA.

CHAPTER 1

Introduction to Business Processes

LEARNING OBJECTIVES

After completing this chapter you will be able to:

1. Define the functional organizational structure, and explain why this structure creates problems for modern businesses.

2. Describe key business processes in an organization.

3. Identify the main integration points between and among processes.

4. Understand the cross-functional nature of processes and their relationship to organizational areas.

5. Adopt and apply an integrated perspective to business processes.

6. Describe organizational structure of Global Bike Incorporated.

7. Explain how the SAP® ERP system promotes an integrated approach to business processes.

At this point in your university career, you have probably begun taking courses in accounting, operations, MIS, and other disciplines. These courses have introduced you to some basic business concepts and exposed you to different aspects of how a business operates. You have also begun to master several technology tools that will be very useful in your future career, such as office productivity tools to create spreadsheets, presentations, and documents. The course for which you are using this textbook deals with *integrated business processes* and the *enterprise systems* (ES) that support them. The concepts and skills you will gain from this course are different from what you have experienced previously, and you will need to approach this course with a different perspective.

■ THE FUNCTIONAL ORGANIZATIONAL STRUCTURE

To successfully master the concepts in this textbook, you must first begin to think holistically about the operations of a business. The most common organizational structure you are likely to encounter is the **functional structure**. Organizations that utilize a functional structure are divided into functions, or departments, each of which is responsible for a set of closely related activities. For example, the accounting department sends and receives payments, and the warehouse receives and ships materials. Typical functions or departments found in a modern organization include *purchasing, operations, warehouse, sales and marketing, research and development, finance and accounting, human resources*, and *information systems*. The vertical columns in Figure 1-1 identify the key functions in a typical company.

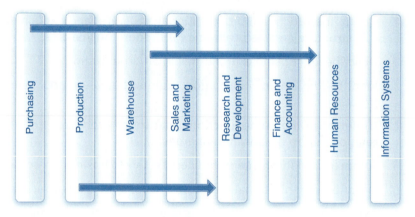

Figure 1-1: The functional structure

Although most companies maintain vertical (or functional) silos to compartmentalize their operational units, the integrated business processes that companies use to perform their work cut across these silos horizontally. Business processes, such as the procurement and fulfillment processes discussed later in the chapter, consist of activities that occur in different, seemingly unrelated functions or departments. In other words, these processes are *cross-functional*, meaning no single group or function is responsible for their execution. Rather, it is a shared responsibility among many functional areas. The cross-functional nature of business processes is also illustrated in Figure 1-1. For a process to be successfully completed, then, the company must rely on each functional group to execute its individual steps in the process in a coordinated way, which, as we shall see, may not be an easy thing to accomplish.

THE SILO EFFECT

The functional structure served organizations well for a number of years because it enabled them to cope with the challenges generated by their rapid growth. Over time, however, this system developed a serious drawback. Put simply, people in the different functional areas came to perform their steps in the process in isolation, without fully understanding which steps happen before and which steps happen next. They essentially complete their part of the process, hand it off to the next person, and then proceed to the next task. By focusing so narrowly on their specific tasks, they lose sight of the "big picture" of the larger process, be it procurement, fulfillment, or any number of other common business processes. This tendency is commonly referred to as the **silo effect** because workers complete their tasks in their functional "silos" without regard to the consequences for the other components in the process.

A key point here is that the silo nature of the functional organizational structure and the cross-functional nature of processes are at odds with each other. That is, while workers focus on their specific function, each business process involves workers located in multiple functional areas. A major challenge facing organizations, then, is to coordinate activities among the different functional areas. Viewing a company from a process perspective requires employees to "think sideways"—in other words, to view the business across functional boundaries and focus on the end-to-end nature of the process and its intended outcomes. Learning to view a process from end to end is essential to understanding how enterprise systems help businesses manage their processes efficiently. Not surprisingly, then, this understanding has become a critical skill that companies have come to demand from their employees.

ENTERPRISE SYSTEMS

As you can see from the previous section, business processes span different parts of an organization. In fact, in today's global economy, the various process steps are increasingly executed by people in multiple locations throughout the world. That is, a company will manufacture its products in different countries, acquire the materials to make these products from different locations, sell the products in many countries, and so on. For example, a bicycle manufacturer may purchase components from Italy, produce bicycles in Germany, and sell those bicycles in the United States. Because the steps in business processes are performed in locations that are geographically dispersed, it is impossible to manage such processes effectively without the use of modern information systems. Systems that support end-to-end processes are called **enterprise systems (ES)**, and they are essential to the efficient and effective execution and management of business process.

Given the significant impact that enterprise systems have on operational efficiency (and, ultimately, profitability), companies have invested enormous sums of capital and effort to plan, implement, and continuously improve enterprise systems over the past 40-plus years. A great deal of research has confirmed that investments in information technology (IT), particularly enterprise systems, have significantly increased the profitability, productivity, and competitiveness of corporations by removing the barriers to sharing information between functional areas and managing processes holistically.[1,2] The key driver for this productivity and efficiency is the ability of modern enterprise systems

---

[1] A. McAfee and E. Brynjolfsson, "Investing in the IT That Makes a Competitive Difference," *Harvard Business Review*, 86, No. 7/8 (2008): 98–107.

[2] E. Brynjolfsson and L. Hitt, "Paradox Lost? Firm-level Evidence on the Returns to Information Systems Spending," *Management Science*, 42, No. 4 (1996): 541–558.

to effectively manage a business process from beginning to end in an integrated, consistent, and highly efficient manner. Further, once a business process is managed by an integrated enterprise system, it can be monitored and improved very easily. As a result, we cannot discuss contemporary business processes without considering the role of enterprise systems. We will discuss enterprise systems in greater depth in Chapter 2.

In this chapter, we begin by identifying the key processes that typically exist in organizations. We then discuss enterprise systems and SAP, the company that produces the most popular enterprise systems globally. We also introduce Global Bike Incorporated, a company that we will use as a case study throughout this textbook to illustrate important concepts in a practical format. We conclude with the plan for the remainder of the book.

■ BUSINESS PROCESSES

Organizations exist either to serve some commercial purpose or to achieve some social objective. They differ depending on the purpose or goal they are trying to achieve, their ownership or management structure, and the regulatory environment in which they operate. Some organizations create and deliver products or services to customers to make a profit. For example, a bicycle manufacturer produces a variety of bicycles and accessories. It then sells these products to numerous retailers who, in turn, sell them to the final consumers. Other companies provide services, such as repairs to the bicycles. Yet others provide the manufacturer with the parts and materials needed to make the bicycles. Achieving the organization's objectives involves many different types of work. For example, the manufacturer must design the bicycles, identify what parts it will use to make them, determine where to obtain these parts, produce the bicycles, identify its customers, and market and sell the bicycles to them. In addition, it must determine how to manage its money, its various facilities such as factories and warehouses, and the many people that it must recruit, employ, train, and retain. This work is completed in numerous processes.

Although organizations exist for many different purposes, vary greatly in size and complexity, and operate in many different industries, they all exhibit similarities in the ways that they operate. Regardless of their type or size, successful organizations and industries use *processes* and *enterprise systems* to complete the work needed to achieve their goals. Processes may vary slightly depending on the unique characteristics of the industry or the structure of the organization, but the basic activities can be recognized by anyone who has developed a process view of business. Likewise, companies may employ different enterprise systems to manage their processes. However, you can apply the principles, concepts, and techniques explained in this textbook to most of the enterprise systems you are likely to work with.

A business process, illustrated in Figure 1-2, is a set of tasks or activities that produce desired outcomes. Every process is triggered by some event, such as receiving a customer order or recognizing the need to increase inventory. The columns in the figure represent different parts, or functional areas, within an organization, such as sales, warehouse, manufacturing, and accounting. Thus, the specific steps in the process are completed in different functional areas. For example, when a retailer (customer) places an order for bicycles, the manufacturer (seller) uses a specific process to ensure that the correct

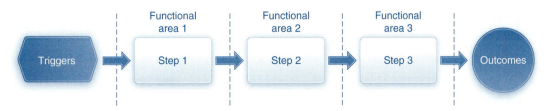

Figure 1-2: A generic business process

products are shipped to the customer in a timely manner and that payment for the order is received. These process steps can include validating the order, preparing the shipment, sending the shipment, issuing an invoice, and recording the receipt of payment. The sales department receives and validates the customer order and passes it on to the warehouse, which prepares and ships the order. The accounting department handles the invoice and payment steps. This is a very simplistic example. However, it highlights the fact that processes consist of interdependent steps that are completed in different parts of the organization.

Because the various process steps are carried out by different functional areas or departments, effective communication and collaboration among the departments is essential to the smooth execution of these processes. Without this interaction, the process cannot be completed efficiently and effectively. For instance, if the customer order is not properly communicated to the warehouse, then it cannot be shipped on time. Similarly, if the order and shipment information is not communicated to the accounting department, billing and payment will not be completed efficiently and accurately. Clearly, completing a process successfully requires more than just communicating information. Close coordination of work among the people involved is also essential. For example, when the salesperson accepts the order, he or she must collaborate with the warehouse to determine when the order can be shipped. Without this collaboration, the salesperson may make promises that the company cannot realistically meet. If this occurs, then, the products will not be available when promised. The salesperson must also collaborate with the accounting department to verify that the customer is credit-worthy. Accepting orders and shipping goods to customers who have not made payments for previous shipments can cause major financial problems for the organization.

An organization uses many processes to achieve its objectives, as illustrated in Figure 1-3. Three processes are directly related to creating and delivering products and services. They are *buy*, *make*, and *sell*. Organizations use specific terms to identify these processes.

- The **procurement process** (*buy*) refers to all of the activities involved in buying or acquiring the materials used by the organization, such as raw materials needed to make products.

- The **production process** (*make*) involves the actual creation of the products within the organization. Whereas the production process is concerned with acquiring needed materials *internally* (by making them), the procurement process is concerned with obtaining needed materials *externally* (by buying them). Each is appropriate for different types of materials, as we will discuss later in the book.

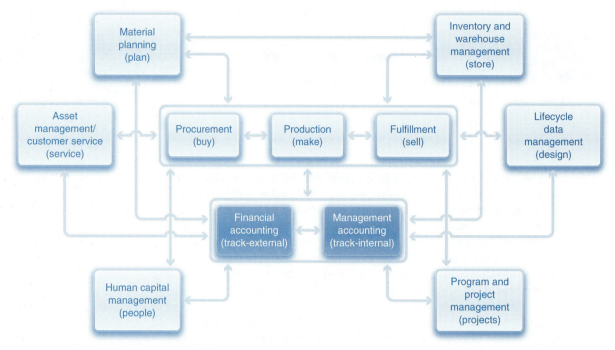

Figure 1-3: Key business processes

- Finally, the fulfillment process (*sell*) consists of all the steps involved in selling and delivering the products to the organization's customers.

Closely related to buying, making, and selling are four processes used to design, *plan, store,* and *service* products. Once again, organizations use specific terms for these processes.

- The lifecycle data management process (*design*) supports the design and development of products from the initial product idea stage through the discontinuation of the product.

- The material planning process (*plan*) uses historical data and sales forecasts to plan which materials will be procured and produced and in what quantities.

- The inventory and warehouse management (IWM) process (*store*) is used to store and track the materials.

- The asset management and customer service processes (*service*) are used to maintain internal assets such as machinery and to deliver after-sales customer service such as repairs.

Going further, two support processes are related to *people* and *projects*.

- Human capital management (HCM) processes (*people*) focus on the people within the organization and include functions such as recruiting, hiring, training, and benefits management.

- **Project management processes** (*projects*) are used to plan and execute large projects such as the construction of a new factory or the production of complex products such as airplanes.

All these processes have an impact on an organization's *finance*. This brings us to the last two processes, which *track* the financial impacts of processes.

- **Financial accounting (FI) processes** (*track–external*) track the financial impacts of process steps with the goal of meeting legal reporting requirements—for example, the Internal Revenue Service (IRS) or the Securities and Exchange Commission (SEC).

- **Management accounting or controlling (CO) processes** (*track–internal*) focus on internal reporting to manage costs and revenues.

Each of these processes can include numerous subprocesses. For example, each of the components of HCM, such as recruiting and benefits management, is itself a process. Similarly, IWM can include complex processes for receiving materials from a vendor and shipping products to a customer. In addition, each process can impact other processes, as illustrated by the arrows between the processes in Figure 1-3. These arrows represent process integration. For example, the procurement of raw materials has an impact on what can be produced and when. Similarly, the production process has an impact on what goods are available to sell and when. Going further, the arrows indicate that all processes have an impact on the organization's financials, a concept we explore throughout this book.

Clearly, then, in addition to understanding the details of how each process works, it is essential to understand the interrelationships among the processes. Significantly, to prevent Figure 1-3 from becoming cluttered with arrows, we did not include every possible integration point. Instead, we highlighted only the key points.

In the next section, we briefly describe the various business processes. We subsequently consider each process at length in separate chapters, where we also examine the linkages among the processes.

PROCUREMENT—BUY

The procurement process includes all of the tasks involved in *acquiring needed materials externally* from a vendor. A very simple example of a procurement process is diagrammed in Figure 1-4. As the figure illustrates, procurement is comprised of five steps that are completed in three different functional areas of the organization.

The process begins when the warehouse recognizes the need to procure materials, perhaps due to low levels of inventory. The warehouse then documents this need in the form of a purchase requisition, which it sends to the purchasing department. In turn, the purchasing department identifies a suitable vendor, creates a purchase order, and sends it to the vendor. The vendor ships the materials, which are received in the warehouse. The vendor then sends an invoice, which is received by the accounting department. Accounting then sends payment to the vendor, thereby completing the process.

Figure 1-4: A procurement process

In the preceding discussion a low inventory of materials was the trigger for the process. This discussion illustrates the link between procurement and the inventory and warehouse management process illustrated in Figure 1-3. Figure 1-3 shows, however, that procurement could be triggered by activity in other processes as well. The figure suggests at least three alternative scenarios.

1. The material planning process could indicate that the company needs to procure materials based on a forecasted demand for products.

2. The asset management or customer service process could trigger the procurement of a part needed to repair a machine or a product previously purchased by a customer.

3. A customer order (fulfillment process) could trigger the need to buy something, such as raw materials or component parts needed to manufacture the product.

PRODUCTION—MAKE

In the preceding discussion the company met the need that triggered the process via external procurement; that is, it purchased the needed materials from a vendor. Other times, however, a company uses the production process to *acquire needed materials internally*. As we explained in the previous paragraph, a customer order can trigger the production process. Alternatively, the material planning process can trigger in-house production. Figure 1-5 illustrates the case where the warehouse notices that its inventory of products is low. Subsequently, it will request production. In turn, the production department will approve the request. The approval authorizes the warehouse to release the materials needed to complete production. Once the production department has completed its task, the warehouse places the finished goods into storage. Note that this last step in the production process, which is concerned with the storage of the finished goods, could trigger IWM processes.

Figure 1-5: A production process

FULFILLMENT—SELL

Fulfillment (Figure 1-6) is concerned with *efficiently processing customer orders*. It is triggered by a customer purchase order that is received by the sales department. Sales then validates the order and creates a sales order. The sales order communicates data related to the order to other parts of the organization, and it tracks the progress of the order. The warehouse prepares and sends the shipment to the customer. Once accounting is notified of the shipment, it creates an invoice and sends it to the customer. The customer then makes a payment, which accounting records.

As this scenario illustrates, fulfillment triggers processes in IWM where the materials are stored. Of course, in many cases the ordered materials are not available in the warehouse. In such cases fulfillment will trigger external procurement and/or production.

Figure 1-6: A fulfillment process

MATERIAL PLANNING—PLAN

The term material encompasses all the products, components, parts, and so on that an organization uses. Businesses use and produce many types of materials. For example, material planning in a bicycle manufacturer would include: (a) *finished goods*, such as bicycles, that are sold to customers; (b) *semifinished goods*, such as wheel assemblies, that are used to make the finished goods; and

(c) *raw materials*, such as the tires, tubes, and wheels that are used to make the wheel assemblies. We examine the major *material types* in greater detail in Chapter 2.

The purpose of material planning is to *match the supply of materials with the demand*. The demand for finished goods is based on external factors such as customer tastes and preferences, economic conditions, and competitors' actions. The demand for the other materials is dependent on the demand for finished goods. Consequently, organizations use different data and processes to plan for different types of materials.

The supply of materials is a function of many internal and external factors. For example, the supply of materials procured externally (e.g., raw materials) depends on availability from vendors as well as the *lead time*, which is the time between placing the order and receiving the shipment. Internally, the supply depends on available production capacity in the factories.

The outcome of material planning is the development of strategic and operational plans that match supply with demand as closely as possible. Excess supply will result in increased inventory costs, which are the expenses associated with storing materials. Insufficient supply will result in a situation called *stock-out* in which the company cannot meet its customers' demands. Both situations can undermine a company's productivity and profits.

Material planning is influenced by the fulfillment process, which provides sales data that companies use to forecast demand for finished goods. It is also influenced by procurement and production, which provide data on lead times and capacities, and by IWM, which provides data on material availability. In turn, material planning will trigger procurement and production processes to ensure that demand is met and IWM processes to ensure that materials are stored until needed.

INVENTORY AND WAREHOUSE MANAGEMENT—STORE

Inventory and warehouse management (IWM) is concerned with the *storage and movement* of materials. For a business to operate efficiently, it is essential that materials be stored so that they can be quickly and easily located when needed. This is especially true for large warehouses where thousands of different materials are stored in large quantities. In addition, companies must be able to move the materials quickly and efficiently to wherever they are needed.

Figure 1-7 depicts four scenarios related to material storage and movement. Quadrant A (top left) shows a request for materials that will be used in the production process. These materials must be located and then issued to the production floor. In Quadrant B, the warehouse receives materials from the production process and then prepares them for storage. This process can include such steps as sorting and determining an appropriate storage location. Finally, the materials are moved into the selected locations. A similar process is used for materials that are received from a vendor via the procurement process (Quadrant C). Finally, when a customer order is processed by the fulfillment process, the warehouse must locate the materials and prepare and send shipments to the customer (Quadrant D).

These examples also clearly illustrate the integration between IWM and procurement, production, and fulfillment. We will discuss integration points with other processes in later chapters.

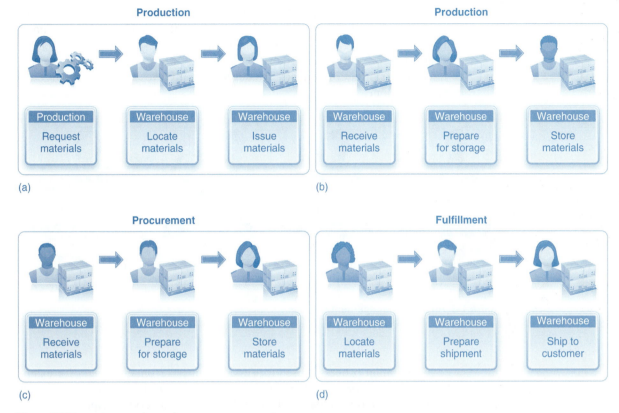

Figure 1-7: Inventory and warehouse management processes

LIFECYCLE DATA MANAGEMENT—DESIGN

A successful organization must constantly improve its products and create new and innovative products that reflect changes in customer tastes and preferences. Lifecycle data management provides a set of tools to *manage product design and improvement* throughout the lifecycle of a product. The product lifecycle begins with idea or concept development; progresses through production, marketing, and service; and concludes when the product is discontinued from the market. It can range from a few months for fad items to many years or even decades for products such as automobiles and bicycles. Products in the latter category typically undergo small but continual improvements over the course of their lifecycle.

Lifecycle data management enables an organization to optimize its product development process, from design to market, while ensuring that it complies with industry, quality, and regulatory standards. At the same time, it provides users—that is, the organization's employees—with access to product data at any point in the product's lifecycle. This capability, in turn, enables the organization to react more quickly to take advantage of market and competitive opportunities.

ASSET MANAGEMENT AND CUSTOMER SERVICE—SERVICE

Asset management is concerned with both the preventive and corrective maintenance of an organization's equipment. *Preventive maintenance* is performed periodically—for example, the routine maintenance of a machine in a factory.

In contrast, *corrective maintenance* is done as needed—for example, repairing a machine when it breaks down. Figure 1-8 illustrates a simplified maintenance process. The trigger is a maintenance request, which can be either preventive or corrective. Production approves the request, and the maintenance is performed. The final stage, settlement, involves an internal charge for the work done.

Figure 1-8: An asset management process

A similar process is used for service requests from customers, for example, to *repair a product* they purchased (Figure 1-9). In such cases, different functional areas may be involved. Sales receives a service request, which it approves and forwards to the department responsible for completing the repairs. Settlement will depend on whether the service is covered by a warranty. If it is, then the organization will absorb the cost of the repair. Otherwise, the organization will send an invoice to the customer and then record payment, similar to the steps in the fulfillment process.

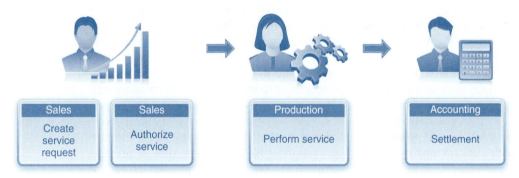

Figure 1-9: A customer service process

HUMAN CAPITAL MANAGEMENT—PEOPLE

Human capital management (HCM) consists of numerous processes related to all aspects of *managing people* in an organization. Examples of HCM processes are *recruitment, hiring, training, compensation and benefits management*, and *payroll administration*. In our brief discussion of processes in this chapter, we focused on tasks and the functional areas where they are completed. Clearly, however, it is the people in the functional areas who actually perform the tasks. Consequently, HCM touches every process in the organization. Moreover, it is not uncommon for people in different functional areas to complete many of the tasks in HCM processes. For example, the trigger for recruitment and hiring is a need for people with the requisite skills to complete process tasks. Consequently, the functional area in need of new employees will be involved in this process.

PROJECT MANAGEMENT—PROJECTS

Most business processes are ongoing or repetitive. For example, the lifecycle data management process spans the life of a product, and the procurement and fulfillment processes are repeated frequently. In contrast, a **project** is temporary in nature and is typically associated with large, complex activities, such as the construction of a factory or an aircraft. As we discussed earlier, project management refers to the processes a company uses to *plan and execute large-scale projects*. It involves the use of tools and techniques for managing complex projects.

Projects can be internal or external depending on the recipient of the final outcome. For internal projects, such as constructing a plant, project management is concerned primarily with costs. This is because the outcome of the project benefits the organization and is not sold to a customer. Because no sales are involved, no revenues are created. In contrast, external projects such as building an aircraft for a customer generate both costs and revenues.

Projects rely on resources and capabilities available in other processes. For example, building an aircraft involves purchasing materials (procurement process), making components from these materials (production), supervising people (HCM), and so on. External projects are also integrated with selling to customers (fulfillment). Figure 1-10 illustrates a simplified project management process. The diagram does not identify the specific functional areas in which the work needed to complete the project is performed because this will vary depending on which other processes are involved.

In the planning phase the scope of the project is defined, and the milestones and deadlines are set. The budgeting phase triggers the accounting processes to calculate and allocate the resources needed to execute the project. The project is not executed until management approves the budget. During

Various functional areas

Figure 1-10: A project management process

the execution phase the needed processes (e.g., procurement and production) are triggered. In addition, accounting processes are used to keep track of costs and revenues and, for external projects, to issue customer invoices. Finally, throughout the life of the project and at the end of the project an accounting process called *settlement* is periodically carried out to assign costs and revenues to the appropriate parties.

FINANCIAL ACCOUNTING—TRACK FOR EXTERNAL REPORTING

Financial accounting is concerned with *tracking the financial impacts of processes* with the primary goal of meeting legal and regulatory reporting requirements. Thus, it is externally focused. Common reports include the income statement or profit and loss (P&L) statement and the balance sheet. The income statement indicates the organization's financial condition within a specified period of time. It identifies revenues, expenses, and net profit (or loss) for the period. In contrast, a balance sheet indicates the financial condition of an organization at a given point in time. It identifies assets, liabilities, and shareholders' equity. All of these reports must comply with prescribed standards, such as the generally accepted accounting principles (GAAP) in the United States and Handelsgesetzbuch (HGB) in Germany. These reports must be submitted to regulatory agencies at prescribed times, such as annually or quarterly. Finally, these reports are country specific. Therefore, an enterprise that operates in multiple countries must track financial data separately for each country, using that country's prescribed standards.

Various steps in the different processes introduced earlier in this chapter have an impact on an organization's financial status. Organizations analyze this impact using four key processes based in financial accounting: general ledger, accounts receivable, accounts payable, and asset accounting. The *general ledger* process records the impacts of various process steps on a company's financial position. The impacts are recorded in a number of *accounts* in the *general ledger* that represent an organization's income, expenses, assets, and liabilities. These accounts are used to store accounting-relevant data from process steps. *Accounts payable* is associated with the procurement process and is used to track money that is owed to vendors. Similarly, *accounts receivable* is used to track money owed by customers. Accounts receivable and accounts payable automate the general ledger entries associated with the procurement and fulfillment processes so that the financial impact of these processes is recorded automatically. Finally, *asset accounting* is concerned with tracking financial data related to assets such as machinery and cars.

MANAGEMENT ACCOUNTING—TRACK FOR INTERNAL REPORTING

Whereas financial accounting is concerned with external reporting that is mandated by laws and regulations, **management accounting**, or **controlling**, is concerned with *tracking costs and revenues* for internal reporting that is intended to help management control costs and revenues and assess the profitability of various products and market segments. Management creates these reports to support its decision making. Unlike financial accounting reports, management accounting reports are produced as needed and can contain any information that management deems necessary.

Among the major costs management accounting tracks are materials costs, labor costs, and overhead costs. Management takes these costs into account when it establishes prices for its products or services. It then combines these data with information concerning revenues to determine the profitability of various products and services in different market segments. Ultimately, management utilizes all of this information to make key strategic decisions that affect the organization's products market mix as well as tactical decisions that influence day-to-day operations.

■ GLOBAL BIKE INCORPORATED (GBI)

Throughout this book, we will use the case of **Global Bike Incorporated (GBI)** to illustrate important concepts, processes, and techniques. GBI is a fictional company, and its operations have been greatly simplified to make its business processes and its SAP ERP system easier for you to work with. Although GBI might seem complex as you progress through the chapters of this textbook, rarely will the business operations of a real-world company be as simple as those found in GBI.

Much the data used in this textbook are based on GBI and represent the many aspects of its fictional suppliers, customers, employees, and materials. In addition, all of the hands-on exercises are intended to be completed in a functioning (live) SAP ERP system that is configured with GBI data. (Enterprise Resource Planning, or ERP, systems integrate a company's various functional and cross-functional business processes. We explain ERP systems in greater detail in Chapter 2.) It is very important that you quickly become familiar with GBI and their business operations in order to master the key concepts in this course and to complete your course assignments.

The following paragraphs provide a brief overview of GBI. However, you must retrieve the detailed GBI Annual Report from the *WileyPLUS* course site (explained later) or the SAP *University Alliances Community (SAP UAC)* at http://uac.sap.com to learn the full story of how GBI came into existence and to familiarize yourself with the specifics of the company's operations. The SAP UAC is a free site for all university students who are enrolled in an SAP course. The registration process is very simple and is free. In addition to the detailed GBI information on the SAP UAC site, you will also gain access to several SAP career services, including certification information and internship and job opportunities. Your instructor can show you where to access the GBI Annual Report on the SAP UAC site once you have registered.

GBI was founded in 2001 following the merger of two bicycle manufacturers, one based in the United Sates and the other in Germany. GBI has three lines of business: deluxe and professional touring bikes, men's and women's off-road bikes, and bike accessories. GBI sells its bikes to a network of specialized dealers throughout the world, and it procures its raw materials from a variety of suppliers globally.

GBI has two manufacturing facilities, one in the United States and one in Germany. It also has three additional warehouses, two in the United States and one in Germany. GBI has more than 100 employees globally. The organization uses SAP ERP to support its processes. Figure 1-11 illustrates GBI's enterprise structure.

Figure 1-11: GBI enterprise structure

● HOW TO USE THIS BOOK

This edition of *Integrated Business Processes with ERP Systems* does not cover all of the processes introduced in this chapter. Chapter 2 is an introduction to enterprise systems, and Chapter 3 discusses financial accounting. Chapters 4-8 address the key logistics processes: procurement, fulfillment, production, warehouse management, and material planning. Finally, a concluding chapter discusses all of these processes from an integrated perspective. In addition, the exercises and demonstrations included in this book are available online via *WileyPLUS*.

CHAPTER STRUCTURE

As the previous paragraph indicates, most chapters will focus on a specific process, such as procurement, financial accounting, and production. Most of these chapters share a common structure. Each chapter begins with a review of the simple presentation of the process introduced earlier in this chapter. The chapter then segues to a detailed discussion of data, key concepts, and process steps. General concepts related to data—*organizational data, master data,* and *transaction data*—will be introduced in Chapter 2. Each subsequent chapter will focus on the specific concepts and data that are relevant to the process discussed in that chapter. Most chapters require you to understand a few fundamental concepts, which are discussed next. Note that many of the concepts related to organizational and master data are relevant to more than one process. In such cases, we do not repeat the discussion of these concepts. Rather, we refer you to previous chapters where they were discussed.

The third main component of each chapter consists of a detailed discussion of the various steps involved in the process. Each process step will be discussed using the following framework:

- Triggers: the event(s) that cause(s) the process step to be initiated

- Tasks: the specific steps needed to complete the process step

- Data: the information associated with each process step

- Outcomes: the specific products or consequences of the process step

The fourth component of each chapter is reporting. This section examines how the data generated during the process steps are converted into meaningful information. It also provides examples of the types of reports that can help managers improve process performance.

Going further, each chapter employs three pedagogical tools—demonstrations, real-world cases, and exercises—to reinforce the material. Demonstrations illustrate either a particular concept or the execution of a process step in the SAP ERP system. These demonstrations are in the form of animations that can be viewed multiple times. Real-world cases are vignettes from actual companies that illustrate a concept or demonstrate how that company executes a process. Exercises to be completed in an SAP system configured with GBI data provide a final reinforcement of the chapter's key concepts.

SAP SOFTWARE

SAP (pronounced by saying each letter individually, like IBM or ABC) is the pioneer in enterprise systems. SAP was the first company to build a packaged enterprise system, which means that it designed a single piece of software that is used by many companies. Prior to that time, software developers had to create customized software for every company, which was prohibitively expensive.

SAP introduced the first integrated, end-to-end enterprise system, called SAP® R/3, in 1992. The "R" in R/3 stands for "real time." Prior to the development of enterprise systems, companies typically employed a number of different systems, each of which supported a single function or department. Thus, there were sales systems, accounting systems, manufacturing systems, and so on. These systems were not integrated, so sharing data between and among them was problematic. As you might expect, this architecture regularly experienced delays in executing business processes because data had to be transferred from one system to the next as the process was being performed.

SAP R/3 was designed to eliminate these inefficiencies by executing an entire process from start to finish and consolidating all of the process data in a *single database*. Consequently, regardless of which individuals were completing a step in the process, all of the data were available to them in real time. In addition, everyone else in the company could see the status of the process in real time as well. In today's age of Twitter and RSS feeds, this development might seem trivial. At the time, however, it was a crucial innovation. SAP R/3 was quickly adopted by one major corporation after another, and it catapulted SAP software onto the "must do" list for nearly every large company. By 2010, SAP had more than 110,000 customers in over 120 countries, including nearly every Fortune 1000 company. In 2008, SAP's market share in the ERP category was equivalent to the market share of the next four largest ERP vendors—combined.[3,4] Today, more than 75% of SAP's customers are small and medium-sized businesses.

---

[3]C. Pang, Y. Dharmasthira, C. Eschinger, and K. Motoyoshi, *Market Share: ERP Software, Worldwide*, 2008, July 2008, Gartner.

[4]A. Pang, *Worldwide ERP Applications 2009–2013 Forecast and 2008 Vendor Shares*, October 2008, IDC.

Enterprises of every size, in every industry, all over the world use SAP software to manage their business operations. Regardless of where you live, nearly every major corporation, government entity, and nonprofit organization you are familiar with runs the same SAP software that you will use in this course.

Before you start to think that this book is a marketing brochure for SAP, you should understand why we have explained SAP's strategic importance in business and have selected SAP ERP as the reference system for this textbook. One of the most lucrative and rewarding careers in the IT industry for nearly 20 years has been that of an SAP consultant.[5] Contrary to what you may have heard, most SAP consultants are *not* programmers. Rather, they are MIS and business majors who have developed a process perspective on business and have become competent in a specific capability of the SAP ERP system. However, even technical programmers who wish to work with SAP must have a deep understanding of how business works in order to program applications that enable business processes to operate more efficiently. In other words, they are people just like you who have mastered the material in this textbook.

Integrated Business Processes with ERP Systems will incorporate a number of demonstrations, examples, and hands-on exercises using SAP ERP. Several other companies offer enterprise systems that have similar capabilities, but it would be very difficult to explain how processes are executed in each of them. We have chosen to include the most prevalent and widely used ERP system that you are likely to encounter in your career. Although some of the concepts in this textbook are specific to SAP ERP, you can easily transfer nearly everything you learn to whichever system is used in the companies where you will work.

When SAP first introduced R/3, almost anybody could claim to be an R/3 expert and thus become a highly paid consultant. Unfortunately, this practice led to quite a few well-publicized project failures. In response, SAP introduced *certifications* for the various modules and technical skills required to be a properly trained consultant. This arrangement enabled consultants who participated in SAP training programs and demonstrated a high degree of skill to distinguish themselves for potential employers. Today, SAP provides more than 100 certification types, classified by solution, focus area, and role. Each certification type specifies three levels of skill: associate, professional, and master. It can take many years and tens of thousands of dollars to progress up to master-level certification. SAP is very proud of the high level of knowledge and skills that are required to earn certification. As you probably suspect by now, the SAP testing process is extremely rigorous. Because an SAP certification is such a highly valued credential, once you have earned one, SAP provides you with a certification number that can be listed on your resume or CV and verified by potential employers—the thousands of consulting companies that implement SAP software and the more than 110,000 (in 2010) companies that run SAP software.

As an added benefit to students enrolled at universities or technical schools that are members of the SAP University Alliances Program, SAP offers special certification academies on campuses around the world where students can earn the same certification as professionals at a reduced cost. This textbook and the additional online materials are based on the content in the

---

[5] J. Sahadi, Hot 6-figure jobs now, 2007 [Online], *CNN/Money.* http://money.cnn.com/galleries/2007/pf/0708/gallery.hot_six_fig_jobs_now/index.html.

SAP course, which results in an official SAP Associate Application Consultant certification and can be used as a supplement to the SAP course materials. Alternatively, students who master the concepts in this textbook and the additional online materials can take the SAP certification exam at one of over 8,000 global testing centers without participating in a certification academy.

Students who pass the exam will receive the same official SAP certification as working professionals who complete an SAP-sponsored training program. Earning this certification is the first step toward a successful and perhaps lucrative career as an SAP application consultant. Speak with your instructor, and consult the certification information on the SAP University Alliances Community and *WileyPLUS* for more details.

WILEYPLUS

WileyPLUS is an important online supplement to this book. It includes four key components: hands-on exercises, SAP ERP system demonstrations, online chapters, and information about preparing for the SAP certification exam.

The hands-on exercises found on the *WileyPLUS* companion site for this textbook will guide you through the execution of the process steps found in each chapter. You will complete these exercises in a live SAP ERP system based on Global Bike, Inc., which you will become very familiar with throughout the chapters. In essence, you will assume the role of the various employees of GBI and complete their tasks in the SAP ERP system, as if you were doing their job. In this way, you will see the processes executed from multiple viewpoints and thus further develop your "process perspective" of the firm. Your instructor will provide you with login information and the SAP interface to complete these exercises in the SAP ERP system. We anticipate that you will encounter some difficulties while completing the exercises. Nearly every student does, so don't become discouraged if this happens to you. Your instructor or lab assistant can provide some help if you are working in an on-campus lab. You can also seek help from fellow students in your class. One of the most valuable sources of assistance is the SAP University Alliances (SAP UAC) discussion forum for this textbook. Go to www.extrabandwidth.com/forum, which will redirect you to the SAP UAC forum, where you can ask questions about the text and the exercises. Students and professors around the world will quickly assist you. If you receive a helpful answer, you can award points to the person who helped you. Not only is this a nice form of recognition, but it helps the community reinforce its focus on mutual support and knowledge sharing.

Throughout each chapter you will see references to demonstrations that will illustrate how a particular concept, task, or data is presented in the SAP system. These demonstrations are meant to enhance your conceptual understanding of the topic by providing you with a visual and physical representation of how the system executes or displays a particular component of the process being discussed. We advise you to follow the demonstrations on the *WileyPLUS* website while reading and reviewing the chapter in the printed textbook. For the online version of the textbook on *WileyPLUS*, the demonstrations are linked directly from the references in the chapter for easy access. Going further, the demonstrations are very similar to the activities required in the exercises. Therefore, it will be helpful to review the demonstrations prior to attempting the exercises so as to familiarize yourself with the navigation, key data, and activities required to complete the process steps.

CHAPTER SUMMARY

This chapter introduced the key concepts related to common business processes in organizations, the typical functional structure that companies employ to manage their operations, and the benefits of adopting a holistic view of integrated business processes and their role in effectively translating corporate strategy into operational efficiency.

Most companies are organized according to functional departments, which group together related activities and assets under specialized management controls. Although this approach enables companies to focus resources on specific activities, it also creates communication difficulties and delays between the highly specialized groups. Business processes cut across the vertical barriers (silos) that characterize the functional structure. For this reason they require cross-functional communication and collaborative execution.

Enterprise systems allow companies to effectively manage business processes across functional areas and institutional boundaries. They perform this task by removing barriers to sharing and accessing information, thereby providing a holistic platform to execute integrated business processes consistently and efficiently. One of the key benefits to managing business processes with an integrated enterprise system is that process data are collected throughout the execution of each step of the process. Managers can then use these data to monitor and improve the organization's processes. Enterprise systems enable companies to achieve operational efficiency through transparency across functional areas, and they provide consistent information for managerial decision making. All business processes have an impact on the organization's financial status, and the real-time impact of process execution can be monitored and analyzed through the use of an integrated enterprise system.

KEY TERMS

Asset management and customer
 service processes

Business process

Controlling

Enterprise systems (ES)

Financial accounting (FI) processes

Fulfillment process

Functional structure

Global Bike Incorporated (GBI)

Human capital management (HCM)
 processes

Inventory and warehouse
 management (IWM) process

Lifecycle data management process

Management accounting or
 controlling (CO) processes

Material

Material planning process

Procurement process

Production process

Project

Project management processes

Silo effect

REVIEW QUESTIONS

1. Describe the functional organizational structure. Why do you think this structure is so widely used?

2. What is the silo effect? Why does it exist? What problems does it create? How can an organization reduce or eliminate the silo effect?

3. What is a business process? Why is adopting a process view of organizations essential to becoming a successful manager?

4. Briefly describe the key business processes included in this chapter in terms of their key steps.

5. Explain the interrelationships among the key processes included in this chapter. Why are these interrelationships important?

Introduction to Enterprise Systems

LEARNING OBJECTIVES

After completing this chapter you will be able to:

1. Discuss the evolution and key business benefits of enterprise systems.

2. Explain the role of enterprise systems in supporting business processes.

3. Differentiate the different categories of data within SAP® ERP.

4. Identify and analyze the major options for reporting.

In Chapter 1 we discussed the key processes executed in organizations. We saw that there is a high degree of integration and interdependence among processes. Even within small organizations it is difficult to execute these processes efficiently using manual techniques. Thus, organizations invariably rely on the use of enterprise systems to ensure that these processes are executed efficiently and effectively. In this chapter we discuss key concepts in enterprise systems, particularly SAP ERP. We begin by expanding on the introduction to enterprise systems and SAP ERP provided in Chapter 1. We follow this discussion with a brief history and evolution of SAP ERP. We then explore the different types of data utilized in SAP ERP. Finally, we conclude the chapter by examining various reporting options enabled by enterprise systems (ES).

ENTERPRISE SYSTEMS

Enterprise systems are one of the most complex and powerful information systems in use today. As we explained in Chapter 1, this book will cover the world's most popular ES—SAP ERP—in great depth. Although you might have studied enterprise systems in a previous course, we provide a quick review of the key concepts to refresh your knowledge and to place these concepts in an appropriate context for the rest of this course. In this section we briefly discuss the architecture of enterprise systems, the SAP® Business Suite, SAP ERP, and the technology platform—SAP® Netweaver—that forms the foundation for these applications.

ARCHITECTURE OF ENTERPRISE SYSTEMS

The architecture of an enterprise system refers to the technical structure of the software, the ways that users interact with the software, and the ways the software is physically managed on computer hardware. Most modern ES have either a three-tier client-server architecture or a service-oriented architecture. There are many different ways to deploy ES in these two architectures. Both models offer distinctive technical and cost benefits, and both models have drawbacks. Nevertheless, the impact of these two models on the management of business processes is largely the same. We examine both types of architecture below.

Client-Server Architecture

Think of a desktop application that you routinely use, such as word processing, spreadsheet, or presentation software. These applications consist of three components, or *layers*: (1) how you interact with the application (using menus, typing, and selecting); (2) what the application allows you to do (create formulas or charts, compose an essay); and (3) where the application stores your work (on your hard drive or flash drive). These layers are the presentation layer, application layer, and data layer, respectively. In the desktop applications mentioned above, all three layers are contained in one system. In contrast, the three-tier client-server architecture separates these layers into three separate systems, as illustrated in Figure 2-1.

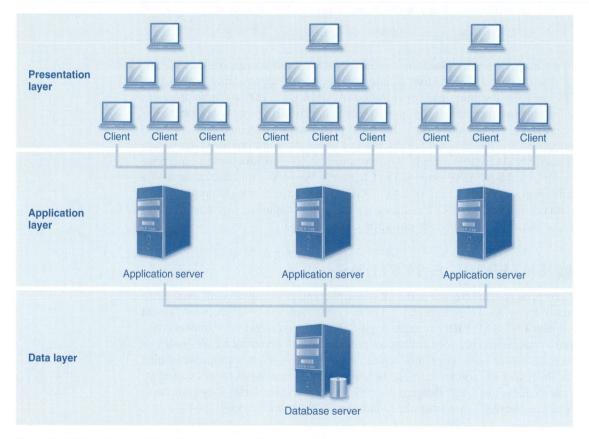

Figure 2-1: Three layers of the client-server architecture

Much of the work you do on the Internet uses a three-tier architecture. Your browser is the presentation layer. Through your browser, you connect to many systems (websites) that provide a variety of capabilities (e-mail, purchasing goods, information sharing). These websites contain the applications that execute the request you send through the browser (via HTTP), and they retrieve and store data in a connected database.

The shift to the three-tier client-server architecture dramatically reduced the costs of acquiring, implementing, and using an ES while significantly increasing the scalability of the systems. *Scalability* refers to the ability of the hardware and software to support a greater number of users easily over time, typically at a decreasing cost per user. These two benefits transformed ES from a capability that only a few large companies could afford into a technology that tens of thousands of companies now utilize.

Service-Oriented Architecture

In the early 2000s, companies began to Web-enable their three-tier applications so that users could access the systems through a Web browser. During these years companies also benefited from new technologies that could help link, or *integrate*, many different client-server systems together in new and valuable ways. These new technologies are collectively labeled **service-oriented architecture**, or SOA. The fundamental concept behind SOA relates to the technical capabilities that allow systems to connect with one another through standardized interfaces called *Web services*. By using Web services, companies could now integrate multiple client-server applications and create enterprise *mash-ups*, or *composite applications*. Composite applications and mash-ups rely on Web services to send and receive data between and among ES in a standardized way, which eliminates a great deal of cost and complexity from integration projects. In addition, they execute newer and more specific processes than are typically found in the standard ES.

Companies such as SAP have invested billions of dollars to service-enable their applications so that these systems can be exposed—that is, their functionality can be made visible to users—and can be connected to a great number of composite applications. By using SOA to integrate and expose the business processes and data inside an ES, companies can now create new composite applications quickly and inexpensively. In essence, SOA enables companies to build composite applications on top of their existing three-tier client-server applications without changing the underlying applications. This capability gives companies an entirely new level of flexibility at an extremely low cost.

ENTERPRISE RESOURCE PLANNING (ERP) SYSTEMS

Enterprise resource planning (ERP) systems are the world's largest and most complex ES. ERP systems focus primarily on *intra-company processes*— that is, the operations that are performed within an organization—and they integrate functional and cross-functional business processes. Typical ERP systems support Operations (Production), Human Resources, Finance & Accounting, Sales & Distribution, and Procurement. As we discussed in Chapter 1, SAP was the first company to create a fully integrated and global ERP system, SAP® R/3, which could manage end-to-end processes for companies that operated in many different countries, with multiple languages and

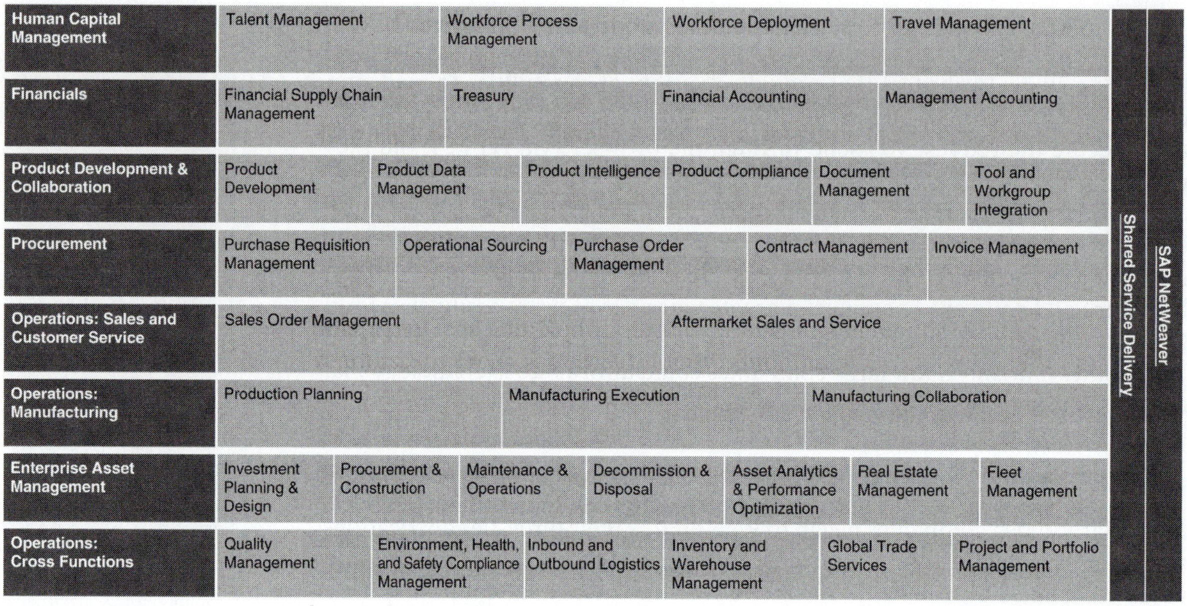

Human Capital Management	Talent Management		Workforce Process Management		Workforce Deployment		Travel Management
Financials	Financial Supply Chain Management		Treasury		Financial Accounting		Management Accounting
Product Development & Collaboration	Product Development	Product Data Management		Product Intelligence	Product Compliance	Document Management	Tool and Workgroup Integration
Procurement	Purchase Requisition Management	Operational Sourcing		Purchase Order Management		Contract Management	Invoice Management
Operations: Sales and Customer Service	Sales Order Management				Aftermarket Sales and Service		
Operations: Manufacturing	Production Planning			Manufacturing Execution		Manufacturing Collaboration	
Enterprise Asset Management	Investment Planning & Design	Procurement & Construction	Maintenance & Operations	Decommission & Disposal	Asset Analytics & Performance Optimization	Real Estate Management	Fleet Management
Operations: Cross Functions	Quality Management	Environment, Health, and Safety Compliance Management	Inbound and Outbound Logistics	Inventory and Warehouse Management		Global Trade Services	Project and Portfolio Management

(Right side vertical bands: Shared Service Delivery | SAP NetWeaver)

Figure 2-2: The SAP ERP solution map. Copyright SAP AG 2011

currencies. Figure 2-2 shows the solution map for the current version of the system developed by SAP, known as SAP ERP.

The solution map identifies the functionality and processes supported by the system. Notice that many of the functional capabilities in the solution map are similar to the business processes that were defined in Chapter 1. In addition, several areas of SAP ERP overlap with functional groups within the company. These overlaps are a result of the tight integration of ERP and the processes that it manages. As companies have adopted more and more ERP capabilities and begun to view their companies from more of a process perspective, the ES world and the functional world have begun to merge. Given the scope and size of the SAP ERP system, we will focus on the core ERP functional modules in this book.

Although companies are moving toward a process view of organizations, and our book takes a process view of business operations, the functional view still persists in many organizations. The capabilities of an ERP system are often described in terms of modules or specific capabilities, and it is still quite common to see or hear SAP ERP referred to in terms of module abbreviations in job advertisements or industry discussions. Figure 2-3 lists the more common

- Production Planning (PP)
- Materials Management (MM)
- Sales and Distribution (SD)
- Plant Maintenance (PM)
- Project Systems (PS)
- Quality Management (QM)
- Financial Accounting (FI)
- Management Accounting / Controlling (CO)
- Human Resources (HR)
- Business Intelligence (BI)

Figure 2-3: SAP ERP modules

modules in SAP ERP and the abbreviations that are typically used for them. For example, a person with expertise in the financial accounting and management accounting modules of SAP ERP is typically called a FICO expert based on the abbreviations of the two modules.

As more companies acquired ERP systems, the next step in the evolution of ES was to connect these systems so they could support *inter-company processes*—that is, processes that take place between and among companies. Examples of inter-company systems are **supply chain management (SCM)** and **supplier relationship management (SRM)** systems, which connect a company's ERP system to those of its suppliers. SCM connects a company to other companies that supply the materials it needs to make its products. Typical SCM systems help companies plan for their production requirements and optimize complex transportation and logistics for materials. SRM systems typically manage the overall relationships with the materials suppliers. SRM systems contain functionality to manage the quotation and contracts processes. These systems act as extensions to the procurement and material planning processes of ERP systems.

On the other side of the manufacturing and sales processes, **customer relationship management (CRM)** systems connect a company's ERP system to those of its customers. CRM systems provide companies with capabilities to manage marketing, sales, and customer service. These systems are an extension of the fulfillment process of ERP systems. **Product lifecycle management (PLM)** systems help companies administer the processes of research, design, and product management. In effect, PLM systems help companies take new product ideas from the virtual drawing board all the way to the manufacturing facility.

The collection of these inter-company systems and the underlying intra-company ERP system is called an **application suite**. Suite vendors, such as SAP and Oracle, provide fairly comprehensive collections of applications that offer an enormous amount of functionality and cover most of the standard business processes.

Figure 2-4 identifies the various capabilities that are part of an application suite and illustrates how they connect to other members of a company's business network. It is important to note that one of the key benefits of utilizing a complete suite of software is that the data and processes are integrated among the systems in the suite. That is, although they are separate systems, they are designed so that they work together in an integrated manner.

Figure 2-4: The ES application suite

The focus of this textbook is on core intra-company processes and ERP systems. Keep in mind, however, that the emergence of inter-company business capabilities is one of the most important developments in the modern business environment. A fundamental understanding of the key business processes and ERP systems is a prerequisite to studying advanced topics such as supply chain management and customer relationship management because those processes are extensions of the core ERP-enabled business processes.

APPLICATION PLATFORMS

Another critical component of ES is application platforms. Much like the role of the operating system for your personal computer, **application platforms** serve as a type of "enterprise operating system" for a company's ES landscape by allowing all of the various systems to communicate seamlessly with one another as well as with systems outside the company. SAP introduced its application platform, SAP NetWeaver, in 2003. SAP NetWeaver is now an integral part of SAP ERP and the SAP Business Suite. It contains the SOA capabilities needed to integrate SAP systems with non-SAP systems. In addition, it provides companies with a toolset to build new composite applications or to plug in independent software vendor (ISV) applications on top of their core ERP and suite applications. Figure 2-5 illustrates how SAP NetWeaver interacts with the SAP Business Suite of applications.

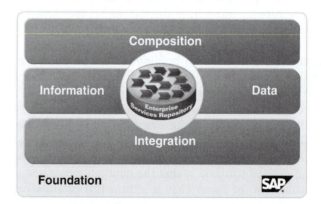

Figure 2-5: SAP NetWeaver. Copyright SAP AG 2011

The SAP Business Suite, which includes SAP ERP, SAP® CRM, SAP® SCM, SAP® PLM, and SAP® SRM, runs on SAP NetWeaver. You can think of the relationship between the SAP Business Suite and SAP NetWeaver in terms of the relationship between Microsoft Office and the Microsoft Windows operating system. The SAP Business Suite consists of the applications that companies use to manage and execute their business processes, just as Microsoft Office contains the applications that you use to accomplish tasks such as creating a presentation, a document, or a spreadsheet. SAP NetWeaver orchestrates the communication among the applications, transporting the master data and technical information needed by the applications at different points in the process. Similarly, Microsoft Windows is an operating system that the Microsoft Office applications use to communicate with one another and to access other capabilities and tools. SAP NetWeaver also contains several technical tools to help companies extend the SAP Business Suite applications, integrate with other non-SAP applications, and build (compose) new applications. In essence, SAP NetWeaver is the "operating system" for a company's entire range of business processes.

■ DATA IN AN ENTERPRISE SYSTEM

As we discussed earlier, a central component of any ERP system is the common database that stores data related to all the processes. Without this function, integrating the various processes would be difficult, if not impossible. Therefore it is essential to understand how data are organized in an ERP system. We address this topic in the following section. We then introduce the different types of data that are stored in an ERP system, and we identify basic data elements that are common to many processes. We will develop these topics and introduce additional data elements in later chapters that discuss specific processes. For the purposes of this chapter we will restrict our discussions to the procurement and fulfillment processes introduced in Chapter 1.

Data in an ERP system are used to represent the physical system in which process steps such as creating a purchase order and receiving goods are carried out. These steps generate data, which represent the outcomes of the steps. There are three types of data in an ERP system: organizational data, master data, and transaction data.

ORGANIZATIONAL DATA

Organizational data are used to represent the structure of an enterprise. Examples of organizational structure are companies, subsidiaries, factories, warehouses, storage areas, and sales regions. The three organizational data elements discussed in this chapter are client, company code, and plant (see Figure 2-6). Note that the terms *organizational data, organizational levels,* and

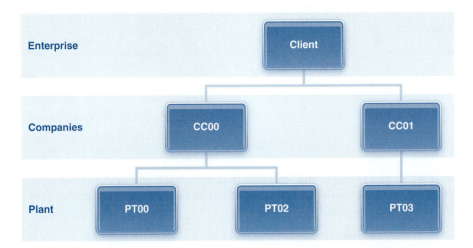

Figure 2-6: Organizational data

organizational elements are often used interchangeably, depending on the context. These data are relevant to many of the processes discussed in Chapter 1. We will introduce additional organizational data as needed in the various process chapters.

Client and Company Code

A client is the highest organizational level in SAP ERP. It represents an enterprise consisting of many companies or subsidiaries. Each company within the enterprise is represented by a company code. Each company code represents a separate legal entity, and it is the central organizational element in financial accounting. That is, financial statements required for legal reporting purposes are maintained at the company code level. A client can have multiple company codes, but a company code must belong to only one client.

Figure 2-7 shows organizational data for GBI. Recall from Chapter 1 that GBI consists of two companies, one in the United States and one in Germany. GBI is represented by a client, and each of the two companies is represented by a company code, US00 and DE00, respectively.

Figure 2-7: GBI organizational data

Plant

A plant is an organizational element that performs multiple functions and is relevant to several processes. It is essentially a facility in which the following functions are performed:

- Products and services are created.

- Materials are stored and used for distribution.

- Production planning is carried out.

- Service or maintenance is performed.

A plant can be a factory, a warehouse, a regional distribution center, a service center, or an office. It can be a part of a building, an entire building, or a collection of buildings. In addition, a single building can house multiple plants. Consider, for example, a company that has several offices in a building. Different services or activities, such as processing customer returns and providing technical support to customers, are performed in these offices. Each of these offices is defined as a separate plant. Just as a client can have multiple company codes, a company code can contain multiple plants. However, a plant can belong to only one company code.

As illustrated in Figure 2-7, GBI operates five plants for the manufacture and storage of bicycles and accessories. Three plants are located in the United States—in Dallas (DL00), San Diego (SD00), and Miami (MI00). The Dallas plant is a manufacturing facility, whereas the other two are distribution centers from which products are shipped to customers. The Dallas plant ships products to customers as well. The other two plants are located in Germany—in Hamburg (HB00) and Heidelberg (HI00). The Heidelberg plant operates as both a manufacturing facility and a distribution center, while the Hamburg plant is exclusively a distribution center.

Business Processes in Practice 2.1: Coca-Cola® Enterprises

Coca-Cola Enterprises provides us with a good example of a company that has several types of plants. Coca-Cola operates factories that produce both raw materials and finished goods. Some factories produce the syrup that forms the basis of the Coca-Cola products you are familiar with. Other factories combine the syrup with carbonated water during the bottling process to make the finished Coca-Cola products. The finished goods, which consist of cases of bottles and cans of Coca-Cola products, are then shipped to regional distribution centers for storage until they are transported to end customers, such as retailers. The syrup factory, the bottling factory, and the distribution center are all considered plants in Coca-Cola's SAP ERP system.

Source: Coca-Cola Company Reports & CCE CIO presentation at SAP Sapphire 2008.

MASTER DATA

Master data represent entities associated with various processes. For example, processes involve buying materials from vendors and selling materials to customers. In this example, customers, vendors, and materials are represented in an ERP system using master data.

The most commonly used master data in an organization is the material master. Materials are used in numerous processes. They are purchased, sold, produced, and planned for. They are used in maintenance and service, and in projects. Consequently, material master data are some of the most complex and extensively utilized data in an ERP system. In contrast, other master data are relevant only to certain processes. For example, vendor master data apply to procurement, and customer master data are utilized in fulfillment. This chapter will focus exclusively on material master data. We will consider other master data in the appropriate process chapters.

Material Master

Although materials are relevant to many processes, each process uses the materials differently. For example, the procurement process buys materials, the production process makes materials, and the fulfillment process sells materials. Each process, therefore, requires data about the material that may or may not be needed by other processes. For example, the procurement process requires data concerning who is responsible for purchasing the material and how much should be ordered. Similarly, the fulfillment process utilizes data concerning product availability and shipping conditions.

It should be evident that because the material master is used in numerous processes, it must include a large amount of data. To manage these data, the material master groups them into different categories or *views*, each of which is relevant to one or more processes. Figure 2-8 illustrates the major views of data in the material master. Basic data, such as *material number*, *description*, and *weight*, are relevant to almost all processes. The other views are relevant only to certain processes. For example, purchasing data are relevant to the procurement process and sales data to the fulfillment process. The data in each of the views will be explained in detail in the appropriate process chapters.

Material Types

Another factor that influences the type of data or view needed is the type of material. Materials are categorized into different **material types** based on the

Figure 2-8: Material master data

way they are used in the firm's operations. Each material type has different characteristics and is used for different purposes and in different ways. The material type determines which business processes are permitted to use the material. This, in turn, determines which types of data must be maintained for the material. Therefore, the data in the material master will vary for different types of materials. Specifically, material type determines, for example, the screens that appear in the material master record, the department or function-specific data that must be maintained, how the material numbers are determined, the appropriate procurement types (in-house or external), and the general ledger accounts that need to be updated. Table 2-1 provides a list of commonly used material types.

Material Type	Description
DIEN	Services
ERSA	Spare parts
FERT	Finished goods
FHMI	Production resources/tools
HALB	Semifinished goods
HAWA	Trading goods
HIBE	Operating supplies
IBAU	Maintenance assembly
KMAT	Configurable material
LEER	Empty containers
NLAG	Nonstock, nonvaluated material
PROD	Product group
ROH	Raw materials
UNBW	Nonvaluated, stocked material
VERP	Customer returnable packaging
WETT	Competitive products

Table 2-1: SAP material types

The four most common material types are raw materials, semifinished goods, finished goods, and trading goods. We describe and discuss these material types below. The terms in parentheses following the names are the SAP ERP abbreviation for that material type. These abbreviations are based on the German term for each type. GBI's product structure (finished goods and trading goods) is presented in Figure 2-9. Table 2-2 lists GBI materials grouped by material type.

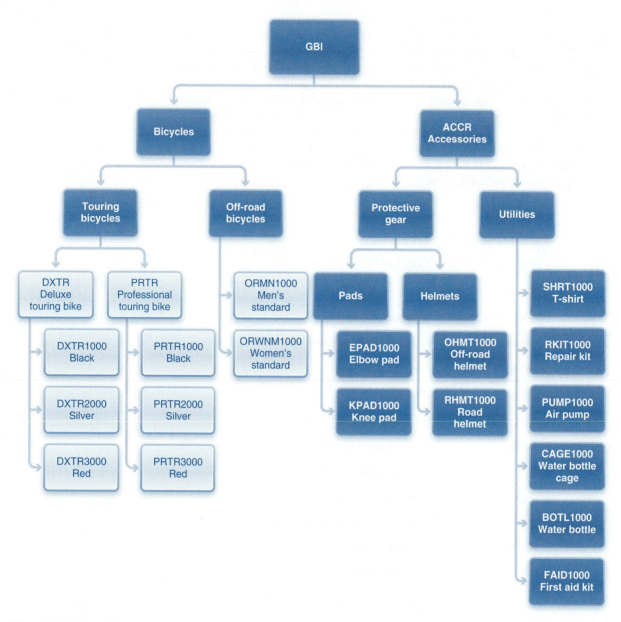

Figure 2-9: GBI product structure

- **Raw materials** (ROH) are purchased from an external source—a vendor—and used in the production process. Typically, raw materials are not sold to end-customers. Consequently, the material master will contain data related to procurement and production but not fulfillment. Examples of raw materials utilized by GBI are frames, wheels, tires, and tubes.

- **Semifinished goods** (HALB) are typically produced in-house from other materials (e.g., raw materials) and are used in the production of a finished good. Consequently, data related to production must be maintained for semifinished goods. Front wheel assemblies are

Raw Materials	Semifinished Goods	Finished Goods	Trading Goods
• Derailleur gear assembly	• Wheel assembly	• Deluxe touring bike (3 colors)	• Elbow ads
• Frame		• Professional touring bike (3 colors)	• Knee pads
• Seat kit		• Men's standard off-road bike	• Off-road helmet
• Handle bar		• Women's standard off-road bike	• Road helmets
• Pedal assembly			• Repair kit
• Chain			• Air pump
• Brake kit			• Water bottle cage
• Warranty document			• First aid kit
• Packaging			• T-shirt
• Tire			
• Tube			
• Wheel			
• Nuts and bolts			

Table 2–2: GBI material list

an example of semifinished goods from GBI. GBI purchases tires, wheels, and tubes and then uses these raw materials to create wheel assemblies.

- **Finished goods** (FERT) are created by the production process from other materials, such as raw materials and semifinished goods. They are generally not purchased. As a result, the material master for finished goods will include data related to production and fulfillment, but not procurement. An example of a finished good from GBI is the deluxe touring bicycle, which is produced from raw materials (e.g., frames) and semifinished goods (e.g., wheel assemblies).

- **Trading goods** (HAWA), like raw materials, are purchased from a vendor. Unlike raw materials, however, trading goods are resold to customers. Significantly, the company does not perform any additional processing of the material prior to reselling it. Therefore, the material master for trading goods will include data related to purchasing and selling but not production. An example of a trading good from GBI is a helmet. GBI simply purchases the helmets from a supplier and resells them to its customers; no other steps are involved.

Material Groups

Related to material type is the concept of a **material group**, which includes materials with similar characteristics. For example, all of the materials used in the production of bicycles, such as tires and tubes—which are raw materials—and wheel assemblies—which are semifinished goods—can be included in one material group called *production*. As another example, all bicycles, which are generally finished goods but can also be trading goods, can be placed into one group called *sales*. Alternatively, bicycles can be grouped based on how they are used, such as *touring* and *off-road*. In the retail industry, material groups represent merchandise categories such as footwear, clothes, and beverages. Materials are grouped so that they can be managed collectively. For example, planning for off-road bicycles is performed for all of the bikes in that material group rather than for individual bikes or brand names.

Organizational Level

A final factor that determines the type of data included in the material master is organizational level. Materials can be defined differently for different organizational levels. For example, the same material can be used in multiple plants, but the ways it is used can vary from one plant to another. If a company exports materials from only one of its plants, for instance, then data related to exporting that material must be included in the material's definition for that plant. These data are not necessary, however, for the other plants. As another example, GBI may choose not to ship bikes to customers from its Dallas plant. Rather, it sends the bikes to its two distribution centers (Miami or San Diego), which then ship them to customers. In this case, sales-related data for the bikes are included in the material master's definition for the Miami and San Diego plants but not for the Dallas plant.

> **Demo 2.1:** Review material types

> **Demo 2.2:** Review material master data

TRANSACTION DATA

Processes are executed in the context of organizational levels, involve master data, and result in transaction data. **Transaction data** reflect the consequences of executing process steps, or *transactions*. Examples of transaction data are dates, quantities, prices, and payment and delivery terms. Thus, transaction data are a combination of organizational data, master data, and situational data—that is, data that are specific to the task being executed, such as who, what, when, and where. The composition of transaction data is illustrated in Figure 2-10.

SAP ERP uses several different types of documents to record transaction data. Some of these documents are created or utilized as the process is being executed; others record data after the process steps are completed. We refer to the first category as **transaction documents**. Examples are purchase orders, packing lists, and invoices. A purchase order communicates the company's order to its vendor. A packing list accompanies the shipment sent by the vendor, and an invoice is a request for payment for materials shipped.

Documents that record data generated after the process steps have been completed include **financial accounting [FI] documents, management**

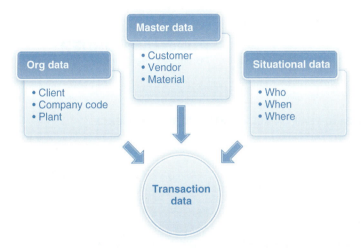

Figure 2-10: Transaction data

accounting or controlling [CO] documents, and material documents. These three documents are "virtual" documents in that they reside in the enterprise system and are printed only occasionally as needed. FI and CO documents record the financial impact of process steps. For example, when a company receives a payment from a customer, there is a financial impact, and an FI document is created. Material documents record materials movements, such as when materials are received from a vendor or shipped to a customer.

Documents typically consist of two sections, a *header* section and a *detail* or *line item* section. Figure 2-11 illustrates the concept of headers and items using an example of a purchase order, which is a type of transaction document. The top part of the document is the header. The three materials included in the purchase order—knee pads, elbow pads, and off-road helmets—are the line items. The header includes data such as purchase order number, date, and payment terms that are relevant to all line items, meaning that these data are relevant to the entire document. In contrast, the data in the line items, such as quantity and price, are specific to each item. A document can include multiple line items, as illustrated in the figure.

Demo 2.3: Review a purchase order

■ REPORTING

As you have probably concluded from the discussions of master data, organizational data, and transaction data, enterprise systems produce and consume massive amounts of data in the day-to-day execution of business processes. In fact, it is not uncommon for companies to have several terabytes (trillions of bytes) of "live" data passing through their ERP systems on a weekly basis. More importantly, after data are no longer needed for process execution, they

Global Bicycle Incorporated

5215 N. O'Conner Blvd.
Dallas, Texas, 75039
Phone: +1.972.555.2000   Fax: +1.972.555.2001

PURCHASE ORDER
Purchase Order Number: 4546

THE PURCHASE ORDER NUMBER MUST APPEAR ON ALL RELATED CORRESPONDENCE, SHIPPING PAPERS, AND INVOICES

TO:
Olympic Protective Gear
2100 Summit Boulevard
Atlanta, GA, 30319

SHIP TO:
GBI San Diego Distribution Center
150 Spear Street
San Diego, 94105
+1.415.555.7700

Header

Purchase Order #	P.O. Date	Delivery Date	Shipped VIA	F.O.B. Point	Payment Terms
4546	July 11, 2009	July 27, 2009	Ground	Destination	Net 30

Quantity	Material #	Material Description	Unit Type	Unit Price	Item Total
100	KPAD1000	Knee Pads	Each	37.50	3,750.00
100	EPAD1000	Elbow Pads	Each	37.50	3,750.00
50	OHMT1000	Off-road Helmets	Each	25.00	1,250.00

Line items

SUBTOTAL	$8,750.00
SALES TAX	Exempt
SHIPPING AND HANDLING	Included
OTHER	N/A
ORDER TOTAL	$8,750.00

Authorized by: _   Date: _ _ _ _ _ _ _ _ _ _
                    Purchasing Manager

Figure 2-11: Purchase order

then become historical data and must be archived securely and made available for many types of data analysis. This process generates many more terabytes of historical data that are stored in complex data repositories called *data warehouses*. With such a massive volume of data to deal with, how can a company extract the meaningful information it needs to make better decisions and operate more efficiently?

At the most basic level, every enterprise system contains transaction and historical data in its main database. Transaction data relate to processes that are currently in use or have been completed recently, within days or weeks.

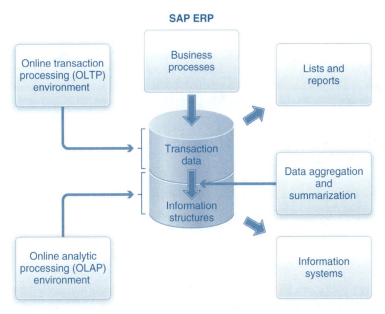

Figure 2-12: Reporting options within SAP ERP

Conversely, historical data are typically comprised of transaction data for processes that have been completed within months or years. **Reporting** is a general term used to describe the ways that users can view and analyze both transaction and historical data to help them make decisions and complete their tasks. Reporting capabilities range from simple lists of information for basic users to analytical tools that can perform powerful statistical analysis and advanced calculations to produce extremely detailed information for specialist users. The data used in the different types of reporting are the same, but the ways in which they are extracted, filtered, and presented differ greatly and involve varying levels of complexity and expertise, depending on how employees plan to use them.

SAP ERP provides two reporting options—simple *lists* of data and documents and *analytics*. Before we examine these options, however, we need to distinguish between the *transactional environment* and the *analytic environment* of SAP ERP (see Figure 2-12). The transactional environment of SAP ERP is an **online transaction processing (OLTP)** system, which, as the name suggests, is designed to capture and store detailed transaction data. The primary function of OLTP is to execute process steps quickly and efficiently; it is optimized for this purpose. OLTP is not used to generate sophisticated reports because it lacks the computing power to parse through and analyze the vast stores of data that most companies accumulate. Consequently, businesses employ OLTP to generate only simple lists and reports.

For detailed data analysis, SAP ERP includes an **online analytic processing (OLAP)** environment in the form of *information systems*. Instead of using detailed transaction data, these systems use information structures to provide analytic capabilities. **Information structures** capture and store specified transaction data in an aggregated and summarized form that enables users to analyze the data as needed. Each information structure in the OLAP environment is defined in terms of three features: characteristics, key figures, and period definition (Figure 2-13). **Characteristics** are the objects for which

Period	Characteristic		Key figures	
Date	**Customer**	**Material**	**Sales quantity**	**Sales amount**
5/12/09	Rocky Mountain Bikes	DXTR1000	23	$64,400
5/19/09	Philly Bikes	PRTR1000	45	$135,000
5/23/09	Beantown Bikes	DXTR1000	34	$95,200
....	....	....	....	....

Figure 2-13: Components of information structures

data are collected. These objects are typically organizational data such as plant and sales organization and master data such as materials, vendors, and customers. An information structure can include up to nine characteristics. **Key figures** are performance measures, such as quantities and counts that are associated with the characteristics. Examples are number of orders, quantities ordered, order value, and invoice amounts. Thus, instead of recording the details of orders and invoices, key figures maintain only statistical summaries, such as the total number of orders placed by a customer. This is one level of aggregation of transaction data, and it is *qualitative* in nature because the selection of key figures is subjective. Finally, data are collected or aggregated for specified time periods, such as daily, weekly, and monthly, which are specified in the **period definition**. In contrast to key figures, period definition represents a *quantitative* aggregation of data. Thus, information structures can be defined as aggregated and summarized forms of transaction data that are periodically updated.

In sum, then, the OLTP environment provides reporting in the form of lists, and the OLAP environment provides reporting in the form of analytics via information systems. Going further, lists fall into two categories—work lists and online lists.

WORK LISTS

Work lists identify tasks that are scheduled to be completed in a process. In the fulfillment process, for example, once customer orders are recorded in the system by the salespersons, warehouse personnel can retrieve a list of orders that are ready for picking. Picking is the first step in preparing a shipment. It involves retrieving, or picking, materials from storage. A *picking due list* (Figure 2-14) identifies all customer orders that must be prepared for delivery so that they can be shipped in a timely manner. The user selects the appropriate data, such as shipping location, due dates, and other relevant parameters (see inset in Figure 2-14). The resulting work list shows three orders that must be picked to ensure that they will be delivered on time. The user will select one of the orders and complete the picking task.

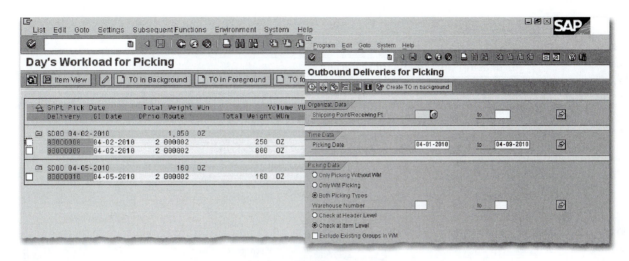

Figure 2-14: Work list—picking due list. Copyright SAP AG 2011

Demo 2.4: Review a work list

ONLINE LISTS

Online lists display lists of master data—such as materials, vendors, and purchasing info records—and documents—such as transaction documents, FI, CO, and material documents—that are generated during the execution of a process. The content and appearance of these lists are defined using selection parameters and scope-of-list parameters. *Selection parameters* determine which documents will be included in the list, while the *scope-of-list parameters* define which data will be included for the selected documents. In addition, numerous other parameters such as dates, master data (e.g., vendors), and organizational data (e.g., plant) can be used to narrow the data in the report. Figure 2-15 shows the initial screen for the display of purchasing documents. The inset shows choices for the selection parameters.

The reports are displayed in one of two available formats—a standard list format using the *SAP list viewer* or a grid format using the *ABAP list viewer (ALV) grid control*. Examples of these formats are provided in Figure 2-16 and Figure 2-17, respectively.

The list viewer and grid control provide several options for displaying the report output. These options are illustrated in Figure 2-18 and are explained as follows.

- The *select detail* allows the user to select a line on the report and drill down for more details.

- The *set filter* option is used to limit the list to only those items that meet specified values. For example, the list can be restricted to purchase orders where the quantity ordered (one of the columns) exceeds a specified value.

- Lists can be *sorted* in ascending or descending order in a selected column.

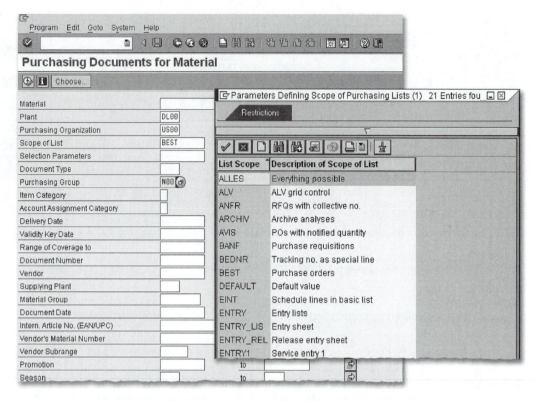

Figure 2-15: Online list—list display for documents. Copyright SAP AG 2011

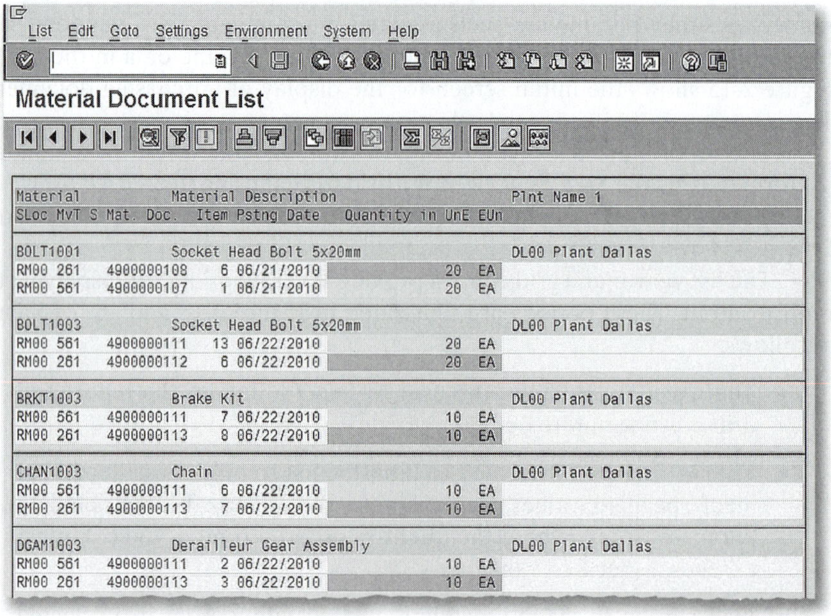

Figure 2-16: Online list—report using SAP list viewer. Copyright SAP AG 2011

Material	Plant	SLoc	MvT	S	Material Doc.	Item	Posting Date	Qty in Un. of Entry	EUn
BOLT1001	DL00	RM00	261		4900000108	6	06/21/2010	20	EA
BOLT1001	DL00	RM00	561		4900000107	1	06/21/2010	20	EA
BOLT1003	DL00	RM00	561		4900000111	13	06/22/2010	20	EA
BOLT1003	DL00	RM00	261		4900000112	6	06/22/2010	20	EA
BRKT1003	DL00	RM00	561		4900000111	7	06/22/2010	10	EA
BRKT1003	DL00	RM00	261		4900000113	8	06/22/2010	10	EA
CHAN1003	DL00	RM00	561		4900000111	6	06/22/2010	10	EA
CHAN1003	DL00	RM00	261		4900000113	7	06/22/2010	10	EA
DGAM1003	DL00	RM00	561		4900000111	2	06/22/2010	10	EA
DGAM1003	DL00	RM00	261		4900000113	3	06/22/2010	10	EA
DGAM9999	DL00	RM00	561		4900000100	1	06/21/2010	5,000	EA
DXTR3003	DL00	FG00	101		5000000005	1	06/22/2010	10	EA
HXNT1001	DL00	RM00	261		4900000108	4	06/21/2010	20	EA
HXNT1001	DL00	RM00	561		4900000104	2	06/21/2010	20	EA
HXNT1001	DL00	RM00	561		4900000104	1	06/21/2010	20	EA
HXNT1003	DL00	RM00	261		4900000112	4	06/22/2010	20	EA
HXNT1003	DL00	RM00	561		4900000111	11	06/22/2010	20	EA

Figure 2-17: Online list—report using ALV grid control. Copyright SAP AG 2011

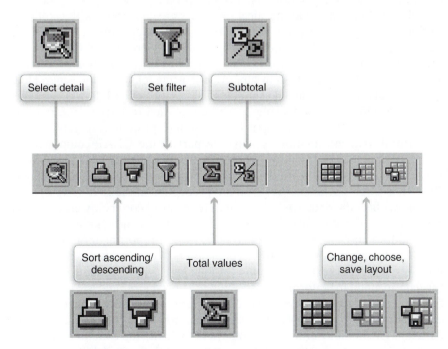

Figure 2-18: Functions of the list viewer and grid control

- The *total values* and *create subtotals* options enable users to calculate totals and subtotals for selected columns, respectively.

- The *layout* options allow users to change the appearance of the display. The layout option displays a list of available fields that can be included in the report. Fields appear as columns in the report and can be added or removed as desired. The modified layout can be saved as a *variant* of the report, which can be used to re-create the report at a later time.

- Several options are available to *export* the data in various formats, such as MS Word, Excel, and HTML. In addition, the data can be e-mailed using the system's messaging capabilities.

Demo 2.5: Review an online list

INFORMATION SYSTEMS

Numerous information systems are available within SAP ERP to support most of the processes that we will discuss in this book. Information systems (IS) can be divided into three broad categories: logistics information systems (LIS), financial information systems (FIS), and human resources information systems (HRIS). Logistics information systems support all of the logistics processes. Recall from Chapter 1 that logistical processes are concerned with acquiring, storing, creating, and distributing materials. The components of LIS include purchasing IS, sales IS, inventory control IS (IWM processes), quality management IS, plant maintenance IS, and shop floor IS (production processes). The financial information system supports reporting related to the general ledger (e.g., balance sheet, income statement, statement of cash flows), accounts receivable, and accounts payable. The HRIS is used to retrieve information about different HR components such as personnel, positions, and jobs.

Recall that information systems are part of the OLAP component of SAP ERP, and they utilize information structures to provide analytic capabilities. There are two types of information structures—standard and user-defined. **Standard information structures** are predefined in the SAP ERP system, and they collect the data needed to generate the most commonly used reports. SAP ERP also enables users to define their own structures, known as **user-defined information structures**, to meet specific reporting requirements.

Finally, information structures enable users to conduct two types of analysis—standard and flexible. **Standard analysis** provides predefined analytics for data in standard information structures. This type of analysis is sufficient for most analytic requirements. When standard analysis is insufficient, users can conduct flexible analysis to customize the reporting. In contrast to standard analysis, **flexible analysis** allows users to define the content and format of the analysis. Specifically, it enables users to combine available characteristics and key figures as needed and to create new key figures using user-specified formulas. It also provides users with several layout options.

To summarize, the OLTP component of SAP ERP offers reporting in the form of work lists and online lists that are based on detailed transaction data. In contrast, the OLAP component offers reporting via information systems, based on aggregated data in information structures. These capabilities are limited to data within the SAP ERP system. Today, however, companies need even more powerful reporting capabilities that combine data from multiple sources. This is the domain of business intelligence, which we discuss next.

Demo 2.6: Review SAP ERP reports

BUSINESS INTELLIGENCE

Business intelligence is a general term that refers to the overall capabilities a company uses to collect and analyze data from a variety of sources to better understand its operations and make better managerial decisions. As we suggested in the previous paragraph, the OLAP environment within SAP ERP cannot perform the powerful analytic capabilities needed to provide business intelligence. For these purposes, businesses utilize SAP® Business Warehouse (SAP BW) (Figure 2-19).

SAP BW is a separate system that receives data from the SAP ERP system, other SAP systems such as SAP CRM and SAP SRM, and other non-SAP systems. These data are stored in the SAP BW database. Whereas the

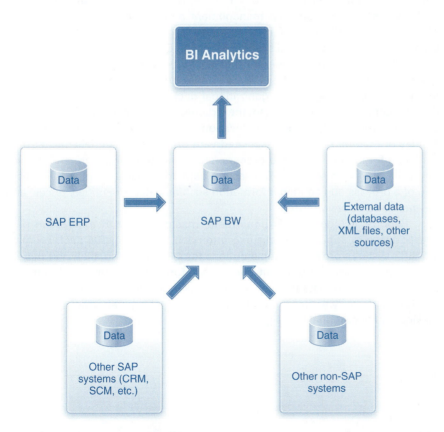

Figure 2-19: Reporting using SAP BW

SAP ERP system is used to execute process steps, the SAP BW system is designed and optimized for processing large quantities of data to provide powerful analytics. Unlike the OLAP environment in SAP ERP, SAP BW is not a real-time or an online system. That is, the data used in BW reporting are not tied to transactions and therefore are not the most current data available.

CHAPTER SUMMARY

This chapter explains the evolution of enterprise systems in terms of the processes they manage and the technical capabilities they possess. In addition, it examines the different types of data that ES collect and utilize to execute processes and enable managerial decision making.

Enterprise systems evolved from the custom-built mainframe applications of the 1960s and 1970s into the three-tier client/server systems of the 1990s. They were then rebuilt to take advantage of the new technical capabilities of service-oriented architectures to expand their reach and value as business platforms. The largest and most complex ES are integrated ERP systems. ERP systems initially managed only intra-company processes. However, their capabilities were later extended to incorporate external or inter-company processes, such as customer relationship management and supply chain management. The combined collection of inter-company process-based applications and intra-company process-based systems forms an ES "application suite."

Enterprise systems generate and consume vast quantities of different types of data in their operations. Data in enterprise systems can be classified into three major categories: organizational data, master data, and transaction data. Organizational data represent the structure of the enterprise. Examples are company code, plant, and storage location. Master data represent the various entities or materials that are associated with processes. Materials master data contain information needed to procure, store, manufacture, ship, and invoice physical goods and services. Transaction data are collected during the execution of a process and contain information such as dates, quantities, prices, and payment and delivery terms.

Reports include organizational data, master data, and transaction data and are used to support process execution and for managerial decision making. ERP systems provide multiple options for extracting and analyzing the different types of data for different purposes. Information systems (IS) combine the various types of data for specific functions in the enterprise. IS also enable employees to easily access relevant data in ways that facilitate efficient decision making and operational oversight.

KEY TERMS

Application layer

Application platforms

Application suite

Architecture

Business intelligence

Characteristics

Client

Company code

Customer relationship management (CRM)

Data layer

Enterprise resource planning

Financial accounting (FI) documents

Finished goods

Flexible analysis

Information structures

Key figures

Management accounting or controlling (CO) documents

Master data

Material documents

Material group

Material types

Online analytic processing (OLAP)

Online lists

Online transaction processing (OLTP)

Organizational data

Period definition

Plant

Presentation layer

Product lifecycle management (PLM)

Raw materials

Reporting

Semifinished goods

Service-oriented architecture (SOA)

Standard analysis

Standard information structures

Supplier relationship management (SRM)

Supply chain management (SCM)

Three-tier client-server architecture

Trading goods

Transaction data

Transaction documents

User-defined information structures

Work lists

REVIEW QUESTIONS

1. Describe client-server and services-oriented architectures. What are the advantages and disadvantages of each architecture?

2. What is an enterprise system application suite? Describe the capabilities of the individual components of the application suite.

3. Discuss the three types of data in an enterprise system and how they are related.

4. Explain the relationship among client, company code, and plant in SAP ERP. What are these organizational levels typically used to represent?

5. Why is material master one of the most complex types of data in an ERP system? Provide some examples of data typically included in a material master.

6. What are material types? Identify the four common material types in SAP ERP, and provide an example of each.

7. What are material groups? How are they different from material types?

8. How are transaction data created in an ERP system?

9. Explain the document concept in SAP ERP. What are the functions of the four types of documents in SAP ERP?

10. Discuss the typical structure of documents in SAP ERP.

11. What are the reporting options available in SAP ERP? How do they differ from one another? How do they differ from the reporting options available in SAP BW?

EXERCISES

Exercises for this chapter are available on *WileyPLUS.*

Introduction to Accounting

LEARNING OBJECTIVES

After completing this chapter you will be able to:

1. Explain the differences between financial accounting and management accounting.

2. Describe the organizational data related to financial accounting.

3. Discuss and analyze the key types of master data involved with financial accounting.

4. Explain and apply basic accounting concepts.

5. Execute key processes in financial accounting.

6. Identify key integration points between financial accounting and other processes.

7. Prepare reports in financial accounting.

In Chapter 1 we briefly introduced numerous processes that most organizations typically perform, such as fulfillment, production, and procurement. A common feature of many—but not all—of these processes is that they have consequences for the organization's financial position. The role of accounting processes is to record the financial consequences of the various process steps. In turn, the organization uses this financial information to plan and manage these processes.

Accounting processes are broadly divided into two main categories: financial accounting and management accounting. Financial accounting (FI) is concerned with recording the financial impacts of business processes as they are executed. Businesses use these data to generate financial statements to meet legal or regulatory reporting requirements. For example, in the United States, the Securities and Exchange Commission (SEC) requires that all publicly traded companies periodically submit financial statements in a prescribed format. Further, certain regulated industries, such as energy and health care, have additional reporting requirements imposed by their respective regulating agencies. These reports are externally focused, meaning they are intended primarily for audiences outside the organization, such as the SEC. However, they are also useful for internal management purposes.

In contrast, management accounting, or controlling (CO), is internally focused, meaning that it provides the information the organization needs to effectively manage the various processes. Management accounting processes, like FI processes, use financial data recorded during process execution to generate reports. Specifically, CO reports focus on costs and revenues which management uses to achieve basic business objectives such as increasing revenues, minimizing costs, and achieving profitability. In contrast to FI, however, the content of these reports is not prescribed by any external entity. Rather, CO reports are based entirely on management's needs. Figure 3-1 highlights the key differences between FI reports and CO reports.

	Financial accounting	Management accounting
Focus	External	Internal
Purpose	Legal reporting (financial statements) Tracking financial impact of processes Communicate with investors	Managing the firm with regard to costs and revenues
Content	Defined by laws and regulations	Defined by management needs

Figure 3-1: Financial accounting vs. management accounting

From an ERP perspective, financial accounting is the "heart" of the system because it must accurately reflect the financial status of the firm at any given point in time. As you learn about processes in later chapters, it is essential that you understand the financial impact of these processes. For this reason, we have included this chapter on accounting early in the textbook. At the same time, however, financial accounting is closely intertwined with management accounting. Consequently, we introduce a few basic management accounting concepts in this chapter.

The key processes in financial accounting are:

- General ledger accounting
- Accounts receivable accounting
- Accounts payable accounting
- Asset accounting
- Bank ledger accounting

The **general ledger (GL)** is used to record the financial impacts of business process steps; it contains much of the data needed for financial reporting. **Accounts receivables accounting** is associated with the fulfillment process and is used to manage money owed by customers for goods and services sold to them. Conversely, **accounts payable accounting** is associated with the procurement process. Companies use accounts payable accounting to record and manage money owed to vendors for the purchase of materials and services. **Asset accounting** is used to record data related to the purchase, use, and disposal of assets such as buildings, equipment, machinery, and automobiles. Finally, **bank ledger accounting** is concerned with recording data associated with bank transactions.

As previously stated, the financial data recorded in the general ledger are used to generate the financial statements needed for external reporting. Typical financial statements are the balance sheet, income statement, and statement of cash flow. A **balance sheet** is a snapshot of the organization at a point in time. It identifies assets, liabilities, and equity. In contrast, an **income statement**, also known as a **profit and loss statement**, indicates the changes in a company's financial position over a period of time. It identifies revenues, costs, and profits or losses. Finally, a **statement of cash flow** displays all cash receipts and payments over a specified period of time. We begin this chapter by examining the organizational data and master data relevant to financial accounting.

■ ORGANIZATIONAL DATA

The organizational data associated with financial accounting are client, company code, and business area. We discussed both client and company code in Chapter 2. Recall that a client is the highest organizational level in the system; it represents an enterprise that consists of multiple companies. Therefore, even the largest enterprise can have only a single client. The various companies within an enterprise are represented by a company code. Applying this scenario to GBI, the global GBI enterprise is represented by a client, while the two companies, GBI US and GBI Germany, are represented by company codes US00 and DE00, respectively. Financial statements are generally prepared at the company code level. Thus, GBI US and GBI Germany will generate separate financial statements to meet the regulatory requirements of each country.[1]

Business areas are internal divisions of an enterprise that are used to define areas of responsibility or to meet the external reporting requirements of an enterprise segment. A **segment** is a division of an enterprise for which management monitors performance (revenue, costs, profitability, etc.) separately from other segments. Financial statements are generated for each business area within the enterprise. A business area is often based on either the enterprise's product line or its geographic division, across company codes. Figure 3-2 illustrates two hypothetical business areas for GBI. The upper part of the figure identifies three companies within the GBI enterprise—GBI US, GBI Germany, and GBI Australia.[2] It also defines two business areas based on product lines—bicycles and accessories. GBI generates financial statements

---

[1] Although the International Accounting Standards Board (IASB) has created a global standard for financial reporting called the International Financial Reporting Standards (IFRS), not all countries have adopted this standard. In addition, local regulatory requirements still mandate that companies maintain financial data in different ways. Consequently, there continues to be a need to generate different financial statements for different countries.

[2] GBI currently only has companies in the United States and Germany. The companies referred to in this section and in Figure 3-2 are only included to facilitate a discussion of business areas.

	GBI US	GBI Germany	GBI Australia
Bicycles	X	X	X
Accessories	X	X	X

	GBI US	GBI Canada	GBI Mexico	GBI Germany	GBI UK
GBI North America	X	X	X		
GBI Europe				X	X

Figure 3-2: Business areas

for both business areas across all three companies. In contrast, in the lower part of the figure, business areas are defined in terms of the geographic locations of the individual companies. Thus, financial statements are generated for all companies in North America and Europe.

Business Processes in Practice 3.1: Apple Inc.

Apple Inc. provides a familiar example of business areas and segments in global public companies. Apple has four main business areas: the Americas, Europe, Japan, and Retail. The Americas business area includes two segments, North America and South America. The Europe business area includes the European countries as well as the Middle East and Africa. Finally, the Retail business area includes all Apple Stores across the globe, which are managed as a separate business area.

Within each business area, Apple operates various units for products, such as Mac computers, iPods, iTunes, and iPads. Thus, Apple must report its financial results in both business areas and product segments so that investors have a great deal of transparency into the company's operations. Were you to examine Apple's annual report, you could locate total sales by business area (e.g., the Americas), by product segment within each business area (e.g., Mac desktops within the Americas), and by product segment globally (e.g., global Mac sales). This level of transparency is critical for investors and regulatory groups to properly analyze and monitor Apple both as an individual company and by comparison with its competitors in the industry.

Source: Apple company reports.

■ MASTER DATA

As previously stated, the goal of financial accounting is to record the financial impact of business activities. These data are recorded in the company's general ledger. More specifically, the general ledger includes many *accounts* that companies use to record financial data. Each account tracks different types of financial data. For example, some accounts record sales revenues, whereas others record the costs associated with producing and selling products. A list of accounts that can be included in a general ledger is called a *chart of accounts*. In this section we take a closer look at charts of accounts and general ledger accounts.

CHART OF ACCOUNTS

A **chart of accounts (COA)** is an ordered listing of accounts that comprise a company's general ledger. There are three types of charts of accounts: operative COA, country-specific COA, and group COA. The *operative or operational COA* contains the *operational accounts* that are used to record the financial impact of an organization's day-to-day transactions. It is the primary COA maintained by an organization.

The accounts in the operative COA are mapped to *alternative accounts in country-specific charts of account.* Companies create these alternative accounts to meet special country-specific reporting requirements. Figure 3-3 illustrates a scenario in which both GBI US and GBI Germany use the INT COA, while each company also maintains its country-specific COA—CANA (North America COA) and GKR (German COA).

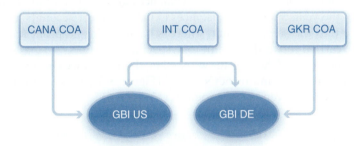

Figure 3-3: Charts of accounts and company codes

Finally, a *group chart of accounts* contains *group accounts* that multiple companies within an enterprise use to consolidate their financial reporting. When an enterprise includes several companies, then, in addition to creating financial statements for each company (company code), it must also create financial statements for the enterprise as a whole. This consolidation is necessary because the enterprise, which is itself a separate legal entity (e.g., parent or holding company), has reporting requirements. Using a group chart of accounts makes it easy to generate consolidated financial statements. Otherwise the enterprise must rely on more complex methods of consolidation. All enterprises must maintain an operative COA in order to record financial data. In contrast, group and country-specific COAs are optional.

GENERAL LEDGER ACCOUNTS

The accounts in the general ledger are defined based on the selected COA. The general ledger is an instantiation of the COA for a particular company and can include some or all of the accounts in the COA. Like most master data, the data in general ledger accounts are segmented by organizational level (Figure 3-4). COA account data include a *COA* or *client segment* and a *company code segment*.

The COA segment typically includes an account number, short and long text, an account group, and an indication as to whether the account is a balance sheet or a profit and loss account. Each account is assigned a unique *account*

COA segment (client)	Company code segment

• Account number
• Long text
• Short text
• Account group
• Balance sheet or
  income statement account
	• Account currency
	• Tax related data
	• Field status group
	• Open item management
	• Line item display
	• Reconciliation account
	  for account type

Figure 3-4: General ledger account data

number to distinguish it from other accounts in the COA. Each account also includes a *long text* (description) and *short text* (brief description) of the account. Designating the account as either a balance sheet or a profit and loss account has implications for the ways the balances in the accounts are treated at the end of the year. Specifically, balances in balance sheet accounts are carried forward into the same account, whereas balances in the profit and loss accounts are carried forward into different, specified accounts.

In the beginning of the chapter we explained that balance sheet accounts include assets, liabilities, and owner's equity (Figure 3-5), whereas profit and loss accounts include revenue and expenses (Figure 3-6).

Assets

Liquid assets
- Cash/Bank
- Receivables
- Prepaid expenses

Material Accounts
- Inventory - Raw materials
- Inventory - Finished goods
- Inventory - Semifinished goods
- Inventory - Trading goods

Fixed assets
- Land
- Building

Liabilities

Short term
- Payables

Long term
- Loans

Equity
- Retained earnings
- Shareholders equity

Assets = Liabilities + equities

Figure 3-5: Balance sheet accounts

Revenue	Expenses
• Sales • Other	• Cost of goods sold • Payroll • Utilities • Taxes

Income = Revenue − Expenses

Figure 3-6: Profit and loss accounts

- **Assets** are what the company owns, such as cash, inventory of materials, land, buildings, and money owed to the company by its customers (receivables).

- **Liabilities** are what the company owes to others, including money owed to vendors (payables) and loans from financial institutions.

- Owner's **equity** refers to the owner's share of the company's assets.

- **Revenues** are the monies the company earns by selling its products and services

- **Expenses** are the costs associated with creating and selling those products and services.

GBI has created a custom COA—GL00—which it uses as the operative COA for all the companies in its enterprise. GBI currently does not utilize a country-specific or group COA. A complete listing of all the accounts in GL00 is provided in Appendix 3A of this chapter. A detailed explanation of these accounts is beyond the scope of this book. Instead, we discuss relevant accounts in the various process chapters.

The final data element in the COA segment is the **account group,** which groups together accounts with similar characteristics. For example, all bank and cash accounts are consolidated in one account group called *liquid assets*. Accounts within each group are numbered within a specified number range. For example, accounts in the liquid assets group are located between 100000 and 110300. Further, accounts in different account groups require different types of data when they are used in a company's general ledger. The data contained in account groups can include dates, tax-related data, and organizational data. These data can be designated as either required, optional, display only, or hidden when the accounts are created.

Demo 3.1: Review chart of accounts

Although the accounts in a COA can be used by more than one company, each company uses the account in different ways. For example, the currency used and the tax-related data in different countries can be different. Therefore, the general ledger account requires certain company code-specific data in addition to the COA data. The typical company code data in general ledger accounts consist of the following elements (refer back to Figure 3-4)

- Account currency

- Tax-related data

- Field status groups

- Open item management

- Line item display

- Reconciliation account data

Account currency determines the currency in which all the transactions are recorded. For example, GBI US uses US$ (USD) as the account currency, while GBI DE uses Euro€ (EUR). Further, each country has to comply with distinctive tax laws that require it to include different *tax-related data* in its general ledger accounts. The *field status group* determines both the screen layout for document entry and the status of each field on the screen. The available field status options are *suppress*, *display*, *required*, and *optional*. If a field is suppressed, then it is hidden; that is, it is not displayed on the screen. A field with the display status is displayed and cannot be changed. The user must provide data for required fields, whereas data entry is optional for fields with the optional status. Different field status groups can be defined for different types of accounts such as liquid asset accounts and expense accounts.

Figure 3-7 illustrates the two segments for GBI's bank account. The chart of accounts segment indicates that the bank account (account #100000) is part of the GL00 COA. Both GBI US and GBI DE use this account, but the two companies use it differently, as specified in their company code segments. For example, the two companies have different company codes (US00 and DE00) and different currencies (USD and EUR).

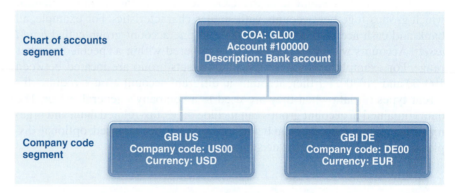

Figure 3-7: General ledger account segments

Another element in the company code segment of a general ledger account is open item management. If *open item management* is enabled, then each item in the account is marked as either "open" or "cleared." An item is designated as open until an offsetting (debit or credit) entry is posted to the account. At that point its status is changed to cleared. For example, when a company ships a product to a customer, the amount owed is recorded in a specific account. This item remains open until the company receives a payment. The payment offsets the open item, which is then marked as cleared. Typically, the open item management indicator is set for *clearing accounts*, which are temporary accounts that hold data until these data are moved to another account.

Finally, when *line item display* is enabled, a link to the line items that are included in account balances is maintained. Line items are the specific debit and credit entries in the account. Maintaining links to the line items is necessary when the company wants to include the specific debit and credit entries in reports. We discuss reporting at the end of this chapter. In the next section we shift our focus to subledger and reconciliation accounts.

SUBSIDIARY LEDGERS AND RECONCILIATION ACCOUNTS

Some financial data are not directly maintained in the general ledger. For example, customer accounts, which track the amounts customers owe and the payments they have made, are maintained separately for each customer. Although it is necessary to track sales and payments separately for each customer, it is not necessary to include each customer account in the general ledger. Similarly, data about each vendor and asset, such as an automobile, are maintained in separate accounts. Vendor accounts track purchases from and payments made to them. Asset accounts are used to track the purchase price as well as increases and decreases in the asset's value over time. Such accounts are maintained in **subsidiary ledgers** or **subledgers**, and they are not part of the general ledger.

Although customer and vendor accounts are not part of the general ledger, the data in these accounts must be reflected in the general ledger. Companies accomplish this task by posting the data from subledger accounts into special accounts in the general ledger called reconciliation accounts. **Reconciliation accounts** are general ledger accounts that consolidate data from a group of related subledger accounts, such as customers and vendors. The reconciliation account for customers is *accounts receivable*, and the reconciliation account for vendors is *accounts payable*. Because the general ledger can include multiple reconciliation accounts, it is necessary to indicate which subledger each reconciliation account is associated with. This information appears in the *reconciliation account for account type* field in the general ledger account master data. These concepts are related to the accounts receivable and payable accounting processes introduced at the beginning of the chapter. These processes will be explained in greater detail later in this chapter.

One special characteristic of reconciliation accounts is that it is not possible to post data directly into them. Rather, data must be posted to subledger accounts, at which point they are automatically posted to the corresponding reconciliation account as well. Thus, when a company sells products or services to a customer on credit, the amount owed is noted in the customer's subledger account and is also posted to the corresponding reconciliation account (accounts receivable). Likewise, when the company owes money to a vendor for purchases it made on credit, this amount is noted in the vendor's subledger account and is simultaneously posted to the corresponding reconciliation account (accounts payable). The balance in the reconciliation account (e.g., accounts receivable and accounts payable) is the sum of the postings in the related subledger accounts (e.g., customers and vendors, respectively).

We will consider subledger and reconciliation accounts in greater detail in the process section of this chapter. We now turn our attention to the key concepts involved in financial accounting, beginning with accounting documents.

Demo 3.2: Review general ledger accounts

■ KEY CONCEPTS

Before we turn our attention to the processes involved in financial accounting, we need to explain two key financial accounting concepts: accounting documents and parallel accounting. We also need to introduce a few key concepts related to management accounting. You must become familiar with these concepts to understand the processes we discuss later in this chapter and in other chapters.

ACCOUNTING DOCUMENTS

We introduced the concepts of documents in Chapter 2. In this chapter we elaborate on financial accounting documents. A **financial accounting document (FI document)** records the impact (financial data) of a transaction step on financial accounting. As Figure 3-8 illustrates, an FI document consists of a header section and a detail or line item section. The header includes data that apply to the entire document, such as document number, document type, various dates, company code, currency used, and a reference number. A *document type* is a two-character code that identifies the specific business process step that generated the document. Commonly used document types include customer invoice (DR), customer payment (DZ), goods issue (WA), and goods receipt (WE). A document type determines the document number range and the account type (explained below) associated with the posting.

Header
- Document date
- Document type
- Document number
- Company code
- Posting date
- Currency
- Reference number

Items (detail)
- Account
- Description
- Posting key (debit or credit)
- Amount

Figure 3-8: Structure of an FI document

The detail section typically consists of two line items: a debit item and a credit item. Each line item includes the account number from the general ledger, a description of the account, an indication of whether the account is debited or credited, and the amount. The debit or credit is indicated by a *posting key,* which is a two-digit code that determines how a line item is posted. Specifically it identifies the account type, indicates whether the line item is a debit or credit posting, and specifies the field status of additional data needed to post the item. Examples of *account types* are customer (D), vendor (K), asset (A), material (M), and general ledger accounts (S). Examples of additional data are cost centers and business areas. Figure 3-9 includes several examples

Posting key	Debit/Credit	Account type
01 (invoice)	Debit	Customer
15 (payment)	Credit	Customer
40 (debit)	Debit	GL account
50 (credit)	Credit	GL account
31 (invoice)	Credit	Vendor
25 (payment)	Debit	Vendor

Figure 3-9: Posting key examples

of posting keys related to debit and credit postings to customer, vendor, and general ledger accounts.

Demo 3.3: Review an FI document

PARALLEL ACCOUNTING

The general ledger is based on the operating chart of accounts. In fact, an organization can implement multiple ledgers in parallel and use each ledger for different purposes. This practice is called **parallel accounting**. In a typical arrangement, an enterprise will implement one set of accounting principles for all companies (company code) in the enterprise (client). These global principles are consolidated in a single ledger known as the *leading ledger*. A leading ledger is required, and all transaction data are posted to it. In addition, the enterprise will define *nonleading ledgers* for each company (company code) based on local accounting practices, such as US GAAP and German HGB.[3]

GBI has implemented a leading ledger based on the GL00 COA. GBI does not maintain additional ledgers. However, Figure 3-10 illustrates how parallel accounting would be implemented within GBI should the enterprise choose to do so at a later date. In addition to the leading ledger, each of the two GBI companies has a nonleading ledger based on local accounting standards. GBI uses the leading ledger to consolidate its financial statements for the global enterprise and the nonleading ledgers to meet local reporting requirements in Germany and the United States.

---

[3] Most countries have their own standards for financial reporting. In the United States, generally accepted accounting principles, or GAAP, are used to prepare financial statements. In Germany, the German commercial law, German Handelsgesetzbuch (HGB) is the standard. A global standard, the international financial reporting standard (IFRS), is available, but it is not adopted by all countries.

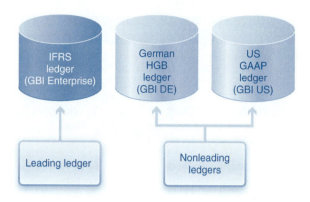

Figure 3-10: Parallel accounting

CONCEPTS IN MANAGEMENT ACCOUNTING

At the beginning of the chapter we explained that financial accounting and management accounting, or controlling (CO), are very closely related. In fact, most of the data used in management accounting are derived from financial accounting. Therefore, we pause here to introduce a few a key concepts in management accounting.

As the name suggests, a key function of management accounting is to manage and allocate costs. Companies incur these costs as they carry out various business processes. For example, the fulfillment process involves costs related to selling products and services, and the production process involves costs associated with manufacturing products. Other costs include supplies, maintenance, and equipment that are consumed by various processes.

To properly allocate and track costs, the organization is divided into cost centers. A **cost center** is associated with a location where costs are incurred. Cost centers can be associated with departments, such as marketing and finance; with locations, such as plants; and with individuals. In essence, a cost center is something that absorbs costs that are generated when companies execute processes. For example, when the company purchases supplies, it assigns the costs of the purchase to a cost center. Thus, if the marketing department purchases office supplies, the company assigns or charges the cost of the supplies to the marketing cost center. Periodically, the company reviews and further allocates these accumulated costs. Think of a cost center as a container or bucket that accumulates costs.

In Chapter 1 we introduced numerous processes in simple terms. One of the common themes across most processes is the need to "authorize" the execution of these processes. This authorization often takes the form of "orders." For example, in introducing the procurement process, we noted that the authorization to acquire materials is typically a purchase order. Likewise, the authorization to fill a customer order is a sales order, and the authorization to produce something is a production order. Like cost centers, costs incurred during processes can be allocated to or absorbed by these orders. Collectively, these orders and cost centers are called **cost objects**. As we discuss various processes beginning with Chapter 4, we will illustrate how companies use cost objects to accumulate costs as they execute these processes.

■ PROCESSES

In the preceding sections, we discussed the master data and key concepts relevant to financial accounting. In this section, we examine the actual processes that companies use in financial accounting. Specifically, we explore general ledger, accounts receivable, accounts payable, and asset accounting.

GENERAL LEDGER ACCOUNTING

General ledger accounting is based on the double entry accounting system, where every transaction has both a debit entry and a credit entry. Recall that accounts are divided into balance sheet accounts (Figure 3-5) and income (profit and loss) statement accounts (Figure 3-6). Balance sheet accounts are grouped into assets, liabilities, and equity, while profit and loss accounts are divided into revenue and expenses. Figure 3-11 illustrates how postings are debited and credited to these accounts using a "T" account. Debits are displayed on the left side of the T account, and credits on the right side. An increase in an asset account or an expense account results in a debit posting, whereas a decrease results in a credit posting. Conversely, an increase in revenue or liability results in a credit posting, whereas a decrease generates a debit posting. Below we present several examples involving GBI to illustrate and clarify the concept of postings. Please refer to Appendix 3A at the end of this chapter for the specific accounts that are included in the examples.

Figure 3-11: Debits and credits

Consider the following scenario. A venture capitalist invests $50,000 in GBI US on January 10, 2010, which GBI deposits into its bank account. In exchange, the investor receives GBI common stock at $1 per share. How is this transaction recorded in the general ledger? The first step is to identify the relevant accounts. For this transaction the appropriate accounts are *bank* (#100000) and *common stock* (#329000). The transaction will generate an increase in both accounts. Because the bank account is considered an asset, there will be a debit posting, while common stock, a liability, will receive a credit posting. This transaction is illustrated in Figure 3-12.

Figure 3-12: Posting example 1: Investment in company

Consider another example. GBI purchases office supplies for $500 with a check. Office supplies are expensed; that is, they are defined as money spent rather than treated as an asset upon purchase, even if some of the supplies remain unused. In this case, the relevant accounts are *bank* and *supplies expense*. This posting is diagrammed in Figure 3-13.

Figure 3-13: Posting example 2: Purchase of supplies with cash

Next, consider a scenario in which GBI purchases $1,000 of office supplies, but on credit rather than with cash. In this case the purchase and payment are recorded separately. One account is *supplies expense,* which is debited by $1,000. The offsetting account is *payables–miscellaneous,* which is credited by $1,000. Payment is made using the *bank* account ($1,000 credit). Finally, the *payables–miscellaneous* account is *cleared* ($1,000 debit). This transaction is illustrated in Figure 3-14.

Figure 3-14: Posting example 3: Purchase of supplies on credit

If a company purchases supplies from multiple sources or vendors, it records all the payable data in one account, *payables–miscellaneous.* One problem with this arrangement is that the company cannot determine how much money it owes to each vendor. If the company needs to track the money it owes to individual vendors, then it uses a separate process known as *accounts payable accounting,* which utilizes subledger accounts. Accounts payable accounting is typically used in conjunction with the procurement process. In the next section we examine accounts payable accounting in simple terms. We provide a more detailed discussion in Chapter 4.

Demo 3.4: Post general ledger entries

ACCOUNTS PAYABLE (AP) ACCOUNTING

In the section on master data we explained that organizations use subledgers to track money owed to individual vendors. We further explained that subledgers are not part of the general ledger but instead are associated with special accounts in the general ledger known as reconciliation accounts. In accounts payable accounting, the accounts payable subledger consists of individual vendor accounts. The subledger account number is created when the vendor master record is created. The vendor master record and the vendor subledger account share the same account number. The associated reconciliation account is a general ledger account that is designated as the reconciliation account. The association between the vendor account and the reconciliation account is established in the definition of the vendor master record. We discuss vendor master data and its link to the general ledger in the context of the procurement process in Chapter 4.

In the GBI general ledger, account #300700, *accounts payable reconciliation,* is the designated account. Let's consider a scenario in which GBI purchases office supplies from three vendors. Each vendor has a designated vendor account number that is also the subledger account number. The purchases are as follows: $2,000 from Vendor 1, $1,000 from Vendor 2, and $4,000 from Vendor 3. Further, GBI makes these purchases on credit and then pays the vendors at a later date via a check. As illustrated in Figure 3-15, Steps 1–3 record the purchases from each vendor. Each purchase results in a debit to the *supplies expense* account and a credit to the appropriate *vendor* account. Postings to the vendor accounts are automatically posted to the reconciliation account, *accounts payable reconciliation*, as indicated by the arrows. Note that the AP reconciliation account does not track the details of each transaction; rather, it maintains only the total values. Payments, recorded in Steps 4–6, result in a credit posting to the *bank* account and a debit posting to the appropriate *vendor* account. Again, these debit postings are also automatically made to the reconciliation account, *accounts payable reconciliation*.

Demo 3.5: Review reconciliation and non-reconciliation AP accounts.

ACCOUNTS RECEIVABLE (AR) ACCOUNTING

Whereas accounts payable accounting is concerned with vendors, accounts receivable accounting is concerned with customers. When businesses need to track money owed by each customer separately, they create an account in the accounts receivable subledger for each customer with a corresponding designated general ledger account (the reconciliation account). The customer subledger account is created when the customer master record is created, and they share the same account number. The association between the customer account and the reconciliation account is established in the definition of the customer master record. We discuss this procedure in the context of

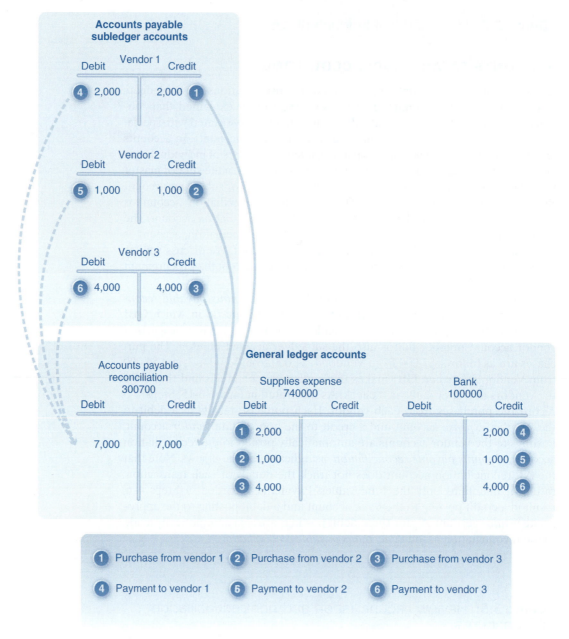

Figure 3-15: Accounts payable accounting

the fulfillment process in Chapter 5. For GBI, the designated reconciliation account is *accounts receivable reconciliation* (#110100).

Let's consider a scenario in which GBI sells bicycles to two customers on credit for $5,000 and $3,000, respectively, and then receives payment at a later date. These purchases are Steps 1 and 2 in Figure 3-16. The relevant accounts are sales revenue and the individual customer accounts. *Sales revenue* is credited by the amount of the sale, and a corresponding debit is made to the appropriate *customer* account. This debit is also automatically posted to the *accounts receivable reconciliation* account as indicated by the arrows in Figure 3-16.

As in the case of the AP reconciliation account, the AR reconciliation account does not track the details of the transactions. When payment is made (Steps 3–4), the *bank* account is debited, and the appropriate *customer* account is credited. At the same time, a corresponding automatic credit is posted to the reconciliation account, *accounts receivable reconciliation*.

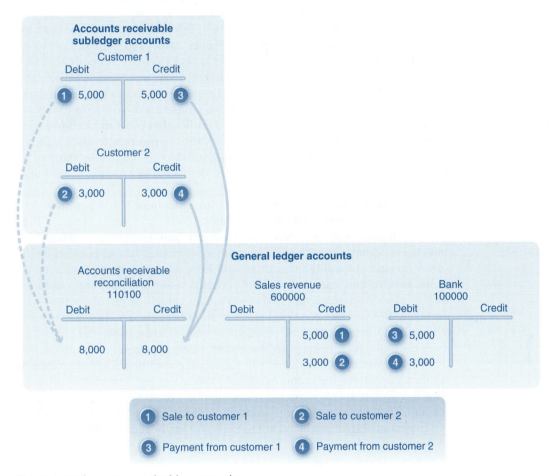

Figure 3-16: Accounts receivable accounting

Demo 3.6: Review reconciliation and non-reconciliation AR accounts

ASSET ACCOUNTING

An organization may possess a variety of assets, including tangible, intangible, and financial assets. *Tangible assets* have a physical form, whereas *intangible assets* are nonphysical. Examples of tangible assets are computers, machinery, and buildings. Examples of intangible assets are intellectual property, patents, and trademarks. *Financial assets* include a variety of financial instruments such as securities, long-term notes (debts), and mortgages.

Companies use asset accounting to track the financial consequences associated with the entire lifecycle of an asset, from acquisition to disposal. In this section we discuss asset accounting as it relates to tangible assets, which can be further categorized as *fixed assets*, *leased assets*, and *assets under construction*. A discussion of how the other types of assets are accounted for is beyond the scope of this book.

Asset accounting is complex, and a thorough discussion is beyond the scope of this book. However, we discuss some key concepts next. Assets are assigned to a company code and, by virtue of this assignment, all asset-related transactions are posted to the general ledger associated with the company code. This arrangement ensures that asset transactions are properly reflected in the company's financial statements. Recall from our previous discussion that financial statements can be created for business areas as well as company codes. Therefore, assets are also assigned to a business area. Finally, assets are associated with cost centers. We explained earlier that companies employ cost centers to accumulate the costs incurred in various processes. In asset accounting, the primary cost is depreciation expense, which is the loss in value of an asset over time. When a company incurs a depreciation expense, it must allocate that expense to a cost center.

Accounting data about each asset are maintained in asset subledger accounts. These data include acquisition costs and depreciation. Like other subledger accounts (such as customer and vendor accounts), asset subledger accounts are created when the asset master record is created. The subledger account and the master record share the same account number. As in the case of customer and vendor accounts, asset accounts are associated with a reconciliation account in the general ledger. However, in contrast with customer and vendor accounts, the association between an asset account and a reconciliation account is not straightforward. Rather, it depends on which asset class the asset belongs to. An **asset class** is a grouping of assets that possess similar characteristics. For example, all computing equipment such as computers, printers, and monitors can be included in one asset class. Each asset class is associated with a specific reconciliation account in the general ledger account. The five reconciliation accounts related to assets that are included in GBI's general ledger are listed in Figure 3-17. Finally, each asset class includes

Account number	Account name
220100	Land
220200	Production machinery, equipment, and fixtures
220400	Office furniture
220600	Office equipment and computers
200800	Vehicles

Figure 3-17: GBI reconciliation accounts for assets

a variety of parameters that determine how an asset belonging to that class is treated. The two most important parameters are *account determination* and *depreciation*. We discuss account determination in the next paragraph, and we consider depreciation a bit later in the chapter.

The reconciliation account for each asset in the asset subledger account is determined by its association with an asset class. This association, referred to as **account determination**, is illustrated in Figure 3-18. The figure shows three of the five reconciliation accounts included in GBI's general ledger as well as four of GBI's asset classes. Note that office equipment and office computers are associated with the same reconciliation account. Thus, two or more asset classes can be associated with the same reconciliation account. Going further, asset class vehicles and asset class office computers both have two assets, which in turn have individual subledger accounts associated with them.

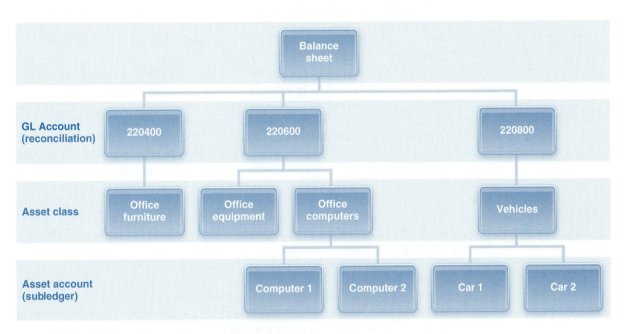

Figure 3-18: Asset accounts and account determination

Demo 3.7: Review asset classes and asset-related accounts

A company typically acquires an asset and keeps it for a certain amount of time, after which it is no longer useful. A variety of activities or *transactions* are associated with the asset during its lifecycle. The most common *transactions types* are acquisition, depreciation, and retirement. We discuss these topics next.

Acquisition

An asset can be acquired either externally or through internal processes (e.g., the production process). For assets produced internally, a special asset class, *assets under construction*, is used during production, and the costs (materials, labor, etc.) are tracked in a corresponding general ledger reconciliation account. For assets obtained externally, three options are available: (1) purchase from an established vendor without using the purchasing process; (2) purchase from an established vendor using the purchasing process; and (3) purchase from a one-time vendor, or a vendor for whom master data (and therefore a subledger account) are not maintained.

In the first scenario, a company purchases an asset from an established vendor but does not employ the full purchasing process. That is, a purchase order is not created. Instead, the accounting impact of the acquisition is *manually* recorded in relevant general ledger and subledger accounts. The process is similar to the one described in the accounts payable accounting process discussed earlier in the chapter. In this scenario, however, the company uses the vendor subledger account and a corresponding accounts payable reconciliation account instead of the supplies expense account.

In the second scenario, a company purchases from an established vendor using the entire purchasing process, which involves a purchase order, a goods receipt, an invoice receipt, and payment. The accounting impact is very similar to the first scenario, but the impacts are *automatically* recorded by the steps in the purchasing process. We examine this process more closely in Chapter 4.

In the final scenario, the asset is purchased from a one-time vendor or a vendor for whom the company does not maintain master data. In this case, a vendor subledger account does not exist. The accounting impact of the acquisition is *manually* recorded using the asset account (subledger), the corresponding reconciliation account, and a specially designated clearing account. Recall that clearing accounts are used to hold data temporarily until the data are moved to another account.

Figure 3-19 illustrates the acquisition of an asset from a one-time vendor. In this illustration, a company purchases a new desktop computer from the vendor for $5,000, with payment to be made at a later date. As a result of this purchase, asset master data for the new computer (*Desktop Computer #14*) are created. This is a subledger account that is associated with the *office equipment and computers* account in the general ledger.

When the purchase is completed (Step 1), the asset subledger account is debited by $5,000, and the *asset acquisition clearing* account is credited by the same amount. At the same time, the *office equipment and computers* account in the general ledger, the reconciliation account, is debited. When the company receives an invoice (Step 2), the clearing account is "cleared" with a debit posting, and a corresponding credit is posted to the *payables–miscellaneous* account. Note that this is not the same account as the one used in the accounts payable process. In that process the accounts payable reconciliation account was used. In this case *payables–miscellaneous* is not a reconciliation account and therefore can be posted to directly. Finally, when the company pays for the computer via a check (Step 3), the *payables–miscellaneous* account is debited, and the *bank* account is credited.

An alternative scenario may involve a loan, in which case there is no accounts payable account or bank account. Rather, a notes payable account is used to clear the asset acquisition clearing account.

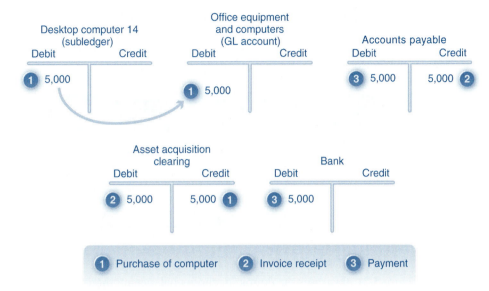

Figure 3-19: Asset acquisition with a clearing account

Demo 3.8: Acquire an asset

Depreciation

The second transaction type is depreciation. Over time, an asset's value diminishes due to wear and tear. This decrease in value is recorded as **depreciation**. Thus, the value of an asset is equal to its acquisition value less accumulated depreciation. Depreciation can be ordinary or unplanned. Ordinary depreciation refers to the planned, periodic, and recurring decrease in the value of an asset due to normal usage. In contrast, unplanned depreciation occurs when extraordinary or unforeseen circumstances cause the asset to lose value faster than normal.

The actual amount of asset depreciation depends on several factors, primarily the type of depreciation method the company employs, the asset's useful life, and its residual value. Companies can select from a variety of *depreciation methods*, for example, straight-line and double-declining balance. In straight-line depreciation, the asset is depreciated by the same amount every year. In declining balance, the asset is depreciated at a fixed percentage rate each year. In contrast to the straight-line method, then, in this method the amount of the depreciation decreases each year because the value of the asset decreases each year.

Going further, every asset has a *useful life*, which specifies how long the company anticipates using the asset. At the end of its useful life, an asset has a *scrap* or *residual value*. This is the amount the company expects to receive when it disposes of the asset. Finally, an asset has a *book value*, which is the value of the asset after it is depreciated.

In the previous section we presented an example in which a company purchases a desktop computer. Let's use this same example to illustrate depreciation. We will assume that the asset was purchased at the beginning of the year, has a useful life of four years, and a residual value of $1,000. Using the straight-line depreciation method, the amount to be depreciated is the asset purchase price ($5,000) less the residual value ($1,000), which is $4,000. This amount is to be depreciated over four years, resulting in an annual depreciation expense of $1,000. This process is outlined in Figure 3-20. The last column in the figure is the *book value* following the depreciation.

Year	Book value (start of year)	Depreciation expense	Accumulated depreciation	Book value (year end)
1	5,000	1,000	1,000	4,000
2	4,000	1,000	2,000	3,000
3	3,000	1,000	3,000	2,000
4	2,000	1,000	4,000	1,000

Figure 3-20: Straight-line depreciation

Figure 3-21 illustrates the double-declining balance method for the same asset. The depreciation rate is equal to double the depreciation rate for the straight-line method. The annual depreciation in the straight-line method is $1,000. Therefore the depreciation rate is $1,000 divided by $5,000, which is 20%. In the double-declining balance method this rate is doubled to 40%. By comparing Figure 3-21 with Figure 3-20, you can see that the double-declining balance method is an accelerated depreciation method that allows the company to expense the asset at a faster rate than the straight-line method. Note that the book value cannot be less than the residual value. Consequently, the depreciation in the fourth year is a fixed amount ($80) needed to bring the book value to the residual value of $1,000.

Year	Book value (start of year)	Depreciation rate	Depreciation expense	Accumulated depreciation	Book value (year end)
1	5,000	40%	2,000	2,000	3,000
2	3,000	40%	1,200	3,200	1,800
3	1,800	40%	720	3,920	1,080
4	1,080	1,080–80	80	4,000	1,000

Percent annual depreciation based on straight line method: 20%
Percent annual depreciation for declining balance = 2 × 20% = 40%

Figure 3-21: Double-declining balance depreciation

A company selects a depreciation method based on a variety of factors including generally accepted accounting principles, tax laws, and regulatory requirements, to name a few. Consequently, an asset can be valued differently for different purposes. For example, the same asset can be depreciated using one method to satisfy legal and regulatory requirements but a different method to address management's needs. Referring back to the computer purchase, for internal purposes the computer can be depreciated over two years using the double-declining balance method. However, tax laws may require that it be depreciated over five years using the straight line method. Thus, an asset can be depreciated using different methods and assumptions *simultaneously*. This practice is called parallel depreciation or parallel valuation of assets, and it is used to support the practice of parallel accounting discussed earlier in this chapter.

These different calculations are maintained in different **depreciation areas**. Common depreciation areas vary across countries. In the United States, the common areas are book depreciation, cost accounting depreciation, and tax or legal depreciation. Book depreciation is used to prepare financial statements for shareholders and to meet regulatory requirements. Cost accounting depreciation is used to allocate the cost of using the asset to a cost center. For example, the depreciation associated with a machine used in a production facility is allocated to the production cost center. Tax depreciation is used to file federal and state income tax returns.

Demo 3.9: Depreciate an asset

Retirement

After an asset has completed its useful life, it is disposed of, or retired. Asset retirement may or may not generate revenue. If an asset does not generate revenue, then it is scrapped. An asset can be sold to an external entity. The company may choose to utilize a fulfillment process similar to the one described in Chapter 5 to dispose its assets.

INTEGRATION WITH OTHER PROCESSES

Because financial accounting is concerned with recording the financial consequences of process execution, it is tightly integrated with all of the processes in an organization, as illustrated in Figure 3-22. Numerous steps in the different

Figure 3-22: Integration of financial accounting with other processes

processes have a financial impact on the firm. The key to recognizing these integration points is to "follow the money." Any time money either leaves or comes into the company—or the company makes an obligation to pay or receive money—there is very likely a financial accounting impact. We have illustrated this point in our examples of financial accounting transactions throughout this chapter. As we discuss the various processes in later chapters, the linkages between financial accounting and these processes will become clearer.

■ REPORTING

Reporting in financial accounting is broadly divided into two categories: displaying account information and generating financial statements.

ACCOUNT INFORMATION

Account information can be obtained at three levels—account balance display, line items display, and original FI document. Figure 3-23 shows the balance display for a bank account for the months of September (Period 9) and October (Period 10). The figure highlights a drilldown for a credit amount of $19,000 in September. The drilldown reveals a list of line items that comprise the credit amount. One of these items is for the value of $5,000. A further drilldown of the $5,000 displays the data in the original FI document—the original debits and credits—associated with the posting. Note that drilling down to the line item level is possible only if the *line item display* indicator, which was discussed earlier, is set in the general ledger account master data.

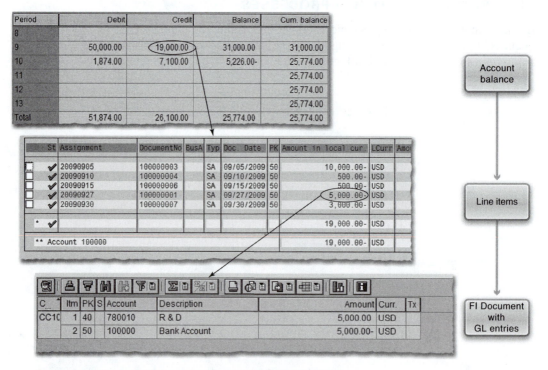

Figure 3-23: Account information. Copyright SAP AG 2011

Demo 3.10: Review account information

ASSET EXPLORER

The data associated with assets is complex and includes information concerning acquisition, depreciation, and retirement. The simple reporting capabilities discussed in the previous section are not adequate for asset accounting. Consequently, companies rely on a reporting tool known as the asset explorer (Figure 3-24). The **asset explorer** provides an overview of all the activities related to the asset, including acquisition data, planned and posted depreciation for different depreciation areas, and comparisons of data across multiple years. It also enables companies to drill down for details regarding master data, transactions, and documents.

The asset explorer distinguishes between *planned values*—depreciation amounts that have not yet been posted to the general ledger accounts—and

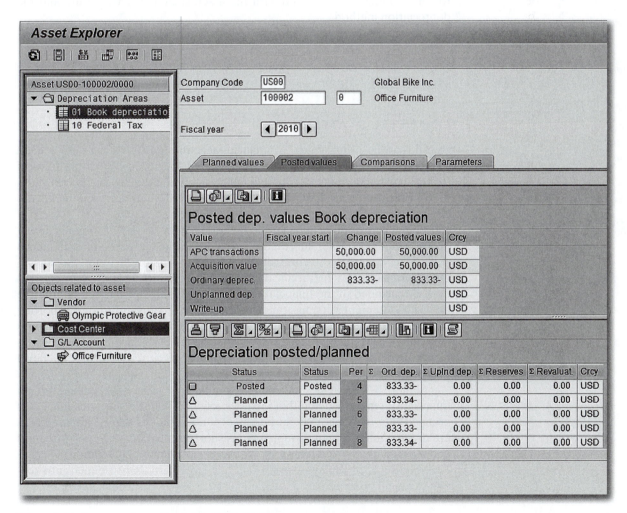

Figure 3-24: Asset explorer. Copyright SAP AG 2011

posted values, which have been posted. Planned values must be periodically posted to the general ledger. Companies accomplish this task by executing a *depreciation posting run*, which posts the planned values for the specified time period for all depreciation areas to the appropriate general ledger accounts. In addition, it charges the appropriate cost centers with the depreciation expenses incurred.

Figure 3-24 is an example of the asset explorer. The top part of the figure identifies the asset and the fiscal year for which the data are displayed (asset #100002, office furniture, and 2010, respectively). The top left part lists available depreciation areas. In the figure, two areas are available: book depreciation and tax depreciation. Book depreciation has been selected. The tabs in the middle part of the figure indicate the types of data that are maintained in the asset explorer. Note that the posted values tab is selected. This tab displays the acquisition value of the asset and depreciation values that were posted by the depreciation run. The planned values tab includes planned depreciation values for all the depreciation areas. The comparisons tab displays data for multiple years, and the parameters tab displays current settings for the parameters associated with the asset, such as the useful life and the depreciation method.

Demo 3.11: Review asset explorer

FINANCIAL STATEMENTS

Recall that the primary goal of financial accounting is to report data needed to meet legal and regulatory requirements. This reporting takes the form of financial statements, including the balance sheet and the profit and loss statement. The specific accounts that need to be included in these statements are determined by the nature and purpose of the requirements.

Financial statements can be generated for different organizational levels, including one or more company codes and business areas. Financial statements are created from financial statement versions. A financial statement version is a hierarchical grouping of general ledger accounts that must be included in the financial statements. A company can define multiple financial statement versions, tailoring each one to satisfy different reporting requirements. Financial statements can be generated from either the operative chart of accounts or the country-specific chart of accounts. These statements also specify additional characteristics such as currency, format, and level of detail.

Figure 3-25 provides an example of a balance sheet. It is defined using a financial statement version that includes relevant balance sheet accounts. It is grouped into two major categories, assets and liabilities/equity, which in turn are divided into account groups such as short-term assets (e.g., raw materials and finished goods) and long-term assets (e.g., land and depreciation).

Figure 3-26 displays a profit and lost statement. It is grouped into revenue accounts, expense accounts, and cost of goods sold accounts.

Financial Statements

Financial Statement (GBI)

0L — Ledger
10 — Currency type Company code currency
USD — Amounts in United States Dollar
2010.01 -2010.16 — Reporting periods
2009.01 -2009.16 — Comparison periods

F.S. item/account	Tot.rpt.pr	tot.cmp.pr	Abs. diff.
▼ ☐ ASSETS	244,208.44	0.00	244,208.44
▼ ☐ Cash & Cash Equivalents	45,050.00-	0.00	45,050.00-
▶ 🖻 100000 Bank Account	52,550.00-	0.00	52,550.00-
▶ 🖻 110000 Trade Account Reveivables	7,500.00	0.00	7,500.00
▼ ☐ Short-Term Assets	30,925.10	0.00	30,925.10
▶ 🖻 200000 Inventory-Raw Materials	232,925.00	0.00	232,925.00
▶ 🖻 200100 Inventory-Finished Goods	133,400.00	0.00	133,400.00
▶ 🖻 200200 Inventory-Trading Goods	76,117.50	0.00	76,117.50
▶ 🖻 200500 Inventory-Suspense (Heaven)	411,517.40-	0.00	411,517.40-
▼ ☐ Long-Term Assets	258,333.34	0.00	258,333.34
▶ 🖻 220100 Land	10,000.00	0.00	10,000.00
▶ 🖻 220400 Office Furniture	150,000.00	0.00	150,000.00
▶ 🖻 220500 Accumulated Depreciation-Offic	1,666.66-	0.00	1,666.66-
▶ 🖻 220800 Vehicles	100,000.00	0.00	100,000.00
▼ ☐ LIABILITIES / EQUITY	202,015.00-	0.00	202,015.00-
▼ ☐ Current Liabilities	202,015.00-	0.00	202,015.00-
▶ 🖻 300000 Payables-Trade Accounts	150,000.00-	0.00	150,000.00-
▶ 🖻 310000 Goods Receipt / Invoice Receipt	52,015.00-	0.00	52,015.00-

Figure 3-25: Financial statement version with balance sheet accounts. Copyright SAP AG 2011

Financial Statements

Financial Statement (GBI)

0L — Ledger
10 — Currency type Company code currency
USD — Amounts in United States Dollar
2010.01 -2010.16 — Reporting periods
2009.01 -2009.16 — Comparison periods

F.S. item/account	Tot.rpt.pr	tot.cmp.pr	Abs. diff.
▶ ☐ ASSETS	244,208.44	0.00	244,208.44
▶ ☐ LIABILITIES / EQUITY	202,015.00-	0.00	202,015.00-
▼ ☐ PROFIT & LOSS STATEMENT	42,193.44-	0.00	42,193.44-
▼ ☐ Revenue	134,715.00-	0.00	134,715.00-
▶ 🖻 600000 Sales Revenue	134,715.00-	0.00	134,715.00-
▼ ☐ Expenses	23,559.06	0.00	23,559.06
▶ 🖻 720000 Raw Material Consumption Exp	44,337.40	0.00	44,337.40
▶ 🖻 720200 Trading Good Consumption Exp	765.00	0.00	765.00
▶ 🖻 720300 Semi-Finished Consumption Ex	760.00	0.00	760.00
▶ 🖻 740000 Supplies Expense	8,000.00	0.00	8,000.00
▶ 🖻 741600 Manufacturing Output Settlemen	1,570.00-	0.00	1,570.00-
▶ 🖻 741700 Manufacturing Output Settlemen	80,400.00-	0.00	80,400.00-
▶ 🖻 741800 Depreciation Expense	1,666.66	0.00	1,666.66
▶ 🖻 770000 Research & Development	50,000.00	0.00	50,000.00
▼ ☐ Cost of Goods Sold	68,962.50	0.00	68,962.50
▶ 🖻 780000 Cost of Goods Sold	68,962.50	0.00	68,962.50

Figure 3-26: Financial statement version—with profit and loss accounts. Copyright SAP AG 2011

Demo 3.12: Generate financial statements

Recall from our discussion of asset accounting earlier in this chapter that in financial accounting an enterprise maintains a variety of depreciation areas simultaneously. As a consequence, the enterprise requires different types of financial statements—for example, one type for external reporting and another type for filing taxes. For this reason it maintains different financial statement versions, each of which includes the appropriate depreciation-related accounts. Figure 3-27 shows a company that uses two depreciation areas to provide data to different financial statements intended for different audiences. Specifically, the company includes book depreciation data in the financial statements presented to shareholders and tax depreciation data in the statements intended for tax authorities.

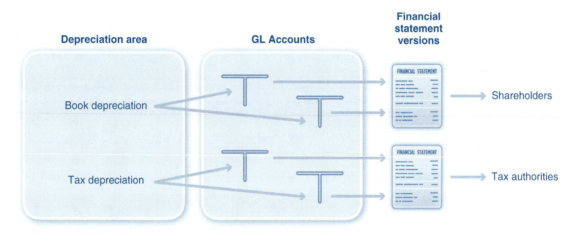

Figure 3-27: Financial statements based on depreciation areas

CHAPTER SUMMARY

In this chapter, we explored various ways in which a firm can use accounting processes to reflect the impact of the other business processes (e.g., procurement and fulfillment) on its financial status. We also considered how the firm can utilize accounting information to better plan and manage its operations.

The two basic categories of accounting processes are financial accounting (FI) and management accounting. Financial accounting is concerned with calculating the impacts of business operations for external reporting, typically to regulatory bodies and shareholders. In contrast, management accounting, or controlling (CO), consolidates process data the firm utilizes for internal management and planning. Both financial and management accounting leverage the same data from an ERP system, but they do so from different perspectives and for different goals.

Financial accounting consists of five key processes: general ledger accounting, accounts receivable accounting, accounts payable accounting, asset accounting, and bank ledger accounting. These processes are closely linked with other operational or logistics processes throughout the firm, and they share a great deal of the common master data found in those processes. Financial accounting uses several unique types of data, such as the chart of accounts, general ledger accounts, subsidiary ledgers, and reconciliation accounts, to provide a complete picture of the firm's financial status.

Management accounting focuses primarily on the allocation of costs and revenues to proper areas within the firm. Costs and revenues that are incurred as the various business processes are executed are accumulated in various cost objects. Firms then utilize these data to manage the organization.

KEY TERMS

Account determination

Account group

Accounts payable accounting

Accounts receivables accounting

Asset accounting

Asset class

Asset explorer

Assets

Balance sheet

Bank ledger accounting

Business areas

Chart of accounts (COA)

Cost center

Cost objects

Depreciation

Depreciation areas

Equity

Expenses

Financial accounting document

Financial statement version

General ledger (GL)

Income statement

Liabilities

Parallel accounting

Profit and loss statement

Reconciliation accounts

Revenues

Segment

Statement of cash flow

Subledgers

Subsidiary ledgers

REVIEW QUESTIONS

1. Explain the difference between financial accounting and management accounting.

2. Briefly describe the key processes in financial accounting.

3. Explain the key organizational data in financial accounting and the relationships between them.

4. What are charts of accounts and the general ledger? How are they related?

5. What are subsidiary ledgers and reconciliation accounts? How are they related?

6. What is an accounting document? What role does it serve?

7. Explain parallel accounting. Why do organizations maintain multiple ledgers?

8. What is the purpose of cost objects? Provide several examples of cost objects.

9. An organization purchases supplies for $3,000 and pays for them via a check. Prepare the T accounts to illustrate the impact of this purchase on the general ledger.

10. An organization purchases office supplies as listed below. The vendor invoices the organization at a later date, and the organization makes payment via a check. Prepare the T accounts to illustrate the impact of these purchases on the general ledger.

    a. Purchase office supplies for $2,500 from Vendor Z.

    b. Purchase office supplies for $1,200 from Vendor Y.

11. An organization sells products to customers as explained below. The customers are sent invoices at a later date, and they make payment for the amount of the invoice. Prepare the T accounts to illustrate the impact of these purchases on the general ledger.

    a. Sell products for $3,500 to Customer A.

    b. Sell products for $3,500 to Customer B.

12. Explain the relationships among asset accounts, asset classes, and general ledger accounts.

13. Explain the three transaction types in asset accounting.

14. What are depreciation areas? Why do firms maintain different depreciation areas?

15. Explain the components of the asset explorer.

16. What are financial statement versions? Explain how they are created.

EXERCISES

Exercises for this chapter are available on *WileyPLUS.*

3A

Accounts In The GL00 Chart of Accounts

PROFIT AND LOSS ACCOUNTS

Account Number	Short Text	Long Text
600000	Sales Revenue	Sales Revenue
610000	Sales Discount	Sales Discount
620000	Misc. Revenue	Miscellaneous Revenue
630000	Revenue Deductions	Revenue Deductions
640000	G or L-Sale of Asset	Gain or Loss on Sale of Assets
650000	Cust. Serv. Revenue	Customer Service Revenue
650100	CS Rev Settlement	Customer Service Revenue Settlement
700000	Labor	Labor
720000	RM Consumpt Expense	Raw Material Consumption Expense
720100	FP Consumpt Expense	Finished Product Consumption Expense
720200	TG Consumpt Expense	Trading Good Consumption Expense
720300	SF Consmpt Expense	Semifinished Consumption Expense
740000	Supplies Expense	Supplies Expense
740100	Utilities Expense	Utilities Expense
740200	Legal and Prof Expense	Legal and Professional Expense
740300	Rent Expense	Rent Expense
740400	Ins. Expense Liability	Insurance Expense—Liability
740500	Payroll Expense	Payroll Expense—Office
740600	Payroll Expense	Payroll Expense—Administrative

(*Continued*)

PROFIT AND LOSS ACCOUNTS (*CONTINUED*)

Account Number	Short Text	Long Text
740700	Sales Expense	Sales Expense
740800	Tax Expense	Tax Expense—Property
740900	Tax Expense	Tax Expense—Income
741000	Misc. Expense	Miscellaneous Expense
741100	Labor Expense	Labor Expense
741200	COGS Expense Acc.	Cost of Goods Sold Expense Account
741300	IT Expense Account	Information Technology Expense Account
741400	PO Var. Expense Acc.	Production Order Variance Expense Account
741500	Utilities	Utilities (electricity & phone)
741600	Manufac. Output Sett.	Manufacturing Output Settlement
741700	Mfac. Output Sett Var.	Manufacturing Output Settlement Variance
760000	Purchase Price Diff.	Purchase Price Difference
760100	Production Var.	Production Variance
780000	R & D	Research and Development
790000	COGS	Cost of Goods Sold

BALANCE SHEET ACCOUNTS

Account Number	Short Text	Long Text
100000	Bank	Bank Account
101000	Alt Bank	Alternate Bank Account
110000	Trade Receivables	Trade Accounts receivables
110100	Misc. A/R	Miscellaneous Accounts Receivable
110200	Int. Receivable	Interest Receivable
200000	Inv-RM	Inventory-Raw Materials
200100	Inv-FG	Inventory-Finished Goods
200200	Inv-TG	Inventory-Trading Goods
200300	Inv-SFG	Inventory-Semifinished Goods

200400	Inv-PS	Inventory-Production Supplies
200500	Inv-SP	Inventory-Suspense (Heaven)
200600	Inv-OP	Inventory-Operating Supplies
210000	PP Ins	Prepaid insurance
215000	PP Rent	Prepaid Rent
220000	N/R	Notes Receivable
220100	Land	Land
220200	Prod Mach/Equip/Fixt	Production Machinery, Equipment and Fixtures
220300	Accum. Depr.	Accumulated Depreciation-Production Mach. Equip. and Fixtures
220400	Office Furniture	Office Furniture
220500	Accum. Depr.	Accumulated Depreciation-Office Furniture
220600	Office Equip & Compu	Office Equip. and Computers
220700	Accum. Depr.	Accumulated Depreciation-Office Equipment
220800	Vehicles	Vehicles
220900	Accum. Depr.	Accumulated Depreciation-Vehicles
221100	Intangible Assets	Intangible Assets
221200	Accum. Amort. - IA	Accumulated Amortization-Intangible Assets
300000	Payables-TA	Payables-Trade Accounts
300100	Payables-In Taxes	Payables-Income Taxes
300200	Payable-Misc	Payables-Miscellaneous
300300	Payables-Int	Payables-Interest
300400	Payables-ST/N	Payables-Short-Term Notes
300500	Payables-LT/N	Payables-Long-Term Notes
300600	Payables-Comm	Payables-Commissions
310000	GR/IR Account	Goods Receipt / Invoice Receipt Account
320000	AT-Output	Accrued Tax-Output
321000	AT-Input	Accrued Tax-Input
322000	Unearned Revenues	Unearned Revenues
329000	Common Stock	Common Stock
329100	Additional Paid Capit	Additional Paid-in-Capital
330000	Retained Earnings	Retained Earnings

The Procurement Process

LEARNING OBJECTIVES

After completing this chapter you will be able to:

1. Describe the major organizational levels associated with the procurement process.

2. Discuss the four basic categories of master data that are utilized during the procurement process.

3. Explain the key concepts associated with the procurement process.

4. Identify the key steps in the procurement process and the data, documents, and information associated with these steps.

5. Effectively use SAP® ERP to execute the key steps in the procurement process.

6. Utilize SAP ERP to extract meaningful information about the procurement process.

In Chapter 1 we presented a simple procurement process, which is reproduced in Figure 4-1. This diagram indicates that the initial step in this process is to create a requisition, which is then converted to a purchase order and sent to a vendor. When the vendor receives the purchase order, it ships the materials, which the ordering party receives in the receive materials step. The ordering party also receives an invoice from the vendor, and it then makes a payment to the vendor.

This simple process has served GBI well until now due to its small size and closely connected operations. However, as GBI has grown and its operations have become more dispersed and complex, GBI's management has come to realize that it needs to reevaluate how GBI procures materials so that the company can take advantage of the most effective and efficient processes. To accomplish this objective, management needs to familiarize itself with the various options available to GBI for executing the procurement process. In addition, it wants to analyze the process steps and their impact in greater depth. Once management has attained a thorough understanding of the tactical and

Warehouse	Purchasing	Warehouse	Accounting	Accounting
Create purchase requisition	Create and send purchase order	Receive materials	Receive invoice	Send payment

Figure 4-1: A basic procurement process

strategic aspects of this current procurement process, it can then design and implement a new process that best meets GBI's needs. It can also determine the best way to manage this process using the SAP ERP system.

In this chapter we examine the procurement process, also referred to as the purchasing or requisition-to-pay process. We begin by discussing the organizational and master data relevant to this process. We then examine some of the key concepts inherent in the procurement process. After considering the concepts, we discuss the process steps in greater detail than we did in Chapter 1. We conclude the chapter with a discussion of reporting options.

To illustrate the various concepts and process steps, we will use the following scenario throughout the chapter. GBI has discovered that the inventory of t-shirts (SHRT1000) in its Miami distribution center is low. Consequently, the company must procure more shirts before it runs out and begins to lose sales (and perhaps customers). GBI procures all of its t-shirts from a company called Spy Gear. Further, it purchases them in quantities of 500.

■ ORGANIZATIONAL DATA

The procurement process is executed in the context of specific organizational levels. Organizational levels relevant to the procurement process include client, company code, and plant. We discussed these levels in Chapter 2. Recall from that discussion that a client represents an enterprise that is comprised of many companies or subsidiaries, each of which is represented by a company code. Most activities in the procurement process occur within a company code. Recall also that a plant fulfills many functions in a company. In the context of procurement, a plant is the location where the materials are received. Therefore we refer to it as a *receiving plant*, as opposed to, say, a manufacturing plant, where goods are actually produced. Three additional organizational data are relevant to purchasing: storage locations, purchasing organization, and purchasing group. We consider each one next.

STORAGE LOCATION

Storage locations are places within a plant where materials are kept until they are needed. A plant can have multiple storage locations, each of which is designated for different purposes (e.g., staging area, inspection area) or stores specific types of materials (e.g., semifinished goods). More specific storage locations include shelves, bins, cabinets, and trays. Locations range from small bins to entire buildings, depending on the size of the materials being stored. For example, the storage location for nuts and bolts will be a small container, whereas the storage location for an aircraft will be a hanger. Organizations with sophisticated inventory management systems can manage their materials on a more detailed level. We address these systems in the chapter on inventory and warehouse management.

Regardless of the nature of the enterprise, however, a plant must have at least one storage location if it needs to track the quantity and value of materials in its inventory. For example, a plant that serves as a production or storage facility must maintain accurate records of the quantity and value of raw materials, semifinished goods, and finished goods. The plant cannot perform this function without storage locations. In other cases, however, this function is not necessary. For example, an enterprise does not typically track the quantity or value of supplies it purchases for a corporate office (a plant). Therefore, a storage location is not essential. Significantly, although one plant can have multiple storage locations, each storage location can belong to only one plant.

Figure 4-2 shows storage locations for the five GBI plants. The Dallas plant has four storage locations. It stores raw materials (RM00), semifinished good (SF00), finished goods (FG00), and miscellaneous materials (MI00). The Miami and San Diego plants, which are distribution centers (DCs), both have three storage locations to store finished goods (FG00), trading goods (TG00), and miscellaneous materials (MI00). The structure of storage locations in Germany is similar to that of the U.S. company. The manufacturing facility in Heidelberg has a structure similar to that in Dallas, and the Hamburg plant has a structure similar to the plants in Miami and San Diego. Note that although

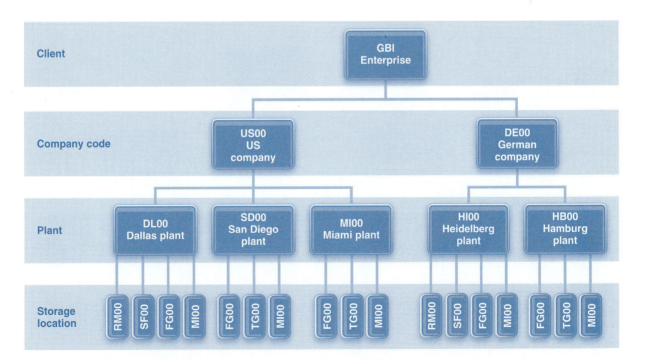

Figure 4-2: GBI Storage locations

the labels of the storage locations are the same in different plants—for example, location FG00 exists in all five plants—they are distinct organizational levels. The combination of plant and storage location must be unique. Thus, the Dallas plant may not have another storage location with the label FG00. It is common to use the same labels across plants and company codes if they represent the same type of storage, such as raw materials and finished materials.

PURCHASING ORGANIZATION

A purchasing organization is the unit within an enterprise that performs strategic activities related to purchasing for one or more plants. It evaluates and identifies vendors, and it negotiates contracts and agreements, pricing, and other terms. An enterprise may have one or more purchasing organizations. Typically, there are three models of purchasing organizations: enterprise level, company level, and plant level. These models range from highly centralized to highly decentralized. We discuss each of these models in greater detail below.

Enterprise-Level Purchasing Organization

The enterprise-level purchasing organization, also known as the *cross-company code* purchasing organization, is the most centralized model. There is only one purchasing organization for the overall enterprise and all of the plants within the enterprise. Figure 4-3 illustrates the GBI organizational structure using the enterprise-level model. There is only one corporate purchasing organization, GL00, and it handles purchasing for all five plants in both company codes (US00 and DE00). In this model, the purchasing organization is assigned to each plant, but not to the company code.

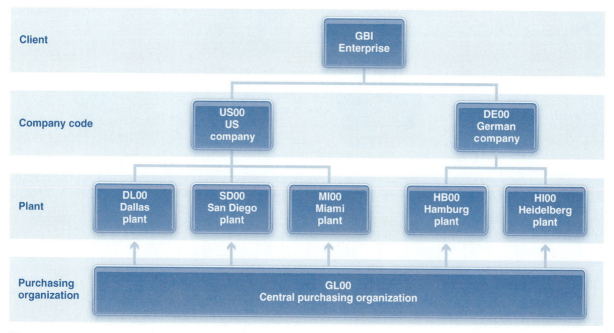

Figure 4-3: Enterprise-level purchasing organization

Company-Level Purchasing Organization

With the company-level purchasing organization, also known as the *cross-plant* model, a single purchasing organization is responsible for multiple plants in one company code. Figure 4-4 illustrates such a model for GBI. In the figure, there are two purchasing organizations: US00 and DE00. US00 is responsible for all three U.S. plants, and DE00 is responsible for the two German plants. This approach is less centralized than the enterprise-level model. In this model the purchasing organization is assigned to both the plant and the company code. However, a purchasing organization can be assigned only to one company code.

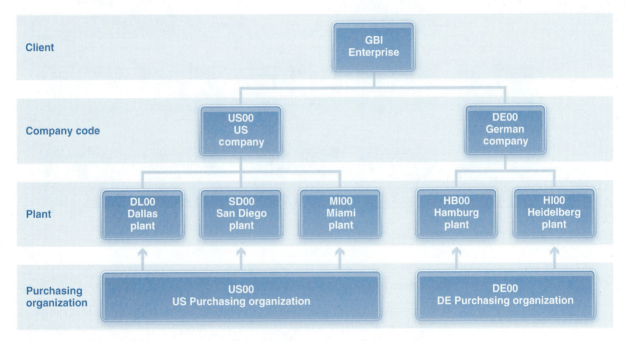

Figure 4-4: Company-level purchasing organization

GBI has one company in the United States and one in Germany, each of which has its own purchasing organization. If GBI had additional companies in other European countries, then each country could have a separate purchasing organization. Alternatively, one purchasing organization could manage purchasing for several countries. In fact, it is fairly common to set up a separate purchasing organization for each country to deal with that country's distinctive set of laws, taxes, and business practices.

Plant-Level Purchasing Organization

The most decentralized model is the plant-level purchasing organization, also known as a *plant-specific* purchasing organization, in which each plant has its own purchasing organization. Figure 4-5 illustrates a plant-specific model for GBI. Note that each plant has its own purchasing organization that is responsible for purchasing materials for that plant. As in the case of the cross-plant model, in this scenario the purchasing organization is assigned to both the plant and its company code.

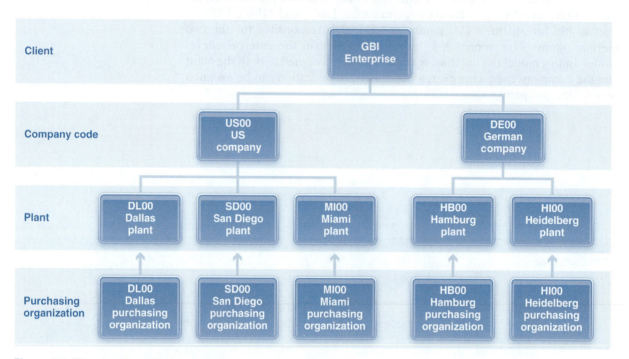

Figure 4-5: Plant-level purchasing organization

Reference Purchasing Organization

Each purchasing organization model has its advantages and disadvantages. A highly centralized model enables an enterprise to negotiate favorable agreements because it purchases materials in large volumes. However, the enterprise may not be able to take advantage of local practices and relationships with which it is not familiar. In addition, it may not be able to react quickly to changes in local conditions. Conversely, a highly decentralized model is preferred when vendors primarily serve a local geographic area and knowledge of local practices and conditions enables the enterprise to make favorable agreements. Ultimately, enterprises frequently adopt a hybrid model that consists of one centralized purchasing organization that can evaluate needs and opportunities for the entire enterprise and negotiate global contracts, which purchasing organizations then use across the enterprise. Such a purchasing organization is called a *reference purchasing organization*.

GBI has adopted a hybrid model to include a single global reference purchasing organization (GL00), as indicated in Figure 4-3, plus multiple company-code-specific purchasing organizations, as indicated in Figure 4-4. In the United States, the purchasing organization (US00) is physically located in the Miami facilities, and in Germany the purchasing organization (DE00) is physically located in the Heidelberg facilities.

PURCHASING GROUP

Whereas purchasing organizations are responsible for the strategic aspects of purchasing, such as negotiating contracts with vendors, purchasing groups carry out the day-to-day purchasing activities. A **purchasing group** is an individual or a group of individuals who are responsible for purchasing activities for a material or a group of materials. These activities include planning, creating purchase requisitions, requesting quotations from vendors, and creating and monitoring purchase orders. A **purchase order** (PO) is a formal communication to a vendor that represents a commitment to purchase the indicated materials under the stated terms. The purchasing group also serves as the main point of contact with vendors.

A purchasing group is not always an entity within the company. Some businesses outsource the group's activities. Consider, for example, a case in which a company needs to acquire land or a building. The company most likely will retain a realtor to find the property that best suits their needs. In this case, the realtor serves as the purchasing group. Similarly, many companies use the services of buyer agents to find suitable vendors and buy materials from them because these agents are more familiar with the vendors. GBI has one purchasing group for North America (N00) and one for Europe (E00).

Business Processes in Practice 4.1: Dell & Intel

Dell Computers and Intel Corporation illustrate how purchasing organizations manage both local and global procurement strategies. Dell has manufacturing facilities in the United States, Brazil, Ireland, Poland, China, Malaysia, and India. The company purchases vast quantities of Intel microprocessors for its various computer product lines (laptops, desktops, and servers). In turn, Intel maintains a dedicated sales force at Dell's headquarters to negotiate purchasing contracts and manage the relationship. Dell has a central purchasing organization that consolidates procurement requirements globally and negotiates pricing centrally with Intel. However, the actual purchase orders are created at the local Dell manufacturing facilities in each region. In other words, Dell US purchases chips from Intel US, Dell China purchases chips from Intel China, and so on. All purchases are based on the global contract and pricing terms negotiated between Dell and Intel headquarters, but they are executed locally by the purchasing groups for the various plants. This arrangement ensures that Dell receives the best pricing and terms due to the aggregate demand and strategic oversight of the centralized purchasing organization. At the same time, however, the local manufacturing facilities maintain control over the tactical purchasing activities because the purchasing organization is located on the same premises. Intel also benefits from this arrangement by gaining global visibility into Dell's purchasing so that the company can better adjust their manufacturing capacity to provide the right amount of chips to Dell when and where they are needed.

Source: Dell & Intel company reports.

■ MASTER DATA

In Chapter 2 we explained that business processes involve multiple types of master data. The four master data types that are relevant to the purchasing process are material master, vendor master, purchasing info records, and conditions. All four types are integrated in various combinations throughout the procurement process.

MATERIAL MASTER

In Chapter 2 we explained that data in the material master are grouped into different views that are relevant to different processes. We also examined one view in detail, namely, basic data, because these data are applicable to many processes. Recall that basic data include material number, description, and weight. Please review Chapter 2 for a complete list of materials that GBI utilizes. In addition to basic data, the views relevant to purchasing are financial accounting, purchasing, and plant data / storage.

Financial Accounting Data

Financial accounting data include the valuation currency, the valuation class, and the price control. Valuation currency is the currency that the materials will be priced in, such as U.S. dollars or euros.

The valuation class identifies the general ledger accounts associated with the material. The general ledger accounts are used to maintain the value of the inventory in stock and are updated as materials are purchased, sold, or used in production. You may wish to review the appendix in Chapter 3 to familiarize yourself with the material accounts that GBI uses. Valuation class provides an important integration point between purchasing and financial accounting because it allows the system to automatically make postings to appropriate stock or inventory accounts in the general ledger. Typically, all materials with similar characteristics are assigned to the same valuation class. Consequently, all financial transactions for these materials are posted to the same general ledger account. For example, because off-road bikes and touring bikes are both finished goods, their transactions could be posted to the same finished goods inventory account. In some cases, however, materials with similar characteristics are assigned to different valuation classes and therefore to different general ledger accounts. Referring back to the previous example, the bikes could be assigned to the off-road bike inventory account and the touring bike inventory account, respectively. Assigning materials with similar characteristics to different valuation classes is appropriate when a company maintains separate general ledger accounts for different materials. The last and simplest option is to assign materials with different characteristics to the same valuation class and therefore the same inventory account. This strategy is appropriate when the enterprise does not need to track the value of the materials separately, as is the case, for example, with office supplies.

Price control identifies the method that is used to value the materials. The two options for price control are moving average price and standard price. Both options define the *price per unit* of materials in stock, such as helmets. In the *moving average price* option, the total value of the materials is divided by the quantity in stock to determine the average price per unit. For example, if a firm has 1000 helmets in stock and they cost $34,000 to purchase, then the moving price is $34 (34,000/1,000). This price is called "moving" because it is updated each time a process step affects the price; it represents an average price of the materials in stock. Thus, if the enterprise purchases an additional 100 helmets for $3,500, then the new moving price increases slightly to $34.09 (($34,000 + $3,500)/(1,000 + 100)).

In contrast, *standard price* is constant for a specified period of time and does not fluctuate, even when an event occurs that causes the value of the materials to change. The standard price is updated periodically — for example, monthly or quarterly — to account for changes in the value of materials. Thus, in our example above, if the firm's policy is to update the standard price at the end of each month, then it does not make any price changes when it purchases the additional helmets. Instead, it updates the standard price at the end of the month.

Purchasing Data

Another key component of the material master is the *purchasing data* or *view*. The key data in the purchasing view are the *purchasing group*, the *goods receipt processing time*, and the *delivery tolerances*. The purchasing group, which we discussed earlier as one of the organizational elements in procurement, is responsible for purchasing the materials.

When a company receives materials from a vendor, it requires a certain amount of time to receive them and place them into storage. For instance, it must unpack the boxes, count the materials, inspect their quality, and physically move them to the appropriate storage location. This is the **goods receipt processing time**. An estimate of this time is included in the material master. The ERP system utilizes this estimate in planning activities, for instance, to determine when an order should be placed so that the materials are available when they are needed.

It is not uncommon for the shipment from a vendor to include either more or less material than the actual quantity ordered. When this occurs, the receiving organization may or may not accept receipt, depending on its policies and its agreements with its vendors. The **delivery tolerances** in the material master specify how much over delivery and under delivery the ordering party will accept. If the quantity delivered is within these tolerances, then the ordering party accepts delivery. If the quantity exceeds the tolerances, then it refuses the shipment and returns it to the vendor.

Some of the data in the material master can vary for each relevant organizational level. In purchasing, the relevant organizational level is the plant. If a company has multiple plants, then the material must be defined for all plants in which it is stored. For example, the purchasing group and goods receipt processing time can vary by plant.

Plant Data / Storage

Most materials that are purchased from a vendor or produced in-house ultimately are received into inventory. For this step to occur, the plant data / storage view must be included in the material master. The *plant data/ storage* view includes data that are needed to properly store materials. Examples of these data are:

- Environmental requirements such as temperature and humidity

- Special containers that are required for storage

- Shelf life; that is, how long a material can be stored before it becomes obsolete or unusable (common in pharmaceutical and food services industries)

- Instructions for special handling, for instance, if the material is fragile or hazardous.

Demo 4.1: Review material master

VENDOR MASTER

Vendor master data include the data needed to conduct business with a vendor and to execute transactions related to the purchasing process. Data in the vendor master are grouped into three segments: *general data*, *accounting data*, and *purchasing data*. The relationships among the three segments and the two departments responsible for the data—accounting and purchasing—are depicted in Figure 4-6. Figure 4-7 highlights the specific data that are included in each segment.

Figure 4-6: Segments of vendor master data

Figure 4-7: Examples of vendor master data

General data include the vendor's name, address, and communication information such as phone and fax numbers. These data are defined at the client level and are consistent across all company codes and purchasing organizations in the enterprise (client). General data are common to the purchasing and accounting departments and can be maintained by either department.

Accounting data include tax-related data, bank data, and payment terms and methods. These data are defined at the company code level (recall from Chapter 2 that financial accounting is maintained at the company code level) and are relevant to all purchasing transactions in the company code. The accounting department will typically complete this segment of the vendor master.

Accounting data must also specify the reconciliation account in the general ledger. Recall from Chapter 3 that a vendor account is a subledger account and that the reconciliation account identifies the accounts payable account in the general ledger associated with the vendor. If the vendor supplies multiple companies (company codes) within the enterprise, then the data very likely will vary for each company. The reconciliation account will be different if each company uses a different chart of accounts and general ledger accounts. Bank data and payment terms may vary as well. Thus, accounting data are maintained separately for each company code with which the vendor had dealings.

Finally, purchasing data include various terms related to determining prices, creating and communicating purchase orders, verifying invoices, and other steps involved in executing purchases with the vendor. The purchasing department will typically complete this segment. Purchasing data are defined at the purchasing organizational level and are applicable only to that organization. If an enterprise has multiple purchasing organizations that deal with the vendor, then it must maintain separate data for each one. For example, delivery and payment terms may vary for different purchasing organizations.

Both GBI US and GBI DE have 12 vendors that supply raw materials and trading goods. These vendors are listed in Table 4-1. Appendix 4A provides additional details about these vendors. Note from the appendix that each vendor supplies specific materials to GBI.

GBI US Vendors	GBI DE Vendors
• Olympic Protective Gear	• Burgmeister Zubehör OHG
• Boomtown Tire & Wheel	• Pyramid Biking
• Dallas Bike Basics	• ABS Brakes GmbH
• Lightbulb Accessory Kits	• Flat Tire and More
• Space Bike Composites	• Gummi Schultze
• Night Rider Aluminum Products	• Lohse Schraube
• Spy Gear	• Thick Spoke
• Rapids Nuts n Bolts	• Main Carbon
• Green Blazers Seats	• Shell Gear
• Fun n the Sun Seats n Bars	• Cologne Bike Supplies
• Sunny Side Up Tire	• Sachsen Stahl AG
• Redwood Kits	• Run & Fun

Table 4-1: GBI vendor list

Demo 4.2: Review vendor master

PURCHASING INFO RECORDS

A purchasing info record is an intersection or a combination of material and vendor data, as illustrated in Figure 4-8. It contains data specific to *one* vendor and *one* material or material group. Purchasing info records include some data that are in the vendor master and the material master, as well as data that are valid for the specific combination of vendor and material. These data are grouped into general data and purchasing organization data. *General data* are applicable to all purchasing groups and include vendor number, material number (or group), and other data used for communication (e.g., contact information, telephone numbers, and reminders). In contrast, *purchasing data* are specific to one purchasing organization, and they are based on agreements with the vendor regarding delivery times, delivery tolerances, quantities, and pricing conditions. Companies use pricing conditions to determine the cost of purchasing the material from that vendor. The info record typically defines a number of different **condition types**, including gross price, discounts and surcharges, taxes, and freight. It also includes text data that are used for notes and instructions to accompany purchase orders, and it keeps track of the last purchase order for the specific material-vendor combination. Finally, the company uses data from the purchasing info record as default values when it creates a purchase order for a specific combination of material and vendor.

Figure 4-8: Purchasing info record

Figure 4-9 illustrates a purchasing info record for vendor 107000 and material SHRT1000 for purchasing organization US00. It indicates that Spy Gear takes four days to deliver the t-shirts. Further, Spy Gear charges $15 per shirt, but it offers a discount of 4% for orders greater than $1,000.

CONDITIONS

The final type of master data relevant to purchasing is **conditions**. These data are very similar to the conditions discussed in the section on purchasing info records, and they are used to determine the appropriate prices, discounts, taxes, freight, and so on for the materials. Unlike the conditions in the purchasing info records, however, these conditions are not defined for a specific combination of vendor and material. Rather, they are based on the overall agreements and contracts in place with vendors. The company uses these conditions to determine pricing when it creates purchase orders.

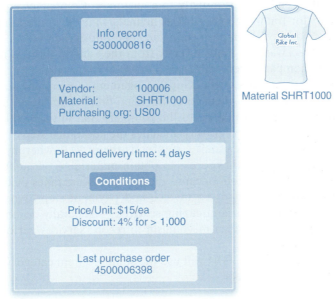

**Spy Gear
Vendor 107000**

Info record
5300000816

Vendor: 100006
Material: SHRT1000
Purchasing org: US00

Material SHRT1000

Planned delivery time: 4 days

Conditions

Price/Unit: $15/ea
Discount: 4% for > 1,000

Last purchase order
4500006398

Figure 4-9: Purchasing info record example

Demo 4.3: Review purchasing info record and conditions

■ KEY CONCEPTS

Before we discuss the procurement process in detail, we pause here to discuss some key concepts that are essential to understanding how the process works. These concepts are related to how the materials are purchased (item categories), how their impact on financials is recorded (account determination), the materials' usability (stock type), and the movement of the materials as they are received, stored, and shipped to customers (goods movements).

ITEM CATEGORIES

Item categories determine which process steps and data are needed when a company purchases materials or services. Common item categories are standard, consignment, subcontracting, third-party, stock transfer, and services.

   Of these categories, standard items are the most common, and the process used to procure them includes the steps portrayed in Figure 4-1. The initial step is to create a requisition, which is then converted to a purchase order and sent to a vendor. When the vendor receives the purchase order, it ships the materials, which the ordering party receives via the goods receipt step. The ordering party also receives an invoice, and it makes a payment to the vendor. In contrast, when a company purchases materials on consignment, it pays the vendor only when it uses or sells the materials. For this category of materials, therefore, there is no invoice receipt step. Third-party order refers to items that the vendor ships directly to a customer. Companies employ third-party orders for trading goods, such as helmets, that they purchase and then resell to customers without performing any operations themselves. Because the customer receives the goods directly from the vendor, there is no goods receipt for the company itself.

Under a **subcontracting** arrangement, a company sends materials to a vendor, who uses them to create semi-finished products. The vendor then sends these products back to the company that initiated the process. In this case, the procurement process includes the additional step of shipping materials to the vendor. A **stock transfer** is the process whereby an organization uses the procurement process to obtain materials from another plant within the same organization. Because the entire process takes place within a single organization, there are no invoice and payment steps. Finally, **services** — such as janitorial or landscaping services — generally do not involve receiving materials. Instead, a mechanism to record services performed – a *service sheet* - is necessary.

In our example, GBI will use the standard item category to purchase the t-shirts from Spy Gear.

Demo 4.4: Review item categories

ACCOUNT DETERMINATION

Businesses typically use the procurement process to purchase materials that they place in inventory until they need them. For example, businesses acquire raw materials for later use in the production process and trading goods for subsequent sales to customers. Such materials are referred to as **stock materials**. Recall from the discussion of financial accounting in Chapter 3 that the general ledger contains multiple inventory accounts, such as raw materials, trading goods, and finished goods. How does an ERP system know which of these inventory accounts must be updated when materials are received? For stock materials, for which a material master must be defined, **account determination** — the process whereby the system determines which general ledger accounts to use in a given situation — is automatic and is based on data contained in the material master, particularly the valuation class.

Companies also use the procurement process to acquire **consumable materials**. As the name suggests, these are materials that are acquired to be consumed by or used within the organization. One example of consumable materials is office supplies, such as pencils and paper, which people in the organization use during the course of their day-to-day work. When a company purchases materials for consumption, the transaction must identify the account assignment object to be charged for the purchase as well as the general ledger accounts to be debited and credited. An **account assignment object** identifies the bearer of the cost of the purchase and is the entity for which the materials were purchased. For example, when a company purchases office supplies for the marketing department, it debits a consumption account, such as the supplies expense account in the general ledger, and it charges the marketing department cost center for the purchase. Recall that a cost center is a cost object used to accumulate costs for a department. In the above example, the account assignment object is the cost center. Companies also use the purchasing process to acquire assets, such as cars, and to obtain materials needed to support processes such as production, fulfillment, and enterprise asset management and projects such as constructing a new factory. The specific accounting data needed are determined by the **account assignment category**. The typical account assignment categories are described below along with the accounting data — specifically, the account assignment object to be charged and the general ledger account number — that are required for each category. The letters in parentheses are the codes used in SAP ERP.

1. ***Asset*** (A). A company uses this category when it acquires a fixed asset, such as a car or land. Recall from Chapter 3 that the value of fixed assets is tracked in separate subledger accounts with corresponding asset master records. When assets are purchased using a purchase order (see Chapter 3 for other ways of acquiring assets), the account assignment object to be included in the purchase order is the asset master record.

2. ***Order*** (F). Companies use this category when they purchase materials for different types of orders. An example of an order is a production order that will be used to produce another material. When a company purchases materials for an order, it must include the order number (the account assignment object) and a general ledger account number in the purchase order.

3. ***Cost Center*** (K). When a company purchases materials (e.g., supplies) for consumption, then the purchase order must include both the cost center to be charged (the account assignment object) and the appropriate general ledger expense account number (e.g., supplies expense).

4. ***Sales Order*** (C). When the purchase is associated with a specific sales order (which is part of the fulfillment process), then the sales order number and a general ledger account number must be provided.

5. ***Project*** (P). When the purchase is related to a project, then the project number and a general ledger account number must be specified.

Note that in several of these categories a general ledger account is necessary. The system can be configured to automatically determine the appropriate account via account determination procedures. It is not always necessary for the user to provide these data.

Figure 4-10 shows the relationship between stock and consumable materials and account assignment categories. It shows the several scenarios related to purchasing – purchase of stock material, purchase of consumable material (with and without material master), and purchase of stock material for consumption. The left side of the figure shows that for stock material, account assignment is automatic and is based on data (valuation class) in the required material master. These data determine which accounts (e.g., which stock account) will be used during the procurement process.

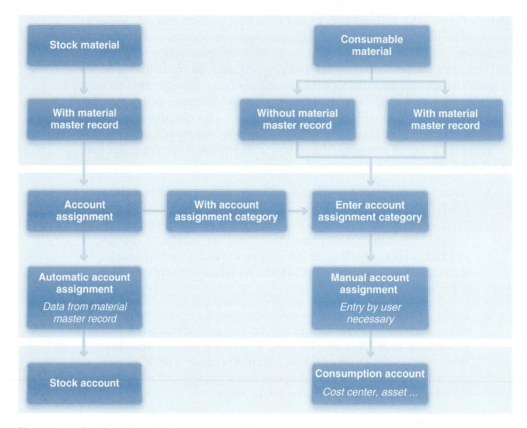

Figure 4-10: Purchase for stock vs. consumption

The right side of the figure shows that, for consumable materials, an account assignment category and specific account assignment objects, such as a cost center, must be provided when the purchase order is created. The data provided by the user determine which general ledger accounts (e.g., consumption account) will be used during the process. Consumable materials may or may not have a material master. If material master data exist, then two options are available. In one, the company doesn't track the quantity of the material in inventory; in the other, it does. It is important to remember, however, that the company can track only the *quantity* of inventory on hand. The *value* of inventory cannot be tracked because a consumption account (refer to Chapter 3), such as supplies expenses, rather than an inventory account is used in the purchasing process.

Finally, the middle of the figure illustrates the scenario in which materials that are typically purchased to stock are sometimes purchased for consumption. For example, GBI normally purchases helmets to resell to its customers; that is, it purchases them to stock. However, GBI occasionally purchases helmets to be distributed as gifts at trade shows. In these cases the transactions are considered purchases for consumption rather than for stock. Consequently, an account assignment category of K (cost center) is provided to override the data that are included in the material master, which would otherwise define helmets as stock material. Because category K is used, a specific consumption account (e.g., advertising expense) and a cost center associated with the trade show are required.

In our example, the t-shirts are purchased to stock. Because material master data for the t-shirts are defined in the ERP system, the data needed for account assignment will be obtained automatically from the material master.

STOCK TYPE OR STATUS

Stock or inventory of materials is classified into different **stock types** or *statuses* that determine the usability of materials— that is, how the company can use the materials in its various processes. Four common stock types are unrestricted use, in quality inspection, blocked stock, and stock in transit. Materials that are classified as **unrestricted use**—as the name implies—can be used in any manner that management feels will benefit the enterprise. They can be consumed internally—for instance, to produce other products—or externally, to meet customer demand. In contrast, materials defined as **in quality inspection** or **blocked stock** can be withdrawn only for sampling or for scrap. A company uses the in quality inspection status when the goods it receives from a vendor must undergo inspection before being released for consumption. Blocked stock is typically used for materials that are damaged or unusable for some reason, such as the when the vendor delivers the wrong materials. Finally, when materials are being moved from one plant to another, they are classified as **stock in transit**.

GOODS MOVEMENT

A process step that results in a change in stock results in a **goods movement**. The goods movement is associated with receiving materials from a vendor, shipping them to a customer, or otherwise "moving" them from one location within the company to another. The four common goods movements are goods receipt, goods issue, stock transfer, and transfer posting. The first three movements involve the physical movement of materials from one location to another. The fourth, transfer posting, is used to change the stock type or status of material (e.g., from in quality inspection to unrestricted use) or to reclassify the material into a different material type.

A **goods receipt** records the receipt of materials into storage, which results in an increase in inventory quantity. A company usually generates a goods receipt when it receives materials either from a vendor or from the production process. The material document created as a result of a goods receipt will show the location (plant and storage location) where the materials are received as well as the specific movement type used. The accounting document will identify the various general ledger accounts that are updated.

In contrast to a goods receipt, a company uses a goods issue when materials are *removed from* storage, in which case inventory is reduced. A company typically generates a goods issue when it (a) ships materials to a customer, (b) uses them for internal consumption (e.g., to produce another material), or (c) designates them for sampling or to scrap. The material document created by the goods issue will record the location from which the materials were issued as well as the quantity involved. The accounting document will indicate the relevant general ledger accounts and amounts. For example, when GBI ships materials to a customer, it removes the materials from inventory and records a goods issue in its SAP ERP system.

A stock transfer is used to move goods from one location to another within the organization. Materials can be transferred between storage locations, between plants within the same company codes, and between plants across company codes. In all cases, one or more material documents are created to record the transfer. In addition, for transfers between plants or company codes, accounting documents are also created. Recall that earlier in the chapter we defined stock transfer as an item category. So, why is it also a goods movement? The reason is that the procurement process can be used to transfer materials from one location to another. However, materials can be transferred outside the procurement process as well. In these cases the transfer can simply be recorded via a goods movement. This approach is quicker and more direct than using the procurement process, but it has limitations. We discuss stock transfers in greater detail in the chapter on inventory and warehouse management.

Finally, an enterprise uses a transfer posting to change a material's status or type. For example, it would use a transfer posting to redefine a material from in quality inspection status to unrestricted use or to change a material type from raw materials to finished goods. A transfer posting may or may not involve the physical movement of materials from one location to another. In either case, a material document is created to record the status change. For example, when the company receives materials from a vendor, it stores them and designates them as in quality inspection. After they pass inspection, it issues a transfer posting to "move" them to unrestricted use status. In this situation a material document is created, but an accounting document is not. As with stock transfers, we will examine transfer postings in greater detail in the chapter on inventory and warehouse management.

A goods movement will always result in the creation of a material document. In addition, a financial accounting document is created if the movement results in a change in valuation. As we discussed in Chapter 2, financial accounting documents record the impact of a process or process step on relevant general ledger accounts.

A material document records data related to a goods movement, such as the receipt of goods from a vendor. As illustrated in Figure 4-11, the material document consists of a header and one or more items or details. The header includes data such as the date, the name of the person who created the document, and the source of the document, that is, what process step or transaction was used to create it. The items identify the materials involved, quantities, location, the movement type used, and other relevant data.

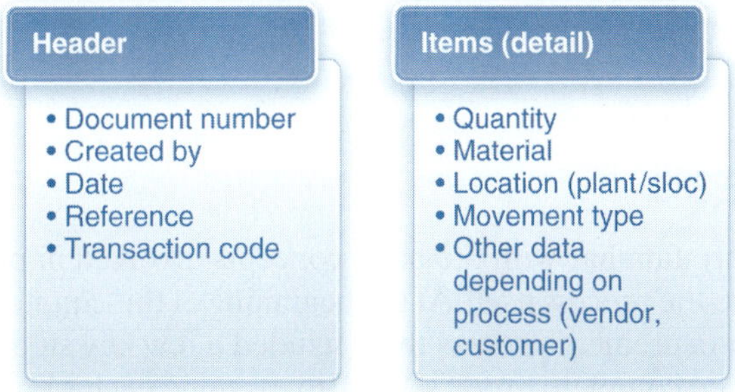

Figure 4-11: Structure of a Material Document

Demo 4.5: Review a Material Document

MOVEMENT TYPES

The four goods movements we just discussed can be accomplished through a number of specific **movement types**. Every goods movement requires a movement type. The movement type determines which category of movement is being executed (e.g., goods receipt or goods issue), what information must be provided when executing the movement (e.g., storage location), and which general ledger accounts will be updated (e.g., finished goods inventory). It also determines how the stock quantity will be affected (e.g., increase or decrease). Because different movement types require different information, they also determine the screen layout used to record the movement. Each movement type has a corresponding cancellation or reversal movement type that is used to reverse its impact. For example, movement type 101 is used to record the receipt of materials for a purchase order, and movement type 102 is used to reverse the receipt. Reversals are typically used to correct an error in recording. If the materials are defective and must be returned to the vendor, then a different movement type, 122, is used to record this movement. Table 4-2 lists examples of movement types in SAP ERP.

Goods Receipt
- 101: Goods receipt for a purchase order
- 102: Goods receipt for a purchase order - reversal
- 103: Goods receipt for a purchase order into blocked stock
- 122: Return delivery to vendor

Goods Issue
- 261: Consumption for production order from warehouse
- 231: Consumption for sales order from warehouse

Transfer Posting
- 321: Quality inspection to unrestricted
- 350: Quality inspection to blocked stock

Stock Transfer
- 301: Plant to plant transfer
- 311: Storage location to storage location transfer

Table 4-2: Examples of movement types

Demo 4.6: Review goods movements and movement types

■ PROCESS

Now that you are familiar with the basic concepts involved in procurement, we shift our focus to the process itself. At the beginning of this chapter we introduced a very simple procurement process that included a few key steps. In this section we discuss a more complete process. We also examine each step in detail.

In this section, we discuss the purchase of a standard item. The steps used to procure standard items are diagrammed in Figure 4-12. The figure indicates that the procurement process is triggered by some event that results in a requirement to acquire materials. The trigger is often a result of an event in another process. For example, the company cannot fulfill a production order (a step in the production process) until it purchases certain necessary materials. Alternatively, the materials planning process may alert the company that it needs to increase its inventory of certain materials. Regardless of the trigger, the result is a requirement to obtain materials. This requirement typically takes the form of a purchase requisition.

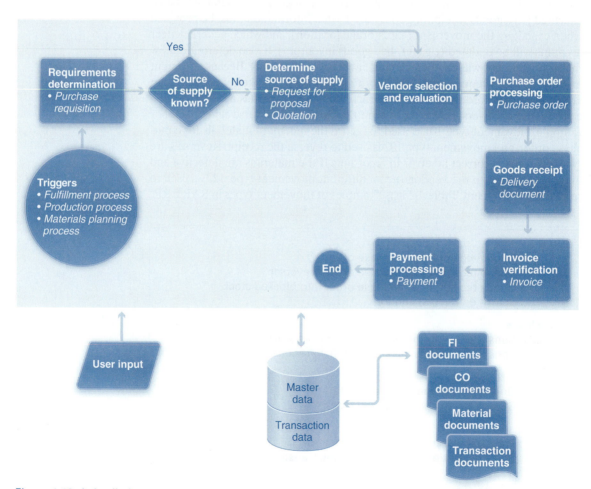

Figure 4-12: A detailed procurement process

Once a requisition is created, the company must select a source of supply. This source can be either external (e.g., a suitable vendor) or internal (e.g., another plant in the company). If the source is external, then the selection process may include additional steps such as requesting and receiving quotations. After the company receives the quotations, it evaluates them and selects a vendor. It then submits a purchase order. Upon receiving the order, the vendor confirms receipt and may provide additional information such as the expected shipment date. The vendor then ships the materials to the company, which receives them into inventory. The vendor also sends an invoice. Once the company verifies the invoice, it sends a payment to the vendor.

If the source of supply is internal, then the process is somewhat different. A *stock transport order* is used instead of a purchase order. We will discuss stock transport orders in greater detail in the chapter on inventory and warehouse management.

The preceding paragraphs convey a very simplistic overview of the basic steps in the procurement process. In reality, procurement is much more complex. In the next section we examine the steps illustrated in Figure 4-12 in detail. We discuss each step in terms of its key elements— *triggers*, *data*, *tasks*, and *outcomes*. A trigger is something that causes the step to be executed. The relevant data typically include organizational data, master data, transaction data, and user input that are specific to the process step. Outcomes include new transaction data and updates to master data, all of which are stored in the database. In addition, financial accounting (FI) documents, management accounting or controlling (CO) documents, and material documents are created. Finally, transaction documents are created or updated.

REQUIREMENTS DETERMINATION

The elements of the requirements determination step are summarized in Figure 4-13. Requirements for materials arise from a need that is identified either automatically by another process or manually by an individual. The process that most commonly generates requirements is the materials planning process. (We will discuss this process at length in the materials planning chapter.) Requirements are also generated by the production and plant maintenance processes. To complete these processes, the company sometimes must purchase non-stock items or services from another organization. In such cases a requirement for the material or service is created. In addition, the need to send materials for external processing during production (e.g., a part to be repaired) will result in a requirement for a subcontracted item.

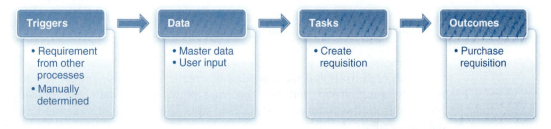

Figure 4-13: Elements of the requirements determination step

Requirements are also created manually for items that are not included in materials planning. This process occurs when an individual manages inventory or when the company needs a nonstock item (e.g., supplies) or a service (e.g., janitorial or repair). Regardless of the trigger or source, the need for materials is documented in the form of a purchase requisition. Note that a purchase requisition is a document that is used for internal purposes—namely, to request needed materials. It is *not* a commitment to purchase the materials or service. Rather, the commitment occurs when a purchase order is created in the next step of the process.

Data

The data needed to create a purchase requisition are the item category, quantity, desired delivery date, and desired delivery location or receiving plant (see Figure 4-14). In addition, a material number is needed for stock items, and an account assignment object may be required depending on the item category selected. The ERP system uses the material number to obtain additional data from the material master such as description, material group, purchasing group, unit of measure, and valuation price. The delivery date and location are typically provided by the requisitioner, but they can also be obtained from the material master.

Figure 4-14: Data in a purchase requisition

The organizational data needed to create a purchase requisition are the purchasing group and the receiving plant. These data are typically obtained from the material master. User input can provide or override these data as needed.

Vendor data are optional. When they are included, they indicate a preference for the source of supply. Vendor data include the vendor number and name.

It is also possible to requisition materials that do not have material master data, but this procedure must be performed manually. Basically, the requisitioner provides a description of the material instead of a material number. In addition, he or she provides data that are normally obtained from the material master, including delivery location, material group, purchasing group, and account assignment category. Further, depending on the account assignment category, additional data such as cost center, asset number, and general ledger accounts can also be included. (At this point you might want to review our discussion of account determination earlier in the chapter.)

Tasks

The only task in this step is to create the purchase requisition using the specified data.

Outcomes

The process document that results from this step is the purchase requisition. The system will assign a unique requisition number to this document, which the concerned parties can use to track its progress through the various steps in the process. Significantly, this step does not generate any financial or management accounting documents because creating a requisition has no financial impact.[1] Moreover, because there is no goods movement (that is, no materials are received), no material document is created either.

In our example, the trigger for the procurement process is low inventory of t-shirts. GBI has determined (through material planning, which we discuss in Chapter 8) that t-shirts must be reordered when there are 50 or fewer left in inventory. In addition, the shirts must be purchased in quantities of 500. GBI was alerted to the need to reorder by an employee in the plant who reviews inventory reports that are printed at the beginning of each day. This individual observed that the inventory of t-shirts at the Miami plant had fallen below 50. As a result, he created a purchase requisition for 500 t-shirts to be delivered to the Miami plant by a specified date.

SOURCE OF SUPPLY DETERMINATION

Once again, a requisition is merely a request for material; it does not represent a legal obligation to purchase anything. In contrast, a purchase order constitutes an obligation to purchase. As Figure 4-15 illustrates, there are three paths to create a purchase order, depending on whether the source of supply is known.

---

[1]Although there is no financial accounting impact when a requisition is created, a requisition typically will result in the purchase of the needed materials. To help with planning for anticipated expenses, when purchasing consumable materials, a requisition will result in an internal record of the potential obligation, called a commitment, if the commitment management process in management accounting is in use.

If it is, then the requisition can be converted into a purchase order without additional steps (Path 1). In such cases the company selects a vendor from a list of potential suppliers, called a **source list**. If the source list contains only one source, then the system will automatically assign the vendor to the requisition. However, if the source list identifies multiple sources, then the system will display a list of vendors for the user to choose from. Alternatively, the requisition can be satisfied through **outline purchase agreements,** which are longer-term agreements between an organization and a vendor regarding the supply of materials or the performance of services within a specified period according to predefined terms and conditions. Outline agreements are subdivided into **contracts** and **scheduling agreements**. During the contract validity period, certain quantities or services are released (called off) against the contract as and when required through the issue of purchase orders. Such purchase orders are thus termed *contract release orders* or simply *release orders*. In some non-SAP systems, they are also referred to as *call-off orders*. In a scheduling agreement, the delivery of the total quantity of material specified in the agreement is spread over a certain period according to a delivery schedule. The delivery schedule specifies the quantities with their corresponding planned delivery dates.

Figure 4-15: Converting a purchase requisition to a purchase order

If a source of supply is not known, then the company must send a *request for quotations* (RFQ) to several potential vendors, receive and evaluate the quotations, and then make a final selection. An RFQ is an invitation to vendors by an organization to submit a quote for the supply of the materials or services. A quotation is legally binding on the vendor for a specified period. It identifies materials or services for which the total quantities and delivery dates are specified. In this case, the organization uses a quotation to create a purchase order (Path 2). Finally, in certain cases the RFQ is directly converted into a purchase order without a quotation (Path 3). This may be the case when a vendor provides a quotation verbally and the company does not consider it necessary to enter the quotation data into the system.

In our example, Spy Gear is the only supplier of t-shirts. This information is ascertained from a source list maintained in the ERP system. Because there is an established supplier, it is not necessary for GBI to request and evaluate quotes from potential vendors.

Demo 4.7: Create Purchase Requisition

ORDER PROCESSING

As we previously discussed, a *purchase order* is a communication sent to a vendor in which a company commits to purchasing the specified materials under the stated terms. Figure 4-16 summarizes the elements of a purchase order.

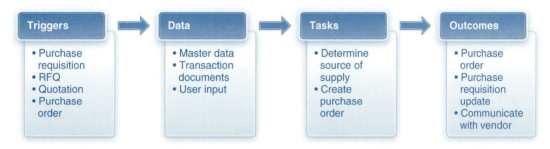

Figure 4-16: Elements of a purchase order

A purchase order is typically created with reference to a requisition, an RFQ, a quotation, or a previously created purchase order. When reference documents are used to create a purchase order, then much of the necessary data is copied from these documents. In addition, a purchase order can be created without reference to any document. In this case, all the necessary data are entered manually.

Data

A purchase order includes data from a variety of sources, as shown in Figure 4-17. Besides the source documents, data from several master records, such as material master, vendor master, info records, and conditions, are also included. In addition, data from specific agreements and contracts with the selected vendor can be incorporated.

Most of the data in a purchase requisition (Figure 4-14) are included in the purchase order. In addition, the purchase order will contain other data depending on how the order is created and which reference documents are used. For example, material characteristics such as weight are included from the material master. Vendor data, such as communication method, contact person, and address, are included from the vendor master or quotation. Pricing data, payment terms, and Incoterms®[2] are included from the quotation, purchasing info record, other condition records, or specific contracts and agreements with vendors, depending on how the process is configured at each company.

---

[2]International Commercial Terms define the roles and responsibilities of buyers and sellers with regard to when ownership of materials changes hands and who bears the costs and risks associated with transporting the materials. See International Chamber of Commerce page on Incoterms at http://www.iccwbo.org/incoterms/ for a more detailed explanation.

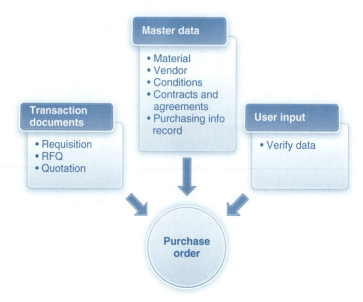

Figure 4-17: Data in a purchase order

If the necessary data are not available from a reference document, then the user must provide this information manually when he or she is creating the purchase order.

As depicted in Figure 4-18, a purchase order document consists of a header section and one or more item details. The header includes data such as the purchase order number, vendor, currency, dates, and payment terms. These data apply to the entire document, including all line items. The item details section includes data specific to each item in the purchase order, such as the material number, description, quantity, delivery date, and price.

Figure 4-18: The structure of a purchase order

Tasks

The primary task in this step is to create and send the purchase order to the vendor. In addition, other steps might be necessary, depending on how the order is created. The most common additional steps involve selecting a vendor and then communicating with the vendor to confirm logistics and delivery details.

Outcomes

The main document created in this step is the purchase order. If the purchase order includes data from reference documents, then multiple documents can be used to generate one order. Conversely, a single reference document can be used to create multiple orders. Thus, as you can see in Figure 4-19, one or more requisitions can generate one or more purchase orders. For example, consider the following scenarios. A purchasing manager receives many requisitions for the same materials and decides to consolidate them into a single purchase order and send the order to one vendor, perhaps to take advantage of volume discounts. Alternatively, the requisitions may include a number of different materials that must be purchased from different vendors. In this case, the purchasing manager creates a different purchase order for each vendor that includes the relevant materials.

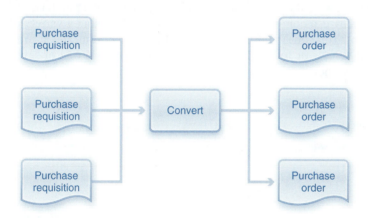

Figure 4-19: Purchase requisition to purchase order

Purchase requisitions are updated to reflect the purchase order number(s) assigned to them. This process enables the requisitioner to easily determine the status of each requisition. He or she can also click on the PO document number now referenced on the purchase requisition to view the purchase order and its status.

Although the purchase order is an obligation to acquire materials from a vendor, no financial accounting documents are created because this step has no impact on the financial condition of the organization. (Despite the commitment to purchase, no money or goods have been exchanged.) Recall, however, our note concerning commitments in management accounting in the case of a requisition for consumable materials. If a purchase order is created without reference to a requisition, then a commitment is created when the purchase order is created. In addition, no material documents are created because no goods movement (goods receipt) has occurred.

Once the purchase order is created, it must be communicated to the vendor. This communication is accomplished using the messaging capabilities of SAP ERP, as depicted in Figure 4-20. SAP ERP utilizes a variety of media, including print, e-mail, EDI, Web services, and fax. Companies also use the messaging capabilities of the system to send reminders and to request that deliveries be sped up. In turn, the vendor uses these capabilities either to accept or reject the order.

Figure 4-20: Communicating with vendors

Figure 4-21 shows the various options related to the purchase order step. To summarize, a company creates a purchase order using a variety of source documents (or none) and user inputs and then communicates it either to an external vendor or to another plant in the company via one of several communication tools.

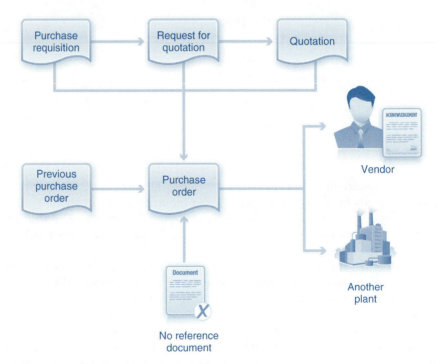

Figure 4-21: Purchase order processing options

In our example, the purchase requisition created in the previous step is used as the source document to create a purchase order for 500 t-shirts. The ERP system automatically selects Spy Gear as the vendor from the source list and utilizes the purchasing info record to determine the gross price of $15 per t-shirt. Thus, the total cost indicated on the purchase order is $7,500.

Demo 4.8: Convert Purchase Requisition to Purchase Order

GOODS RECEIPT

The next step in the procurement process is goods receipt, which records the receipt of the materials from the vendor. The elements of this step are summarized in Figure 4-22.

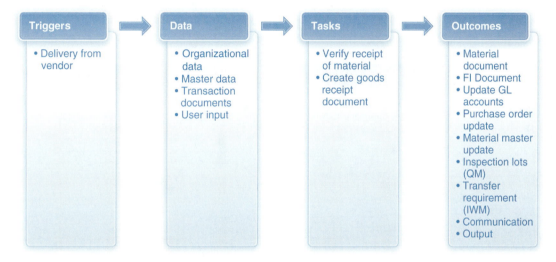

Triggers	Data	Tasks	Outcomes
• Delivery from vendor	• Organizational data • Master data • Transaction documents • User input	• Verify receipt of material • Create goods receipt document	• Material document • FI Document • Update GL accounts • Purchase order update • Material master update • Inspection lots (QM) • Transfer requirement (IWM) • Communication • Output

Figure 4-22: Elements of the goods receipt step

The materials are accompanied by a **delivery document** — also known as a **packing list**—that identifies the materials included in the delivery and the purchase order. The recipient uses this document to verify that the correct materials have been delivered in the correct quantities.

A single purchase order can result in multiple deliveries. This can occur, for example, when the materials are very bulky or the quantities are too great for a single shipment. Alternatively, the materials ordered in multiple purchase orders can be delivered in one shipment. In our example, the vendor, Spy Gear, delivers all 500 t-shirts in one shipment. The accompanying delivery document indicates that there are 5 boxes of 100 t-shirts in the delivery.

When a shipment is received, it is matched against the indicated purchase order(s). Checking the shipment against a purchase order offers several benefits. First, it allows the receiving company to verify that the materials delivered are what it ordered. Second, the relevant data from the purchase order, such as material data and quantities, are automatically copied into the **goods receipt document** that is created in this step. This makes the goods receipt step more efficient and less prone to error. Of course, the data copied into the goods receipt can be edited if the quantity delivered is not the same as what was ordered. A company can accept a delivery without requiring a purchase order. In these cases, however, it will not enjoy the benefits identified above.

Data

Most of the data needed to complete the goods receipt task are contained in the delivery document and the purchase order. These data are shown in Figure 4-23. The purchase order provides data about the materials that the company ordered, and the delivery document contains data about the materials that it actually received. Additional data regarding where the materials are to be stored (plant and storage location) and the specific movement type are also necessary. The system will suggest values for these data, and the user will make changes to the data as needed.

Figure 4-23: Data in the goods receipt step

Tasks

The essential task in the goods receipt step is to verify and record the materials included in the shipment in the goods receipt document. The user will log into the system and create a goods receipt document by providing the purchase order number. The system will retrieve the purchase order and automatically add the relevant data to the goods receipt document. The user will then verify that the data are correct. That is, the materials and quantities delivered match what the company ordered. As we previously discussed, one purchase order can generate multiple deliveries. In such cases, the user will modify the data to reflect the materials and quantities that the company actually received. When partial deliveries are recorded, the purchase order can be used again when the rest of the materials are delivered.

Recall from the earlier discussion of stock types that goods can be received and designated as one of three stock statuses: unrestricted use, in quality inspection, and blocked stock. The default option is to receive materials into unrestricted use. Receipt into quality inspection status can be accomplished in several ways. If the materials are usually subject to quality inspection, then the "post to inspection stock" indicator in the purchasing view of the material master is enabled (checked). This will automatically result in a goods receipt into in quality inspection status. It will also cause the stock status to be included in both the purchase order and the goods receipt document for the material. If inspection is required only in unusual cases, then the stock status can be specified in the purchase order or during goods receipt. Finally, the materials can be designated as blocked stock if they are not what the company ordered or if they are unacceptable for any reason.

In our example, GBI has received a shipment from Spy Gear. The shipment includes a delivery document that states that there are 5 boxes in the shipment, each containing 100 t-shirts. A GBI employee verifies the contents against the delivery document and records the receipt in the ERP system. He does this by retrieving the purchase order identified in the delivery document and indicating that the ordered materials have been received.

Outcomes

In addition to creating the goods receipt document, the goods receipt step has numerous consequences for multiple areas of the organization. Significantly, it is the first step in the procurement process that has an impact on financials, specifically, on general ledger accounts. Figure 4-24 illustrates the financial impact of receiving the 500 t-shirts in our example. The trading goods inventory account is debited by the value of the goods received, that is, $7,500. A corresponding credit is posted to the goods receipt/invoice receipt (GR/IR) account. If the purchase is for a consumable material, then the appropriate consumption account, such as the supplies expense account, is debited rather than a stock account.

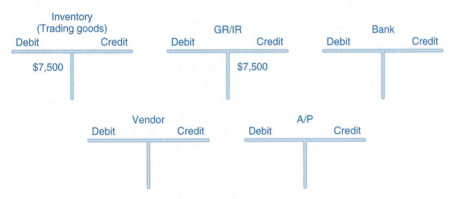

Figure 4-24: Financial impact of goods receipt

A material document and an accounting document are also created; they are illustrated in Figure 4-25. In the material document the header includes the material document number, the date, and the associated delivery document number. The items identify the materials received, the quantity received, the location (plant), and the movement type. In the accounting document the header section consists of the document number, date, currency, and a reference to the delivery document. The item details section shows the two general ledger accounts that are impacted by the goods receipt – a debit in the inventory (trading goods) account and a credit in the GR/IR account. The accounting document is a record of the postings made to the accounts in the general ledger.

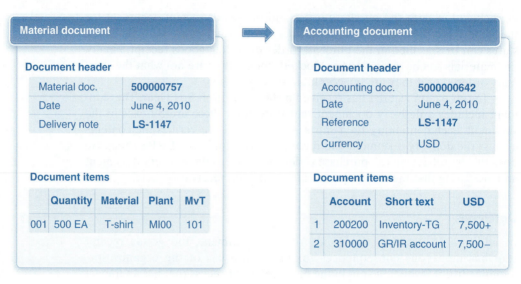

Figure 4-25: Material and accounting documents from a goods receipt

The goods receipt step also results in updates to the purchase order and the material master. The purchase order history is modified to include the material document number. A user is able to retrieve the purchase order (or the purchase requisition, which, if you recall, includes a link to the purchase order) and display the purchase order history. The history will show the material document number, which the user can access to view details. In the material master, the quantity, value, and the moving average price are updated.

Several optional steps can follow the goods receipt step, including the creation of inspection lots, transfer requirements, notifications, and outputs. Significantly, SAP ERP includes certain optional capabilities that enable firms to implement these steps. One of these capabilities, *quality management*, creates an inspection lot from the goods received and triggers various steps in the quality management process. An *inspection lot* is a request for a quality inspection of the materials received. It includes details such as how many of the materials to inspect and which characteristics to inspect. In contrast, *warehouse management*, another optional capability, generates a transfer requirement. A *transfer requirement* documents the need for the warehouse to store or withdraw materials. It therefore serves as a trigger for warehouse management processes. We discuss warehouse management in Chapter 7. An example of a *notification* is when appropriate persons in the organization, such as the original requisitioner, are informed that the materials have been received. Finally, an example of an *output* is a *goods receipt slip,* which is a document that warehouse personnel use to make certain they store the materials in the correct locations.

Demo 4.9: Receive goods against a purchase order

INVOICE VERIFICATION

The next step in the process is **invoice verification**, which is summarized in Figure 4-26. When a company receives a vendor invoice, it verifies that the invoice is accurate before it makes payment. The most common method of invoice verification is a **three-way match** between the purchase order, the goods receipt or delivery document, and the invoice. The objective is to ensure that the quantities and price in all three documents are consistent. An alternative is a two-way match between a purchase order and the goods receipt document. This method is not very common, and it requires a high degree of trust and cooperation between partners. In our example, GBI placed a purchase order for 500 t-shirts from Spy Gear. The Miami plant received the Spy Gear shipment of 5 boxes of 100 t-shirts (500 total). Spy Gear sent GBI an invoice for 500 t-shirts. Further, the price in the purchase order and invoice are the same. Thus, GBI can make a three-way match between the 500 units it ordered for $15 each, the 500 units it received, and the 500 units it was invoiced for $15 each.

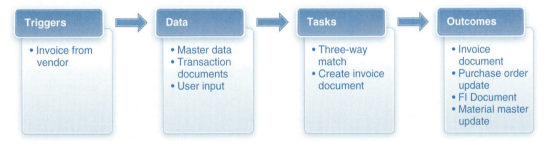

Figure 4-26: Elements of the invoice verification step

Data

Figure 4-27 identifies the data that are needed to complete the invoice verification step. The data obtained from the invoice include the vendor number, invoice date, invoice quantity, and invoice amount. The data from the purchase order include vendor number, materials, quantities, and price. Finally, the materials and quantities received are obtained from the material document created during the goods receipt step.

Figure 4-27: Data needed for invoice verification

Tasks

To complete this step, the user will provide the data from the invoice (vendor, date, and amount) and the purchase order number. The system will then retrieve all the needed data from the purchase order (vendor, materials, quantities, and price). It will also retrieve the goods receipt data for the purchase order. The user will verify that the data are correct and, if they are, will approve the invoice. Occasionally, there will be *discrepancies* among the three sets of data. For example, the quantity delivered or price may vary somewhat. Whether these discrepancies are acceptable will depend on the organization's purchasing and accounting policies, which are specified in the material master or other master data in the form of over- and under-tolerances. If the discrepancies are within tolerances, then the invoice is approved for payment. If not, then the invoice will be blocked, and further action from the accounting or purchasing department will be required before it can be released.

Outcomes

As you can see in Figure 4-28, invoice verification has an impact on the general ledger. The figure illustrates the data for our example. Specifically, a debit of $7,500 is posted to the GR/IR account, and the vendor account is credited by the same amount. Because the vendor account is a subledger account, an automatic credit posting is also made to the corresponding reconciliation account in the general ledger—the accounts payable reconciliation account. A corresponding financial accounting document is created. In addition, an invoice document is created.

Figure 4-28: Financial impact of invoice verification

The purchase order history is also updated, and a link to the invoice document is added. Finally, if the invoice price is different from the price in the purchase order, then the material master must be updated to reflect this discrepancy, if the moving average price is used for price control. Recall that when a goods receipt is recorded, the quantity, value, and moving average price are updated in the material master. When an invoice is received and the price is different from the one listed in the purchase order, the material value and moving average price must be adjusted to reflect the new values.

Invoice verification provides the linkage between materials management and accounting. It authorizes payment of the invoice to the vendor, which is the next—and final—step in the procurement process.

Demo 4.10: Receive and verify an invoice

PAYMENT PROCESSING

Figure 4-29 diagrams the elements of the final step in the procurement process—namely, paying the vendor. This step is triggered by the receipt and verification of an invoice.

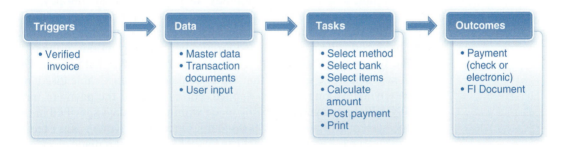

Figure 4-29: Elements of the payment step

Payments can be made manually or automatically via a *payment program*. Typically, an organization will have a number of invoices to pay, and the most common method is to execute a payment program periodically, such as daily or weekly. The program will retrieve all authorized invoices over a specified timeframe and automatically create payments.

Data

Figure 4-30 highlights the data needed to process vendor payments. Data from the invoice include the date, the vendor number, and the invoice amount. In addition, payment terms, method, and address are obtained from the vendor master. The dates of the invoices are compared with the payment terms and the date of the next scheduled run of the payment program in order to determine which invoices are due for payment.

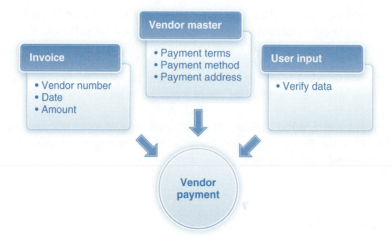

Figure 4-30: Data needed for vendor payment

Tasks

Processing payment involves several steps: selecting a payment method and a bank, deciding which invoices are ready for payment, calculating payment amounts, posting the payment documents, and printing the payment medium. When making payments manually, the user will select the payment method and the bank and will provide the vendor number and the amount of the payment. The system will then display a list of open invoices for that vendor. The user will next select the invoices that are to be paid. Any applicable discounts based on payment terms are then applied. For example, if the payment term is 2%/10Net 30[3] and payment is being made within the 10 days specified in the terms, the system will apply a 2% discount. Once the payment is posted in the general ledger, the actual payment can be sent. If payment is made electronically, the system will automatically send the payment. If it is to be made via a printed check, the user will print and send the check to the vendor.

If the company has an automated payment program, then the program will retrieve and process all of the invoices that are due for payment using the parameters specified in the payment program. Users typically become involved only if there are exceptions that require special resolution.

Outcomes

One obvious outcome of this step is payment to the vendor, either electronically or via a check. Appropriate general ledger accounts are also updated, as shown in Figure 4-31, and a corresponding financial accounting document is created. As the figure indicates, the bank account is credited by the amount of the payment, and the vendor account is debited, as is the associated accounts payable reconciliation account.

---

[3]The term 2%/10Net30 indicates that payment is due within 30 days of receipt of the invoice and that a 2% discount may be taken if payment is made within 10 days of receiving the invoice.

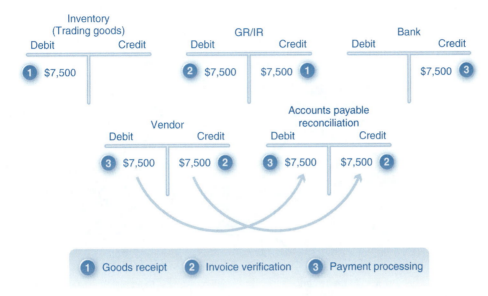

Figure 4-31: Financial impact of vendor payment

Demo 4.11: Make payment to vendor

INTEGRATION WITH OTHER PROCESSES

It should be clear from the preceding discussion that the procurement process is highly integrated with several other processes within an organization. Some of these integration points, such as with financial accounting, were explained in detail, while others were briefly mentioned. We elaborate on these other integration points in later chapters. Below we briefly summarize how procurement is linked with the other processes. Figure 4-32 illustrates these linkages.

The vendor master record is jointly maintained by purchasing and accounting. In addition, several steps in the procurement process, such as goods receipt, invoice verification, and payment processing, impact general ledger accounts. Further, when a company purchases materials for consumption, it uses a controlling object such as a cost center — which is related to management accounting — to charge groups or departments for the purchase.

Activities in materials planning, production, fulfillment, enterprise asset management, and project management generate purchase requisitions that are processed by the procurement process. Objects in these processes, such as sales orders and production orders, are then charged for the materials purchases. Finally, procurement involves materials movements and quality inspections that are the domain of inventory and warehouse management.

■ REPORTING

Standard reporting tools in the transactional system are used to generate both online lists based on selected master data and documents and work lists to identify pending work associated with various process steps.

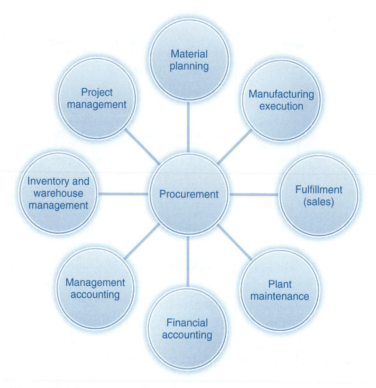

Figure 4-32: Integration with other processes

ONLINE LISTS

Online lists can be manipulated using the various functions of the list viewer or grid control that were explained in Chapter 2. An example of an online list is provided in Figure 4-33, which displays a series of invoices for a specified date range. Double-clicking on the document number will display the invoice document. Data in the list can be sorted, grouped, and summed, as explained in Chapter 2.

| | List | Edit | Goto | Settings | System | Help | | | | | | | | |

Display List of Invoice Documents

Follow-On Documents ...

Doc. No.	Year	T.	Doc. Date	Posting Date	User Name	Entered at	T.	CoCd	Invoicing Pty	Crcy	Gross inv. amnt	Unpl. del. csts	Value-Added Tax Amt
5105600111	2010	RE	03/31/2010	03/31/2010	CLAUSP	20:24:16	RD	US00	100120	USD	14,100.00	0.00	0.00
5105600101	2010	RE	03/23/2010	03/23/2010	HOLSTECO	18:52:27	RD	US00	100150	USD	14,100.00	0.00	0.00
5105600112	2010	RE	03/31/2010	03/31/2010	HOLSTECO	22:46:56	RD	US00	100950	USD	5,000.00	0.00	0.00

Figure 4-33: List of invoices. Copyright SAP AG 2011

WORK LISTS

Recall that work lists display work that is to be completed. An example of a work list in purchasing is provided in Figure 4-34. This figure shows a list of purchase requisitions that are open. The task to be completed is to assign a source of supply, that is, a vendor who will supply the needed materials.

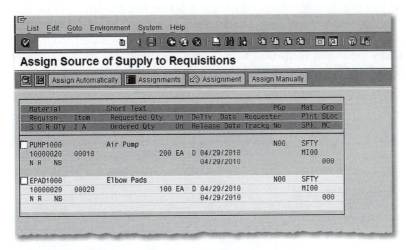

Figure 4-34: List of requisitions. Copyright SAP AG 2011

Demo 4.12: Reporting – lists

PURCHASING INFORMATION SYSTEMS

Recall from Chapter 2 that the purchasing information system (IS) is one of the components of the logistics information system. Purchasing IS provides both standard and flexible analysis capabilities.

In standard analysis, the characteristics are organizational levels and master data relevant to the procurement process. Key figures include quantities, such as the amount of a material ordered or delivered; value, such as the value of material ordered or delivered; and counts, such as the number of purchase orders. Companies combine the characteristics and key figures over a specific time period to generate meaningful information that they can use to evaluate the performance of the process. Examples of this type of information are:

- The quantity of a particular material ordered in the last 30 days

- The quantity of a material delivered by a particular vendor last week

- The number of purchase orders send to a particular vendor last month

- The average time between sending a purchase order and receiving the materials in the last year, for each vendor

- The average value of purchase orders sent to a particular vendor in the last quarter

Figure 4-35 provides an example of standard analysis using the purchasing information system. In this example, the characteristic selected is purchasing group, and the key figures are purchase order value and invoice amount, for two months (February and March). The top part of the resulting report shows two purchasing groups (the United States and Europe) and the key figures (order value and invoice amount) for each one. The figure illustrates the drilldown feature, showing that the United States purchased from two vendors, Spy Gear and Redwood Kits. It also highlights the data for one of the vendors, Spy Gear, for each of the two months.

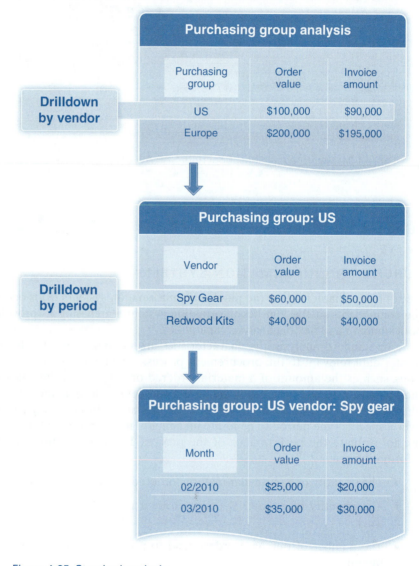

Figure 4-35: Standard analysis

Demo 4.13: Reporting - standard analysis using the purchasing information system

In contrast to standard analysis, flexible analysis enables the user to define the content and format of the analysis. We explained in Chapter 2 that in flexible analysis, characteristics and key figures can be combined as needed. Figure 4-36 is an example of flexible analysis using the purchasing information system. The report in the figure is based on combining the characteristics of vendor, material, and month with the key figures order value and number of items in the order. Vendor and material are displayed in the rows, while the month, order value, and number of order items are shown in the columns.

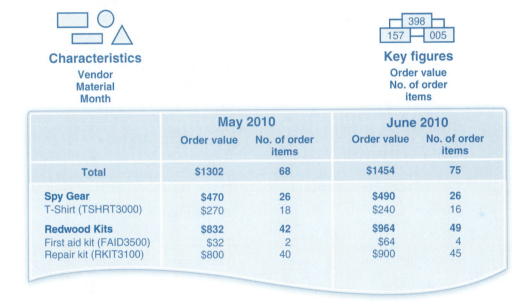

Characteristics
Vendor
Material
Month

Key figures
Order value
No. of order
items

	May 2010		June 2010	
	Order value	No. of order items	Order value	No. of order items
Total	$1302	68	$1454	75
Spy Gear	$470	26	$490	26
T-Shirt (TSHRT3000)	$270	18	$240	16
Redwood Kits	$832	42	$964	49
First aid kit (FAID3500)	$32	2	$64	4
Repair kit (RKIT3100)	$800	40	$900	45

Figure 4-36: Flexible analysis

CHAPTER SUMMARY

The procurement process involves the activities required to purchase, receive, and pay for the goods and services that an organization needs for its operations. A company's procurement process is typically optimized for both the types of goods and services it purchases and the location and use of those goods by other processes, such as manufacturing. Because the procurement process involves significant amounts of collaboration and commerce with suppliers, it must be strategically linked with the manufacturing and material planning processes to ensure that the proper amount of the correct materials are procured at the right price for the right time. In addition, given the amount of money that companies spend during the procurement process, many of the data and requirements associated with purchasing are designed to ensure proper financial accounting and controlling compliance.

The procurement process consists of six key steps: requirements determination, supplier selection, order processing, goods receipt, invoice verification, and payment processing. To function properly, procurement requires organizational data such as plant, storage locations, purchasing organization, and purchasing group. Master data are also needed to account for the value of the goods and services that are purchased as well as for controlling purposes to manage the process efficiently. Tolerances, controls, and conditions are predetermined data qualities that enable the procurement process to operate in a more automated fashion. Materials that have been received by the company must be assigned to a material account in order to properly record the financial impact of the procurement and use of the material. In addition, materials that have been received into stock must be classified according to their availability status to ensure that they are properly allocated to the processes that utilize them.

Likewise, when materials are moved within the organization, either from one process to another or from one storage location to another, the movement must be recorded to properly account for the quantity, value, and location of the goods.

KEY TERMS

Account assignment category

Account assignment object

Account determination

Accounting data

Blocked stock

Company-level purchasing organization

Conditions

Condition types

Consignment

Consumable materials

Contracts

Delivery document

Delivery tolerances

Enterprise-level purchasing organization

Financial accounting data

General data

Goods issue

Goods movement

Goods receipt

Goods receipt document

Goods receipt processing time

In quality inspection

Invoice verification

Item categories

Material document

Movement types

Outline purchase agreements

Packing list

Plant-level purchasing organization

Price control

Purchase order

Purchasing data

Purchasing group

Purchasing info record

Purchasing organization	Storage locations
Scheduling agreements	Subcontracting
Services	Third-party order
Source list	Three-way match
Standard	Transfer posting
Stock in transit	Unrestricted use
Stock materials	Valuation class
Stock transfer	Valuation currency
Stock transfer	Vendor master data
Stock types	

REVIEW QUESTIONS

1. Explain the key organizational levels relevant to the purchasing process.

2. Explain the differences between the various types of purchasing organizations. Under what conditions is each type appropriate?

3. Explain the data in the material master that are relevant to the purchasing process.

4. Explain the data in the vendor master that are relevant to the purchasing process.

5. What are purchasing info records? What is their role in the purchasing process?

6. What are conditions used for?

7. Explain the relationship between organizational levels and master data in purchasing.

8. What are item categories in purchasing? Explain how each of the following item categories impacts the purchasing process: consignment process, third-party item, subcontracting item.

9. What is the role of account assignment categories in purchasing?

10. How is account determination different when purchasing stock items and consumable items?

11. What are the stock types or statuses based on the usability of materials? What is the significance of these statuses?

12. Explain the four goods movements discussed in this chapter. How are goods movements related to movement types?

13. What is a material document? List some key data included in a material document.

14. Briefly describe the steps in the procurement process explained in this chapter. What are some possible variations to this process?

15. Explain the different steps in the procurement process in terms of their triggers, required data, tasks completed, and outcomes.

16. Which steps in the procurement process have an impact on financial accounting? Explain these impacts.

17. During which steps in the procurement process are material documents created. Why?

18. What is meant by source of supply determination? What are the different ways of identifying a source of supply?

19. What are the different paths from a purchase requisition to a purchase order? What determines which path is selected?

20. Figure 4-21 illustrates the different purchase order processing options. Explain this figure.

21. A purchase requisition can result in multiple purchase orders, and multiple requisitions can be combined into one purchase order. Explain the circumstances when these two scenarios are possible. Provide examples.

22. What is a delivery document? What is the significance of a delivery document in purchasing?

23. Explain the outcomes of the goods receipt step of the procurement process

24. Explain the outcomes of the invoice verification step of the procurement process.

25. What is a three-way match? What is its purpose? What documents are involved in a three-way match?

26. Explain how the procurement process is integrated with other processes within an organization.

27. Provide two examples of online lists and work lists. Explain what these reports are used for.

28. Provide two examples of reports generated via standard analysis. Explain what these reports are used for.

EXERCISES

Exercises for this chapter are available on *WileyPLUS*.

The Fulfillment Process

G BI currently uses a very simple process to fill customer orders. This process, introduced in Chapter 1, is reproduced in Figure 5-1. The process begins when GBI receives a customer's purchase order, which it validates and authorizes via a sales order. The warehouse then prepares and sends the shipment, after which accounting forwards an invoice. The process ends when GBI receives payment from the customer.

This simple process has worked well for GBI up to this point. Because GBI has grown rapidly, however, the company wants to utilize the new ERP system it acquired to enhance its process for filling customer orders. Specifically, it wants to make the process more efficient and customer friendly as well as more transparent by keeping track of the status of every order throughout each step in the process. In addition, it wants to incorporate other sales-related activities, such as developing leads and responding to inquiries, into the new process.

Figure 5-1: A basic fulfillment process

In this chapter, we discuss the fulfillment process in detail, with a special focus on how an ERP system supports the process. We begin by identifying the key organizational levels and the master data related to the process. Next we examine the process steps in detail, and we explain how fulfillment is integrated with other processes. We conclude by discussing the various reports related to fulfillment. Unlike the previous chapter, this chapter does not include a separate section on key concepts. The reason for this is that the basic concepts associated with fulfillment, such as goods movement, have been addressed in previous chapters.

To illustrate the various concepts and process steps, we will use the following scenario throughout the chapter. Rocky Mountain Bikes (RMB), a GBI customer located in Denver, Colorado, has placed an order for 40 silver deluxe touring bikes and 100 t-shirts that it plans to sell at two racing events in Colorado Springs, one to be held on May 15 and the other on June 20. Because the bikes represent a significant inventory and storage expense, RMB wants GBI to deliver them directly to the racing location just a few days before each race. Further, RMB anticipates that the May race will attract a much larger crowd, so it expects to sell more bikes and t-shirts at that race. It has therefore requested that GBI deliver 30 of the bikes on May 10 and the remaining 10 on June 10. However, it wants GBI to deliver all 100 t-shirts in May so that it can sell as many as possible at the first race and then sell the remaining ones at the second race. Unlike the bikes, t-shirts are relatively inexpensive and are easy to store between races.

● ORGANIZATIONAL DATA

Several organizational elements are essential to the fulfillment process. These are client, company code, sales area, plant, storage location, shipping point, and credit control area. Three of these—sales area, shipping point, and credit control area—are unique to fulfillment. A sales area is a combination of three other organizational elements—sales organization, distribution channel, and division—that are also unique to fulfillment. We discuss all of these organizational elements in this section.

Some elements—namely, client, company code, plant, and storage location—are also relevant to other processes and have been discussed in previous chapters. In this section we have included a discussion of plant and storage locations as they relate specifically to fulfillment. No additional discussion of client and company code is necessary.

SALES ORGANIZATION

A company (company code) is divided into several **sales organizations**, each of which is responsible for the sale and distribution of goods and services for a particular geographical area, such as a regional or national market. Specifically, a sales organization is:

- Responsible for negotiating terms and conditions of sales for that market.

- Responsible to customers with regard to liability and rights of recourse in cases of disputes.

- The highest level of aggregation in sales-related reporting. That is, sales data can be summarized up to the level of the sales organization.

A company code must have at least one sales organization, although it can have many. The latter arrangement is appropriate if the sales processes are substantially different in the different sales organizations, for instance, to handle regional differences in practices and customs. In other cases a company might use multiple sales organizations simply to make sure that the geographic area covered remains manageable. Although a company can include multiple sales organizations, a sales organization can belong to only one company code. The sales organizations for GBI are depicted in Figure 5-2. As the figure indicates, GBI US has two sales organizations, one each for the Eastern and Western US. GBI Germany also has two sales organizations, one each for the Northern and Southern territories.

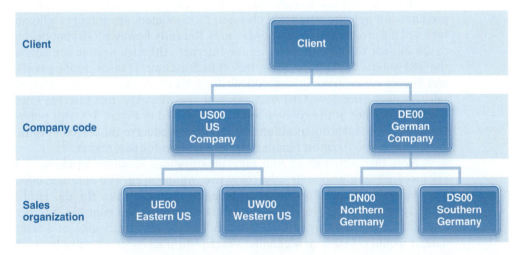

Figure 5-2: GBI sales organizations

Business Processes in Practice 5.1: Intel's Organizational Structure

Intel Corporation has six independent operating groups that manufacture products, each of which operates four sales organizations: Asia-Pacific, the Americas, Europe, and Japan. Intel locates its sales organizations close to their largest clusters of customers. Each of the 24 sales organizations has two distribution channels, direct and reseller. Thus, there are 48 combinations through which Intel sells its products to its customers globally.

Source: Intel company reports.

DISTRIBUTION CHANNEL

A distribution channel (DC) is the means by which a company delivers its goods and services to its customers. Typical channels are wholesale, retail, and online (Internet sales). Just as a company can have multiple sales organizations, it can also have multiple DCs. Each channel has its own strategies, approaches, and constraints for getting the goods and services to the customer. More specifically, each channel has its distinctive responsibilities, pricing systems, plants from which shipments are made, and other characteristics. For example, a wholesale channel has the following characteristics (among others):

- It does not include sales taxes in calculating prices (in the United States).

- It requires a minimum volume of purchase and offers volume discounts.

- It may designate a specific plant or plants from which deliveries are made.

In addition, reporting can be consolidated at the DC level. That is, statistics can be summarized and aggregated based on distribution channels. A sales organization must have at least one distribution channel, although it can have more than one. In addition, a distribution channel can be assigned to multiple sales organizations.

Because GBI is a manufacturing organization, it historically has sold its products through the wholesale channel. Its customers are retailers who, in turn, sell the products to the end-consumers. Recently, however, GBI has begun to sell directly to end-customers via the Internet. Although anyone can access the GBI website to purchase a bike, factors such as complex taxes, shipping costs, and import duties make it very difficult for GBI to operate a global Internet sales channel. Therefore, GBI manages both the wholesale and Internet sales channels together at the country level, as illustrated in Figure 5-3. This policy ensures that the sales organization that ships the product to the customer is the group that is also the most familiar with the tax laws for that region.

Note that, although all four sales organizations identified in Figure 5-3 are involved with wholesale sales, only two are involved with Internet sales. The Western US sales organization manages Internet sales for the entire United States, and the Northern German sales organization manages Internet sales for all of Germany. If GBI were to venture into retail sales at a later date, it would create a new channel—retail—to manage these sales because the strategies for retail sales, such as pricing, minimum quantities, and taxes, will be different from the other two channels.

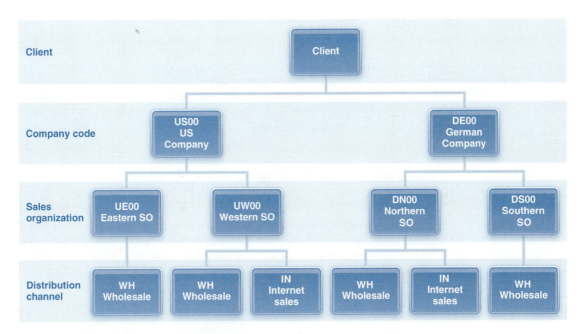

Figure 5-3: GBI US distribution channels

A unique combination of a sales organization and distribution channel is called a **distribution chain**. Some master data, such as material master and pricing conditions, are maintained at the distribution chain level.

Business Processes in Practice 5.2: Distribution Channels at Apple

Apple Inc. provides a good example of a company that utilizes multiple distribution channels. Apple sells its products through its online store (Internet), its Apple stores (retail), and third-party retailers (wholesale). Apple uses each of these channels to resolve different issues within the fulfillment process.

Because Apple places a priority on the customer's buying experience, it tries to establish either an Apple-owned retail store or a mass-market retail store in every major market. This policy ensures that the majority of consumers in most developed nations live within a short distance of a retail store that sells Apple products.

Although retail stores offer the best opportunity for consumers to examine the products before purchasing them, maintaining an extensive network of physical stores entails many major expenses, including real estate, local taxes, and retail staff. Therefore, Apple very carefully evaluates new locations for its stores based largely on the local demographics of those consumers who are the most likely buyers.

When it is not feasible for Apple to establish a retail store in an area with a strong potential consumer base, the company must partner with another retailer to resell its products. Although this arrangement eliminates many of the retail costs identified above for Apple, it also reduces Apple's profit per unit, because Apple must now share its sales revenues with the reseller.

Online retailing eliminates a great deal of the costs associated with operating physical stores. In addition, because the online channel sells directly to consumers, Apple does not have to share its profits with a reseller. However, because online retailers sell to any number of locations around the world, they must deal with shipping, taxes, and import costs that the retail channel does not have to. In addition, they must invest in the technical infrastructure that supports a global online retail site. Apple's online retail operations, including the Apple store and iTunes, are based on SAP ERP.

Source: Apple company reports.

DIVISION

Most companies consolidate materials and services with similar characteristics within a unit known as a division. Typically, each division is associated with a company's product line. A product or material can be assigned to one division only. Each division can employ its own sales strategies, such as pricing agreements with customers. In addition, it is possible to aggregate reports at the division level.

A sales organization must have at least one division. A division can be assigned to multiple sales organizations, and a sales organization can include many divisions.

GBI currently has two divisions, the bicycles division and the accessories division. Recall from Chapter 2 that GBI's material list includes different material types. The finished goods—that is, bicycles—are managed by the bicycles division, while the trading goods—such as helmets—are managed by the accessories division. In the future, if GBI expands into other product lines, such as skateboards, it will create additional divisions. The divisions for GBI US and GBI DE are illustrated in Figure 5-4 and Figure 5-5, respectively.

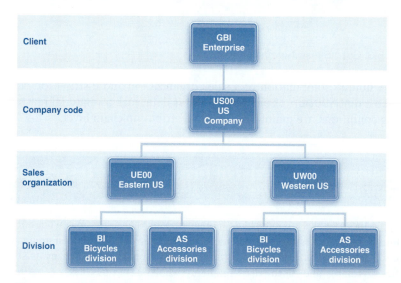

Figure 5-4: GBI US divisions

Business Processes in Practice 5.3: Multiple Divisions in a Major Publishing Company

John Wiley & Sons, the publisher of this textbook, has three main divisions that serve different reading markets around the world. Wiley publishes college textbooks through the Higher Education division. The Professional/Trade division contains the For Dummies, Frommer's, Betty Crocker, CliffsNotes, and Webster's Dictionaries series, as well as several other popular brands. Wiley's third division is the Scientific, Technical, Medical, and Scholarly (STMS) division, which is the world's largest publisher of professional and scholarly journals and books. Although the physical products (books/journals) and the geographic regions are similar for all three divisions, the audience, authors, and distribution channels for each division vary greatly. Wiley has learned that by grouping its brands and the employees who are responsible for their success into three divisions, they can achieve greater synergies and operate more efficiently.

Source: John Wiley & Sons company reports.

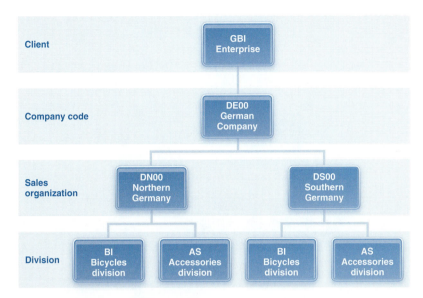

Figure 5-5: GBI DE divisions

SALES AREA

A **sales area** is a unique combination of sales organization, distribution channel, and division. In other words, it defines which DC a sales organization uses to sell the products associated with a particular division. A sales area can be assigned to only one company code. All of the documents associated with the fulfillment process, such as quotations and packing lists, belong to one sales area.

Figure 5-6 illustrates the six sales areas for GBI US. For example, one sales area (UE00+WH+BI) is responsible for the sale of products in the bicycles *division* for the Eastern US *sales organization* via the wholesale *channel*. This sales area is highlighted in the figure. A second sales area (UW00+WH+AS) manages the sale of products in the accessories division for the Western US sales organization via the wholesale channel. As a third example, sales area UW00+IN+BI manages the sale of products in the bicycles division for the

Business Processes in Practice 5.4: The Sales Structure at Apple

As we discussed in a previous example, Apple sells its products through a combination of online stores, Apple retail stores, and reseller stores. Apple contains several hardware divisions, including Mac computers, iPods, iPhones, servers, and accessories. Apple also operates several sales areas for different types of customers, such as education, government, enterprise, and consumer. Each of these customer segments has unique needs and requires a distinctive sales approach, even though they are buying the same products. Therefore, Apple must plan its sales strategies by product globally while paying close attention to the unique characteristics of both the channels (retail, online, reseller) and the customer (education, government, enterprise, and consumer). This strategy is typically reflected in a matrix, which allows Apple to pinpoint opportunities and manage their global sales efforts effectively.

Source: Apple company reports.

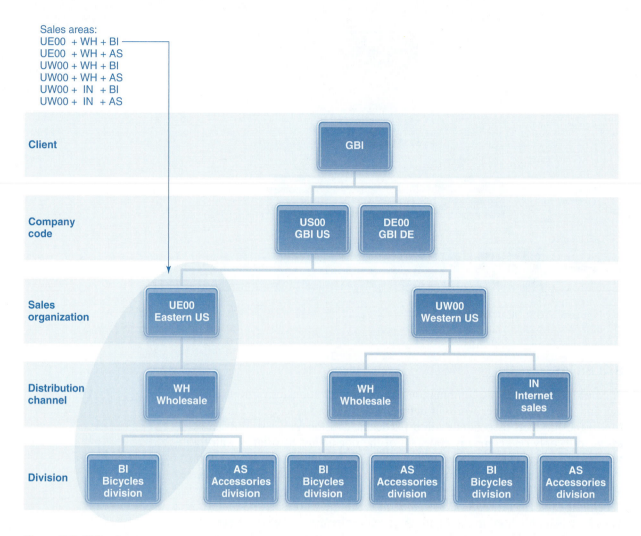

Sales areas:
UE00 + WH + BI
UE00 + WH + AS
UW00 + WH + BI
UW00 + WH + AS
UW00 + IN + BI
UW00 + IN + AS

Figure 5-6: GBI sales areas

Western US sales organization via the Internet channel. The German company also has six sales areas. They are not depicted in the figure, however.

PLANT

We have discussed plants in previous chapters in the context of other processes. In the fulfillment process a *delivering plant* is a facility from which the company delivers products and services to its customers. In the case of products, a plant is typically a manufacturing and/or storage facility. In the case of services, it can simply be an office. A plant can be assigned to more than one distribution chain. Recall that a distribution chain is a unique combination of sales organization and distribution channel. Conversely, a distribution chain can be associated with more than one plant.

In Figure 5-7, plant 1 delivers only for distribution chain 1 and plant 3 only for distribution chain 3. In contrast, plant 2 delivers for all three distribution chains. Viewed from a different perspective, distribution chains 1 and 3 use two plants to deliver materials to their customers, whereas distribution chain 2 uses only one plant.

Recall from Chapter 2 that GBI has three plants in the United States and two in Germany. In the United States, the Dallas plant is the sole manufacturing

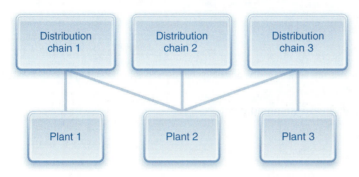

Figure 5-7: Plants

site, while the plants in San Diego and Miami serve as distribution centers. Finished goods are shipped from the Dallas facility to the other two facilities as needed. In contrast, trading goods are shipped directly to the two regional distribution centers by the vendors. The Dallas plant does not hold an inventory of trading goods. Normally, the Miami plant delivers products to customers in the Eastern United States and the San Diego to the Western United States. However, the Dallas plant serves as an overflow facility to the two other plants and can ship finished goods anywhere in the country, as needed. In Germany, the Heidelberg plant ships to locations in the South and the Hamburg plant to locations in the North.

SHIPPING POINT

A shipping point is a location in a plant from which outbound deliveries are shipped. It can be a physical location, such as a loading dock, a rail depot, or a mail room. It can also be a designated group of employees who, for example, handle express or special deliveries. A shipping point is associated with one or more plants, and a plant can have more than one shipping point. A plant must have at least one shipping point from which to process deliveries, although the shipping point does not have to be physically located within the plant.

Figure 5-8 diagrams a scenario in which multiple plants access one shipping point. The figure represents a campus for a company that includes a factory and two storage facilities, all of which are plants. Note that the only plant that has a shipping point is the storage facility located by the front office. Therefore, all materials from the factory and the main storage facility must first be moved to this facility and then shipped to their destinations.

In contrast, Figure 5-9 illustrates a scenario in which several plants share three shipping points. Storage facility #1 has one shipping point, and facility #3 has two. Storage facility #2 has none, so it uses the shipping points located in the

All shipments are sent from one shipping point, which is in the storage facility located by the front office.

Figure 5-8: Shared shipping point

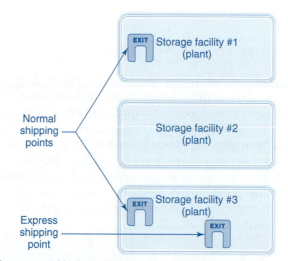

The express shipping point is used by all plants, as needed.
Facility 2 uses the shipping points located at the other two facilities.

Figure 5-9: Multiple shipping points

other plants. In storage facility #3, one of the shipping points handles normal deliveries, while the other one is reserved for express deliveries or for deliveries that require special handling.

In GBI, each of the five plants has a single shipping point. All customer deliveries are shipped from one of these locations. Each shipping point is a loading dock, which is a facility that trucks can back into so they can be loaded. Figure 5-10 illustrates a loading dock. Other facilities that can operate as shipping points include rail depots (Figure 5-11) and shipyards or ports (Figure 5-12). In the case of a rail depot, the rail cars are pulled up to the facility and loaded. When the storage facility is located by a waterway, a shipyard serves the same purpose.

Figure 5-10: Loading dock as a shipping point. ©iStockphoto

Figure 5-11: Rail depot as a shipping point. ©iStockphoto

Figure 5-12: Port as a shipping point. ©iStockphoto

CREDIT CONTROL AREA

A **credit control area** is an organizational level that is responsible for customer credit. Specifically, it determines customers' creditworthiness, establishes credit limits, and monitors and manages the actual extension of credit to customers. An enterprise can choose to manage credit in either a centralized or a decentralized manner. In a centralized system, a single credit control area manages credit for customers across all company codes in the enterprise. This arrangement is particularly useful if customers conduct business with multiple company codes within the enterprise. As an example, Figure 5-13 illustrates a centralized model that GBI employs for customers who purchase bicycles and accessories from both GBI US and GBI DE. In such cases, GBI manages the

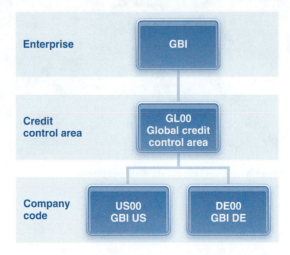

Figure 5-13: Centralized credit control area

credit limit at the enterprise level, meaning that it assigns all company codes to one credit control area.

In contrast, an enterprise that utilizes a decentralized model maintains multiple credit control areas, each of which manages credit for one or more companies within the enterprise. For example, in the hypothetical scenario illustrated in Figure 5-14, GBI has two credit control areas, one for all companies in North America (GBI US, GBI Canada, and GBI Mexico) and one for all companies in Europe (GBI DE and GBI Great Britain). If GBI were to expand operations into the Asia-Pacific region, it likely would create a third credit control area to supervise credit for customers of those companies. Even when using a decentralized approach, however, it is possible—and prudent—to establish credit limits for customers at the enterprise level and for each credit control area. This policy ensures that customers purchasing from companies belonging to different credit control areas (e.g., GBI US and GBI DE in Figure 5-14) do not exceed credit limits across the enterprise.

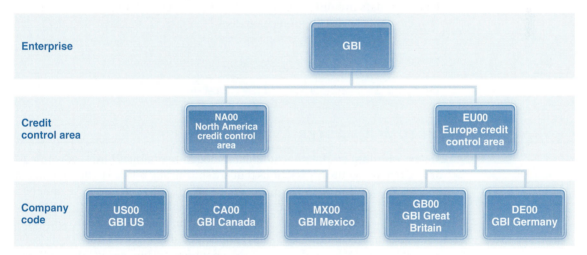

Figure 5-14: Decentralized credit control areas

■ MASTER DATA

In Chapter 4 we discussed the material master, pricing conditions, and output conditions from the perspective of procurement. In this section we will explore these master data as they pertain to fulfillment. In addition, we will discuss master data that are relevant only to fulfillment, namely, customer master, customer-material information record, and credit management master record.

MATERIAL MASTER

The key organizational elements in fulfillment for which material master data are defined are client, sales organization, distribution channel, and plant. Recall that material master data are grouped into views and that each view is relevant to one or more processes and defined for specific organizational levels. The three views relevant to fulfillment are basic data, sales organization data, and sales plant data.

Basic data, which are relevant to all processes, are defined at the client level. **Sales organization data** are defined for combinations of sales organizations and distribution channels. Examples of sales organization data are the delivering plant, sales units, and minimum quantities. The delivering plant is the preferred plant from which deliveries are made for the particular sales organization and distribution channel. Sales units are the units of measure, such as cartons, barrels, containers, cases, pallets, and crates, in which the materials are sold. Quantities include minimum order quantities and delivery quantities. In addition, a link to pricing conditions (discussed later) is available. Because the data are defined for each combination of sales organization and DC, each DC can have different values for these data to support different sales strategies. **Sales plant data** provide details on how the material will be shipped from that plant. Examples are specific transportation requirements (e.g., refrigeration) and the methods of loading the material (e.g., a hand cart, forklift, or crane). Note that it is necessary to define materials for every combination of sales organization and distribution channel, as well as for every plant if the data are different. Very often, the material data will be unchanged between plants or distribution channels.

Demo 5.1: Review material master

CUSTOMER MASTER

Customer master data include data needed to conduct business with customers and to execute transactions that are specifically related to the fulfillment process. The data in the customer master are divided into three segments—general data, accounting data, and sales area data. The relationships among these three segments and the two departments in an organization responsible for these data (accounting and sales) are depicted in Figure 5-15.

General data are defined at the client level. They are valid for all of a client's sales areas and company codes. Examples of general data are a customer's name, address, and account number. **Accounting data** are specific to

Figure 5-15: Segments of customer master data

a company code and include data such as payment terms and the reconciliation account in the general ledger. Recall from Chapter 3 that (1) customer accounts are subledger accounts, (2) subledger accounts are linked to the general ledger via reconciliation accounts, and (3) the accounts receivable account is typically used as the reconciliation account for customers. The accounting department will typically complete this part of the customer master data. **Sales area data** are specific to a particular sales area, which, as we discussed earlier in this chapter, is made up of one sales organization, one distribution channel, and one division. Sales area data relate to sales, shipping, billing, and partner functions. Examples are the sales office and the currency in which the transaction is conducted. Shipping data specify the preferred delivering plant, priorities, and methods. They also define delivery tolerances and policies for dealing with partial deliveries. Billing data include billing terms and tax-related data.

If a customer is served by multiple sales areas, then the data must be defined separately for each sales area. This arrangement permits a company to apply different terms and conditions for different areas. Figure 5-16 illustrates this approach for a hypothetical customer with offices in both the United States and Germany. The customer purchases materials from both GBI's US and Germany companies. The general data for the customer apply across both GBI companies—that is, the GBI enterprise that is represented by the client. However, accounting data for the customer must be defined separately for each GBI company. Recall that one piece of data in the customer master record is the reconciliation account, which is based on the chart of accounts. If GBI US and GBI DE use different charts of accounts, then they may have different reconciliation account numbers. Further, the currencies and tax-related data are also different. Thus, the accounting data are different for each country (company code).

Finally, the customer purchases materials for its facilities throughout the United States. Consequently, it deals with both US sales organizations (UE00 and UW00). In addition, the customer purchases exclusively on a wholesale basis. Therefore, master data for this customer must be defined for two sales areas in the United States UE00+WH+ BI and UW00+WH+BI (see Figure 5-16).

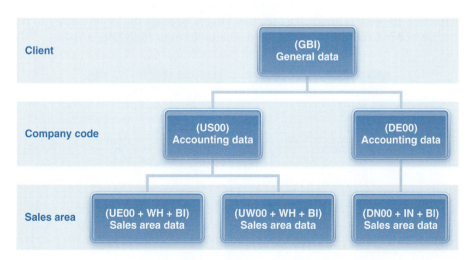

Figure 5-16: Multiple definitions of a customer

In contrast, the customer in Germany deals only in the northern part of the country and purchases exclusively via the Internet. Therefore, only one set of sales area data is defined for that customer.

Customers can play different roles or **partner functions** in the fulfillment process. The four required partner functions are *sold-to party*, *ship-to party*, *bill-to party*, and *payer*. One customer may fill all four roles, or each role may be filled by a different customer. The customer who submits the order is the **sold-to party**. This is the primary type of business partner. The order may indicate that the materials should be shipped to a different location or that the invoice should be sent to someone else. These are the **ship-to party** and **bill-to party** functions, respectively. For example, the customer may request that the material be shipped to one of *its* customers. In this case, the party that actually receives the shipment is considered the ship-to party. However, the invoice will be forwarded to the customer that ordered the materials—that is, the bill-to party. Alternatively, the bill-to-party may be another company that processes invoices for the customer. As another example, a large enterprise may be comprised of a number of companies, such as franchises. An order may be placed by headquarters, the sold-to party, with instructions to deliver the materials to numerous franchises, the ship-to parties. The invoice may be sent to headquarters, which also serves as the bill-to party. Finally, the payment may be outsourced to another company, which will be the **payer** of the invoice.

GBI US has 12 customers, and GBI DE has 7. These customers are listed in Figure 5-17. Additional details of the master data for each customer are provided in Appendix 5A. Rocky Mountain Bikes (RMB), the customer used in our example, is located in Denver, Colorado, and therefore is serviced through GBI's Western US sales organization. In addition, RMB purchases via the wholesale channel. Therefore, it is associated with the sales area made up of the Western US sales organization (UW00), the wholesale channel of distribution (WH), and the bicycle division (BI) (look back to Figure 5-6). Further, because RMB is a small company, its partner functions are usually all located at the same address. However, it is not uncommon for RMB to request that materials be shipped directly to various racing events or to its retail customers. In our example, RMB has requested that the materials be delivered to the RMB booth at the racing location in Colorado Springs, not to its head office in Denver. In this case, RMB is the sold-to party, bill-to party, and payer, but the ship-to party is the racing location. Finally, because the materials are to be delivered in Colorado, they will be delivered from the San Diego plant.

GBI US Customers	GBI DE Customers
• Beantown Bikes	• Berliner Cykel, Berlin
• Big Apple Bikes	• Bicicletas Madrileños, Madrid
• DC Bikes	• Cykel Zurich, Zurich
• Furniture City Bikes	• Frankfurter Cycle, Frankfurt
• Motown Bikes	• Munich Bikes, Munich
• Northwest Bikes	• Vélos Parisienne, Paris
• Peachtree Bikes	• Ye Olde Bike, London
• Philly Bikes	
• Rocky Mountain Bikes	
• Silicon Valley Bikes	
• SoCal Bikes	
• Windy City Bikes	

Figure 5-17: GBI customers

Demo 5.2: Review customer master

CUSTOMER-MATERIAL INFORMATION (INFO) RECORD

A customer-material information record is comprised of master data specific to one customer and one material. In contrast to data in a material master, which apply to all customers, and data in a customer master, which apply to all purchases made by a particular customer, data in a customer-material info record relate to purchases of a *specific material* by a *specific customer*.

Some data in a customer-material info record are not found elsewhere. One example is the *customer material number*, which cross-references the company's material number with the customer's material numbers. Figure 5-18 provides some examples of material numbers used by GBI and its customer RMB. RMB's material numbers are noted as the customer material number in the info record. This cross-referencing of material numbers enables the customer to place an order based on its internal material numbers, which the info record then translates into the company's material numbers. Remember that most customers also have enterprise systems that manage their procurement process. Consequently, the customer material number is the link between the seller's master data and the buyer's master data.

Material	GBI Material number	RMB Material number
Deluxe touring bike-black	DXTR1000	G1000BL
Deluxe touring bike-silver	DXTR2000	G1000SL
Deluxe touring bike-red	DXTR3000	G1000RD

Figure 5-18: RMB and GBI material numbers

In certain cases the data in a customer-material info record supersede data found in other master data, such as the material master and customer master. For example, preferences related to shipping, such as delivering plant, tolerances, and partial deliveries that are included in the customer master apply to all materials purchased by the customer. However, if these preferences vary for different materials, then they are included in the customer-material info record. For example, if deliveries are normally sent to one specified plant but deliveries for a particular material must be sent to a different plant, then this preference is noted in the customer-material info record for that material, not in the customer master.

The customer-material info records for RMB also note that RMB prefers the bikes to be shipped via special ground freight (truck) due to the weight and size of the shipping boxes. In contrast, the company requests that GBI ship the shirts via standard air freight (FedEx or UPS 2-day). Finally, the info records indicate that RMB will accept partial deliveries for shirts but not for bikes, because shirts have a very short lead time and can be reordered quickly if needed.

> **Demo 5.3:** Review customer–material info record

PRICING CONDITIONS

Pricing conditions are master data that companies use to determine the selling prices of their products. Companies create conditions for various components of the final selling price, including *gross prices*, *discounts*, *freight*, *surcharges*, and *taxes*. Conditions can be fixed amounts, percentages, or based on a sliding scale, and they can be either independent of or relative to other conditions. For example, the price of a product can be material specific and customer independent, meaning that the seller charges the same price to all of its customers. Alternatively, the price can be customer specific, in which case the company charges different customers different prices, perhaps based on some agreements between the company and the customer. Similarly, discounts can be uniform, or they can be based on the quantity or value of the purchase. For example, GBI offers a 10% discount for purchases of between 100 and 500 units and a 20% discount for purchases of more than 500 units. Freight is generally based on the weight of the shipment, and it may be waived for purchases greater than a predetermined amount. Thus, the final price to the customer is a function of, or *conditioned* on, numerous variables.

Because numerous conditions are defined for a product, a company must have a procedure to determine which conditions apply to a particular customer order. This procedure, called the *condition technique*, consists of identifying available *condition types* (gross price, customer-specific price, discounts, freight, surcharges, etc.) and determining which ones apply to the particular circumstances of the order.

Recall that in our example, RMB wishes to purchase 40 bikes and 100 t-shirts. The bikes do not qualify for a discount, so GBI will charge the standard price of $2,800 per bicycle. However, the t-shirts qualify for a 10% discount, so the price will be $27 per shirt, reduced from the standard price of $30.

> **Demo 5.4:** Review pricing conditions

OUTPUT CONDITIONS

A variety of outputs that are generated during the fulfillment process, such as quotations, confirmations, and invoices, must be communicated to customers. The data needed to perform this task are included in output conditions. The condition technique used to determine pricing is also used to determine how outputs from the process are communicated to the customer.

Output conditions are defined separately for the different output types (quotations, invoices, etc.). Data in the condition master include the output medium (e.g., print, fax, EDI), partner function (e.g., sold-to party, ship-to party), and transmission time (e.g., immediately, or periodically using a program).

RMB prefers to receive order confirmations via e-mail within 4 hours of acceptance or shipment of an order. It also prefers to receive paper invoices. GBI must maintain all of these output conditions in its ERP system.

CREDIT MANAGEMENT MASTER RECORD

The credit management master record is an extension of the customer master record that includes data relevant to managing credit for that customer. The data contained in this record are grouped into three segments: general data, credit control area data, and an overview. The *general data segment* includes data applicable at the client level, that is, across multiple credit control areas. Examples of general data are address, communication data, and total credit granted to the customer across the enterprise. The *credit control area segment* includes data applicable to a single credit control area. An example is the credit granted to the customer for companies in a particular credit control area and risk category. *Risk category* is a classification used to determine how risky it is to extend credit to the customer. Companies use this classification to assess the likelihood that the customer will pay its invoices. Finally, the *overview segment* includes key data from the other segments from the credit master record. Companies use the overview segment to access the most important data they need to make decisions regarding extending credit to customers.

■ PROCESS

Figure 5-19 illustrates the steps in the fulfillment process. The process begins with presales activities and concludes with the receipt of payment from the customer. *Presales activities* are optional and are designed to identify and develop customer relationships. Very often, the process begins with *sales order processing*, which is triggered by the receipt of a customer's purchase order. As the name suggests, sales order processing involves creating a *sales order*, which is an internal document used to manage and track the order as it flows through the process. After a company creates the sales order, it prepares a *shipment* and sends it to the customer. The next step is *billing* the customer for the materials shipped. Finally, the company receives a *payment* from the customer. As you can see in Figure 5-19, each step involves several tasks. Further, depending on the circumstances, additional steps can be necessary, including activities to be completed by other processes in the organization. Note that in this example, we have not explicitly included credit management. We will assume that the customer has sufficient credit and that the order will be processed. We will, however, consider credit management activities and their impact in greater detail later in this chapter.

A variety of documents are created during the fulfillment process. As previously discussed, documents are categorized as *material documents, financial accounting* (FI) *documents, management accounting* (CO) *documents*, and *transaction documents*. Recall that documents can be printed or can exist in electronic form. The data contained in these documents are categorized as organizational data, master data, and transaction data. Some data are provided by the user, while other data are automatically retrieved from the relevant master data and the exsiting transaction documents.

This overview of the fulfillment process is highly simplified. The following discussion highlights each process step in detail in terms of its key elements: *triggers, data, tasks*, and *outcomes*.

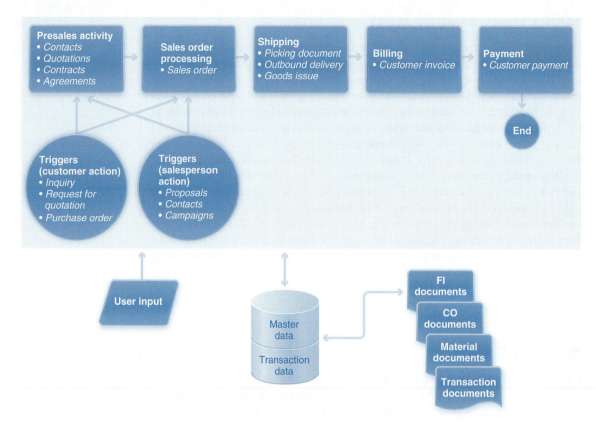

Figure 5-19: Fulfillment process steps

PRESALES ACTIVITY

Presales activity is often triggered by a communication from a customer such as an inquiry or a request for quotation (RFQ). The outcome is a quotation that is sent to the customer making the inquiry. The key elements of this inquiry–quotation activity are illustrated in Figure 5-20. An **inquiry** is a request for information regarding a potential order that the customer might place with the company. In our example, RMB inquires whether GBI can deliver 40 silver deluxe touring bikes and 100 t-shirts by the specified dates. If so, then RMB requests information on pricing, shipping costs, and discounts. In response, GBI creates a quotation and forwards it to RMB. A **quotation** is a binding agreement to sell the customer specific products under clearly defined delivery and pricing terms. Because these terms can change, a quotation will typically include a validity date, that is, a date up to which the quotation remains in effect.

Figure 5-20: Elements of the presales activity

Besides sending quotations in response to inquiries, presales activities can include managing customer contacts and creating outline agreements (explained in the next paragraph). SAP ERP provides some capabilities to track data pertaining to *established* customers, such as their preferences and purchasing history. Companies can analyze these data to create marketing and sales strategies designed to encourage customers to place additional orders. In addition, the system can track *potential* customers. ERP systems typically manage basic presales activities. Companies utilize customer relationship management (CRM) systems, discussed in Chapter 2, to manage very detailed presales, sales-pipeline, sales prospects, and marketing activities that generate a quotation in the ERP system. The handoff between the presales processes in a CRM system and the quotation-to-cash process in the ERP system is a critical integration point for most companies because failures, such as missed sales opportunities, can significantly reduce sales revenues.

Just as quotations are binding agreements made by sellers, **outline agreements** are binding agreements made by *customers* to purchase specific quantities or values of materials. An example is a GBI customer who enters into an outline agreement to purchase 1,000 standard touring bicycles over a six-month period for a specified price. Alternatively, the agreement may specify value instead of quantity. In this case, the customer agrees to purchase bicycles valued at $30,000 over the next six months. These types of outline agreements are called **contracts**. Another form of outline agreement includes specific delivery schedules. For example, a GBI customer could agree to purchase 1,200 bicycles over the next six months and to accept delivery of these bicycles on a specific schedule. In this case, the agreement is called a **scheduling agreement**.

Data

Several types of organizational and master data are necessary to process an inquiry and create a quotation. These data are presented in Figure 5-21. Particularly important are data concerning the customer, the materials, and pricing. User input consists of the customer number, material numbers, quantities, and dates. The SAP ERP system uses these inputs to obtain the necessary organizational data, such as sales area, from the various master data in the system. Recall that the material master and customer master are associated with specific organizational elements. SAP ERP also uses the customer number to obtain necessary customer data, such as contact information, from the customer master. Finally, the system uses material numbers to obtain availability and pricing data from available pricing conditions or customer-material info records.

The preceding paragraph deals with existing customers. If the inquiry is from a new customer, then the system will not contain either master data or a customer-material info record for that customer. In such cases, the company must first create the customer master data in the system. The info record is not essential because pricing data are available via pricing conditions.

The quotation can be created with or without reference to existing documents. If the quotation is created without reference, then all of the necessary data must be provided when the quotation is created. However, if a reference document—such as a previously created inquiry, quotation, sales order, or an outline agreement—is used, then data from these documents are automatically included in the quotation. These data are then updated as needed before the quotation is completed. Figure 5-22 diagrams the process of incorporating existing data into the quotation.

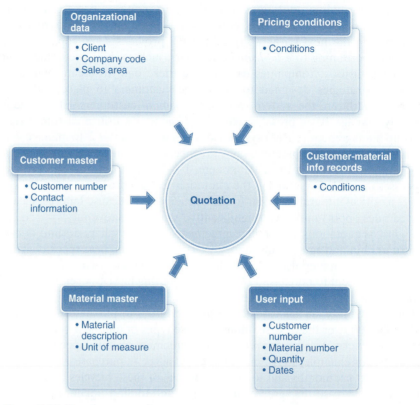

Figure 5-21: Data in a quotation

Figure 5-22: Reference documents for a quotation

Tasks

The key tasks in the presales step are to receive inquiries and to create quotations. Additional tasks include tracking customers and their buying patterns and creating long-term agreements with them.

Outcomes

Presales activity frequently results in the creation of two transaction documents: the inquiry and the quotation. The inquiry document is simply a record of the customer's inquiry in the SAP ERP system. Although creating an inquiry is not essential, it does provide certain benefits. For example, the company can use the inquiry as a reference document when it creates a quotation. Further, it can analyze inquiry data to identify lost potential sales and then devise strategies to prevent similar losses in the future.

Presales activity can also generate contract and scheduling agreement documents. No material documents are created because there is no movement of materials. No accounting documents (FI or CO) are created because presales activities have no impact on the company's financial position.

A final outcome of presales activity is the communication of the quotation to the customer. The manner in which the quotation is communicated is determined by the output conditions associated with the quotation. Recall from the discussion earlier in this chapter that the output conditions determine the following elements:

- The output medium by which the quotation is sent (e.g., print, fax, or EDI)

- The recipient, meaning the company with the appropriate partner function who receives the quotation

- The date on which the quotation is sent

In the case of Rocky Mountain Bikes, GBI receives a request for a quotation for 40 bikes and 100 t-shirts. In response, it creates a quotation. It chooses not to use any existing documents as a reference. Therefore, it must either input the RMB customer number directly or search for RMB in the list of customers for its sales area. It must also provide a valid-to date for the quotation and then input the material numbers and quantities for the materials that RMB has requested. When the customer and the materials are linked to the quotation, the system automatically imports data from the relevant master records—customer, material, pricing conditions, and customer-material information records—into the quotation. When GBI has completed the quotation and is ready to send it to RMB, the output conditions indicate that RMB prefers to receive quotations immediately via e-mail.

Demo 5.5: Create a quotation

SALES ORDER PROCESSING

One of the goals of the presales activities is to encourage customers to place orders for materials or services. These orders typically take the form of a purchase order (PO) sent by the customer to the company. A customer PO triggers the sales order processing step, which results in the creation of a sales order in the SAP ERP system. A **sales order** is an internal document that contains information necessary to fill the customer order in a standardized form. Figure 5-23 illustrates the key elements of the sales order processing step.

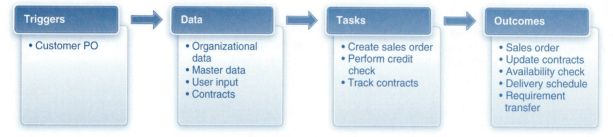

Figure 5-23: Elements of a sales order

In our example, RMB has received a quotation from GBI and several other suppliers. It has decided to place the order with GBI. Accordingly, RMB prepares a purchase order using its procurement process and communicates it to GBI via e-mail, fax, or other means. Note that had RMB selected another supplier, then the quotation that it received from GBI would have expired on the valid-to date with no impact on either GBI or RMB. The PO represents a commitment to purchase the stated materials under the specified terms and conditions. When GBI receives the purchase order, it will retrieve the quotation that was previously sent to RMB and create a sales order using the data in the quotation. As part of this process it will verify that the data in the quotation match the data in the purchase order.

Data

If you compare Figure 5-21 with Figure 5-24 below, you will notice that much of the data contained in the sales order is also found in the quotation. In addition,

Figure 5-24: Data in a sales order

the sales order includes data related to shipping, billing, partner functions, and, if relevant, data from contracts with customers. Shipping and billing data are obtained from the customer master or the customer-material info record. Partner functions are obtained from the customer master based on the specified sold-to party. Recall that contracts are agreements made by customers to purchase a specified quantity or value of materials over a certain time period. Therefore, data regarding quantities, prices, and delivery dates are obtained from contracts. In addition, the delivery plant is obtained from the customer-material info record, the customer master, or the material master, in that order.

Tasks

The key task in this step is to create a sales order. Like a quotation, a sales order can be created using one of several reference documents. The illustration in Figure 5-22 is applicable for a sales order as well. Thus, a sales order can be created with reference to a customer inquiry, a quotation, an agreement, or a previously created sales order. Data from multiple reference documents can be combined to create one sales order. Conversely, a single reference document can generate several sales orders. Figure 5-25 illustrates this relationship for the case of quotations. In our example, the quotation received from RMB is used as the source document to create the sales order. Further, one sales order is created from one quotation.

Figure 5-25: Relationship between quotations and sales orders

If the credit management capabilities of the ERP system are in use, then a check of the customer's credit is conducted. If the credit is approved, then the fulfillment process continues. If not, then additional steps are necessary. The steps related to credit management are discussed later in this chapter. If the sales order is associated with a customer contract then an additional task is to link the customer's purchases against the terms of the contract. This action allows both the company and the customer to monitor and track sales to ensure that the terms of the contract are met.

Figure 5-26 represents a standard sales order. The left side illustrates the structure of a sales order, and the right side indicates some of the data contained in the sales order that GBI created for RMB.

The document header in a sales order includes data that are valid for the entire sales order. Examples are customer data such as partner functions and customer PO number, dates, and order total. Each sales document can

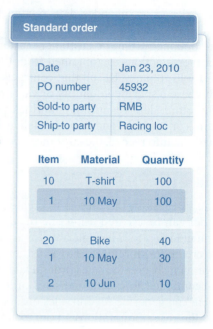

Figure 5-26: Structure of a sales order

include one or more sales document items, which contain data about each item included in the sales order. Examples of item data are material number, description, and quantity. Each item can be associated with a different item category, such as *standard item*, *text item*, and *free-of-charge item,* which determines how the item is handled with regard to pricing, billing, and shipping. For example, there is no charge for free-of-charge items. Finally, each document item can include one or more schedule lines, which specify delivery quantities and dates.

Some of the data in our example are illustrated on the right side of Figure 5-26. For example, the figure shows the PO date and PO number for RMB's order. It also indicates two partner functions, sold-to party and ship-to party. RMB is the sold-to party, and the racing location where the materials are to be shipped is the ship-to party. The order consists of two items, one for the 40 bikes and one for the 100 t-shirts. The bikes have two schedule lines, one for 30 bikes to be delivered by May 10 and the other for 10 bikes to be delivered by June 10. In contrast, the shirts have one schedule line because RMB requested that GBI deliver all 100 shirts by May 10.

Outcomes

A sales order is the only transaction document generated by this step. No material or accounting documents are created. If a contract is associated with the sales order, then it is updated to include the quantity or amount of the sale. There are four additional consequences—*availability check, delivery scheduling*, and *transfer of requirements*—which we consider next.

Availability check is a procedure to determine whether the required materials are available or will be available in time for the desired delivery date (per the schedule lines). Further, if the materials are not available, the availability check will determine the earliest possible delivery date. The decision to conduct an availability check, as well as the type and scope of the check, is based on settings in the material master. For example, the system can be configured to calculate availability based on current stock levels as well as planned receipts of material from either procurement or production. In addition, the system can create a *material reservation,* which reserves the needed materials so they cannot be used to fulfill any other requirements.

The availability check must also take into account the amount of time needed to perform relevant activities such as material staging, transportation planning, loading, and goods issue. *Material staging* refers to preparing the material for shipment. It involves picking the materials from their storage locations and packing them in suitable containers. *Transportation planning* is the process whereby firms determine how best to transport the materials to the customer based on weight, volume, transportation mode (e.g., truck, rail), and other variables. *Loading* involves moving the materials from the plant onto the truck. *Goods issue* is largely concerned with recording the financial impact of shipping goods. We will discuss goods issue later in the shipping step. The time needed to complete these steps is calculated using **backward scheduling,** in which the company begins with the required delivery date and then works in reverse order to determine when each process step must be performed. Figure 5-27 diagrams the backward scheduling process. Note that loading is preceded by picking/packing and transportation planning, which in turn are preceded by material staging. Significantly, these steps can overlap, as the figure illustrates. Consequently, the greater of these two times (transportation lead time and pick/pack time) is included in the calculation.

Finally, creating a sales order can generate a **transfer of requirements** to the material planning process. These data are used by the material planning process to plan materials procurement and production.

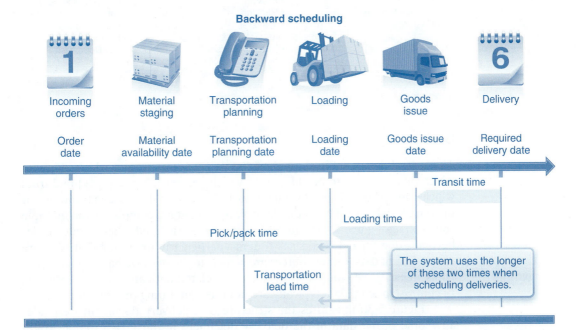

Figure 5-27: Backward scheduling

In our example, after GBI creates the sales order for RMB, the system automatically performs an availability check to determine whether the materials can be shipped as requested. In addition, it transfers the sales data to the material planning process to ensure that the materials are available as needed so that they will be shipped to RMB in a timely manner.

Demo 5.6: Create a sales order

SHIPPING

The shipping step is triggered when orders become due for delivery. Shipping consists of several tasks that are necessary to prepare and send shipments. Specifically, a *delivery document* is created which authorizes the delivery of orders that are ready to be shipped. Then, the necessary materials are *picked* from storage and placed in a staging area where they can be *packed* appropriately. If these tasks are completed through the warehouse management process, then additional steps in that process are triggered. After the order is shipped, a *goods issue* is recorded in the system, which triggers processes in accounting. These elements of the shipping step are diagrammed in Figure 5-28.

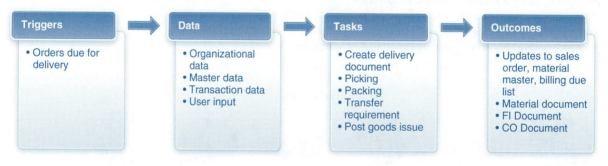

Figure 5-28: Elements of the shipping step

Data

The central document in shipping is the **delivery document**, which identifies which materials are to be shipped to which partner (ship-to party) and from which plant. The delivery document further identifies the storage locations for these materials. The data in the delivery document are compiled from multiple sources (see Figure 5-29). Because shipping is triggered when a sales order becomes due for delivery, sales orders—particularly the schedule lines—are one source of data. Other sources are similar to the ones we have seen for previous steps. As we would expect, shipping-related data are the most relevant. In contrast, pricing data typically are not relevant during the shipping step.

Figure 5-30 illustrates the structure of a delivery document (left side) and some of the data in the delivery document in our GBI example (right side). The header includes data applicable to the entire document, such as the

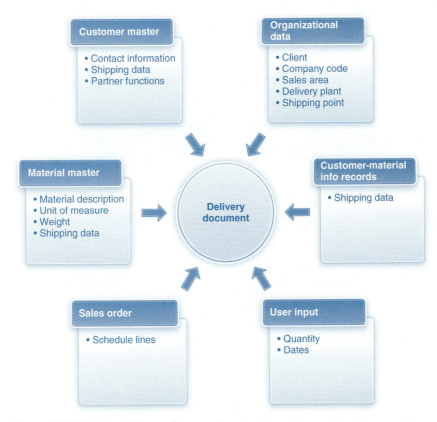

Figure 5-29: Data in a delivery document

Figure 5-30: Structure of a delivery document

ship-to party, shipping address, dates, and totals (weight, number of items). Data about each item in the shipment, such as material number, delivery quantity, and weight, appear as separate line items. Each schedule line in a sales order is a line item in the delivery document. Figure 5-31 illustrates the relationship between schedule lines and delivery document items.

Figure 5-31 displays an order with two items. Item 1 in the sales order has two schedule lines, and item 2 has one. The delivery document includes one schedule line for item 1 and one schedule line for item 2. Note that a delivery can include schedule lines from different orders. We discuss the requirements for combining items from multiple deliveries in the next section.

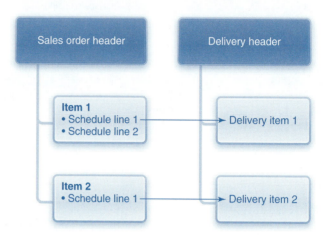

Figure 5-31: Relationship between schedule lines and delivery items

In our example, a separate delivery is created for each date. The delivery for May 10, which is re-created in Figure 5-30, shows two line items, one for 30 bikes and the other for 100 t-shirts. Note that the materials are shipped on May 5 so that they reach Colorado Springs by the desired data of May 10. Thus, the items in this delivery are associated with schedule lines from two items in one sales order. This principle is illustrated in Figure 5-31. The other delivery will include only one item—10 bikes—to be delivered by June 10.

Tasks

As identified earlier, the specific tasks completed during the shipping step are (1) creating a delivery document, (2) picking, (3) packing, and (4) post goods issue. Creating a delivery document serves as an authorization for delivery. As Figure 5-32 illustrates, schedule lines from multiple sales orders with similar characteristics can be combined into one shipment or delivery. Specifically, the

Figure 5-32: Relationship between sales orders and deliveries

sales orders must have the same *ship-to address*, *shipping point*, and *due date*. Conversely, items in one order can be split into more than one shipment.

The picking step is optional and is part of the warehouse management process. We will discuss warehouse management in Chapter 7. However, although picking is a part of the warehouse management process, it is triggered during the shipping step when a delivery document is created. The delivery document serves as a request for picking. The delivery document is converted into a *transfer order* in warehouse management, and the transfer order is then used to complete the physical movement of the materials needed for the shipment.

Items from multiple delivery documents can be included in a single transfer order, as illustrated in the left side of Figure 5-33. This approach can optimize the work of the pickers in the warehouse by grouping requests for materials that are located in the same area. Alternatively, a delivery document can generate multiple transfer orders, as illustrated in the right side of the figure. Data from the delivery documents are copied to the transfer order, as illustrated in Figure 5-34. The delivery quantity from the

Figure 5-33: Relationship between delivery documents and transfer order

Figure 5-34: Delivery quantity vs. pick quantity

delivery document becomes the *pick quantity*, which is the quantity needed to be picked from storage. Once the picking is completed, the quantity picked is automatically transferred back into the delivery document.

After picking has been completed, the materials are placed in a staging area where they are packed appropriately. Materials are packed using a variety of *shipping units* such as cartons, pallets, and containers. Each shipping unit can be packed into another shipping unit to consolidate the shipment. Typically, GBI ships each bike in an individual box and consolidates 20 boxes into one carton. It then packs several cartons into a pallet. Pallets are usually too heavy to lift by hand, so the workers must use a pallet jack or a forklift to load them into a shipping container.

Packing is diagrammed in Figure 5-35, which illustrates a delivery consisting of four items or materials. Item 1 is packed into one carton, items 2 and 3 are combined and packed into one carton, and item 4 has to be split and placed into two cartons. Two cartons are subsequently loaded onto one pallet, and the other two cartons onto a second pallet. Finally, both pallets are placed in a single container.

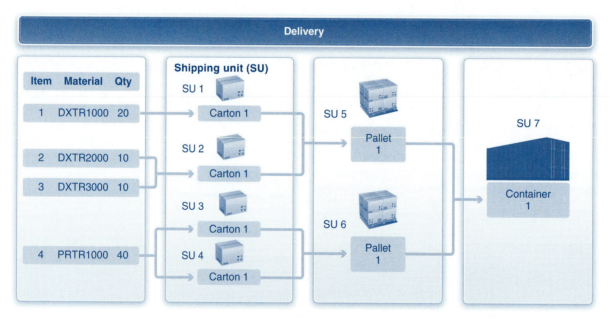

Figure 5-35: Packing options

The final task in shipping is to **post goods issue** in the ERP system. The goods issue indicates that the shipment has left the facility. It also results in several outcomes, which we discuss in the next section.

Outcomes

The shipping step, which ends with the goods issue, has numerous outcomes (see Figure 5-36). These outcomes fall into three broad categories: (1) accounting impacts, (2) creation of documents to record transaction data, and (3) updates to master data and previously created documents.

Shipping is the first step in the fulfillment process that has an impact on financials. Specifically, the *inventory accounts* of the materials shipped are

Figure 5-36: Outcomes of shipping (goods issue)

credited, and the *cost of goods sold* account is debited. These amounts are based on the cost of making or buying the materials. In the case of trading goods, the amount is based on the moving average price of the material, which we discussed in Chapter 4. In the case of finished goods, the amount is based on the standard price which takes into account production costs such as material, labor, and overhead. An FI document is created to record these data. Figure 5-37 illustrates these outcomes for the GBI example after the goods issue for the first delivery has been posted. As the figure indicates, the cost of each bike is $1,400, and the cost of each shirt is $15. Therefore, the inventory accounts for bikes and t-shirts are credited by $42,000 ($1,400 × 30) and $1,500 ($15 × 100), respectively, and the cost of goods sold account is debited by the sum of the two, $43,500. A similar impact will be recorded after the goods issue is posted for the second delivery in June. Note that the other accounts listed Figure 5-37 are relevant in later steps in the process. In addition, a controlling document may be created if a management accounting (controlling) relevant activity, such as profitability analysis is in use.

Note: Inventory and COGS values are based on cost, not selling price.
Cost of bikes: $1,400 per bike (30 bikes)
Cost of t-shirts: $15 per shirt

Figure 5-37: FI impact of the shipping step

Shipping involves a movement of materials that reduces the quantity of those materials in inventory. Therefore, in addition to the reduction of inventory *value* in the general ledger, the inventory *quantity* is also reduced in the material master for the delivering plant. A material document is created to record this movement.

Relevant sales documents, such as quotations and sales orders, are updated with the details of the shipment. Finally, the billing due list is updated. The *billing due list* is a list of deliveries for which the billing step can be executed. We now turn our attention to billing.

Demo 5.7: Process shipment for a sales order

BILLING

The purpose of the billing step is to create a variety of documents such as invoices for products or services as well as credit and debit memos. The billing step is also used to cancel previously created documents. Billing can be based either on deliveries that have been shipped to customers or on orders that have not yet been delivered. This step utilizes organizational data, master data, and transaction data from previous process steps. Like shipping, billing has several outcomes, some of which impact other processes. Figure 5-38 illustrates the elements of the billing step.

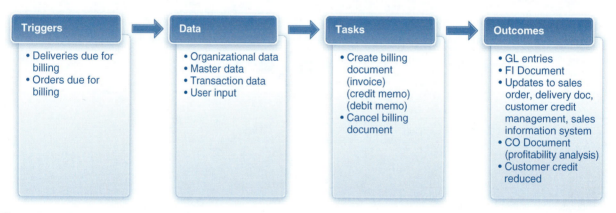

Figure 5-38: Elements of the billing step

Data

Billing, with reference to delivery documents, utilizes data from the delivery document and the sales order, such as material number and quantities (Figure 5-39). Master data, such as customer master and pricing conditions, are the source of pricing data and partner function (bill-to party). In addition, billing utilizes organizational data relevant to the fulfillment process, client, company code, and sales area.

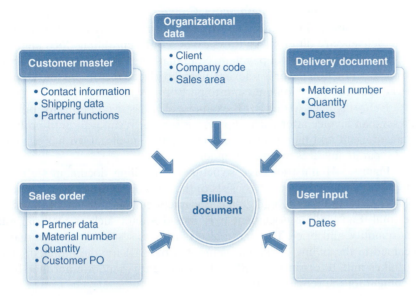

Figure 5-39: Data in a billing document

Tasks

The key task in the billing step is to generate a billing document, typically an invoice for materials or services. As previously mentioned, the invoice can be created on the basis of either a delivery or a sales order. Figure 5-19 depicts a scenario in which shipment is sent prior to billing. However, if the company wishes to be paid before it ships the materials—which is frequently the case when the customer is new or has a poor payment history—then the process can be modified so that billing will take place prior to shipment. Our discussion focuses on billing that is based on deliveries.

Other billing documents that are sometimes created are credit and debit memos. A *credit memo* is a refund the company issues if the customer returns the materials or if the initial invoice overcharged the customer. The company uses a *debit memo* when the customer was undercharged in the original invoice. A debit memo increases the amount owed by the customer.

As you can see in Figure 5-40, multiple deliveries can be combined to create one billing document. This process can be employed only when the deliveries share the same characteristics with respect to *payer* (partner function),

Figure 5-40: Relationship between deliveries and billing

billing date, and *country of destination*. Conversely, one delivery can result in multiple invoices. This is the case when the terms of payment for the items in the delivery are different. In these cases, a different billing document must be created for each term of payment. Note that when deliveries are combined, the partner function payer is relevant, not who placed the order (sold-to party) or who received the shipment (ship-to party).

Referring back to our RMB example, GBI has two options for billing: It can send an invoice after each shipment is sent, or it can wait until both shipments are sent and then prepare one cumulative invoice. GBI has elected to send separate invoices for each shipment.

Figure 5-41 illustrates the structure of a billing document (left side). The billing document header consists of the partner identification such as the sold-to party and payer, billing date, document currency, payment terms, and the total. Each billing document item includes data such as material number, quantity, and price. The figure also illustrates some of the data that are included in the billing document generated by GBI for the initial shipment (30 bikes and 100 t-shirts). GBI will subsequently generate another billing document for the remaining 10 bikes.

Figure 5-41: Structure of a billing document

Outcomes

Like shipping, billing has several outcomes related to accounting, creating documents, and updating master data and documents. These impacts are presented in Figure 5-42.

Figure 5-42: Outcomes of the billing step

When the billing step is completed, accounts receivable reconciliation and sales revenue accounts in the general ledger are updated. The accounts receivable account is debited by the amount of the invoice, which is the amount the customer owes, and the sales revenue account is credited by the same amount. Recall, however, that because accounts receivable is a reconciliation account, the amount of the invoice cannot be posted directly to the accounts receivable account. Instead, the amount is posted through the corresponding subledger account, in this case, the customer account. An open item is created in the customer's account via a debit entry, which automatically creates an entry in the accounts receivable account. In addition to postings to the general ledger, an FI document is created to record these data. Finally, because the billing step increases the amount receivable from the customer, the available credit decreases by a corresponding amount.

Figure 5-43 illustrates the financial impact of the invoice sent in our example. The invoice includes 30 bikes and 100 t-shirts. The bikes are billed at $2,800 each and the t-shirts at $27 each ($30 less 10% volume discount), for a total of $86,700 ($84,000 + $2,700). This total is debited to RMB's account, which results in an automatic posting to the accounts receivable account. Finally, the revenue account is credited in the amount of $86,700. It is worth noting that inventory and cost of goods sold are updated during the shipping step, while revenue and customer/receivables are updated at billing. Further, gross profit is calculated as revenue minus cost of goods sold. If revenue is less than the cost of goods sold, then the result is a loss rather than a profit. In our example, GBI has a gross profit of $43,200 ($86,700 – $43,500).

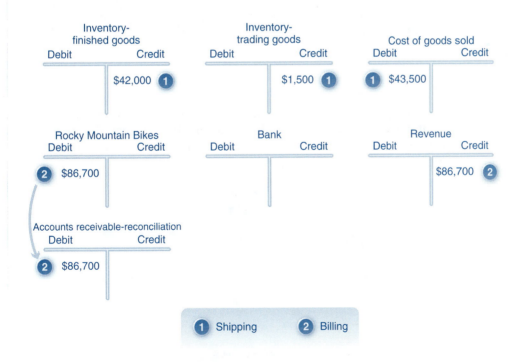

Note: Revenue, customer, and A/R amounts are based on selling price.
Selling price of bikes: $2,800 per bike
Selling price of t-shirts: $27 per shirt ($30 - 10% discount)

Figure 5-43: FI impact of the billing step

Billing has potential consequences in management accounting or controlling. For example, profitability analysis uses revenue data from the billing step that are recorded via a controlling document. Finally, billing generates updates to several sales documents, such as sales orders and deliveries, the customer's credit account, and statistics (information structures) in the sales information system.

Demo 5.8: Process billing for a sales order

PAYMENT

The final step in the fulfillment process is the receipt of payment from the customer. The payment is applied to the appropriate open items—that is, items that have not yet been paid—in the customer's account. The elements of the payment step are diagrammed in Figure 5-44.

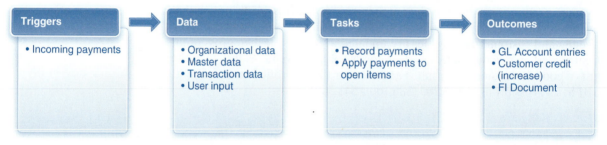

Figure 5-44: Elements of the payment step

Data

When a company receives payment from a customer, it retrieves the customer account to identify the open items. It then applies the payment to these items. Therefore, the payment step involves customer master data as well as organizational data.

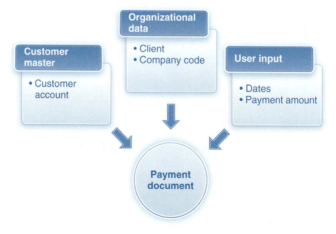

Figure 5-45: Data in a payment document

Tasks

The tasks in the payment step are to identify the open items and to apply the payment to these items. Customers make payment based on terms that were previously agreed upon. Further, customers can pay multiple invoices at once, or, conversely, can divide a single invoice into multiple payments.

Outcomes

When a customer payment is recorded, relevant general ledger accounts are updated, and a corresponding FI document is created. In our example, RMB has sent a payment for the first invoice in the amount of $86,700. Figure 5-46 exhibits the general ledger impact of this payment. The bank account is debited and RMB's account is credited by the amount of the payment. This transaction clears the open item in the customer's account that was created during the billing step. Because the customer account is a subledger account, the corresponding reconciliation account, accounts receivable, is also automatically credited. Finally, because the payment reduced the amount receivable from the customer, the customer's credit limit increases by a corresponding amount.

Figure 5-46: FI impact of the payment step

In the above example, the customer pays the full amount owed. Very often, however, the amount paid is not the amount owed. This is the case, for instance, when the customer is entitled to discounts based on the payment terms. Under the terms 1%10/Net 30, for example, payment is due no later than 30 days of receiving the invoice, and the customer is entitled to a 1% discount if it makes payment within 10 days. If the customer meets the terms for the discount, then the payment received will be less than the invoiced amount. Consequently, additional postings are included to reflect the discount. Specifically, the bank account is debited by the amount of the payment, and the sales discount account[1] is debited by the amount of the discount. The customer account and the accounts receivable reconciliation account are credited by the amount of the invoice, as shown in Figure 5-47. The only differences between Figure 5-47 and Figure 5-46 are that in Figure 5-47 the bank account is debited by a smaller amount (amount owed less discount), and the difference (discount) is debited to the sales discount account. The customer account and the A/R account are credited by the amount owed.

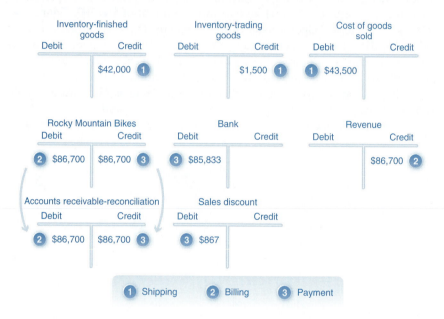

Figure 5-47: Customer payment with discount

In cases where the payment is not equal to the amount of the invoice and no discount is applicable, then two scenarios are possible. In one scenario, the amount of the difference is so small that it is insignificant. In such cases, the company either charges off or writes off the difference using an appropriate general ledger account, and the invoice is considered paid. A difference is generally considered small if it falls within the tolerance limits specified in the system. When the difference falls outside tolerance limits and therefore is considered significant, the payment is handled either through the partial payment technique or the residual item technique. Under the *partial payment* technique, the payment is posted to the customer account, and the original invoice item remains open. Under the *residual item* technique, the original item is closed, and a new item for the balance is posted to the customer account (and the corresponding reconciliation account). Figure 5-48 diagrams all of these scenarios.

---

[1] GBI records all discounts related to sales in one account, the sales discount account. This includes discounts offered at the time of receiving the sales order as well as discounts related to payment. It is not uncommon to record these in different accounts, depending on the reporting needs of the company.

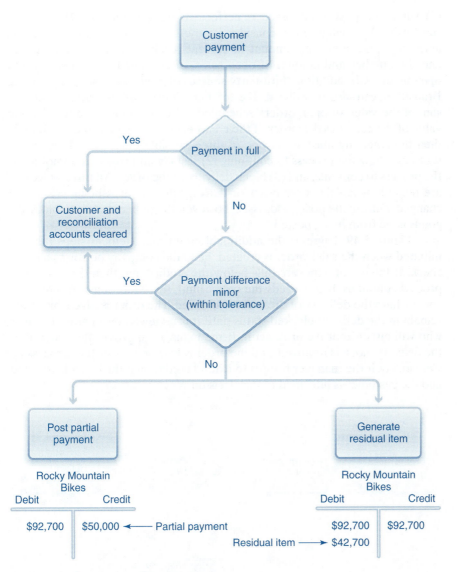

Figure 5-48: Processing customer payment

Demo 5.9: Process payment for an invoice

● CREDIT MANAGEMENT PROCESS

In our discussion of the fulfillment process, we assumed that the customer has sufficient credit. In this section we briefly discuss the credit management process, which businesses use to assess whether a customer should be granted credit to purchase and receive goods prior to payment. The credit management process can be configured to make this assessment at three points during the fulfillment process: (1) when the sales order is created or changed, (2) when the delivery is authorized (delivery document created) or changed, and

(3) when the post goods issue is performed during shipping. The process can further be configured to consider a variety of criteria when making this assessment, including the amount of current receivables from the customer and the number and amount of open sales orders, scheduled deliveries, and open invoices. In addition, third-party sources of credit data, such as Dunn & Bradstreet, can also be utilized. The total *credit exposure* is calculated as the sum of the value of open orders, scheduled deliveries, open invoices, and the value of the current sales order. If the credit exposure exceeds the credit limit, then the company must select one of three possible outcomes: (1) warn the user and allow the process to continue, (2) display an error and do not allow the process to continue, and (3) block delivery of the order. All three outcomes are possible when the sales order or delivery document is being created or changed. During the post goods issue, however, the only option is to block the goods issue from being posted.

Figure 5-49 diagrams the additional credit management steps that are initiated when the sales order is created. First, the company performs a credit check. If the credit exposure falls below the credit limit, then the fulfillment process continues. If it exceeds the credit limit, the figure illustrates the outcome where the delivery of the order is blocked. The order is saved, but it will remain in the delivery blocked status until it is reviewed by a credit manager, who will either approve or reject it. If the manager approves the order, then the delivery block is removed, and the order is released for further processing. Conversely, if the manager refuses to extend credit, then the order is rejected, and the customer is informed of this decision.

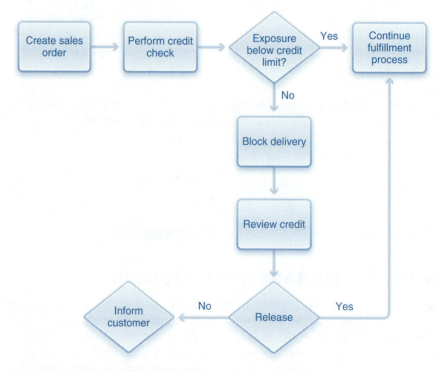

Figure 5-49: Credit management process

■ INTEGRATION WITH OTHER PROCESSES

The fulfillment process is tightly integrated with many other processes. We identified numerous integration points in the discussion of the process steps and will elaborate on them in other chapters. Below we summarize the key integration points, which are presented in Figure 5-50.

Figure 5-50: Integration with other processes

Because fulfillment involves both revenues and payments, a clear relationship exists between fulfillment and financial accounting. For example, some of the master data utilized in fulfillment, such as customer master and material master, are jointly maintained by sales and accounting. In addition, the shipment, billing, and payment steps have an impact on the general ledger. Fulfillment can also impact the profitability analysis process in management accounting, which utilizes sales revenue data.

Going further, during sales order processing, when the company conducts availability checks it employs data from inventory management, production, and purchasing, which are the sources of the materials for shipment. Sales data are also used by materials planning to schedule the procurement and production of materials. Another fulfillment step, goods movement, is related to inventory management. In addition, warehouse management processes (such as picking) can be initiated during shipment.

Fulfillment is also related to project systems. Recall from Chapter 1 that enterprises use projects to create complex products for customers, such as an aircraft. Customer orders for such products are processed using the fulfillment process. However, instead of preparing and sending shipments, as described in this chapter, the customer requirements are transferred to the project management process. In turn, project systems influence deliveries and billing.

Finally, in the process section we explored the relationship between the fulfillment process at GBI and the procurement process at RMB. These processes are executed in different companies using different ERP systems. Nevertheless, for both processes to operate efficiently, the two companies must integrate on a process level and a technical level at multiple stages.

■ REPORTING

As discussed in previous chapters, SAP ERP provides several reporting options including online lists, work lists, and analytics. An additional reporting option in fulfillment is the document flow, which identifies all the documents related to a customer order. We examine these options in this section.

DOCUMENT FLOW

Throughout this chapter we have examined many of the documents associated with the fulfillment process, including inquiries, sales orders, delivery documents, billing documents, and payment documents. Significantly, all of the documents related to one inquiry or sales order are linked together in a document flow. A **document flow** displays all of the documents associated with the steps that have been completed for a single customer inquiry or order. The document flow is updated after each process step is completed. Figure 5-51 illustrates a document flow for a completed process that started with a sales order (rather than an inquiry). The document flow essentially displays the history and status of the sales order. For example, if a delivery document is included in the document flow but a goods issue is not, then we can conclude that delivery is in progress and the shipment has not yet left the shipping point. This conclusion assumes, of course, that the data in the ERP system are up to date and accurately reflect the activity in the physical system. Any of the underlying documents, such as the sales order or invoice, can be retrieved and displayed from the document flow, if more details are necessary.

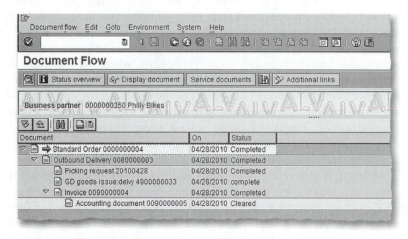

Figure 5-51: Document flow. Copyright SAP AG 2011

Demo 5.10: Display document flow

WORK LISTS

Work lists identify tasks that are ready for completion. These lists can be generated for each task involved in fulfillment, such as preparing deliveries, picking, post goods issue, and billing. Figure 5-52 displays a series of work lists associated with fulfillment tasks.

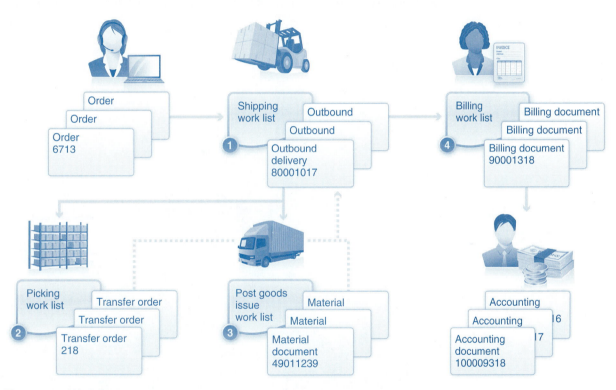

Figure 5-52: Work lists

One example of a fulfillment work list is a delivery due list or a shipping work list, which is essentially a list of orders that are scheduled to be shipped by a specific date. Another example is a list of orders that have been shipped but not billed. Lists can be generated for specific dates and for specific organizational elements, such as a shipping point. In addition, tasks included in the list can be selected for processing individually or collectively. For example, a delivery due list will display all sales orders that should be shipped for on-time delivery. The user can select a single a sales order for individual processing and create a delivery document for that order. Alternatively, the user can select several sales orders for collective processing and create delivery documents for all of them simultaneously.

Demo 5.11: Display a work list

ONLINE LISTS

Online lists are used to generate lists of documents associated with specific master data. In the context of fulfillment, any of the documents discussed earlier can be displayed for specific customers or materials or a combination of the two. Figure 5-53 is an example of a list of sales orders for a particular sold-to party. The figure displays three orders, labeled 1241, 1549, and 1600. Recall that online lists are displayed using a list viewer or an ALV grid. These techniques provide several options for displaying results, such as sorting and summation.

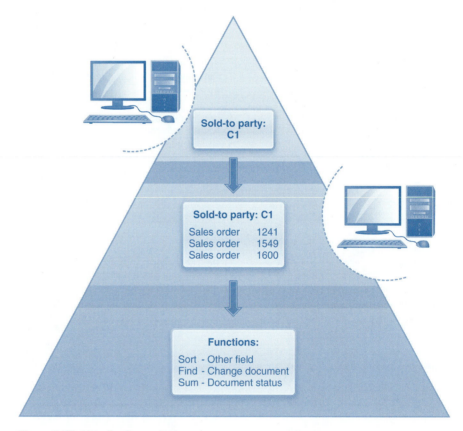

Sold-to party:
C1

Sold-to party: C1
Sales order   1241
Sales order   1549
Sales order   1600

Functions:
Sort - Other field
Find - Change document
Sum - Document status

Figure 5-53: List of sales orders

Other examples of online lists are:

- List of delivery documents for a specific customer

- List of sales orders for a specific combination of customers and materials

- List of delivery documents for a specific material or material group

Demo 5.12: Display online list

ANALYTICS

Figure 5-54 depicts the information structures used in the sales information system. Standard information structures store data based on organizational elements—sales organization and shipping point, for example—as well as master data such as customer and material.

Figure 5-54: Information structures

Information structures are used to generate both standard and flexible analyses. Figure 5-55 provides an example of standard analysis, specifically, an analysis of sales that includes sales organizations, order value, and invoiced amount. It further demonstrates a drilldown to display customers (Philly Bikes and Motown Bikes) for a selected sales organization (UE00). Drilling down for one customer (Philly Bikes) reveals data for each time period (month).

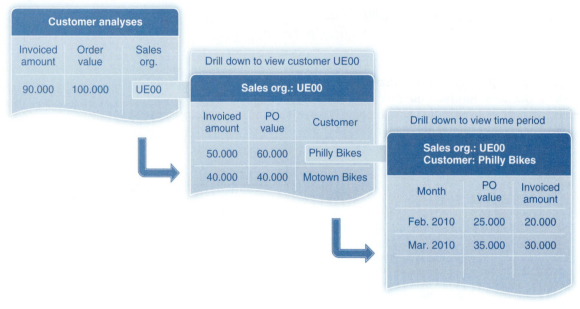

Figure 5-55: Example of standard analysis

CHAPTER SUMMARY

The fulfillment process involves the activities required to receive and respond to a customer inquiry, process a sales order, ship goods, and bill and receive payment from customers. A company's fulfillment process is typically optimized for the type of goods it sells and the sales channels (wholesale or retail) that it utilizes. The fulfillment process is the lifeblood of any company due to its clear focus on generating revenues and driving requirements for many other processes such as production and purchasing. In addition, the company must make certain that all revenues resulting from the fulfillment process are properly reflected in the financial statements and that billing and receiving payments from customers are carried out efficiently.

The fulfillment process consists of five key steps: (1) receipt of a customer inquiry or RFQ, (2) preparation of a quotation in response to the inquiry, (3) sales order processing, (4) shipping, and (5) billing and payment processing. Many types of data are required to execute these steps properly and to account for the goods and financial impact of the fulfillment process.

Sales area, shipping point, and credit control area are categories of organizational data that are unique to the fulfillment process. A sales area is a combination of three additional organizational data: sales organization, distribution channel, and division. The configuration of these data for each company is a reflection of the industry, the product, and any customer requirements that a company must meet.

In contrast, the material master data and customer master data are more operational in scope. These data are used to execute the various steps of the fulfillment process and can vary among customers, plants, and sales organizations to meet the specific requirements of those situations.

Customer master data are critical to ensure that (1) orders are shipped to the correct location, (2) customers have sufficient credit to pay for orders, and (3) invoices are sent to the proper accounts payable group for prompt payment. In addition, pricing conditions are master data that are maintained for specific materials, quantities, or individual customers, depending on the specific contractual and business conditions.

Transaction data are collected at each step of the fulfillment process to enable process and instance-level reporting for improved process management. Multiple lists and reports are generated to provide management with operational visibility into every aspect of the fulfillment process.

KEY TERMS

Accounting data

Availability check

Backward scheduling

Bill-to party

Contracts

Credit control area

Credit management master record

Customer master data

Customer-material information record

Delivery document

Distribution chain

Distribution channel

Division

Document flow

General data

Inquiry

Item category

Outline agreements

Output conditions

Partner functions

Payer

Post goods issue

Pricing conditions

Quotation

Sales area

Sales area data

Sales order

Sales organization data

Sales organizations

Sales plant data

Schedule lines

Scheduling agreement

Shipping point

Ship-to party

Sold-to party

Transfer of requirements

REVIEW QUESTIONS

1. Briefly discuss the organizational levels relevant to the fulfillment process. Be sure to explain the relationships among the various levels.

2. What is a distribution chain? How is it relevant to the fulfillment process?

3. Explain the relationships among the following organizational levels: sales organization, distribution channel, division, and sales area.

4. What is a credit control area? Explain the difference between a centralized and a decentralized model of credit control areas.

5. Briefly discuss the master data relevant to the fulfillment process.

6. Explain the relationship between the master data and organizational data in the fulfillment process.

7. Describe, with examples, the data in the three segments of a customer master.

8. At what organizational levels are the material master defined as it relates to the fulfillment process? Provide examples of data in the material master.

9. Explain the role of each partner function in the fulfillment process.

10. What is the purpose of a customer-material info record? Provide examples of the types of data it contains.

11. How is pricing determined in the fulfillment process? Provide examples of data relevant to pricing.

12. What is the credit management master record? How is it related to the customer master record?

13. Describe the steps in the fulfillment process in terms of triggers, data, steps, and outcomes.

14. Describe the structure of the following documents

    a. Sales order

    b. Delivery document

    c. Billing document

15. Explain the relationship between each of the following pairs of key elements of the fulfillment process:

    a. Quotations and sales orders

    b. Sales orders and deliveries

    c. Deliveries and transfer orders

    d. Deliveries and billing documents

16. Explain how the steps in the fulfillment process impact the general ledger accounts.

17. How do companies manage payments that are less than the amount of the invoice?

18. Briefly describe the credit management process. Which steps of the fulfillment process are relevant to credit management?

19. Briefly explain how the fulfillment process is integrated with other processes.

20. What is a document flow?

21. Provide examples of works lists and online lists associated with the fulfillment process.

22. Provide an example of reporting using standard analysis in fulfillment. Make certain to include the concept of drill down.

EXERCISES

Exercises for this chapter are available on *WileyPLUS.*

GBI US Customer List

Customer Number	Customer Name and address	Sales Organization	Delivering Plant
1000	Rocky Mountain Bikes 6400 Fiddler's Green Circle, Denver CO 80111 USA	UW00	SD00
2000	Big Apple Bikes 95 Morton St, New York City, NY 10014 USA	UE00	MI00
3000	Philly Bikes 3999 West Chester Pike, Philadelphia, PA 19073 USA	UE00	MI00
4000	Peachtree Bikes 1001 Summit Boulevard, Atlanta, GA 30319 USA	UE00	MI00
5000	Beantown Bikes 3 Van de Graaff Dr, Boston, MA 18033 USA	UE00	MI00
6000	Windy City Bikes 3010 Highland Parkway, Chicago, IL 60515 USA	UE00	MI00
7000	Furniture City Bikes 401 W Fulton, Grand Rapids, MI 49504 USA	UE00	MI00
8000	Motown Bikes 1550 One Towne Square, Detroit, MI 48076 USA	UE00	MI00
9000	SoCal Bikes 18101 Von Karman Ave, Irvine, CA 92612 USA	UW00	SD00
10000	Silicon Valley Bikes 3410 Hillview Ave, Palo Alto, CA 94034 USA	UW00	SD00
11000	DC Bikes 1300 Pennsylvania Ave, Washington, DC 20004 USA	UE00	MI00
12000	Northwest Bikes 601 108th Ave, Seattle, WA 98004 USA	UW00	SD00

The Production Process

LEARNING OBJECTIVES

After completing this chapter you will be able to:

1. Describe the master data associated with the production process.

2. Identify the key steps in the production process and the data, documents, and information associated with them.

3. Effectively use SAP® ERP to execute the key steps in the production process.

4. Effectively use SAP ERP to extract meaningful information about the production process.

The production process consists of the various steps and activities involved with the manufacture or assembly of finished goods and semifinished goods. Organizations implement a variety of production or manufacturing processes, depending on the type of material being produced and the manufacturing strategy used to produce it. Among the most common production processes are discrete, repetitive, and process manufacturing. Discrete and repetitive manufacturing involve the production of tangible materials such as cars, computers, and bicycles. Each unit produced is a "discrete" unit, meaning it is distinct from other units and it can be counted. Further, the component materials from which the unit is made, such as wheels and bolts in a bike, are identifiable. There is, however, a fundamental distinction between repetitive and discrete manufacturing. In *repetitive manufacturing*, the same material is produced repeatedly over an extended period of time at a relatively constant rate. In *discrete manufacturing*, the company produces different materials over time in batches, often alternating between materials on a production line.

In contrast, *process manufacturing* refers to the production of materials such as paint, chemicals, and beverages that are not manufactured in individual units. Rather, they are produced in bulk, and they are measured in quantities such as gallons and liters. Further, the component materials cannot be identified after production because they are mixed together in the final product. Imagine, for example, attempting to identify the raw materials in a gallon of paint. The real-world example below illustrates discrete, repetitive, and process manufacturing as implemented by Apple, Intel, and Valero, respectively.

Business Processes in Practice 6.1: Types of Production Processes

Apple Inc. produces its Macintosh computers using a discrete production process. Apple[1] manufactures several models of Mac laptop and desktop computers on the same production lines in batches of varying quantities. For example, the Mac desktop production line might produce 10,000 units of the iMac 21.5-inch models and then switch the line to produce 15,000 units of the 27-inch model.

In contrast, Intel produces most of its processors in a repetitive production process. Due to the immense costs and technical complexity associated with semiconductor production, Intel must construct dedicated production lines for each of its microchips. Often, switching a production line from one chip to another can cost tens of millions of dollars. Therefore, to maximize cost efficiencies, Intel attempts to run continuous production of a specific chip for as long as possible. To successfully implement this strategy, Intel must plan its production very carefully.

Finally, a prominent example of process manufacturing is Valero Energy Corporation, the largest independent petroleum-refining company in North America. Valero produces fuel, chemicals, and other petroleum products in 15 refineries across North America. The company's refineries operate 24/7 in a continuous production process, converting a total capacity of nearly 3 million barrels of raw petroleum into multiple products. Once a refinery starts full production, it can be many months or years before Valero shuts it down for maintenance.

Source: Apple, Intel, and Valero company reports.

---

[1] Technically, Apple uses contract manufacturers to execute the physical production, but retains a great deal of visibility and control, effectively using the contract manufacturers as "virtual" Apple manufacturing facilities.

Regardless of the particular production process used, however, companies typically employ two common production strategies, make-to-stock and make-to-order. In **make-to-stock** production, the production process is triggered by a need to increase inventory. Inventory is typically stored in a warehouse until it is used to fulfill customer orders. When inventory falls below certain predefined levels, the make-to-stock process is initiated, even if there is no pending customer order. In contrast, under the **make-to-order** strategy, production is triggered by the need to fill a specific customer order. In other words, production does not begin until a customer orders a product.

Business Processes in Practice 6.2: Make-to-Stock vs. Make-to-Order

A good example of a company that uses the make-to-stock strategy is Apple Inc. Apple uses the make-to-stock process for Macs sold in its Apple stores. The company first estimates the consumer demand for its Mac computers. It then calculates its available manufacturing capacity and the quantities of raw materials it will need to build enough computers to meet consumer demand. Apple's strategy is to purchase raw materials and reserve manufacturing capacity ahead of time

to maximize the cost efficiencies of buying materials in bulk quantities and doing large production runs. Apple and its contract manufacturers then produce a specific quantity of each Mac model and ship them from the factory to the Apple stores and other retail outlets for sale. When customers come into an Apple store, they expect that the computer they want to buy will be there and that they can take it home immediately after purchasing it.

Because Apple uses a make-to-stock strategy, the company must pay extremely close attention to both its retail sales and the amount of finished goods inventory it has in stock in order to estimate its demand as accurately as possible. If Apple overestimates the demand for a particular product, the company will be stuck with a large inventory of very expensive finished goods that customers don't want to buy and that will decrease in value while they sit on the shelf. Conversely, if it underestimates the demand for a product, customers who want to purchase the computer will be told it is out of stock. They will then have two options: place a back order and wait until the store gets resupplied with inventory, or shop for the product at a different store. Either outcome will make consumers unhappy and could result in lost sales.

In contrast, one of Apple's major competitors—Dell—employs a make-to-order production strategy. Dell was the first company in the industry to build computers only after they had received a firm order and thus knew exactly what product the customer wanted. Because Dell does not have many retail outlets like Apple (although it has recently tested some retail partnerships), the company relies primarily on telephone and Internet sales channels for the majority of their sales. In contrast to Apple customers, then, when Dell customers place an order, they anticipate that they will have to wait a few days for the computer to be produced and delivered.

After the customer places an order, Dell typically assembles the computer from raw materials it has on hand and then ships it directly to the customer. Unlike Apple, then, Dell does not need to be very concerned with estimating demand for its finished products because it knows exactly what customers want based on customer orders. However, Dell must be extremely careful in purchasing raw materials and managing its production capacity. Because its production runs are very small—sometimes one computer at a time—it must estimate its raw material needs and production scheduling based on an unknown customer demand. If Dell mismanages its production planning process, it is especially susceptible to an oversupply or undersupply of raw materials and shortages or idleness in production capacity. If Dell does not have sufficient raw materials or production capacity, customers will have to wait much longer for their computers to be shipped.

Conversely, if the company has excessive raw materials or unused production capacity, it loses money.

Although Dell's customers are accustomed to waiting a few days for their computers to arrive, they probably will be upset if their deliveries are delayed for several weeks due to a shortage of raw materials or a backlog of production orders. Alternatively, Dell's profitability will suffer if its production lines are idle or its warehouses are filled with unused raw materials.

Both Apple and Dell have chosen a production strategy that maximizes their profitability. Apple believes that by controlling the entire buying experience through their Internet and physical stores, they can attract more customers. This strategic objective drives Apple to place a much higher emphasis on having products available in the store when a customer comes there to shop, which increases the likelihood that she or he will make a purchase. In addition, Apple realizes significant cost savings through large, planned production runs and close coordination with retail sales data generated by their online and physical stores. For all these reasons, the make-to-stock production process is probably the best strategy for both Apple and its customers.

In the case of Dell, the make-to-order production process fits well with the company's rapid assembly and standardized products. Dell's customers are comfortable ordering a computer that they have never seen because they know that Dell uses high-quality, industry-standard components. They also trust Dell to ship them a finished computer in just a few days, and they are willing to wait for it to arrive rather than pick it up in a store.

In essence, the preferences and behaviors of each company's customers determine, to a great extent, the production process for each company. Apple's customers want to touch and experience the product in a retail store, whereas Dell's customers are content to buy something over the phone or the Internet. Each company has optimized its production process to match both its specific set of customer requirements and its internal profitability goals and cost structure.

Source: Adapted from Magal and Word Essentials of Business Processes and Information Systems. John Wiley & Sons, Inc. (2009).

In Chapter 1, we introduced a simplified production process. We reproduce this process in Figure 6-1. The process is triggered by a request for production. The request is authorized, which allows the warehouse to issue the raw materials. Production uses these materials to manufacture the requested goods, which are then moved to storage.

Warehouse	Production	Warehouse	Production	Warehouse
Request production	Authorize production	Issue raw materials	Create product	Receive finished goods

Figure 6-1: A basic production process

In this chapter, we discuss the production process in detail. GBI utilizes a make-to-stock production strategy. Further, it employs a discrete production process to make the different types of bicycles in specified quantities or lots.

We begin our discussion by identifying the master data related to the production process. We then examine the specific process steps in detail. We conclude by considering reporting as it relates to production. The major organizational data relevant to production are client, company code, plant, and storage location. We already have discussed all of these data in previous chapters. Consequently, we will not cover them in this chapter.

■ MASTER DATA

The master data relevant to production are bills of material, work centers, product routings, material master, and production resource tools. Let's look at each of these more closely.

BILL OF MATERIALS

A bill of materials (BOM) identifies the components that are necessary to produce a material. In discreet and repetitive manufacturing, the BOM is a complete list of all the materials, both raw materials and semifinished goods, that are needed to produce a specified quantity of the material. In process industries, such as chemicals, oil and gas, and beverages, the BOM is often referred to as a *formula* or *recipe*, and it includes a list of ingredients needed to create a specified quantity of the product. In this book, we will limit our discussion to discrete manufacturing.

A BOM is a hierarchical depiction of the materials needed to produce a finished good or semifinished good (see Figure 6-2). BOMs range from very simple to very complex, depending on the material. For example, a BOM for a ball-point pen consists of only a half dozen or so materials or items.

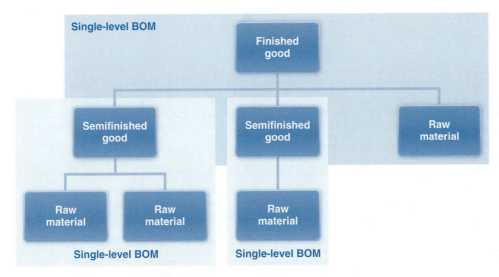

Figure 6-2: Single- and multi-level BOMs

In contrast, the BOM for a Boeing 747 aircraft is exceedingly complex, containing more than 6 million materials. In addition, BOMs can be either single level or multi-level. A single-level BOM contains only one level in the hierarchy, whereas a multi-level BOM has more than one. An aircraft, for example, may have more than 50 levels in its BOM.

BOMs in SAP ERP are defined as single level. However, SAP ERP can construct multi-level BOMs by nesting several single-level BOMs. *Nesting* refers to a hierarchy in which a component in a bill of material has its own bill of material. This structure is illustrated in Figure 6-2, where a multi-level BOM is comprised of three single-level BOMs. The BOM for the finished good shows three items: two semifinished goods and one raw material. In turn, each semifinished good has a BOM consisting of one or more raw materials. (The raw materials have no BOM and are acquired from an external source.)

Significantly, a BOM is defined for a material at the plant level. In other words, different plants may use a different BOM to produce the same material. This is the case when some of the materials used in producing the material are different. For example, one plant may use a slightly different bolt than another plant in making a finished good.

Recall from Chapter 1 that GBI makes deluxe and professional touring bikes. The BOM for the touring bikes (Figure 6-3) displays the materials required to assemble the bikes. The professional touring bikes include a professional wheel assembly made from aluminum wheels, while the deluxe touring bikes include a deluxe wheel assembly made from carbon composite wheels. The frames for both the professional and deluxe bikes are made of carbon composite material and come in three colors—red, black, and silver.

GBI also manufactures men's and women's off-road bikes using aluminum frames and aluminum wheels. The frame for the men's bikes is a different size than the frame for the women's bikes. The BOM for off-road bikes is shown in Figure 6-4.

Figure 6-3 and Figure 6-4 represent multi-level BOMs. In both figures, the wheel assembly is a semifinished good that is manufactured using three raw materials. The other component materials are all raw materials. Should

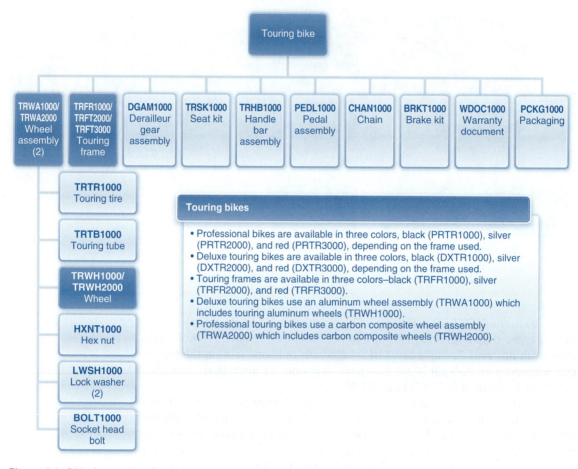

Figure 6-3: Bill of materials for touring bikes

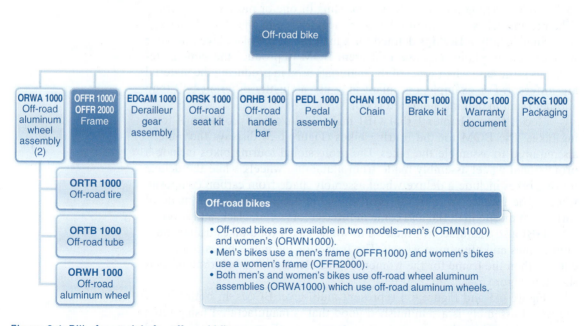

Figure 6-4: Bill of materials for off-road bikes

GBI decide to produce the pedal assembly rather than purchase it, then the BOM will be modified to indicate that the pedal assembly is a semifinished good. In addition, the raw materials needed to make the pedal assembly will be included as a second level in the BOM.

Figure 6-5 identifies the data contained in a bill of material. The BOM consists of a *header* section and an *items* section. The header section includes data that apply to the entire BOM, such as the *material number, description, plant, usage, validity, status,* and *base quantity.* The material number in the header identifies the finished good or semifinished good described in the BOM. The BOM is valid from the date specified in the header. A validity date is appropriate when changes are planned for a future date, for example, due to changes in the product design. In such cases the current BOM is valid until the new BOM goes into effect. Because a BOM can be used in several processes, the usage field in the header identifies the purpose for which the BOM can be used. For example, the BOM in Figure 6-5 displays a usage code of 1, meaning that the BOM is to be used in production. Other purposes for which BOMs are used are engineering, sales and distribution, and plant maintenance.

Going further, regardless of the specific usage, a BOM's status can be active or inactive. An active BOM can be used in the production of a material; an inactive BOM cannot. Finally, the base quantity indicates the quantity of goods that will be produced by the materials specified in the BOM items section. For instance, the BOM illustrated in Figure 6-5 identifies the materials needed to make one bike.

The items section of a BOM identifies all the materials needed to make the finished good or semi-finished good identified in the header. Figure 6-5 includes some of the items in the BOM for the off-road bike. Examples of data for each item are *material number, description, quantity,* and *item category.* Material number and description identify the necessary materials. The quantity specifies how many of these materials are needed. For example, 2 wheel assemblies are needed for each bike. A BOM can contain different types of items, which are distinguished by the item category. The **item category** identifies the type of material and influences how the material is to be used in the

Header

BOM	
Material	DXTR1000
Plant	DL00
Usage	1
Validity	Date
Status	Active
Base quantity	1 pc

Items (detail)

Item	Item cat.	Material	Description	Qty
0010	L	TRWA1000	Touring aluminum wheel assembly	2
0020	L	TRFR1000	Touring frame - black	1
0030	L	DGAM1000	Derailleur gear assembly	1
0040	D	WDOC1000	Warranty document (instead of assembly instructions)	1
0050	L	CHAIN1000	Chain	1

Figure 6-5: BOM structure

BOM. Common item categories are *stock item*, *nonstock item*, *variable-size item*, *text item*, *document item*, *class item*, and *intra material*.

- A stock item (L) is a material for which stock or inventory is maintained; therefore, it must have a material master.

- A nonstock item (N) is one for which inventory is not maintained; therefore, it does not need a material master defined.

- If a material is available in different sizes, such as sheet metal or fabric, then the different sizes can be represented by the same material number. In these cases the item category used is variable-size item (R), and data concerning the needed size or dimension must be specified in the BOM.

- A text item (T) is used to include notes and comments within the BOM. Notes may explain how to use the material or identify any unusual assembly requirements.

- A document item (D) is used to include documents such as engineering drawings, assembly instructions, and photographs.

- Class items (K) are used in *variant BOMs* to identify a class or group of items. Companies use variant BOMs to create multiple versions or variants of the same material rather than prepare a separate BOM for each version. A class item is a placeholder for an actual item that must be specified when the BOM is used. For example, GBI could use a class item to identify the different colors of frames used in the touring bikes. The specific color frame would then be selected either during production for a production BOM or during sales for a sales BOM.

- Intra material (M), or *phantom items*, are a logically grouped set of materials that could collectively be considered as a single material. The material is created temporarily during production, between two subprocesses, and is immediately consumed as production continues. In the case of GBI, a bicycle always will need two wheels — a front wheel and a rear wheel. The two wheels could be logically considered a set, so GBI could use a phantom item to represent this set.

Business Processes in Practice 6.3: How Large Can a BOM Be?

The bill of materials for the Boeing 747 includes more than 6 million parts, half of which are small fasteners or rivets. A 747-400 contains 171 miles (274 km) of wiring and 5 miles (8 km) of tubing. The body of a 747-400 consists of 147,000 pounds (66,150 kg) of high-strength aluminum. To make things even more complex, all those parts are subject to intensive quality and reliability checks, and they are inspected multiple times before, during, and after they are installed. In addition, Boeing must stock more than 6.5 million spare parts in eight global distribution centers for airlines that need to make repairs to aircraft that are currently in operation.

Source: Boeing Corp.

Demo 6.1: Review BOM for bike and wheel assembly

WORK CENTER

A **work center** is a location where value-added work needed to produce a material is carried out. It is where specific operations, such as drilling, assembly, and painting, are conducted. A work center can also be a machine or a group of machines; an entire production line; a work area, such as an assembly area; or a person or group of people who are responsible for completing operations in different parts of the plant. Regardless of its composition, however, it is a resource that can be used for a variety of purposes and for multiple processes. For the purposes of this chapter, we define a work center as a resource used to produce a material.

Figure 6-6 illustrates the data associated with a work center. The *basic data* section includes the *name and description* of the work center and the *person or people responsible* for maintaining the master data for the center. It also identifies which task lists can use the work center. A **task list** is simply a list of operations that are required to accomplish a task. **Operations** are the specific tasks that must be completed, such as drilling, cutting, painting, inspecting, and assembling. Different types of task lists are associated with different processes.

In production a task list takes the form of a *product routing* or a *master recipe*. We discuss product routings later in this chapter because they are used in discrete and repetitive manufacturing. Master recipes are used in process

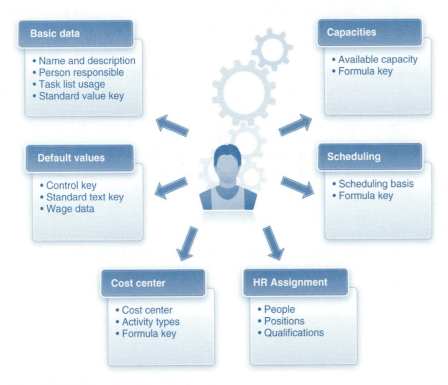

Basic data
- Name and description
- Person responsible
- Task list usage
- Standard value key

Capacities
- Available capacity
- Formula key

Default values
- Control key
- Standard text key
- Wage data

Scheduling
- Scheduling basis
- Formula key

Cost center
- Cost center
- Activity types
- Formula key

HR Assignment
- People
- Positions
- Qualifications

Figure 6-6: Work center data

manufacturing and therefore are not discussed in this chapter. There are many other types of task lists. We will discuss some of them in later chapters in the context of other processes. Others are beyond the scope of this book. Finally, *standard value keys* are used to assign standard or planned values for the normal time elements—that is, the activities that consume time—associated with the work center. Typical *time elements* are setup time, processing time (machine and labor), and teardown time. The keys utilize specific formulas to calculate how much time must be allotted for each of these elements.

Work center data also include *default values* for operations performed at the work center. Examples of default values are control keys and wage data. *Control keys* specify how an operation or a suboperation is scheduled, how costs will be calculated, and how operations will be confirmed once they are completed in the work center. For example, a control key can indicate that confirmation of an operation is required and must be printed before the next operation can be performed. *Wage data* are associated with processes in human capital management, such as payroll.

Available *capacity* defines how much work can be performed at the work center during a specified time. A work center can include more than one resource or capacity, such as labor and machine. In this case, the *scheduling basis* determines the specific capacity to be utilized for production.

A work center is associated with a *cost center*. Recall from Chapter 3 that a cost center is a container or bucket that accumulates costs that are then allocated or further processed by management accounting processes. Costs associated with operations completed in a work center are calculated using formulas that utilize the costs and the standard values associated with each *activity type* (e.g., setup, labor, and machine).

GBI has three work centers, as illustrated in Figure 6-7 and Figure 6-8. Figure 6-7 shows the layout of the production facility in Dallas. It identifies the three work centers (ASSY1000, INSP1000, and PACK1000) and the four storage locations (RM00, FG00, SF00, and MI00). All three work centers are associated with one cost center, the production cost center (NAPR1000).

Figure 6-8 provides details of the three work centers. ASSY1000 is the assembly work center. It has 8 hours of labor capacity. Labor is used to complete three operations—stage or prepare materials, construct the wheel assembly, and assemble the finished bike. INSP1000 is the inspection work center. Here the bike is placed on a machine that tests its suspension and balance. Meanwhile, the employee visually inspects the entire bike, checking for defects. In contrast to the assembly work center, then, the inspection work center utilizes both labor and machine capacity. Once testing has been completed, the bike is disassembled into the frame assembly and the wheel assemblies. These components are then packed separately in the final work center (PACK1000), which, like assembly, involves only labor. The final assembly is typically completed at the retailer's location or by the customer after he or she purchases the bike.

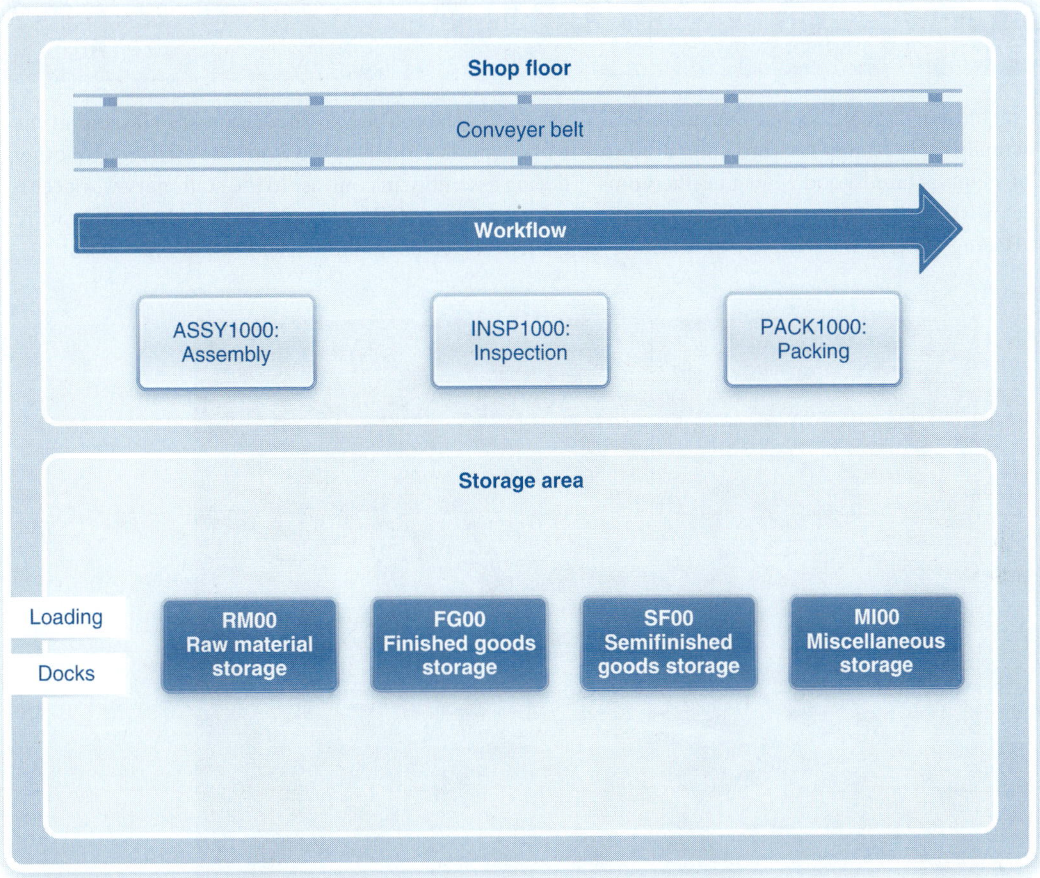

Figure 6-7: GBI Dallas production facility

Figure 6-8: GBI work centers

Business Processes in Practice 6.4: Aircraft Work Centers

Although it might not appear to be simple, bicycle assembly is actually quite straightforward compared to other types of manufactured goods. Imagine the complexity of the work centers and tasks involved with assembling a Boeing 757 (Figure 6-9). Aircraft assembly is so complex and the finished good is so large that the work centers actually move from one aircraft to another during assembly, in contrast to the stationary work centers used in our GBI example. Notice the mobile work centers (carts and mobile machines) in the figure.

Figure 6-9: Assembling a Boeing 757. ©Kevin Horan/Getty Images, Inc.

Demo 6.2: Review GBI work centers

PRODUCT ROUTINGS

In our discussion of work centers we defined a **product routing** as a list of operations that a company must perform to produce a material (Figure 6-10). In addition, the product routing specifies the *sequence* in which these operations must be carried out, the *work center* where they are to be performed, and the *time* needed to complete them. It can also list additional resources, known as *production resource tools*, which the company needs to complete the operations.

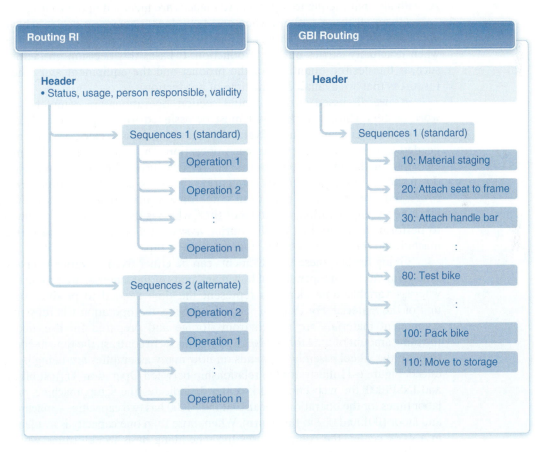

Figure 6-10: Structure of a routing

The left side of Figure 6-10 illustrates the general structure of a routing. Like a BOM, a routing includes a *header* that contains data applicable to the entire routing, such as status and validity. The routing shows two sequences, each of which identifies the required operations and the order in which they are performed. All operations in a routing must be performed in some type of sequence, and many operations can be completed in a variety of sequences. This routing, for example, displays a *standard sequence*, in which Operation 1 is performed prior to Operation 2, and an *alternate sequence*, in which Operation 2 is performed first.

The right side of Figure 6-10 shows the routing for GBI's deluxe touring bike. The routing indicates that operations needed to produce this bike can be performed in only one possible (standard) sequence. For example, the seat is attached to the frame first, followed by the handle bar.

GBI uses prebuilt components such as the brake kit and pedal assembly that it purchases from vendors. If GBI were to manufacture these two components in-house, then it would have to assemble them from raw materials before it attached them to the bike frame. Significantly, GBI would not have to build either of these components before the other. Instead, it could build them simultaneously, or in parallel. This process is referred to as *parallel sequences*. As with alternate sequences, parallel sequences are included in the routing.

Given all these options, when and how does a company decide which approach to utilize? The answer is that it selects the appropriate sequence when it actually carries out the production. It bases this decision on factors such as the desired quantities of the product and the equipment and other resources that are available at the time of production.

As we discussed in the previous section, operations are completed in work centers. Thus, a work center must be assigned to an operation. Recall that work centers have standard values keys and formulas to calculate the time needed to complete the steps in each operation. There are three basic time elements in the production process: setup time, processing time, and teardown time. *Setup time* involves configuring the work center and equipment. *Processing time* can refer both to machine time, which involves the use of a machine for an operation, and to labor time, which is the human work needed to perform the operation. Finally, during *teardown time*, workers return the machines to their original state—that is, before setup.

Going further, these time elements can be either fixed or variable. Fixed time elements are independent of how many units of the material are produced, whereas variable time elements represent the time needed to produce one unit of the material. For example, material staging, the operation whereby the component materials are moved from storage and prepared for use, takes the same amount of time for 10 bikes as for 15 bikes. In contrast, the time needed to build the wheel assembly depends on how many assemblies are being produced. Figure 6-11 illustrates the relationship between Operation 80 (test bike) and INSP1000, the inspection work center. It indicates the setup, machine, and labor times for the operation. Recall that INSP1000 has two capacities—machine and labor (001 and 002 in the figure). When more than one capacity is available in a work center, the company uses the scheduling basis to determine which capacity it will utilize to complete the production order.

Figure 6-12 illustrates the routing for GBI's deluxe wheel assembly. The figure identifies the required operations, the work center where the operation will be completed, the times associated with the operation, and the components assigned to each operation. The wheel assembly has three operations— stage material, assemble components into wheel assemblies, and move to storage—all of which are completed in work center ASSY1000. Wheels are assembled in batches or lots of 50. It takes 5 minutes to stage the materials for 50 wheels, 3 minutes to assemble each wheel, and another 5 minutes to move

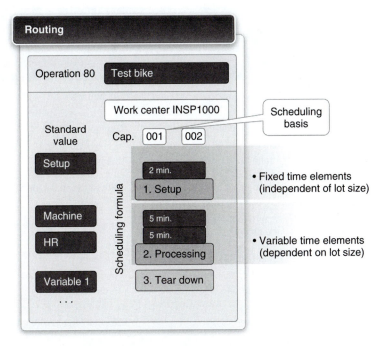

Figure 6-11: Routings and work centers

Material Name: Touring aluminum wheel assembly					Material number: TRWA1000
Operation no.	Work center	Setup time (minutes)	Processing time (minutes)	Operation	Materials allocated
10	ASSY1000	0	5 per 50	Stage material	Touring tire, touring tube, touring aluminum wheel, hex nut 5 mm, lock washer 5 mm, socket head bolt 5 × 20 mm
20	ASSY1000	0	3 per wheel	Assemble components	Touring tire, touring tube, touring aluminum wheel, hex nut 5 mm, lock washer 5 mm, socket head bolt 5 × 20 mm
30	ASSY1000	0	5 per 50	Move to storage	Wheel assembly

Figure 6-12: Routing for deluxe touring wheel assembly

the 50 wheels assemblies into storage. Because these operations are performed manually, they do not involve any setup time. Consequently, all the time spent on these operations is labor time. Overall, it takes 160 minutes (5 + 50*3 + 5) to assemble 50 wheels, an average of 3.2 minutes per wheel.

Figure 6-13 presents the routing for the deluxe touring bike. In contrast to the wheel assembly, this routing includes 11 steps. Further, the operations are completed in three different work centers: ASSY1000, INSP1000, and PACK1000. Finally, one operation—#80, Test bike—includes a setup time of 2 minutes. This is the amount of time it takes to place the fully assembled bike

Material name: Deluxe touring bike					Material number: DXTR1000
Operation no.	Work center	Setup time (minutes)	Processing time (minutes)	Operation	Materials allocated
10	ASSY1000		10 for 15 bikes	Material staging	All materials
20	ASSY1000		1	Attach seat to frame	Frame, seat kit
30	ASSY1000		2	Attach handle bar	Handle bar
40	ASSY1000		2	Attach derailleur gear assembly to rear wheel	Wheel assembly, derailleur gear assembly
50	ASSY1000		5	Attach front and rear wheels and chain	Wheel assemblies, chain
60	ASSY1000		2	Attach brakes	Brake kit
70	ASSY1000		2	Attach pedals	Pedal assembly
80	INSP1000	2	5	Test bike	Assembled bike
90	PACK1000		4	Disassemble (remove wheels and chain)	Assembled bike
100	PACK1000		4	Pack bike (individually packed)	Disassembled bike, warranty document, packaging
110	PACK1000		5 for 15 bikes	Move to storage	Packed bike

Figure 6-13: Routing for deluxe touring bike

on the testing machine. Bikes are produced in batches of 10 or 15. For both quantities the material staging operation and move to storage step operation take the same amount of time (10 minutes and 5 minutes, respectively). The other times in the figure are per bike. Thus, it takes 305 minutes[2] to make 10 bikes—an average of 30.5 minutes per bike—and 450 minutes to make 15 bikes—an average of 30 minutes. For planning purposes, GBI uses the following data:

- Wheel assembly: 3 hours per 50 wheels (3.6 minutes per wheel assembly.

- Bike assembly: 5 hours per 10 bikes (30 minutes per bike)

- On the days wheels assemblies are assembled, only 10 bikes are assembled; on other days, 15 bikes are assembled

The routing indicates how to produce a specified product. The BOM indicates which materials are used to manufacture that product. There is, therefore, an obvious relationship between a BOM and a routing. This relationship is defined via the **component assignment**, a technique that assigns components in a BOM either to a routing or to a specific operation within the routing.

---

[2]The total of variable time operations (#s 20-100) for one bike is 29 minutes. For 10 bikes it is 290 minutes and 15 bikes, it is 435 minutes. The fixed time operations (#10 and #110) take 15 minutes regardless of quantity. Thus total time for 10 bikes = 290 + 15 and for 15 bikes = 435 + 15.

Figure 6-14 presents a component assignment that includes three operations in the routing and three materials in the BOM. Material A is assigned to Operation 20, while materials B and C are assigned to Operation 30. The right side of the figure indicates that the materials are consumed at the beginning of the operations. Any materials that are not explicitly assigned to an operation are automatically assigned to the first operation and consumed at the beginning of that operation.

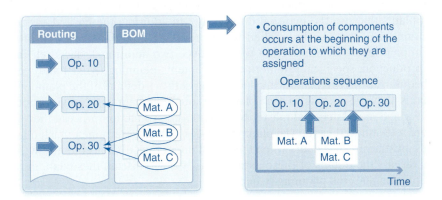

Figure 6-14: Component assignment

In addition to indicating how and from which materials finished goods or semifinished goods are produced, the data contained in bills of material, work centers, and routings are used to determine production capacity. **Production capacity** is a measure of how many units of a material a plant can produce within a given timeframe. For example, GBI's Dallas plant can produce either 15 bikes or 10 bikes and 50 wheel assemblies per day. Figure 6-15 presents an example of a production plan for the Dallas plant, utilizing its full capacity.

	M	T	W	T	F	M	T	W	T	F	M	T	W	T	F	M	T	W	T	F	M	T	W	T	F
Wheels production	50	0	50	0	50	0	50	0	50	0	50	0	50	0	50	0	50	0	50	0	50	0	50	0	50
Wheels inventory	30	0	30	0	30	0	30	0	30	0	30	0	30	0	30	0	30	0	30	0	30	0	30	0	30
Bikes production	10	15	10	15	10	15	10	15	10	15	10	15	10	15	10	15	10	15	10	15	10	15	10	15	10
Bikes inventory	10	25	35	50	60	75	85	100	110	125	135	150	160	175	185	200	210	225	235	250	260	275	285	300	310

Assumptions			
Number of shifts	1	Bikes per week	50
Hours per shift	8	Bikes per year	2500
Days per week	5	Wheels per week	100
Weeks per year	50	Wheels per year	5000

Figure 6-15: Sample GBI production plan

Demo 6.3: Review routing for a bike and wheel assembly

MATERIAL MASTER

We introduced the concept of the material master in Chapter 2. Recall that the material master data are grouped into different views or segments based on three factors: (1) the process that uses the materials, (2) the material type (e.g., raw materials, finished goods), and (3) the organizational level (e.g., different plants that use the material differently). In addition, the basic data view contains data that can be applied to all processes, material types, and organizational levels. In this section we introduce two additional views relevant to production; specifically, material requirements planning (MRP) and work scheduling. Both MRP and work scheduling data are defined at the plant level. That is, they are specific to each plant. Although the data in these views must be defined in the material master to execute the production process, they are more relevant to the material planning process, which determines which materials must be produced and when they must be produced. Consequently, we do not discuss the details of these data instead, we will discuss these data in the chapter on material planning (Chapter 8).

PRODUCTION RESOURCE TOOLS

The final master data relevant to production are **production resource tools (PRT)**. PRTs are *movable* resources that are shared among different work centers. Examples of PRTs are calibration or measurement instruments, jigs and fixtures, and documents such as engineering drawings. It is not feasible or economical to keep these tools in every work center because they are not used very often. Instead, a limited number are available for use in the work centers as they are needed.

● PROCESS

In this section we will discuss the production process in detail (Figure 6-16). The process begins with a request for production that is typically triggered by another process such as fulfillment, which needs to complete a customer order (make-to-order strategy), or material planning, which has determined that the company needs to increase inventory levels (make-to-stock strategy).

The request is then authorized for production by the production supervisor. The next step is to release the order for production so that the materials needed to produce the bikes are issued from storage. Very often, production involves the use of external systems, such as plant data collection (PDC) systems, that utilize data from the ERP system to execute production on the shop floor. In such cases, data about the order are transmitted to the external system. After the finished goods have been produced, the actual production is confirmed in the system, signaling that the steps required to manufacture the materials have been completed. The materials are then moved to storage, and the system reports that they are now available for consumption by other processes (e.g., fulfillment). In addition, several activities are performed

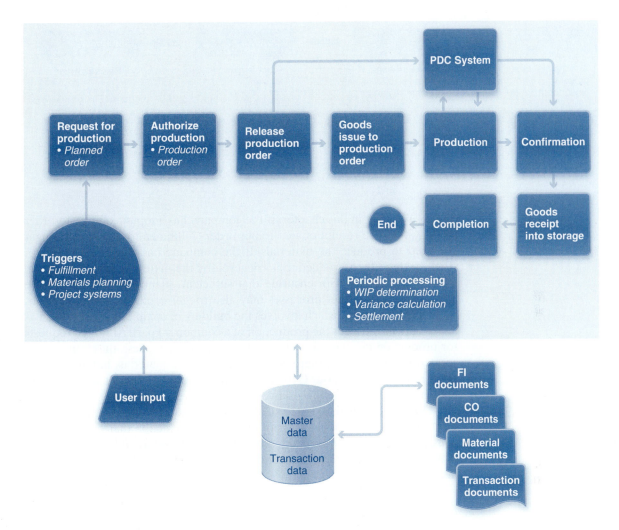

Figure 6-16: The production process

periodically during the process, including overhead allocation, work in process determination, and order settlement. Now that we have a general understanding of the various process steps involved with production, we examine these steps in terms of triggers, data, tasks, and outcomes.

Our discussion will use the following make-to-stock GBI scenario. The inventory for the men's off-road bike (ORMN1000) has fallen below its minimum level. Consequently, GBI must produce more of this model. Going further, the company has determined that the optimum quantity for a single production run is 25 bikes. We will assume that the raw materials needed to make these bikes and the needed capacity in the various work centers are both available.

REQUEST PRODUCTION

Figure 6-17 illustrates the elements of the request production step. A request for production is triggered by a need to produce materials. Typically, this trigger is a result of activity in another process. Consider the two production strategies

Figure 6-17: Elements of the request production step

discussed earlier in this chapter. If the company has adopted a make-to-order strategy, then the receipt of a customer order (fulfillment process) will trigger the need to produce the materials. If the company has adopted a make-to-stock strategy, then production is triggered by the material planning process, which is concerned with ensuring that sufficient quantities of materials are always available. Other processes may also trigger production. For example, project management, which involves the building of complex products such as an aircraft, may trigger the production of a component part. Although requests for production are typically triggered from another process, they can also be created manually when there is a need to produce materials independent of other requirements. In our GBI scenario, the request for production is created manually based on a review of inventory levels.

Regardless of the source of the trigger, the outcome of this step is a **planned order**, which is a formal request for production that indicates *what* materials are needed, *how many* units are needed, and *when* they are needed. It is similar to a purchase requisition (discussed in Chapter 4) in that it does not become a commitment until someone acts on the request.

Data

Various organizational data, master data, and user-specified data are included in a planned order. The key data are listed in Figure 6-18. The individual making the request specifies which materials are needed, how many, and when they are needed. At this point the ERP system automatically incorporates both the master data related to the materials and the bill of material in the planned order. The system uses these data, along with configuration options specified in the system, to calculate additional data, such as order dates and material availability. If the planned order was created by another process, then the user-specified data explained above are provided by the process that created the planned order.

Tasks

The only task in this step is to create the planned order. Planned orders remain in the system until they are acted upon by the authorized person in the company, typically the production manager. The production manager can reject the order, modify it, combine it with other orders, or authorize the production. For our purposes we will assume that he or she authorizes the production. We discuss authorizing production in the next section.

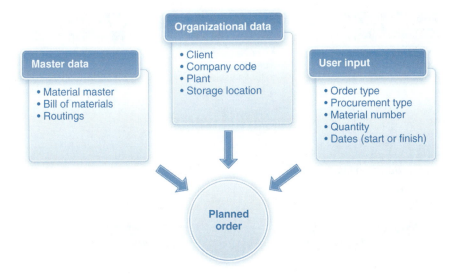

Figure 6-18: Data in a planned order

Outcomes

The obvious outcome of the request production step is a planned order, which is a transaction document. Because this step generates no financial impact, no FI or CO documents are created. Likewise, because there is no movement of materials, no material documents are created. In our example, the planned order will indicate a request to produce 25 men's off-road bikes (ORMN1000) in the Dallas plant (DL00).

Demo 6.4: Create a planned order

AUTHORIZE PRODUCTION

Whereas a planned order is simply a request, a **production order**, which is created in the authorize production step, represents an actual commitment to produce a specific quantity of materials by a certain date. Numerous resources, such as materials, work centers, and PRTs, are committed to producing the materials specified in the production order. A production order is typically created by converting a planned order. However, it can also be generated directly without using a planned order. This process is similar to creating a purchase order without reference to a purchase requisition or creating a sales order without reference to a quotation. Figure 6-19 displays the key elements of the authorize production step.

Data

Figure 6-20 illustrates the key data needed to create a production order. Note that much of this information is also included in the planned order. User input is generally needed only if a planned order is not used as a reference or if the data in the planned order, such as quantity and dates, must be changed.

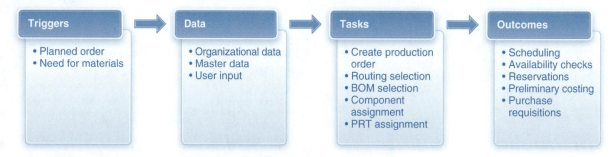

Figure 6-19: Elements of the authorize production step

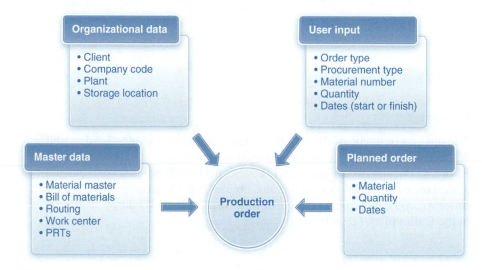

Figure 6-20: Data in a production order

Typically, a production order includes references to a BOM, routing, work centers, and PRTs to be used in production. As explained earlier in this chapter, a BOM identifies the materials or components to be used in production, and a routing identifies the operations needed to produce the material. Work centers are where the operations are to be performed; they define the capacity requirements for the order.

Figure 6-21 illustrates the structure of a production order. The data contained in a production order are quite extensive. Companies use these data to plan, schedule, and execute the production of the specified material. Specifically, a production order includes the following data.

- The *order header* includes basic data such as a unique order number, the plant where the material is to be produced, the person (scheduler) responsible for scheduling production, and the status of the order. The status is significant because it determines which steps in the process can be completed. When the order is initially saved, the status is "created" (**CRTD**). As the order is executed, the order status is changed to reflect its current state. Other production order statuses are partially released (**PREL**), released (**REL**),

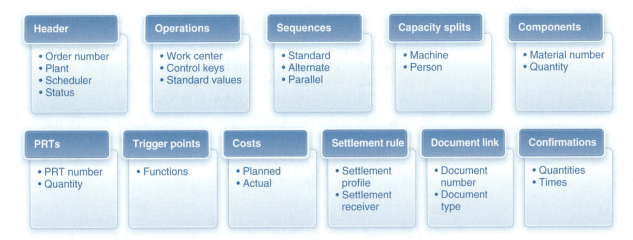

Figure 6-21: Structure of a production order

partially confirmed (**PCNF**), confirmed (**CNF**), partially delivered (**PDLV**), and delivered (**DLV**).

- A production order includes the specific *operations* needed to produce the material, along with data on the designated work centers. It also identifies the specific *sequences* for the operations. Note that a production order must include at least one operation.

- *Capacity splits* are used to determine how the work to be performed is distributed or "split" among the machines and/or people involved in producing the material.

- The production order identifies the *components* needed to produce the specified quantity of the material. Typically, the components are obtained from the BOM. However, they can be added or adjusted manually, as needed.

- The *PRTs* to complete one or more operations are identified.

- As the name suggests, *trigger points* initiate or "trigger" some activity or function. An example of a trigger point is the completion of a specified operation. When this occurs, subsequent operations in the routing are released for execution, or some activity in another process is triggered.

- A production order includes preliminary estimates for various *cost* components, such as material and overhead. These costs are associated with the appropriate accounts in the general ledger, such as material consumption accounts. As production is executed, the actual costs are also included as data in the production order along with the preliminary cost estimates. These data are used in product costing, which is a process in management accounting.

- After the production order has been completed, the costs accumulated in the production order must be *settled*. During settlement the actual costs incurred are allocated to cost objects based on specified *settlement rules*. We discuss settlement in more detail later in this chapter.

- A production order may contain references to various documents. For example, the BOM may include a document item, or a PRT may refer to a document. In these cases, the production order includes links to the documents in the *document management system* (DMS). Using the DMS ensures that the most current versions of the documents are employed during production.

- When the production order has been executed and the materials have been created, the materials actually produced are recorded in the production order via *confirmations*. We discuss confirmations in greater detail later in this chapter.

Tasks

As we discussed earlier, the principal task in the authorize production step is to create a production order. There are several possible scenarios for performing this task. We have already seen that a production order can be created with or without reference to a planned order. Further, planned orders can be converted individually, collectively, or partially. With *individual conversion*, one planned order is converted to one production order. In *collective conversion*, multiple planned orders are processed at once, that is, collectively. The outcome can be one or multiple production orders. Finally in *partial conversion*, only a portion of the quantities listed in the planned order are included in the production order. Partial conversion often generates multiple production orders, each one reflecting a partial quantity of the material in the planned order.

Another task in creating a production order is to select the appropriate master data, such as BOM, routing, and PRTs. Recall that a routing identifies the operations needed to produce the material. In some cases the ERP system automatically selects an appropriate routing. The system then transfers the operations from the selected routing into the production order. A routing can also be selected manually. In these cases the system displays the available task lists or routings for the material, and the person creating the production order decides which one is most appropriate. Significantly, it is possible to create a production order without specifying a routing. In this case, the system automatically generates a default operation, which is incorporated into the production order.

Recall that the BOM identifies the components needed to produce the material. Once again, the system automatically selects a suitable BOM and transfers the components into the production order. If a BOM is not available, then the components must be added to the production order manually.

Now consider a scenario in which (1) the production order is created with reference to a planned order and (2) the planned order includes the BOM and the routing data. In this case the system automatically transfers these data into the production order. Note that the actual BOM and routing data are not retrieved again from the material master. Rather, the data pertaining to the components and operations are copied directly from the planned order into the production order. Further, once these data have been incorporated into the production order, they are not automatically retrieved from the material master again, even when either the BOM or the routing changes. To reflect changes to the BOM and routing data, the system must be manually instructed to re-read or retrieve these data.

A final task is to assign components and PRTs to specific operations. For example, the routing for the deluxe touring bike illustrated earlier in Figure 6-13 indicates that different components are assigned to different operations. Typically, components are automatically assigned by the ERP system, based on the data in the routing. However, they can also be manually assigned or reassigned to specific operations as needed. Any component or PRT that is not assigned to a specific operation is automatically assigned to the first operation.

Outcomes

The creation of a production order generates several outcomes, including scheduling, availability checks, reservations, preliminary costing, and creating necessary purchase requisitions. The *scheduling* function calculates the dates when the various operations are to be performed and the capacities that are needed in the work centers. The scheduling function uses data from the production order (e.g., quantity and dates) and work center parameters previously discussed (e.g., control keys and standard value keys) to complete this task. If the scheduling data in the production order (e.g., dates) are subsequently changed, the system can be configured to automatically reschedule the order.

In addition, the system performs an *availability check* to determine whether the resources (components, PRTs, and capacity) needed to execute the production order are available. If they are, then the system creates material and machine *reservations* to set aside the necessary resources so they cannot be used for other purposes. Unlike scheduling, availability checks usually are not repeated automatically if the production order is changed. Rather, the system must be instructed manually to perform this check.

Finally, the *preliminary cost estimates* for the production order are calculated. Typical costs include *direct costs*, such as materials and production, and *indirect costs* in the form of overhead. Material costs are based on the costs of the components assigned to the production order; these costs are maintained in the material master for each material. Production costs are based on data in the work center such as activity types and formulas that identify which activities (e.g., labor and setup) are required and in what quantities.

If the production order requires nonstock items, such as consumable materials, then the system automatically generates purchase requisitions to acquire them. We discussed the purchase of consumable materials in Chapter 3, in the sections on account assignment categories. Recall that to purchase consumable materials, an account assignment category is required in the purchase order. In the context of production, the appropriate account assignment category is production order (F), and the production order number is included in the purchase requisition. The production order acts as a cost object. Recall from Chapter 3 that a cost object is something that absorbs costs or to which costs can be allocated.

In addition, production sometimes involves operations that are performed by another company. For example, a component might have to be painted or polished by a business that specializes in these tasks. For these operations the company issues a purchase requisition. The requisition will indicate sub contracting as the item category (see Chapter 4 for a discussion of item categories). Once again, the production order is included in the requisition as the cost object.

In our example, GBI creates a production order for the requested 25 bikes. When the order is saved, the system reserves the necessary materials as well as capacity in the three work centers in the Dallas plant, based on the BOM and routing for the bikes. The production order also includes an initial cost estimate. Figure 6-22 displays the cost estimates for the materials needed to build one bike. For each bike, raw materials are expected to cost $350, wheel assemblies (semifinished goods) $230, and labor $25. Thus, the estimated cost for the production order is $15,125. (For the sake of simplicity, we will include only material and labor costs in our example and will not take into account other direct costs [e.g., machine and setup] or indirect overhead costs.) When the production order is created, these estimates are copied to the production order (Figure 6-23). The other columns in the figure—actual, target, and variance—will be discussed in later steps in the production process.

- Material (RM $350 + SFG $230) * 25 = $14,500

- Labor 30 min. @ $50/hr * 25   = $625

- Total planned direct cost   = $15,125

Figure 6-22: Production cost estimates for men's off-road bike

Production order

	Planned (estimate)	Actual (debit)	Target (credit)	Variance (debit-credit)
Material	$14,500.00			
Labor	$625.00			
Total	$15,125.00			

Figure 6-23: Cost estimates in a production order

Demo 6.5: Create a production order

ORDER RELEASE

An order status of created limits the process steps that can be executed. For example, goods movements and confirmations cannot be performed. An order must be *released* for production before subsequent steps can be carried out. The system can be configured to release an order automatically as soon as it is created. However, if the company needs time to verify the order or to prepare for production, then the order remains in the created status until it is ready for release. In this case, the order must be released manually. Figure 6-24 diagrams the elements of the order release step.

Data

The data that are required to release an order are the order number(s) and system parameters that determine which steps are performed automatically and which ones require manual interventions.

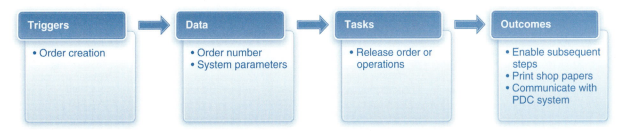

Figure 6-24: Elements of the order release step

Tasks

A production order can be released at either the header level or the operations level. This decision is also determined by the system's configuration. When the order is released at the header level, all operations are also released. When release occurs at the operations level, however, only certain operations are affected. These operations have the released status, and the order itself has a partially released status. The remaining operations can be released either manually as needed or automatically, based on trigger points. In our GBI example, the order is released at the header level, meaning that all operations can proceed.

Recall that the BOM and routing data are not automatically reentered into the production order if they are changed after the order is created. Instead, the system must be manually instructed to reenter these data. However, if the BOM or routing data are reentered into the production order after the order has been released, then the order status reverts to created, and the order must be re-released.

Production orders can be released individually or collectively. Several orders with similar characteristics, such as material, location (plant), and dates, can be selected and released together.

Outcomes

When a production order is released for production, subsequent steps identified in Figure 6-16 can be executed. In addition, *shop floor papers* that are needed to execute the steps in the work center can be printed. Examples of shop floor papers are *material withdrawal slips*, which are used to obtain the materials needed for production; *time tickets*, used to record the amount of time required to complete various operations; and *operations lists*, which specify the operations required to produce the material. Printing shop papers is another task that can be automated. In addition, the SAP ERP system can directly communicate with external shop floor control systems or PDC systems that automate the exchange of data between the SAP ERP system and other systems that control physical activity on the production floor and work centers.

GOODS ISSUE

The next step in the process is **goods issue**, in which materials or components are issued to the production order from storage. Figure 6-25 illustrates the elements of the goods issue step. The trigger is the release of the production order. The data, tasks, and outcomes of the goods issue step are the focus of this section.

Figure 6-25: Elements of the goods issue step

Data

The data needed to complete the goods issue step (Figure 6-26) are the production order number, data about the materials to be issued, organizational data regarding the locations involved, and user input.

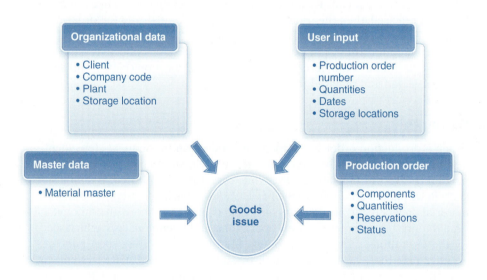

Figure 6-26: Data in a goods issue step

Essentially the system must know which materials or components are to be issued, the desired quantities, and the operations to which they are assigned. Recall that when a production order is created, the materials required for production are reserved. At this point the only materials that can be issued are those that have been (1) included in the reservations and (2) assigned to operations that have been released. The production order includes much of the data related to the goods issue. User input specifies the actual materials and quantities issued. The materials, quantities, and location (plant, storage location) can be changed as needed during this step.

Tasks

The principal task in the goods issue step is to issue materials from storage to the production order. An additional step, *material staging*, is sometimes necessary if materials must be prepared for use.

Many companies do not explicitly track the issue of materials to each production order. Instead, they employ **backflushing**, a technique that automatically records the goods issue when the order is confirmed. Thus, the materials issued are *not* recorded at the time they are withdrawn from inventory. Consequently, there is a time lag between the actual issue of the materials and the recording of the issue in the ERP system. Nevertheless, many companies prefer this technique because it eliminates a step and can make the production process more efficient. Backflushing can be specified in the material master, routing, or work center data.

Outcomes

There are several significant consequences of a goods issue to a production order.

- The material master is updated to reflect a reduction in the quantity on hand and the inventory value of the material issued.

- General ledger accounts are updated. Specifically, the relevant material consumption account(s) and inventory account(s) are updated to reflect an increase in consumption and a reduction in inventory.

- Material reservations are updated. Specifically, reservation quantities are reduced by the quantity of materials issued.

- Because this step involves a goods movement, a material document is created to record the data associated with the movement.

- Because the general ledger accounts are affected, an FI document is created to record financial accounting data.

- Actual costs associated with material consumption are calculated and added to the production order. Recall that the production order is a cost object and serves as a collector of costs incurred during production. During the goods issue step, material costs are debited to the production order. A corresponding management accounting document is created.

- A goods issue document that notes the materials and quantities issued can be created, although it is not required. This document is included with other shop papers that have already been printed, and it serves as a record of which goods were issued. Note that a goods issue document is not the same as a material document. It is used when paper records of the process are maintained.

In our example, the quantities in the material master for all the component materials are reduced by the quantity issued. A corresponding reduction in value is also made. The raw material consumption account (720000) is debited by the total value of the raw materials issued, and a corresponding credit is posted to the raw material inventory account (200000). Similar postings are made to the semifinished goods consumption account and the semifinished goods inventory account for the wheel assemblies issued to the production order. The actual cost of raw materials needed to produce one bike is $369.50, and each wheel assembly costs $115.00. For 25 bikes, raw materials cost $9,237.50, and the wheel assemblies cost $5,750. (Each bike requires 2 wheel assemblies.) Thus, the total material cost for the production order is $14,987.50 (see Figure 6-27). These material costs are also debited to the production order as actual costs.

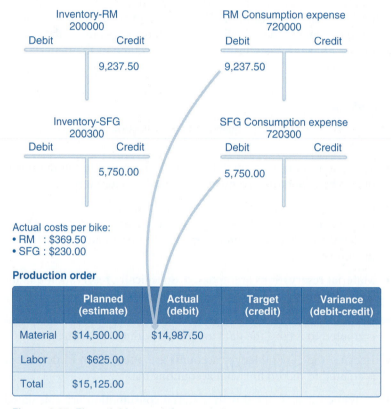

Figure 6-27: Financial impact of a goods issue

Demo 6.6: Goods issue to production order

CONFIRMATIONS

Once the materials are issued to the production order, the actual production takes place on the shop floor, in the work centers. When the finished goods have been produced, the person completing the work records a **confirmation** of the work completed in the SAP ERP system. A confirmation indicates how much work was completed, where it was completed (work center), and who completed it. Figure 6-28 displays the elements of the confirmation step.

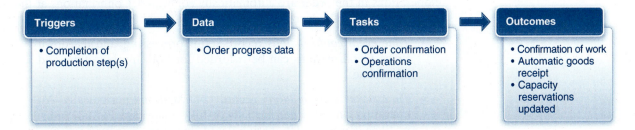

Figure 6-28: Elements of the confirmation step

Data

The data included in a confirmation are highlighted in Figure 6-29 and explained below.

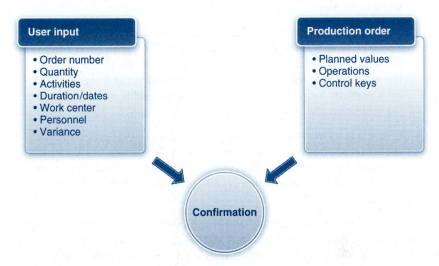

Figure 6-29: Data in a confirmation

- Quantities: How many goods were produced, how many were scrapped, and how many require rework.

- Operations completed: Which operations were completed, such as those involving setup and machines.

- Durations: The dates and times when the operations were started and completed, or the duration of the activities.

- Work center: The physical location in which the operations were carried out.

- Personnel data: Who completed the operations.

- Reason for variance: A reason why the confirmed quantity is different from the planned quantity, if this is the case.

Tasks

Confirmations can be recorded for the entire order or for specific operations or suboperations. When a confirmation is recorded for the entire order, then all operations in the order are automatically confirmed. Confirmations at the operations level can be recorded in several ways, as explained below.

- *Time event confirmations* record setup, processing, and teardown times. Confirmations can be recorded for both machine time and labor time.

- *Time ticket confirmations* record confirmations periodically. An operation can be either partially or fully confirmed. Partial confirmations consist of data accumulated since the previous confirmation. Consider, for example, a production order in which 30 units of a material are to be processed. The work center employee decides to enter two confirmations. If the first confirmation is for 20 units, then the second one will reflect the quantity subsequently produced, that is, 10 units.

- *Collective* and *fast entry* confirmations confirm multiple operations at the same time.

- In *milestone confirmation*, the confirmation of an operation automatically confirms the preceding operations. Imagine, for example, that one of the operations in a sequence is an inspection operation. Those units that pass inspection are confirmed, while the remaining units are sent for rework. In this case, the preceding operations are confirmed for the quantity that passed inspection.

- *Progress confirmation* periodically indicates the total progress of an operation at the time of the confirmation. Revisiting our example of 30 units of a material, when using progress confirmation, the initial confirmation will indicate 20 units, and the second will indicate 30 units.

The above discussion assumes that confirmations are entered into the system manually. As previously stated, the production process may involve the use of external systems such as PDC systems. In such cases, the PDC system automatically provides the confirmation data.

Outcomes

The obvious outcome of the confirmation step is that the data associated with the work actually completed are recorded. In addition, the production order is updated to reflect the quantity of materials that were produced, the activities and operations that were completed, and the dates when the work was performed. The order status is set to either completely confirmed or partially confirmed, depending on whether the entire order quantity was produced. In cases of partial confirmation, the work center employees can make additional confirmations as they produce more of the material. Because confirmation indicates that production in one or more work centers has been completed, capacity reservations in these centers are reduced. The work centers can then be used for other purposes.

Recall that a work center is associated with a cost center and includes various activities, such as labor and setup. As these activities are consumed during production and the times are confirmed in the production order (e.g., labor hours and setup hours), the costs associated with the activities are allocated to the production order, which, as previously explained, serves as an accumulator of costs. Note that there is no financial accounting impact at this point. The FI impact occurs when the shop floor employees are paid (e.g., weekly). At this time the labor costs are assigned to cost centers associated with the work centers where the employees completed the work. Thus, the cost centers are accumulating labor (and other direct) costs. When a production order is confirmed, the cost centers are credited, and the production order that consumed the labor is debited.

Finally, if the control keys in the last operation permit a goods receipt to be automatically recorded, then this occurs when the last operation is confirmed. We discuss goods receipt in the next section.

In our example, a confirmation is recorded for the 25 bikes. The labor costs are debited to the production order, and the cost center where the work was completed (work centers) is credited (Figure 6-30). The actual time (labor) required to build the bikes was 775 minutes. Thus, the production order is debited by $645.83, which is the total cost of labor at a previously established hourly rate of $50 (775/60 * 50). Note that the bikes took 31 minutes each to produce and therefore cost more than the planned amount. The production order has accumulated a total of $15,633.33 for material and labor consumed.

Work center (cost center)

Labor cost: $645.83
Accumulated when incurred

Actual labor
• Total order : 775 minutes
• Per bike   : 31
• Pay rate   : $50

Production order

	Planned (estimate)	Actual (debit)	Target (credit)	Variance (debit-credit)
Material	$14,500.00	$14,987.50		
Labor	$625.00	$645.83		
Total	$15,125.00	$15,633.33		

Figure 6-30: Financial impact of a confirmation

Demo 6.7: Confirm production

GOODS RECEIPT

After production has been completed and confirmed, the materials produced are placed in finished goods inventory. This step is accomplished via a **goods receipt** against the production order. Figure 6-31 highlights the elements of the goods receipt step.

Figure 6-31: Elements of a goods receipt

Demo 6.8: Goods receipt from production

Data

The data associated with a goods receipt are illustrated in Figure 6-32. The production order number, quantity received, date, and location (plant and storage location) are provided by the user based on the completed work. Organizational data associated with the location and master data associated with the material are obtained automatically by the system. The material master is used to determine which inventory account needs to be updated and how the material is to be valued (e.g., standard price or moving average price). It also indicates whether the material can be stored in the specified location and whether there are any special storage requirements.

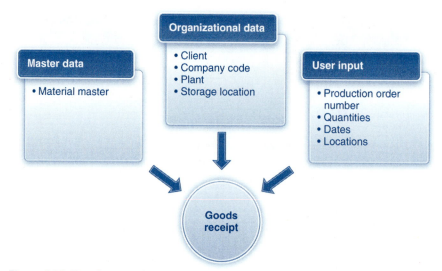

Figure 6-32: Data in a goods receipt

Tasks

The primary task in goods receipt is to physically receive the materials from the shop floor and place them in the appropriate storage location. If the storage location employs a warehouse management (WM) system, then a transfer requirement is created to trigger additional WM steps. We discuss WM processes in Chapter 7.

Outcomes

The goods receipt step generates several significant outcomes. To begin with, the quantity on hand and the value of the inventory are updated in the material master. The price control field in the material master determines how the material is valued (i.e., standard price or moving average price). Appropriate general ledger accounts are also updated to reflect the financial consequences of the goods receipt. For example, the inventory account determined by the data in the material master is debited, and the manufacturing output settlement account is credited. If the price control in the material master is set to standard price and the actual production costs differ from this price, then this difference or *variance* is accounted for when the order is settled. (We discuss order settlement in the next section.) A corresponding FI document is created. The manufacturing output settlement account represents a "cost of goods manufactured" account. Other labels for this account include "plant activity account" and "factory output account." If the price control is set to moving average price, then the material is valued at a price that is determined by the system based on how the system is configured. Details of this technique are beyond the scope of this book.

The postings related to our example are illustrated in Figure 6-33. Postings are based on the target cost of the production order. Recall that planned cost is the cost expected to be incurred when the *planned quantity* is produced. In contrast, the *target cost* is the cost expected to be incurred for the *actual quantity* produced. Note, however, that both planned costs and target costs are based on the standard cost estimates, when the price control in the material master is standard cost. In our example, the target cost is the same as the planned cost because the actual quantity produced is the same as the planned quantity. However, if the actual quantity produced had been 20 instead of 25, then the target cost would be less than the planned cost. Specifically, the target material cost would be $11,600, and the labor cost would be $500 (refer to Figure 6-22, which illustrates cost calculations for 25 bikes).

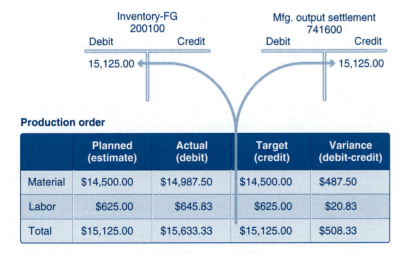

Inventory-FG 200100		Mfg. output settlement 741600	
Debit	Credit	Debit	Credit
15,125.00			15,125.00

Production order

	Planned (estimate)	Actual (debit)	Target (credit)	Variance (debit-credit)
Material	$14,500.00	$14,987.50	$14,500.00	$487.50
Labor	$625.00	$645.83	$625.00	$20.83
Total	$15,125.00	$15,633.33	$15,125.00	$508.33

Figure 6-33: Financial impact of a goods receipt

In our example, the target cost is the same as the planned cost, and the production order is credited by $15,125. At the same time, the finished goods inventory account is debited by this amount, and the manufacturing output settlement account is credited. These steps leave a balance of $508.33 in the production order. This amount, which is the difference between the debits (actual cost) and credits (target cost) in the production order, constitutes a variance. We discuss variances in the next section.

After the goods receipt step has been completed, the status of the production order is updated to either delivered or partially delivered. Like goods issue, goods receipt can be automated to save time and enhance efficiency. In such cases the ERP system automatically records a goods receipt at the time of confirmation.

PERIODIC PROCESSING

Several steps related to production are completed periodically during the process. *Periodic processing* is also known as *period-end closing*. Companies define specific periods, such as months or quarters, when they complete certain accounting steps to update the data in financial statements. Periodic processing includes *overhead allocation*, *work-in-process* determination, and *order settlement*.

The production order accumulates the direct costs associated with production. Other costs that are not directly associated with production are labeled *indirect costs* or *overhead costs*. Examples are the costs associated with the facility such as utilities and maintenance, and the salaries of people, such as supervisors and managers, who are not directly involved in the production in the work centers. These costs are accumulated in specified cost centers and are periodically allocated to the production orders based on preestablished rules.

When materials are issued to production, a reduction in the inventory of these materials is recorded. However, the finished goods are not completed and placed in inventory until a later point in time (at the time of good receipt). During this interim period, neither the component materials nor the finished goods appear as inventory items in the balance sheet. Rather, they are classified as **work-in-process (WIP)** inventory. WIP is not a significant issue if the production process is relatively short and the value of the materials is not high, as in the case of GBI. However, for products such as aircraft and buildings, production can take months or even years, and the value of the inventory involved in production is quite substantial. In such cases, the materials used in production are considered WIP inventory and must be properly accounted for in the general ledger. To accomplish this task, a company will periodically calculate the value of WIP and make postings to the general ledger so that the financial statements accurately reflect the current inventory. A company can use several techniques to determine WIP. However, a discussion of these techniques is beyond the scope of this book.

We noted earlier that the difference between total debits and total credits in the production order is called a variance. Either periodically or when the production order is completed, these variances must be settled, meaning they must be posted to appropriate general ledger accounts. The manufacturing output settlement account is credited by the variance amount. Recall that this account was credited during the goods receipt step and therefore reflects the full cost of production. An offsetting entry is made to a variance account, such as a manufacturing output settlement variance account or a price difference

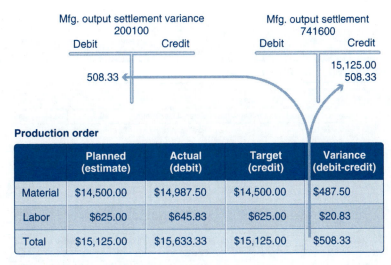

Figure 6-34: Financial impact of settlement

account. In our example, the variance of $508.33 was settled using the accounts indicated in Figure 6-34.

COMPLETION

The final step in the production process, **order completion**, can be viewed from both a logistics perspective (technically complete) and an accounting perspective (closed). A production order is set to a *technically complete* (**TECO**) status when it is no longer necessary or possible to continue with the production. At this point no further execution of the production process steps is possible. All resource reservations that are still open are deleted. Any consequences to other processes, such as purchase requisitions for material needed for production, are also removed. The materials in the order are not expected to be produced and are no longer included in any planning. However, financial postings related to the order, such as those associated with settlement, can still be made.

After a production order has been completed and settled, it is set to a status of *closed* (**CLSD**). Before this step can occur, the order must be in released or technically complete status, and it must be fully settled. After the order is closed, no further processing or financial postings are possible.

Periodically, production orders are *archived* for record-keeping purposes and deleted from the system. Archived orders can be retrieved as needed.

■ REPORTING

Reporting options for the production process are similar to those available for the other processes. A variety of lists, reports, and analytics are available via the production information system, which is a component of the logistics information system. Recall that work lists identify tasks to be completed, whereas online lists display documents for specific combinations of organizational levels and master data. Production reports can be generated to identify the status of planned orders and production orders, capacity availability and utilization, material consumption, and so on. The report illustrated in Figure 6-35 displays the status of component (material) utilization for several orders. Note

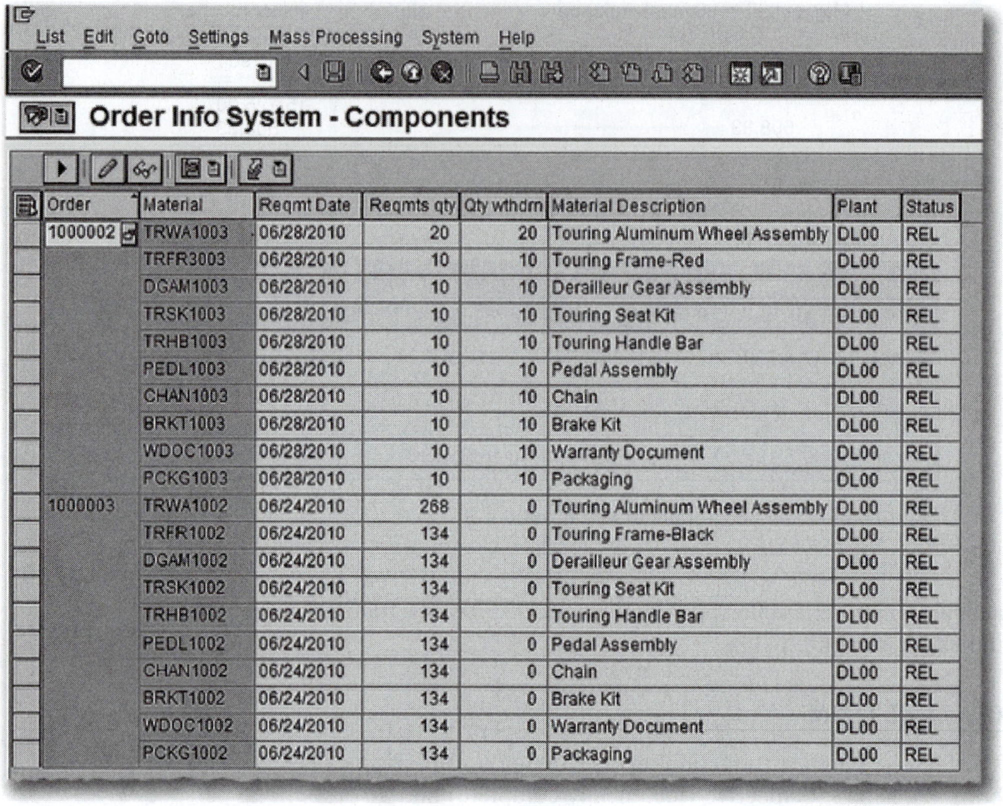

Order	Material	Reqmt Date	Reqmts qty	Qty wthdrn	Material Description	Plant	Status
1000002	TRWA1003	06/28/2010	20	20	Touring Aluminum Wheel Assembly	DL00	REL
	TRFR3003	06/28/2010	10	10	Touring Frame-Red	DL00	REL
	DGAM1003	06/28/2010	10	10	Derailleur Gear Assembly	DL00	REL
	TRSK1003	06/28/2010	10	10	Touring Seat Kit	DL00	REL
	TRHB1003	06/28/2010	10	10	Touring Handle Bar	DL00	REL
	PEDL1003	06/28/2010	10	10	Pedal Assembly	DL00	REL
	CHAN1003	06/28/2010	10	10	Chain	DL00	REL
	BRKT1003	06/28/2010	10	10	Brake Kit	DL00	REL
	WDOC1003	06/28/2010	10	10	Warranty Document	DL00	REL
	PCKG1003	06/28/2010	10	10	Packaging	DL00	REL
1000003	TRWA1002	06/24/2010	268	0	Touring Aluminum Wheel Assembly	DL00	REL
	TRFR1002	06/24/2010	134	0	Touring Frame-Black	DL00	REL
	DGAM1002	06/24/2010	134	0	Derailleur Gear Assembly	DL00	REL
	TRSK1002	06/24/2010	134	0	Touring Seat Kit	DL00	REL
	TRHB1002	06/24/2010	134	0	Touring Handle Bar	DL00	REL
	PEDL1002	06/24/2010	134	0	Pedal Assembly	DL00	REL
	CHAN1002	06/24/2010	134	0	Chain	DL00	REL
	BRKT1002	06/24/2010	134	0	Brake Kit	DL00	REL
	WDOC1002	06/24/2010	134	0	Warranty Document	DL00	REL
	PCKG1002	06/24/2010	134	0	Packaging	DL00	REL

Figure 6-35: Production information system—components. Copyright SAP AG 2011

that the materials have been withdrawn for order number 1000002 but not for order number 1000003. Figure 6-36 shows the operations for the same orders. It indicates that all the operations for order number 1000002 have been confirmed and therefore shows start and end dates for the operations in the order. It also shows that order number 1000003 has a status of released, although the work has not yet started.

One of the most important reports in production is the **stock/requirement list** (Figure 6-37), which identifies all of the activities in the system that can potentially impact the quantity of material in inventory. Figure 6-37 shows the stock/requirements list for the deluxe touring bike (DXTR1000) in the Dallas plant (DL00). The list indicates that there are no deluxe touring bikes in inventory. It further shows that there are three independent requirements for the material. These are the rows with the abbreviation "IndReq" in the column labeled "MRP e." We will discuss independent requirements in the material planning chapter. For the purposes of this discussion, think of independent requirements as a need to increase inventory, which is one of the triggers for production that we discussed earlier. To address this need, the company has created three planned orders (PldOrd). As these orders are processed, the stock/requirements list will indicate their current status until production has been completed. At that point, the quantity available in inventory will increase. Although not illustrated in the figure, a stock/requirements list also includes activities that consume the materials, such as sales orders from the fulfillment process.

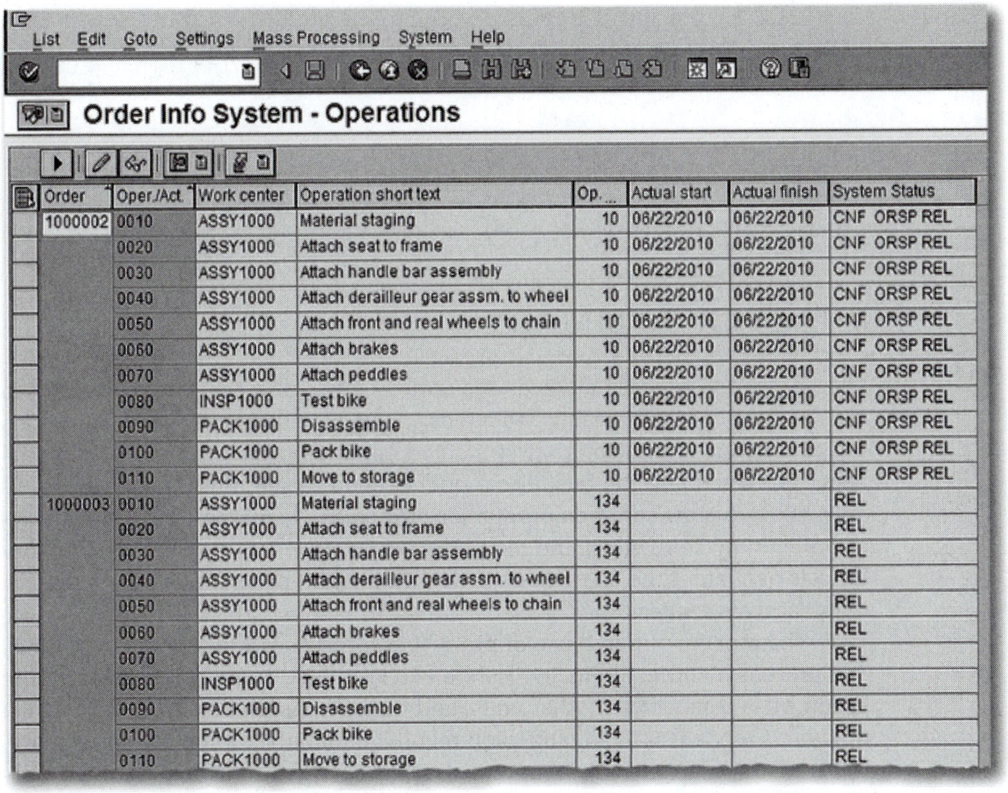

	Order	Oper./Act.	Work center	Operation short text	Op.	Actual start	Actual finish	System Status
	1000002	0010	ASSY1000	Material staging	10	06/22/2010	06/22/2010	CNF ORSP REL
		0020	ASSY1000	Attach seat to frame	10	06/22/2010	06/22/2010	CNF ORSP REL
		0030	ASSY1000	Attach handle bar assembly	10	06/22/2010	06/22/2010	CNF ORSP REL
		0040	ASSY1000	Attach derailleur gear assm. to wheel	10	06/22/2010	06/22/2010	CNF ORSP REL
		0050	ASSY1000	Attach front and real wheels to chain	10	06/22/2010	06/22/2010	CNF ORSP REL
		0060	ASSY1000	Attach brakes	10	06/22/2010	06/22/2010	CNF ORSP REL
		0070	ASSY1000	Attach peddles	10	06/22/2010	06/22/2010	CNF ORSP REL
		0080	INSP1000	Test bike	10	06/22/2010	06/22/2010	CNF ORSP REL
		0090	PACK1000	Disassemble	10	06/22/2010	06/22/2010	CNF ORSP REL
		0100	PACK1000	Pack bike	10	06/22/2010	06/22/2010	CNF ORSP REL
		0110	PACK1000	Move to storage	10	06/22/2010	06/22/2010	CNF ORSP REL
	1000003	0010	ASSY1000	Material staging	134			REL
		0020	ASSY1000	Attach seat to frame	134			REL
		0030	ASSY1000	Attach handle bar assembly	134			REL
		0040	ASSY1000	Attach derailleur gear assm. to wheel	134			REL
		0050	ASSY1000	Attach front and real wheels to chain	134			REL
		0060	ASSY1000	Attach brakes	134			REL
		0070	ASSY1000	Attach peddles	134			REL
		0080	INSP1000	Test bike	134			REL
		0090	PACK1000	Disassemble	134			REL
		0100	PACK1000	Pack bike	134			REL
		0110	PACK1000	Move to storage	134			REL

Figure 6-36: Production information systems—operations. Copyright SAP AG 2011

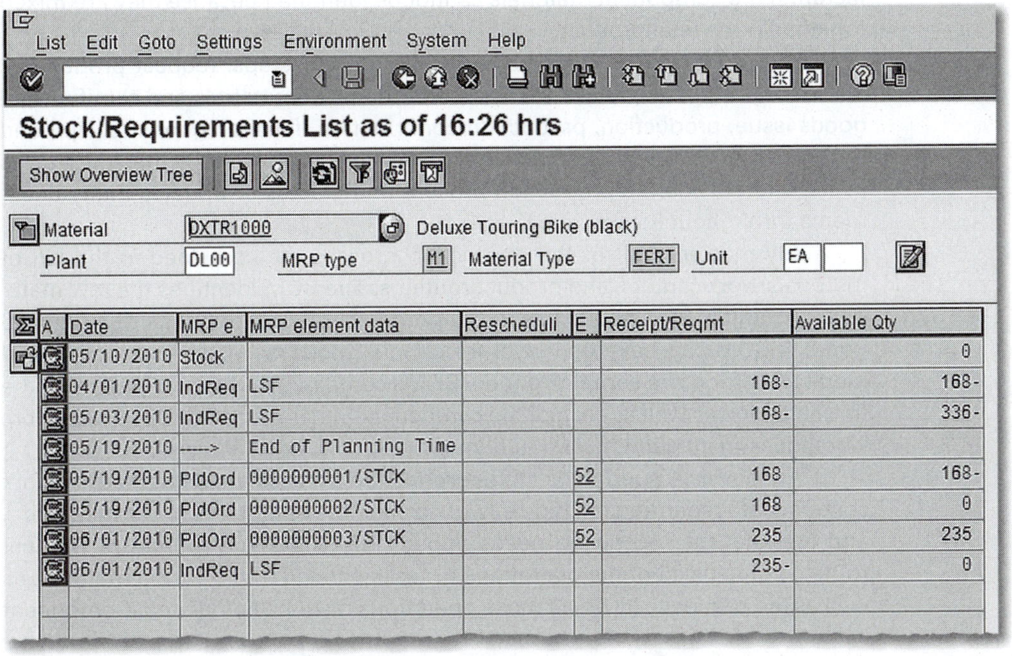

Stock/Requirements List as of 16:26 hrs

Material DXTR1000 Deluxe Touring Bike (black)
Plant DL00 MRP type M1 Material Type FERT Unit EA

A	Date	MRP e	MRP element data	Rescheduli	E	Receipt/Reqmt	Available Qty
	05/10/2010	Stock					0
	04/01/2010	IndReq	LSF			168-	168-
	05/03/2010	IndReq	LSF			168-	336-
	05/19/2010	---->	End of Planning Time				
	05/19/2010	PldOrd	0000000001/STCK		52	168	168-
	05/19/2010	PldOrd	0000000002/STCK		52	168	0
	06/01/2010	PldOrd	0000000003/STCK		52	235	235
	06/01/2010	IndReq	LSF			235-	0

Figure 6-37: Stock/requirements list. Copyright SAP AG 2011

CHAPTER SUMMARY

The production process involves the various steps and activities necessary to manufacture or assemble finished goods and semifinished goods. Organizations utilize different manufacturing strategies depending on the type of material being produced and the business model needed to sell those materials profitably. The two most common production strategies are make-to-stock and make-to-order. In make-to-stock, the materials are produced and stored in inventory for sale at a later time. In make-to-order, production occurs only after the company receives a sales order.

The most common types of production processes are discrete, repetitive, and process manufacturing. In discrete and repetitive manufacturing, each unit produced is distinct from other units, and the component materials from which the unit is made can be identified. In repetitive manufacturing, the same material is produced repeatedly over an extended period of time at a relatively constant rate. In discrete manufacturing, the company produces different materials over time in batches, often alternating between materials on the same production line.

Process manufacturing refers to the production of materials in bulk volumes (liters, gallons, barrels, etc) rather than individual units. In process manufacturing the component materials cannot be identified because they are mixed together in the final product.

The production process consists of eight key steps: request production, authorize production, release production order, raw materials and semifinished goods issue, production, production confirmation, finished goods receipt, and production order completion. Each of these steps is affected by many variables inside and outside the production process and creates or updates many documents throughout its execution.

Key master data for the production process are contained in the bill of materials work centers, and product routings. The BOM identifies the raw materials or semifinished goods needed to produce one or more units of a finished good. A BOM can have one level for simple goods or many levels of nested hierarchies for more complex goods. BOMs contain detailed information on the finished good as well as each of the component materials needed for production, warehouse management, and fulfillment.

The physical operations in the production process are carried out in work centers. Data regarding the type of work center, the operations performed there, and the relevant scheduling needs appear in the product routing. A product routing contains all of the operations or tasks needed to produce a material, as well as the sequence in which those operations must be completed. Component assignment ties together the materials listed in the BOM that are needed for production, the work centers where the final product will be manufactured, and the operations in the routing that the company will use to manufacture it.

The production information system provides detailed reports to monitor and manage the production process. Companies utilize a stock/requirements list to view the different activities that impact the quantity of materials in inventory.

KEY TERMS

Backflushing

Bill of materials (BOM)

Component assignment

Confirmation

Goods issue

Goods receipt

Item category

Make-to-order

Make-to-stock

Operations

Order completion

Planned order

Product routing

Production capacity

Production order

Production resource tools

Stock/requirement list

Task list

Work center

Work-in-process (WIP)

REVIEW QUESTIONS

1. Explain the function of a bill of materials in the production process.

2. What is the significance of item categories in a bill of materials?

3. Explain the structure of a bill of materials.

4. What is the function of a work center in production?

5. Briefly discuss the key data in a work center master record.

6. What is a product routing? What is it used for?

7. Explain the relationship between operations and sequences.

8. Explain the relationship between bills of materials, work centers, and product routings.

9. Which material master data are relevant in production?

10. What are production resource tools?

11. Briefly describe the steps in the production process in terms of triggers, data, tasks, and outcomes.

12. Explain the financial impact of the steps in the production process.

13. What are the different production order statuses? What is the significance of the order status?

14. Briefly describe the structure of a production order.

15. What are the different options for production order confirmations?

16. What is a stock/requirements list? What information does it provide?

EXERCISES

Exercises for this chapter are available on *WileyPLUS.*

CHAPTER 7

Inventory and Warehouse Management Processes

LEARNING OBJECTIVES

After completing this chapter you will be able to:

1. Discuss the four goods movements associated with inventory management.

2. Describe the organizational levels in warehouse management.

3. Analyze the master data associated with warehouse management.

4. Identify and explain the key steps in the warehouse management processes.

5. Demonstrate how inventory and warehouse management processes are integrated with other processes.

6. Effectively use SAP® ERP to execute the key steps in the warehouse management process.

7. Extract and analyze meaningful information about the warehouse management process utilizing SAP ERP.

In Chapter 1 we introduced **inventory and warehouse management (IWM)** processes, which are concerned with the storage and movement of materials within an organization. We indicated that IWM is closely related to the procurement, fulfillment, and production processes. Then, in Chapter 4 we introduced the underlying activity in **inventory management (IM)**, namely, goods movement. Specifically, we introduced the four goods movements—goods receipt, goods issue, stock transfer, and transfer posting—as well as specific movement types. In our discussion of material movement in the preceding chapters, we focused on the simpler processes associated with IM. In addition, we explained that **warehouse management (WM)** involves processes that enable companies to manage materials more effectively using sophisticated techniques. Business Processes in Practice 7.1 illustrates how a large global enterprise, Steelcase, Inc., uses inventory and warehouse management to efficiently move materials across various facilities.

Business Processes in Practice 7.1: Inventory and Warehouse Management at Steelcase, Inc.

Headquartered in Grand Rapids, Michigan, Steelcase is the leading global workplace furniture manufacturer with approximately 11,000 employees and a total revenue of approximately $2.3 billion in FY 2010. The company relies on a network of more than 650 independent and company-owned dealers to market, deliver, and install many types of office furniture products (e.g., desks, chairs, and cabinets) for its customers. Steelcase has manufacturing operations dispersed throughout North America, Europe, and Asia. In North America, Steelcase has ten manufacturing plants and six regional distribution centers (RDCs). Each plant has a small warehouse to store raw materials and, temporarily, finished goods. Steelcase orders raw materials through the procurement process, which are delivered directly to the manufacturing plants. The production process consumes the raw materials at the manufacturing plant, after which it ships the finished goods to the RDCs. The RDCs manage the logistics activities of the fulfillment process, including planning shipments, allocating and routing trucks, and consolidating, preparing, and loading shipments. The key goal of inventory and warehouse management at Steelcase is to optimize warehouse space and efficiently execute the fulfillment process by balancing the inbound flow of goods to its manufacturing plants with the outbound delivery of customer shipments from the RDCs. Steelcase uses the IWM capabilities of SAP ERP extensively to monitor, assess, and manage the efficient flow of goods in and out of their warehouses.

The warehouses at the manufacturing plants and at the RDCs utilize two different IWM processes to address the distinctive storing needs of raw materials versus finished goods. The warehouses at the manufacturing plants store raw materials from the procurement process until these goods are consumed in the production process. They also store finished goods from the production process until they are consumed by the fulfillment process. In the best case scenario, raw materials are stored at the manufacturing plant only for a few hours before they are used in production, and finished goods are stored only for a few hours before they are shipped to the RDCs. The RDCs receive materials from many manufacturing facilities and store those goods until a customer order has been filled. They then pick, pack, and ship the finished goods to the customer.

Each Steelcase RDC receives daily shipment forecast reports from the manufacturing plants. The RDCs use these reports to plan space for shipments and to manage the logistics activities of the fulfillment process. Customer orders are typically filled from multiple factories, a process that requires consolidating multiple inbound deliveries into a single outbound delivery. A large RDC can process more than 100 outbound customer shipments per day, with many more inbound deliveries from the manufacturing plants arriving simultaneously. This constant flow of inbound and outbound deliveries and material movements generates a very complex routing of trucks, pallet loaders, forklifts, and packing materials that are constantly moving in and around the warehouse. Steelcase orchestrates this complex ballet with the IWM capabilities of SAP ERP.

Source: Steelcase, Inc. Materials Planning Group

In this chapter we will review and elaborate on the IM-related goods movements introduced in previous chapters. We will then discuss the organizational data, master data, and processes associated with WM processes in the context of the procurement, fulfillment, and production processes. In these discussions we will also highlight the linkages between IM and WM. We will conclude with a discussion of reporting options. Immediately following the end-of-chapter material is Appendix 7A, which discusses procedures for creating storage bins automatically.

■ INVENTORY MANAGEMENT

Figure 7-1 illustrates the four goods movements involved in inventory management. We have already discussed goods receipt (indicated with a "1" in the figure) in the context of the procurement and production processes. Similarly, we discussed goods issue ("2" in the figure) in the context of the fulfillment and production processes. We also addressed stock transfers ("3") and transfer postings ("4") in prior chapters. In this section, we will review and extend the discussions of these goods movements. Recall that companies perform goods movements using specific movement types that determine what information is needed to execute the movements and which general ledger accounts will be affected by the movements.

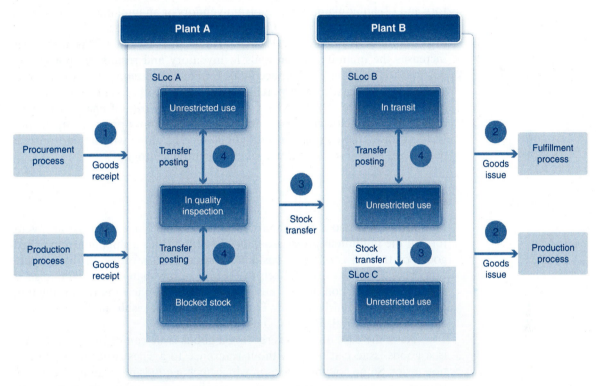

Figure 7-1: Goods movements

The key organizational level associated with inventory management is the storage location. We initially discussed storage locations in Chapter 4, in the context of the procurement process. Recall that storage locations are associated with plants, which in turn are associated with company codes. Further, because inventory management is concerned with material movements, the material master—and, more specifically, the plant/data storage view of the material master—is the most relevant master data in IM. We also discussed the plant/data storage view of the material master in Chapter 4.

GOODS RECEIPT

A goods receipt is a movement of materials into inventory; it therefore results in an increase in inventory. Recall from Chapter 4 that a goods receipt occurs during the procurement process when a business receives raw materials and trading goods into inventory from a vendor. In addition, as we discussed in Chapter 6, a goods receipt takes place in the production process when a company receives finished goods into inventory from the shop floor. Both of these movements result in the creation of material and financial accounting documents. Also, in both processes, when materials are received into inventory, they are placed in an appropriate storage location with an appropriate status, such as unrestricted use or in quality inspection.

The procurement and production chapters focused on a goods receipt that is generated against a purchase order and a production order, respectively. It is not uncommon, however, to record a goods receipt without reference to an order. Two scenarios in which this occurs are (1) the initial receipt of inventory and (2) an unplanned receipt from vendors or an unplanned return from customers. The *initial receipt of inventory* involves a movement type that an organization uses when an SAP ERP system is first installed. This movement increases the quantity of materials in inventory and results in appropriate postings to the general ledger accounts. *Unplanned receipts* occur when a reference document, such as a purchase order or a production order, does not exist. For example, a vendor may deliver materials free of charge (perhaps as samples), or a customer may return materials without prior arrangements. In these cases, the company uses a goods receipt, along with an appropriate movement type, to receive these materials into inventory.

GOODS ISSUE

In contrast to a goods receipt, a goods issue results in a decrease in inventory. In the fulfillment process, a goods issue indicates a shipment of finished goods or trading goods to a customer against a sales order. In the production process, a goods issue reflects the issuing of raw materials or semifinished goods to a production order. These materials are then used in the production process to create finished goods. Finally, a goods issue results in the creation of appropriate material, FI, and CO documents.

As in the case of a goods receipt, a goods issue can be *unplanned*. That is, a goods issue can occur without reference to a sales order or a production order. Some common cases in which such a goods movement occurs are issuing materials to scrap, sampling, and using the materials for internal consumption. When materials are no longer usable due to age or obsolescence, they are discarded or *scrapped*. *Sampling* involves testing the quality of the materials. If the testing is destructive—that is, the testing procedure renders the materials unusable—or if the materials are expensive, then, rather than examine all of the materials, the company tests only a small sample. Finally, materials may be withdrawn for *internal consumption*, for example, for research and development. In all these cases, an appropriate movement type is required.

TRANSFER POSTINGS

Businesses use transfer postings to change the status or type of materials in stock. Recall from Chapter 4 that there are four common stock statuses that determine the usability of materials—unrestricted use, in quality inspection, blocked, and in transit. Recall further that a transfer posting need not include a physical movement of materials. Figure 7-1 provides three examples of transfer postings, indicated by the number "4."

A transfer posting is used in several other situations that do not necessarily involve a physical movement of materials. Here we consider two scenarios: material-to-material posting and consignment-to-warehouse stock posting. A *material-to-material* posting is used to change the material number of a material. This process is common in industries such as pharmaceuticals and chemicals where the characteristics of a material change over time. For example, one of the steps in the process of brewing beer is to boil and cool grains and water. This material, called wort, is combined with yeast and placed into a fermentation vessel. Once the wort is fermented, it becomes beer. Thus one material (wort) changes over time into another (beer). In addition, a company occassionally will change a material number for a material. In both cases, the company uses a transfer posting to change the material number from the old number to a new number, using an appropriate movement type.

The second scenario in which a transfer posting is not accompanied by a physical movement of materials involves *vendor-owned inventory*—that is, materials that are stored in the customer's facilities although the vendor retains ownership. This arrangement is common for large companies such as Walmart. Let's use GBI to illustrate this process. Consider a scenario in which GBI has an agreement with one of its vendors to provide GBI with raw materials on a consignment basis. In this case, when the goods receipt is posted, the quantity of materials in inventory is increased, and the status of the materials is set to consignment stock. However, GBI does not owe any money to the vendor, and the materials are not valued in GBI's balance sheet. Thus, the goods receipt does not affect GBI's financial position. There is no impact on the vendor's account, the accounts receivable reconciliation account, or the inventory account. At a later point in time, when GBI uses the raw materials in the production process, it will change the status of the materials from *consignment* to *warehouse stock* (either unrestricted use or in quality inspection). At this point there is a financial impact—GBI now owes the vendor for the quantity of materials used—which is recorded in the general ledger using an appropriate movement type. (You might want to review our discussion of the invoice verification step of the procurement process in Chapter 4.)

STOCK TRANSFERS

Whereas a transfer posting need not involve an actual movement of materials, a stock transfer is used to physically move materials within the enterprise from one organizational level or location (e.g., a storage location in a plant) to another. A stock transfer can involve movements under three scenarios: (1) between storage locations within one plant, (2) between plants in one company code, and (3) between plants in different company codes. Figure 7-1 provides two examples. The arrow marked "3" in the middle of the figure illustrates a stock transfer between two plants (A and B). Although not indicated in the figure, the plants may be in the same company code or in different company codes. The arrow marked "3" near the bottom right part of the figure illustrates a transfer between two storage locations in the same plant.

Regardless of the organizational levels involved, three options are available for moving materials: using a one-step procedure, a two-step procedure, and a stock transport order. We discuss stock transport orders at the end of this section. The one-step and two-step procedures are illustrated in Figure 7-2.

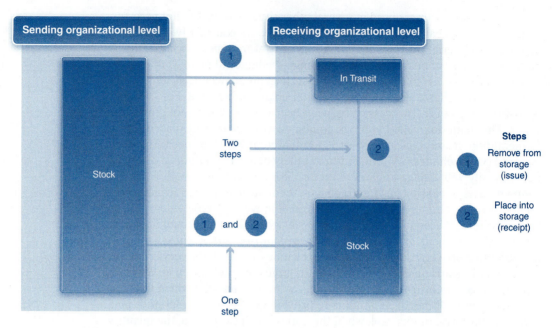

Figure 7-2: One-step and two-step procedures

Material movements consist of two tasks: issue and receipt. Issue refers to removing the materials from storage at the supplying or sending location, and receipt involves placing them into storage at the receiving or destination location. In the one-step procedure, as the name implies, both tasks are accomplished in a single step. Consequently, a decrease in quantity at the supplying location and an increase at the receiving location are recorded simultaneously. This strategy is appropriate when the two locations are physically close to each other and there is no significant time lag between issue and receipt.

By contrast, in a two-step procedure the two tasks are completed in separate steps. The first step (issue) occurs when the materials are removed from storage. At this time the quantity of inventory is reduced at the supplying location and simultaneously increased by the same amount at the destination location. However, because the materials do not arrive immediately at the destination location, they are placed in the in-transit stock status at this location. Later, when they are physically received at the destination location, a second step (receipt) changes their status from in transit to unrestricted use (or another status). Companies utilize the two-step movement when there is a time lag between the two steps, for example, when the locations are geographically separated by distance. The in-transit status alerts the destination location that materials are due to be received. Another situation in which the two-step movement is used is when the same person does not have authorization to make changes at both locations. Significantly, although stock transfers and transfer postings are conceptually different, they are both accomplished via a transfer posting in SAP ERP. The distinction is in the specific movement type that is used.

As in any goods movement, a material document is created during both the one-step and two-step procedures. In the one-step procedure, one material document is created. This document contains two line items for each material moved, one for the issue at the supplying location and one for the receipt at the receiving location. During the two-step procedure, two material documents are created, one at the time of issue and one at the time of receipt. The material document created during the first step includes two line items for each material moved, one for the issue and one for receipt into in-transit status. The material document created at the time of the second step has only one line item for each material moved because the movement (from in transit to unrestricted use) occurs only at the receiving location.

Whether there is a financial accounting impact (and, therefore, FI documents are created) depends on the organizational levels involved in the movement. Three combinations of organization levels are possible: storage location-to-storage location, plant-to-plant, and company code-to-company code. We discuss these next.

Storage Location-to-Storage Location Transfer

A stock transfer between two storage locations within the same plant is referred to as a storage location-to-storage location transfer. There are several reasons for moving materials within the same plant. In some cases, materials received from a vendor or from production are initially stored in a temporary staging area and then moved to a more permanent location at a later date. The staging area is designated as a storage location, so the movement from this location to the permanent location is accomplished via a stock transfer. Another possible scenario is when all materials received from a vendor must be inspected for quality before being placed in their permanent locations. These materials are initially placed in the location where the inspection is performed. Like the staging area just discussed, this inspection area is designated as a storage location. When the inspection is completed, the company uses a stock transfer to move the materials to the more permanent location.

A transfer within a plant can be accomplished via a one-step or a two-step procedure, as illustrated in Figure 7-3. The numbers on the arrows indicate specific movement types. Note that in the one-step procedure, the materials can be in any stock status in the supplying location and can be moved into any stock status in the receiving location. In contrast, a two-step procedure is possible only when the materials are in unrestricted use at the supplying location. Moreover, the materials can be received only into unrestricted use. Finally, as explained earlier, when the first step (issue) is posted, the quantity in unrestricted use in the supplying location is reduced, and a corresponding increase is noted in the receiving location. However, the stock at the receiving location has a status of in transit. When the materials are physically received, their status is changed to unrestricted use.

Because materials are typically valued at the plant level rather than the storage location level, a transfer between storage locations in the same plant does not affect valuation. Therefore, no FI document is created. This observation is true when all quantities of the same materials are valued in the same way. In some cases, however, different quantities of the same material are valued differently. For example, materials purchased from different vendors are valued differently, and materials produced in house are valued differently than those purchased externally. When materials are valued differently, through a practice known as *split valuation*, the company maintains different material accounts for each valuation type. If the material being moved is split-valued and the valuation type changes as a result of the transfer, then the transfer has a financial accounting impact, and an FI document is created.

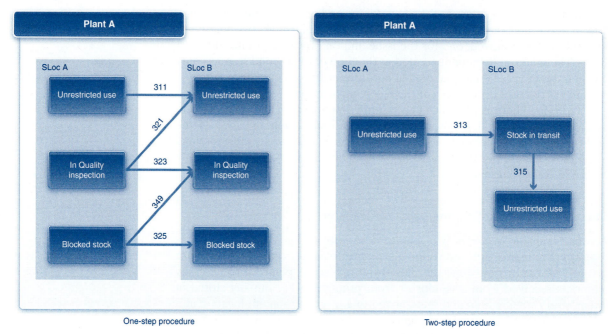

Figure 7-3: Stock transfer within a plant

Plant-to-Plant Transfer

A movement of materials between two plants *within the same company code* is called a **plant-to-plant transfer**. As diagrammed in Figure 7-4, plant-to-plant transfers can be carried out as either one-step or two-step procedures. Typically, only materials in the unrestricted use status can be moved between plants. In both the one-step and two-step procedures, the quantity of materials in inventory is reduced in the issuing plant (Plant A in the figure) and increased at the receiving plant (Plant B). The difference is in the stock status at the receiving plant. In the one-step procedure the materials are placed in unrestricted use at the receiving plant. In contrast, in a two-step procedure, the materials are placed in the stock in-transit status at the receiving location after the first step (issue) and then changed into unrestricted use when the materials are actually received.

Plant-to-plant transfers, like storage location-to-storage location transfers, result in the creation of material documents. In the one-step procedure, one material document is created with two line items for each material moved. In the two-step procedure, two material documents are created, one at the time of issue and one at the time of receipt. The material document created at the time of receipt has only one line item.

Because materials are valued at the plant level, a plant-to-plant transfer represents a change in the value of the materials. Consequently, there is an FI impact. One FI document is created in both one-step and two-step movements. In the two-step method, the FI document is created at the time of issue, when the accounting impact occurs. Therefore, no FI document is created at the time of receipt. Further, the material is valued at the valuation price of the supplying plant.

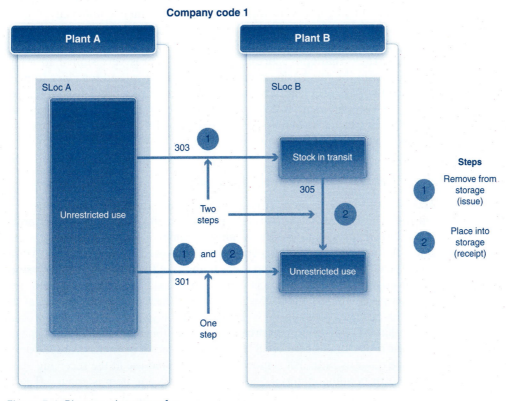

Figure 7-4: Plant-to-plant transfer

Demo 7.1: Plant-to-plant stock transfer (1 step)

Company-Code-to-Company-Code Transfer

A movement of materials between two plants in different company codes is called a **company code-to-company code transfer**. This type of transfer can be accomplished via both the one-step and two-step procedures. In both cases the movements are very similar to plant-to-plant transfers. The obvious difference is that, in this scenario, the two plants are located in different company codes. Consequently, two FI documents are created, one for each company code. One line item is for the material account, and the other (offsetting) line item is for a clearing account created to accommodate such a transfer.

STOCK TRANSPORT ORDERS

The plant-to-plant movements discussed above are simple, straightforward ways of moving materials. However, they have limitations. Among their major limitations are the following:

- They cannot take into account the cost of transporting materials between plants.

- They cannot track the progress of the transfer.

- Valuation can only be based on the book value of the materials at the sending plant and not a negotiated value or price between plants.

When moving materials from one plant to another requires any of these capabilities, the company utilizes a process in which one plant essentially "purchases" the materials and another plant "sells" them. This process involves the use of a **stock transport order (STO)**. An STO is very similar to a purchase order in the purchasing process, except that it is used for plant-to-plant movements. An STO can involve steps from three previously discussed processes—procurement, fulfillment, and inventory management—depending on the specific scenario. In this section we discuss the following three scenarios: STO without delivery, STO with delivery, and STO with delivery and billing.

Stock Transport Orders without Delivery

This scenario involves steps from purchasing and inventory management, as illustrated in Figure 7-5. The receiving plant creates a stock transport order, either directly or with reference to other documents such as a purchase requisition. At the supplying plant, a goods issue is posted against the STO. At this point the quantity in unrestricted use is reduced at the sending plant, and stock in transit is increased at the receiving plant. A material document with two line items is created to record this movement. When the materials arrive at the receiving plant, a goods receipt is recorded, just as in the procurement process. Recall that in the procurement process the goods receipt was recorded against a purchase order. In this case, the STO is used instead of a purchase order. At this time, the quantity in transit is moved to unrestricted use at the receiving plant, and a corresponding material document with one line item is created. The FI impact (and therefore material valuation) occurs at the time of the goods issue

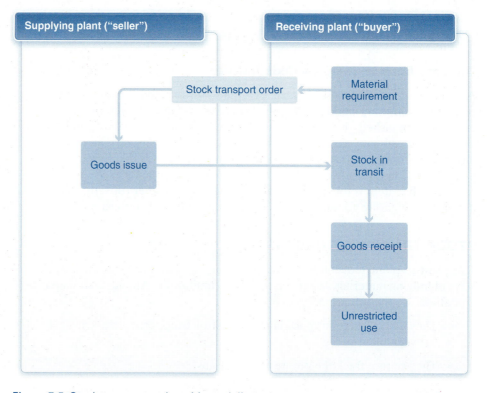

Figure 7-5: Stock transport order without delivery

using the valuation price of the supplying plant. As in the case of stock transfers, one FI document is created if the two plants are in the same company code, and two FI documents are created if the plants are in different company codes. The general ledger accounts affected are the material accounts and a clearing account. Note that the procedure described above is a two-step procedure. In fact, only a two-step procedure is possible for STO without delivery.

Demo 7.2: Stock transport order without delivery

Stock Transport Orders with Delivery

In the previous scenario, the only shipping-related task that is included is the goods issue. Recall from Chapter 5 that the shipping step can include additional tasks, such as creating a delivery document, picking, and packing. When a company uses the stock transport with delivery scenario, the sending plant will first create a delivery document prior to goods issue. Recall that in the fulfillment process, this document is used to pick, pack, and ship the materials to the customer. Thus, when a business uses an STO with delivery, it treats the order like a sales order with the receiving plant taking on the role of a customer, and the sending plant acting as a vendor. After the delivery document is created, the rest of the shipping tasks (pick, pack) are completed, and a goods issue is posted. These steps are illustrated in Figure 7-6. An STO with delivery can utilize both the one-step and two-step procedures for the goods movement. When the company uses a two-step movement, the material movement and financial

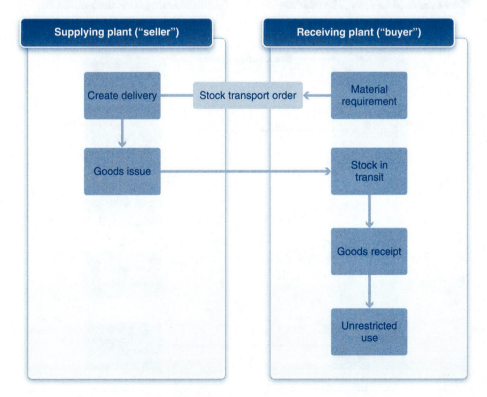

Figure 7-6: Stock transport order with delivery

impact are identical to those associated with an STO without delivery. When it uses a one step movement, only one material document is created, and the materials are placed in unrestricted use at the receiving plant.

Demo 7.3: Stock transport order with delivery

Stock Transport Orders with Delivery and Billing

The third scenario involving STO includes both the delivery document (shipping step) and the billing step from the fulfillment process at the sending plant. In addition, it includes the invoice verification step from the procurement process (see Chapter 4) at the receiving plant. This scenario is most appropriate for inter-company transfers. Figure 7-7 illustrates this scenario with a two-step procedure, although a one-step procedure could also be used. A stock transport order is created at the receiving plant in response to a need to acquire materials. In contrast to the previous two scenarios, a purchase price is included in the STO based on pricing conditions and info records, as we discussed in the Chapter 4. In response, the supplying plant then creates a delivery document authorizing the shipment. As in the fulfillment process, when the goods issue is posted, the quantity designated as unrestricted use is reduced at the supplying plant. In addition, material accounts are credited by the value of the shipment, and the cost of goods sold account is debited. Corresponding material

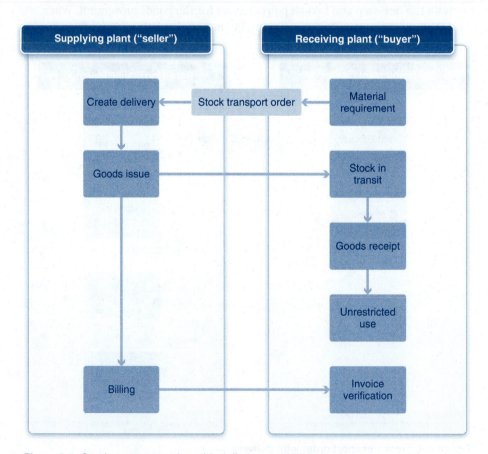

Figure 7-7: Stock transport order with delivery and billing

and FI documents are created. However, the materials shipped technically do not belong to the receiving plant in the other company code. Therefore, the value of inventory is unchanged at the receiving plant. The materials are classified as "in-transit CC," which is different from the "in-transit" category previously discussed. Materials in the in-transit category are included in valuation, whereas those in the in-transit CC category are not.

When the company receives the materials at the receiving plant, it records a goods receipt against the STO. As in the procurement process, the quantity held in unrestricted use increases, material accounts are debited by the value of the materials received, and the GR/IR account is credited. Corresponding material and FI documents are created. Note that, in contrast to the other two scenarios involving STOs, the valuation in this scenario is based on the purchase price in the STO. The supplying plant then creates an invoice based on this price, which is the selling price from the perspective of the fulfillment process. Thus, the valuation of materials does not reflect the valuation price of the delivery plant. Rather, it is based on an agreed-upon transfer price between the companies within an enterprise. When the billing document is created, the system updates the appropriate revenue and receivables accounts in the sending plant's general ledger.

The receiving plant then verifies the invoice, as in the procurement process. The system updates appropriate accounts payable and GR/IR accounts in the receiving plant's general ledger. Corresponding FI documents are created as well. In contrast to the purchasing process, the receiving plant does not make any explicit payments to the supplying plant. Rather, when the invoice verification step is completed, it makes payment via a transfer of funds between appropriate accounts in the two company codes. At this time, the accounts receivable account and accounts payable account are also updated. As usual, corresponding FI documents are created.

Using an STO to move materials between plants, as compared to using stock transfers, has numerous advantages.

- When an STO is created, the company can carry out an availability check to assess material availability in the supplying plant.

- Delivery costs and the selected carrier can be added to the STO.

- Quantities in the STO and planned deliveries and receipts can be included in material planning in both plants.

- Purchase requisitions can be converted to STOs rather than POs.

- The history of the various tasks associated with the STO can be monitored via the purchase order history section of the STO.

- Goods can be received into different stock statuses, such as in quality inspection and blocked stock.

- Goods received can be posted to consumption rather than material accounts. (Refer to the discussion of stock versus consumable materials in Chapter 4.)

To review, inventory management is concerned with managing and moving materials between storage locations within a plant or between two plants. The plants can belong to the same company code or to different company codes. Several options for moving materials are available depending on the type of movement. However, in all the options we have considered, the movement is at the storage location level. Recall that storage locations are places where materials are kept until they are needed. Storage locations can be very large spaces, such as a room in a plant or even a specific area in a large room. It is important to note that although IM keeps track of the *quantity* of materials in a storage location, it cannot determine their *exact location*. For example, GBI's Dallas plant has a storage location for raw materials (RM00), where it stores numerous materials such as tires, tubes, frames, and wheels until it needs them for production. Although IM can track the quantities of these materials in the storage location, it cannot determine exactly where each of these materials is stored. Thus, when production needs the raw materials, the plant employee must manually locate them.

In earlier chapters we alluded to a more granular management of materials using warehouse management processes. We also referred to links between previously discussed processes—procurement, fulfillment, and production—and warehouse management. We now shift our focus to a detailed examination of warehouse management. We begin with organizational data relevant to warehouse management followed by master data and process steps.

● ORGANIZATIONAL DATA IN WAREHOUSE MANAGEMENT

The key organizational data in warehouse management is the **warehouse**. A warehouse is associated with one or more combinations of plant and storage location. For example, in Figure 7-8 the warehouse (100) is associated with three storage locations (FG00, TG00, and MI00) in the San Diego plant (SD00). The association between storage locations and a warehouse provides the linkage between IM processes and WM processes. When linking warehouses to storage locations, the following rules apply.

- A warehouse must be linked to at least one storage location.

- A warehouse can be linked to storage locations across multiple plants.

- A storage location can be linked to only one warehouse.

- Not all storage locations must be linked to a warehouse.

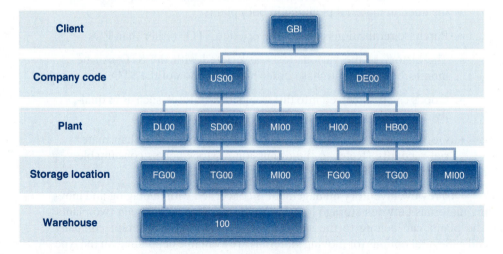

Figure 7-8: Organizational data in warehouse management

GBI has enabled warehouse management only in the San Diego plant, and all three storage locations in that plant are assigned to warehouse number 100. If GBI wished to enable WM in other plants, then the storage locations in the other plants could also be assigned to the same warehouse number. Alternatively, GBI could create additional warehouses for other storage locations. Although all three storage locations in the San Diego plant are assigned to warehouse number 100, GBI could choose to assign the finished goods and trading goods storage locations, but not the miscellaneous storage location, to the warehouse. This setup would be appropriate if the miscellaneous storage location were a small area that did not contain many materials.

A warehouse is divided into smaller areas, in a hierarchical manner, as depicted in Figure 7-9. More specifically, a warehouse is comprised of *storage types*, which are further divided into *storage sections*. In turn, storage sections contain *storage bins* where the materials are ultimately stored. Note that storage bins are actually master data. We introduce them in this section, however, to clarify the relationships among the various elements in a warehouse. Finally, storage types are sometimes divided into picking areas rather than storage sections. We examine all of these concepts in the following sections.

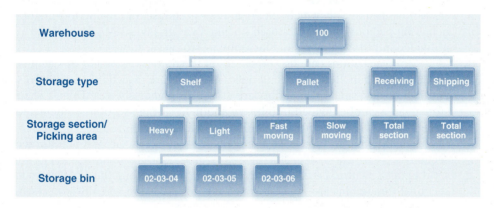

Figure 7-9: Structure of a warehouse

STORAGE TYPE

A warehouse must include at least one storage type. A **storage type** is a division of a warehouse based on the characteristics of the space, materials, or activity. For example, the space in the warehouse can be divided into storage types based on how the materials are stored. In such cases the storage types could include *shelf storage*, *pallet storage*, and *rack storage*. Some materials may need to be handled carefully (e.g., hazardous material) or to be kept in environmentally controlled areas (e.g., specified temperature). In these scenarios the storage types would reflect these specifications. Thus, storage types could be designated as hazardous storage and cold storage. In Figure 7-9 there is one area for shelf storage and one for pallet storage.

Recall that the assignment of storage locations to a warehouse links IM activities to WM activities. To illustrate this point, consider a simple procurement scenario in which a company receives a shipment from a vendor. When materials are managed only at the storage location level, the company uses a goods receipt to record the receipt of the materials, which are then placed in the specified storage location. When WM is enabled, however, additional steps must be completed. We will discuss these steps later in the chapter. For now, the key point is that until these WM steps are completed, the materials are placed in specially designated storage types that serve as **interim storage areas** in the warehouse (e.g., a receiving area). Interim storage areas are also utilized in the fulfillment process when the materials are to be shipped from a warehouse managed storage location. These areas represent the physical links between IM and WM. Figure 7-9 includes one storage type for shipping and one for receiving.

STORAGE SECTION

Storage types can be further divided into storage sections, which group bins with similar characteristics. Examples of storage sections are fast-moving, slow-moving, heavy, light, large, and small. An organization may have some materials that are shipped out very soon after they are received in the warehouse. These materials are designated as fast-moving materials, and, logically, they should be placed close to the receiving and shipping areas. In contrast, slow-moving materials, which remain in the warehouse for long periods before being shipped out, should be stored further away. In Figure 7-9, the pallet area is divided into slow-moving and fast-moving storage sections.

Storage sections can also be based on the material's weight or size. For instance, in a shelf area, heavy and bulky materials are placed in lower shelves, and lighter and smaller materials are stored in higher shelves. Thus, a shelf storage area can be divided into heavy and light storage sections, as depicted in Figure 7-9. The receiving and shipping storage areas have one storage section each, the total section. Each storage type must include at least one storage section.

Finally, Figure 7-9 shows three storage bins within the light storage section. Storage bins are areas in which the materials are actually stored. We discuss storage bins in the section on master data.

PICKING AREA

Storage areas can be divided into picking areas rather than storage sections. A storage section is a division of a storage area based on storing or putting away materials. In contrast, a **picking area** is a division of a storage area based on removing or picking materials. A picking area groups storage bins based on similar picking strategies. For example, picking areas can be assigned to specific employees who are responsible for picking from the specified bins. As another example, a delivery to a customer can be allocated to multiple picking areas to facilitate parallel picking. This arrangement makes the picking step more efficient, and it enables the company to deliver the materials to the customer more quickly.

Figure 7-10 displays the layout of GBI's San Diego distribution center, and Figure 7-11 displays its structure. GBI has two storage types—shelf storage (001) and pallet storage (002)—and two interim storage types—receiving (003)

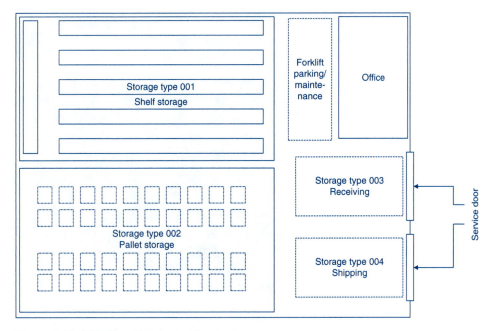

Figure 7-10: GBI's San Diego plant layout

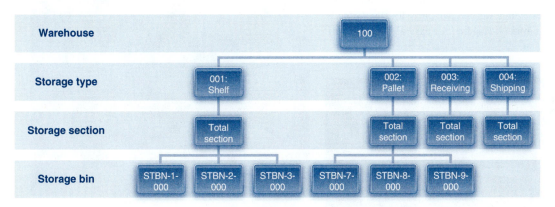

Figure 7-11: Structure of GBI's warehouse in San Diego

and shipping (004). Note that whereas Figure 7-9 displays multiple storage sections for the shelf and pallet storage areas, GBI has elected to not divide the storage types in the San Diego warehouse into multiple sections. Rather, each storage type has one storage section—the total section, as illustrated in Figure 7-11. Going further, GBI does not have picking areas defined in its warehouse. Finally, both the shelf storage and pallet storage have multiple bins. Note that interim storage types do not require bins to be created in advance.

Business Processes in Practice 7.2 describes the structure of a warehouse at Steelcase.

Business Processes in Practice 7.2: Warehouse Organization at Steelcase, Inc.

In its massive manufacturing plants, Steelcase might have to store and maintain inventory for more than 30,000 unique raw materials for production. These materials are classified into multiple storage types, such as plastic, rolled steel, wood, and fabric. Because each of these materials has unique characteristics, each one requires different types of storage. For example, plastic parts are typically very small and can be stored in large bins in bulk quantity on a rack (Figure 7-12). A single Steelcase warehouse can have up to 15,000 storage bins for small raw materials. Rolls of fabric require a different type of space for storage (Figure 7-13). However, the rolled steel, which is formed into cubicle walls or file cabinets, is delivered in massive rolls that weigh several tons each. These materials are bulky and heavy and require special equipment to store and move around the plant, so they require unique storage and handling space on the warehouse floor (Figure 7-14). In addition, raw materials must be stored in two types of storage locations—standard storage, which is located in the warehouse, and line storage, which is located directly next to the manufacturing line for easy access. Typically,

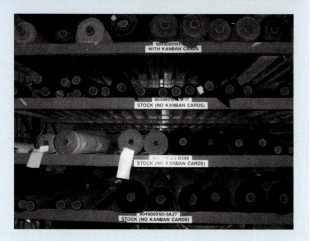

©Angela D. Gustaf, Steelcase, Inc.

Figure 7-13: Fabric storage at the Kentwood East Manufacturing plant, Steelcase, Inc.

©Angela D. Gustaf, Steelcase, Inc.

Figure 7-14: Rolled steel storage at the Kentwood East Manufacturing plant, Steelcase, Inc.

Steelcase prefers to have at least a 24-hour supply of raw materials located next to the production line to ensure a constant flow of materials and to avoid any disruptions to the manufacturing process.

Source: Steelcase, Inc. Materials Planning Group.

©Angela D. Gustaf, Steelcase, Inc.

Figure 7-12: Bins in rack storage at the Kentwood East Manufacturing plant, Steelcase, Inc.

■ MASTER DATA IN WAREHOUSE MANAGEMENT

The key master data in warehouse management are material master and storage bins. We examine these data types in this section.

MATERIAL MASTER

We have previously discussed the material master in the context of several other processes. In these discussions we have explored several views, including basic, purchasing, and sales. If a company stores a material in a storage location that is associated with a warehouse, then it must include additional data in the master record for that material. These data are included in the **warehouse management view** of the material.

Recall that master data are typically defined for specific organizational levels. The organizational levels relevant to the warehouse management view of master data are *warehouse*, *plant*, and *storage type*. A warehouse is required; that is, materials must be defined for each warehouse. However, plant and storage type are optional and are included only when the warehouse data for the material are different in different plants or storage types. Three types of data are relevant to the warehouse management view:

- Basic data

- Data used in defining stock placement and removal strategies

- Data regarding the storage bins where the materials will be stored

Basic data are relevant to all processes, as we discussed in Chapter 2. Some of these data, however, are redefined for WM. An example is the *warehouse management unit of measure*, which can be different from the base unit of measure discussed in Chapter 2. For example, a material can have a base unit of measure in single units (e.g., one helmet) but be managed in larger quantities (e.g., box of dozen helmets) in the warehouse. Data related to *placement and removal strategies* indicate priorities and sequences in which the storage types, storage sections, and picking areas are to be searched. *Bin-related data* indicate which bins are to be used to store materials as well as the minimum and maximum quantities allowed in the bins.

> **Demo 7.4:** Review WM view of material master

STORAGE BINS

Storage bins are the smallest unit of space in a warehouse. They are the areas where materials are physically stored. Storage bins can vary in size from small containers (for nuts and bolts) to large areas for bulky materials (pallets of soft drink cases). They can be containers on shelves or designated spaces on a warehouse floor where pallets of materials are stored. Storage bins have unique addresses that identify their location in a warehouse. These addresses are frequently based on a coordinate system. In a shelf storage environment, for example, a bin address can include a row (or an aisle) number, a stack number, and a shelf number. Consider a library that has rows of shelves that hold books, as illustrated in Figure 7-15. The figure displays two rows, each of which has three stacks. In turn, each stack has six shelves. Each unique shelf, such as Row 1, Stack 1, Shelf 3, is a bin. If further granularity is needed, then each shelf can be further divided into smaller areas. Figure 7-16 depicts storage bins at the warehouse at a Steelcase manufacturing plant.

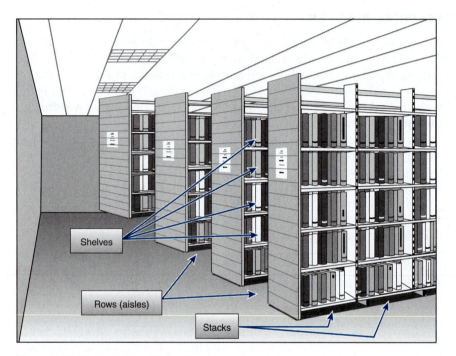

Figure 7-15: Storage bin addressing

©Angela D. Gustaf, Steelcase, Inc.

Figure 7-16: Storage tubs (bins) at the Kentwood East manufacturing plant, Steelcase, Inc.

A bin can be used to store different materials. To distinguish between quantities of different materials, the materials with the same characteristics are grouped into quants. A **quant** is a specific quantity of materials that have similar characteristics and are stored in a single bin. For example, if road helmets and t-shirts are stored in one bin, each material will be identified by a different quant. Figure 7-18 illustrates the use of quants. In the top left quadrant there is one quant of material A. Two materials—A and B—are stored in the bin in the top right quadrant. Each material is identified by a separate quant. Quants are also used when the same material with different characteristics is stored in one bin. In the pharmaceuticals industry, for example, drugs are produced in batches, and each batch has both a specific expiration date and a unique batch number. When different batches of the same material are stored in the same bin, each batch is identified by a different quant. This arrangement is illustrated in the bottom left quadrant of the figure. Finally, the bottom right displays an example in which some quantities of the material are of the stock type unrestricted use and other quantities are designated as in quality inspection. The quantity of each type of material is associated with a different quant.

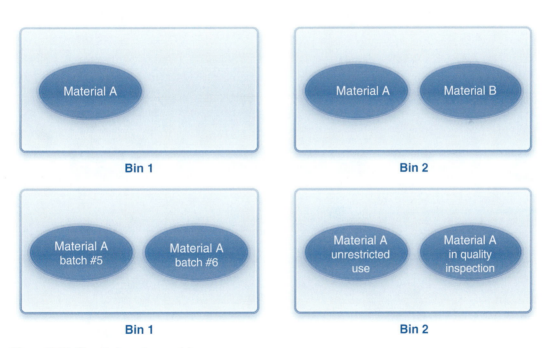

Figure 7-17: Quants in a storage bin

Quants are created as needed by the ERP system when materials are moved into bins. After a quant has been created, the quantity of materials can be increased or decreased only by a goods movement. Moreover, when the quantity is reduced to zero, the system automatically deletes the quant. Because quants are generated as needed, they are categorized as transaction data. We discuss them here, however, to emphasize the relationship between quants and storage bins.

Demo 7.5: Review storage bins, and display stock in storage bins

● PROCESSES IN WAREHOUSE MANAGEMENT

Figure 7-18 illustrates steps in the warehouse management process. Typically, the WM process is associated with a goods movement in another process, such as procurement, fulfillment, production, and inventory management. Recall from our discussion earlier in this chapter that a goods movement is an IM activity. When a goods movement involves a storage location that is warehouse managed, however, additional steps are required to transfer the materials into (putaway) or out of (pick) storage bins in the warehouse. In most cases, an IM goods movement automatically generates a *transfer requirement*. Transfer requirements are used to *plan* the movement of materials in and out of a warehouse. The actual *execution* of the movement is accomplished via a *transfer order*. After a transfer order is created, the materials are physically moved between interim storage areas and the storage bins, to complete putaway or picking activities. At that point the transfer order is *confirmed*.

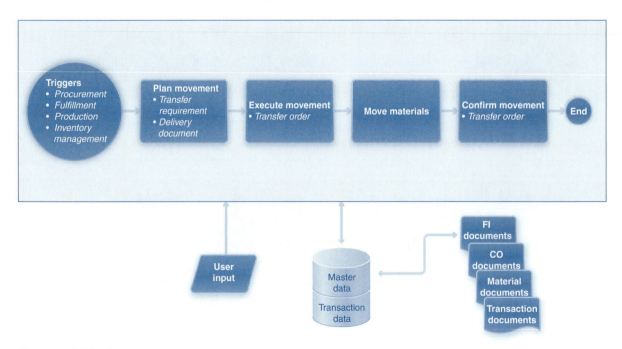

Figure 7-18: Warehouse management process

In this section we will consider the steps in the WM process. We will first discuss these steps in general terms. We will then delve into the details of these steps as they relate to the procurement, fulfillment, production, and inventory management processes. We will assume that all the storage locations involved in our discussion are warehouse managed.

PLAN WAREHOUSE MOVEMENT

A **transfer requirement (TR)** is a document that companies use to plan the movement of materials into and out of bins in a warehouse. In most cases the trigger is either an activity in inventory management or a need to transfer materials within a warehouse. The ERP system automatically creates a transfer requirement when an IM activity involving a warehouse-managed storage location occurs. The transfer requirement communicates data from the IM processes to the WM processes. Figure 7-19 illustrates the elements of the plan warehouse movement step.

Figure 7-19: Elements of the plan warehouse movement step

Data

Figure 7-20 highlights the data included in a transfer requirement. Master data include data about the materials and bins involved in the movement. Organizational data include the client, company code, plant, storage location, and warehouse number. Transaction data include the materials to be moved, quantity, date, transfer type (putaway, pick, or transfer), and the source of the requirement. The source is included when the requirement was not created manually and is typically a result of specific activity in IM such as a goods receipt.

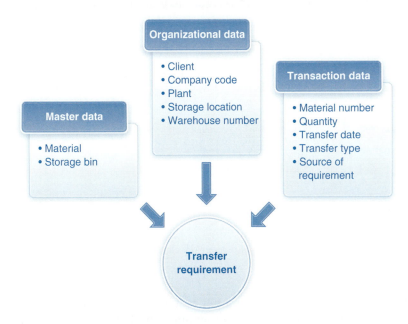

Figure 7-20: Data in a transfer requirement

Tasks

The only task involved in this step is to create the transfer requirement. Although the ERP system is generally configured to create a transfer requirement automatically as a result of activity in IM, the requirement can also be manually created. In the case of a transfer posting, a posting change notice (explained below) is created instead of a transfer requirement. Posting change notices can be created either manually or automatically by the ERP system as a result of a transfer posting in IM.

Recall from previous chapters that IM activities occur in procurement, fulfillment, production, and inventory management processes. In procurement, when a goods receipt against a purchase order is created, a transfer requirement is automatically generated as well. Two steps in the production process can potentially generate a transfer requirement. First, when a production order is released, a transfer requirement for the materials needed for production is created. Then, when the materials have been produced and received into inventory, the receipt of finished goods (or semifinished goods) against the production order triggers a transfer requirement. In inventory management, the stock transfer process uses a transfer requirement. Planning a warehouse movement in fulfillment is a little different than in other processes. Recall that a delivery document is created in the shipping step of the fulfillment process to facilitate picking of materials. The delivery document serves as a transfer requirement and is used to plan the warehouse movement.

In the case of a transfer posting, however, the system creates a posting change notice rather than a transfer requirement. A **posting change notice** is a request to change the status of the material, for example, from in quality inspection to unrestricted use. Finally, a transfer requirement can be created manually to facilitate an internal movement of materials from one bin to another within the warehouse. Thus, the source of the requirement for warehouse movement is typically a material document or a production order, as illustrated in Figure 7-21.

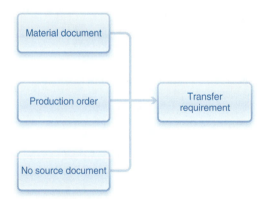

Figure 7-21: Reference documents for a transfer requirement

Outcomes

The outcome of this step is either a transfer requirement or a posting change request. Note that there is no financial accounting impact. In IM the FI impact occurs when a goods movement takes place. At that time, IM inventory is increased or decreased and the FI impact is recorded, as we discussed in the chapters on procurement, fulfillment, and production.

EXECUTE WAREHOUSE MOVEMENT

Figure 7-22 diagrams the elements of the execute warehouse movement step. Common warehouse movements include picking, putting away, and posting changes. The document that is used to execute these movements is the **transfer order (TO)**. The creation of a TO is generally triggered either by a transfer requirement or by a posting change notice. However, TOs can also be created directly from delivery and material documents generated by other processes. Finally, they can be created manually to facilitate internal warehouse transfers.

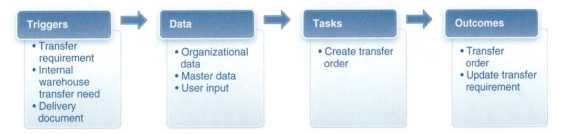

Figure 7-22: Elements of the execute warehouse movement step

Data

Figure 7-23 presents the data involved in a transfer order. The master data and organizational data are the same as those contained in a transfer requirement. If a reference document, such as a transfer requirement, is used, then data from this document are copied into the transfer order. The data in a transfer order include the material number, quantity, data, and transfer type. In addition, identifying the source and destination bins is necessary to execute a WM transfer. The source and

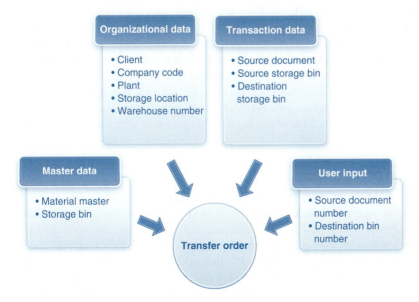

Figure 7-23: Data in a transfer order

distination bins are often proposed automatically by the ERP system. However, they can also be provided by the individual who is executing the transfer.

A transfer order consists of a header and one or more line items, as illustrated in Figure 7-24. The header includes data that are applicable to all line items. Examples are the transfer order (TO) number, reference document number, dates, and warehouse movement type. Line item data include material number; source storage type, bin, and quant; destination storage type, bin, and quant; target quantities; and actual quantities moved. Note that a particular material can have more than one line item if the material has to be moved from multiple source bins or to multiple destination bins. This scenario can occur in the case of picking when there is insufficient quantity in one source bin and in the case of putaway when the destination bin is not large enough to hold all of the materials moved.

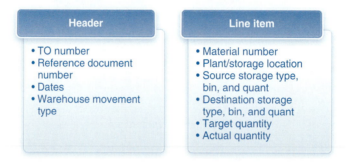

Figure 7-24: Structure of a transfer order

Tasks

The key task in the execute warehouse management step is the creation of a transfer order, with or without a reference document, as illustrated in Figure 7-25. Transfer orders can be created either manually or by the ERP system. When they are created manually, the user selects the appropriate reference document or documents, verifies the data in these documents, and then creates the orders. When a reference document is not used, the user must provide all of the data that would have been contained in the reference document. The ERP system can create the TOs automatically, but only when a reference document exists. The system also can be configured to *automatically* create transfer orders from reference documents that meet certain criteria (e.g., transfer date). Finally, the system can be programmed to *directly* create transfer orders as soon as a material document or an outbound delivery for shipment to a customer is created.

Outcomes

The obvious outcome of this step is a transfer order. When the TO is created, the reference document used to generate it is updated to indicate that this step has been completed. In addition, the storage bin data for the source and destination bins are updated to note planned movements (an example of this is provided in the section on reporting later in this chapter). As in the case of a transfer requirement, creating a TO has no FI impact. The transfer order essentially is a transaction document that authorizes warehouse employees to physically move the materials from the source storage bin(s) to the destination storage bin(s) indicated in the document.

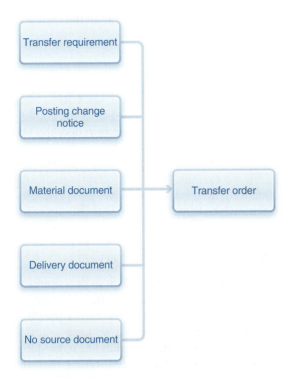

Figure 7-25: Reference documents for a transfer order

CONFIRM WAREHOUSE MOVEMENT

Generating a transfer order allows the warehouse employees to physically move the materials from the source bins to the destination bins. After the employees have completed this movement, they retrieve the transfer order and confirm the movement. The elements of the confirm WM movement step are presented in Figure 7-26.

Figure 7-26: Elements of the confirm warehouse movement step

Data

Confirming the warehouse movement involves the same transfer order created in the previous step. Consequently, this step utilizes the same data concerning the materials being moved and the bins.

Tasks

Confirming the movement involves updating the transfer order to indicate that the movement was completed. The quantities moved from and to various bins are entered into the transfer order, and the order is saved. If all of the materials have been moved, then the step is complete.

Outcomes

When a confirmation of warehouse movement is recorded, the ERP system automatically updates the associated reference documents such as the delivery document, transfer requirement, and posting change notice to reflect the fact that the transfer of materials has been completed.

In this section we explained the warehouse management process in general terms. In the following sections we examine WM as it relates specifically to procurement, fulfillment, production, and stock transfers. We also review the financial and material impact of the various steps. We begin with procurement.

WAREHOUSE MANAGEMENT IN PROCUREMENT

To illustrate the warehouse management steps as they relate to procurement, we will use the following scenario. GBI wishes to increase the inventory of t-shirts in its San Diego plant. To accomplish this task, it has sent a purchase order for 1,000 t-shirts to its vendor, Spy Gear. Recall that we used a similar scenario in Chapter 4. In this scenario, however, the materials are to be delivered to the San Diego plant, which is warehouse managed, rather than the Miami plant, which is not. We will assume that GBI has 500 t-shirts in stock. Figure 7-27 illustrates the inventory impact of the steps in the procurement process. It indicates that GBI has 500 t-shirts in storage location inventory and in the warehouse prior to the start of the process (column 2).

	Prior to process execution	Plan warehouse movement - record GR - create TR	Execute warehouse movement - create TO	Confirm warehouse movement - confirm TO
Storage location	500	1500	1500	1500
Interim storage area	0	1000	1000	0
Warehouse bins	500	500	500	1500

Figure 7-27: Inventory impact—procurement

Plan Warehouse Movement

Figure 7-28 diagrams the steps in the procurement process. The figure includes both IM activities and WM activities. The bottom part of the figure illustrates the physical movement. Recall from Chapter 4 that the procurement process involves a goods receipt from a vendor and that the materials are placed into a specific storage location. In our example, when GBI receives the 1,000 t-shirts from Spy Gear, the warehouse personnel place them in the interim receiving storage area and record a goods receipt into the trading goods storage location the ERP system. (You might want to refer back to the San Diego plant layout illustrated in Figure 7-10 and the discussion on storage types regarding the use

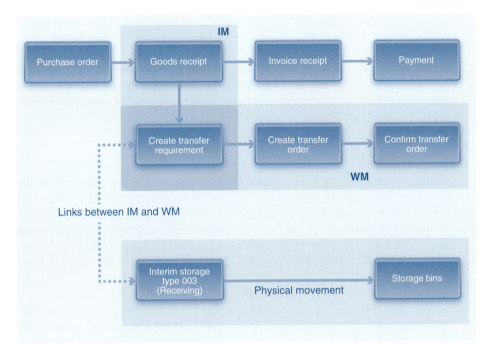

Figure 7-28: IM and WM steps in procurement

of storage type 003, receiving, as the interim storage area for goods received.) The interim storage area is the *physical link* between the procurement and warehouse management processes. When the goods receipt is recorded, financial accounting and material documents are created, as explained in Chapter 4. In addition, the system automatically generates a transfer requirement because the trading goods storage location is warehouse managed. The transfer requirement is created by an IM activity and serves as the *information link* between the procurement process and the warehouse management process.

A review of inventory at this point in the process (column 3 in Figure 7-27) will show that there are 1,500 t-shirts in the trading goods storage location—the initial 500 plus the 1,000 received from Spy Gear. Warehouse (bin) inventory is unchanged because the shirts have not yet been moved into the warehouse. Instead, inventory in the interim (receiving) storage area increases by the 1,000 t-shirts received.

Execute Warehouse Movement

When a warehouse employee is ready to putaway the materials from the interim storage area into warehouse bins, he or she creates a transfer order to facilitate this movement. In our example, the order authorizes the warehouse employees to transfer the 1,000 t-shirts from the interim receiving storage area to specific bins in the warehouse. The reference document for this order is the transfer requirement created at the time of goods receipt. When the order is generated, the ERP system proposes destination bin numbers into which the employees can place the t-shirts. Alternatively, the employees can specify the destination bins manually.

A review of inventory (see Figure 7-27, column 4) will not indicate any change in the number of t-shirts in the storage location, interim storage area, or warehouse bins. This is because the impact on storage location inventory occurs when the goods receipt is recorded in IM. In addition, at this point nothing has actually been moved from the interim bins to the warehouse bins. However, the transfer order will indicate the planned (target) quantities and bins.

Confirm Warehouse Movement

Creating a transfer order authorizes GBI warehouse employees to physically move the materials from the interim receiving storage area into warehouse bins. After this step has been completed, the TO is updated to confirm the quantity and locations (bins). In our example, the t-shirts are moved from the interim receiving storage area into the warehouse bins proposed by the ERP system in the TO. The employee then updates the TO to indicate that 1,000 t-shirts were moved.

A review of inventory (see Figure 7-27, column 5) will indicate that storage location inventory remains unchanged at 1,500. The quantity in the interim receiving storage area is reduced by the 1,000 t-shirts moved and is now zero. Finally, the warehouse bins now contain 1,500 t-shirts, the original 500 plus the 1,000 that were just moved.

As illustrated in Figure 7-28, the remaining steps in the procurement process (e.g., invoice receipt and payment) can continue while the WM process steps needed to putaway the materials into bins are completed. These steps can continue because they are based on the material and financial accounting documents that were created at the time of the goods receipt, which is an IM activity and is not dependent on WM activities.

You may have noticed that inventory is tracked at both at the storage location level and the warehouse level. Warehouse inventory is the sum of the inventory in the interim storage areas and the warehouse bins. Note in Figure 7-27 that warehouse inventory is always equal to storage location inventory.

Demo 7.6: Procurement process with warehouse movements

WAREHOUSE MANAGEMENT IN FULFILLMENT

To illustrate warehouse management in fulfillment we will employ a different GBI scenario. Rocky Mountain Bikes (RMB), a GBI customer, has sent a purchase order for 50 bikes, which GBI will ship from the San Diego plant. Recall that we used a similar example in Chapter 5. The significant differences here are (1) GBI will deliver all of the bikes in one shipment and (2) the transaction will include WM steps that were omitted in Chapter 5 to keep the discussion simple. We will assume that GBI has 500 bikes in inventory before the fulfillment process is executed. We depict this scenario in Figure 7-29. Column 2 in the figure indicates the inventory status prior to process execution.

	Prior to process execution	Plan warehouse movement - Create delivery	Execute warehouse movement - create TO	Confirm warehouse movement - confirm TO	At goods issue
Storage location	500	500	500	500	450
Interim storage area	0	0	0	50	0
Warehouse bins	500	500	500	450	450

Figure 7-29: Inventory impact—fulfillment

Plan Warehouse Movement

Figure 7-30 illustrates the steps in the fulfillment process, including both IM and WM activities. In this case, the creation of an outbound delivery for a sales order triggers the WM activities. Whereas in the case of procurement the transfer requirement served as the *information link* between the procurement process (IM) and the WM process, in fulfillment the delivery document serves this role. In our scenario, GBI first generates a sales order in response to RMB's purchase order. The company then creates an outbound delivery, which triggers the need to move 50 bikes from storage bins to the interim (shipping) storage area, for shipment to RMB. A review of the storage location and the bin inventory will not indicate any change in the quantity of materials because no physical movement has occurred yet (see Figure 7-29, column 3).

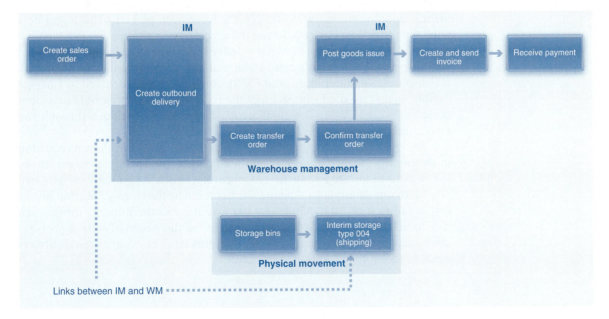

Figure 7-30: IM and WM steps in fulfillment

Execute Warehouse Movement

When a warehouse employee is ready to pick materials from the warehouse, he or she generates a transfer order based on the delivery document. At this time, the ERP system proposes bins from which to move the materials. In our example, the employee creates a TO to pick 50 bikes from the warehouse. Significantly, no physical movement has yet taken place. Consequently, a review of the storage location and warehouse inventory will not show any change in quantities (see Figure 7-29, column 4).

Confirm Warehouse Movement

After the TO is created, warehouse employees pick the bikes from the proposed storage bins and place them in the interim shipping storage area. They then update the TO to indicate the quantity picked and the bins from which they were taken. Again, refer to Figure 7-10 and the discussion of storage types for an explanation of the shipping area. In our example, the 50 bikes are picked from bins in the warehouse and placed in the interim shipping storage area. As in the case of procurement, the interim storage area is the *physical link* between the fulfillment and WM processes.

At this point, a physical movement of materials has occurred. Consequently, a review of warehouse inventory will show a reduction of inventory in the warehouse bins and an increase in the bins in the interim storage area. In our example (see Figure 7-29, column 5), 450 bikes remain in the warehouse bins, and 50 bikes are available in the interim shipping storage area. No goods issue has occurred, so the quantity in storage location inventory is unchanged (500).

After the transfer order is updated, it is confirmed and saved. At this point the reference document that triggered the warehouse movement is updated to indicate the quantity of materials moved. In our example, the delivery document is updated to indicate that 50 bikes have been picked. (This might be a good time to review Figure 5-34 and the accompanying discussion in Chapter 5 regarding the relationship between a delivery document and a transfer order.) At this point the materials can be shipped and a goods issue can be posted, which generates material, FI, and CO documents, as we discussed in Chapter 5. Note again that the FI impact and the recording of the material movement occur in IM, not WM. The fulfillment process then continues through the invoice and payment steps.

A review of warehouse inventory after goods issue will show a reduction in the interim storage area of inventory. Further, the storage location inventory will now indicate a reduction in inventory, because a goods issue has been posted. In our example (see Figure 7-29, column 6) the storage location inventory is reduced by 50 to 450 bikes, and inventory in the interim storage area is reduced to zero. Note that, as explained in the discussion of WM in procurement, the total warehouse inventory (bins plus interim storage area) is always equal to the storage location inventory.

WAREHOUSE MANAGEMENT IN PRODUCTION

The production process triggers the warehouse management process in two places, as indicated in Figure 7-31. Recall from Chapter 6 that production involves both a goods issue (when raw materials and semifinished goods are issued to the production order) and a goods receipt (when finished goods are placed into storage). Figure 7-31 assumes that these materials are issued from and received into a warehouse-managed storage location. The production order generates a transfer requirement for the materials that are needed for production. In response, a TO is created, the materials are moved into an interim storage area, and the TO is confirmed. The accompanying goods issue has all the financial and material outcomes that we discussed in Chapter 6.

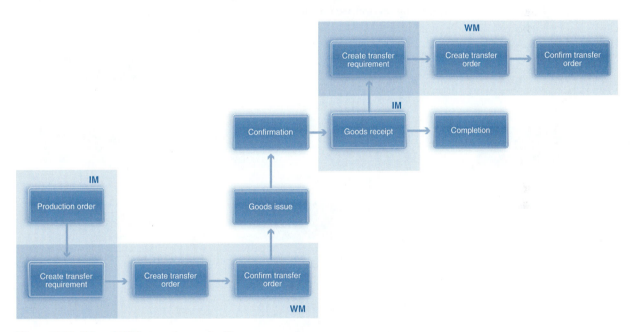

Figure 7-31: IM and WM steps in production

After the production process is completed and confirmed, the finished goods are received into storage. At this point the WM process steps are similar to those that occur within the procurement process. A goods receipt is recorded, as explained in Chapter 6. However, the materials are physically placed in an interim storage area, and a transfer requirement is automatically created by the system. A transfer order is then created, the materials are moved from the interim storage area into bins, and the TO is confirmed. Meanwhile, the remaining steps in the production process, such as completion and variance calculation, can be executed.

WAREHOUSE MANAGEMENT IN STOCK TRANSFERS

In addition to the scenarios we have already discussed, WM activities are also initiated by stock transfers and transfer postings. We addressed these topics earlier in this chapter in the context of inventory management. Figure 7-32 illustrates five scenarios under which stock transfers involving warehouse movements can occur. The first four scenarios involve movement between two storage locations. Recall that IM processes are responsible for managing inventory at the storage location level. Consequently, these four scenarios will require a stock transfer that is initiated in IM. When these goods movements involve warehouse-managed storage locations, the transfer requirements are automatically generated by the ERP system. The fifth scenario involves movement between two bins in the same warehouse and thus does not involve any IM activity. In the following section we consider each of these scenarios in greater detail.

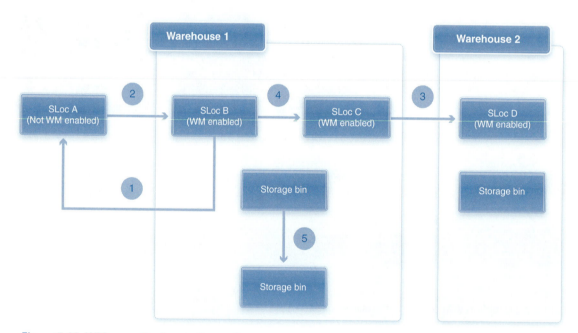

Figure 7-32: WM scenarios for stock transfers

The first scenario involves a stock transfer from a plant where the storage location is warehouse managed (storage location B associated with warehouse 1) to a plant where it is not (storage location A). In this case, a goods issue at the sending plant triggers WM process steps, as explained earlier in the chapter. At the receiving plant, a simple goods receipt is recorded in IM.

The second scenario depicts the opposite movement; namely, a stock transfer from a plant where the storage location is not warehouse managed (storage location A) to a plant where it is (storage location B associated with warehouse 1). In this case, a goods issue (IM) records the shipment of materials at the sending location. At the receiving location, a goods receipt triggers WM process steps.

The third and fourth scenarios involve a stock transfer between two warehouse-managed storage locations. Specifically, they involve a goods issue from and a goods receipt to warehouse-managed storage locations. Therefore, WM processes are triggered at both the goods issue (sending location) and the goods receipt (receiving location).

Finally, in the fifth scenario materials are moved from one bin to another within the same warehouse. This is an internal transfer and thus does not involve IM. Consequently, a transfer requirement is not automatically generated and therefore must be created manually. After it is created, the rest of the WM process steps are completed as in the other scenarios.

Note that in the first four scenarios, material documents are created when IM activities (goods issue and goods receipt) are involved. In contrast, the last scenario does not involve any IM activities, so no material document is created. Also, the first four scenarios may result in a financial impact. If so, appropriate FI documents are created. In the last scenario, there is typically no financial impact, so no FI documents are created.

Demo 7.8: Internal warehouse transfer

ORDER OF POSTINGS IN WM AND IM

The scenarios considered in the preceding section are summarized in the first two rows of Figure 7-33. Goods receipt postings for purchase or production orders trigger putaway activity in WM. Delivery documents (for sales orders) and production orders trigger picking activity in WM, which are followed by goods issue postings.

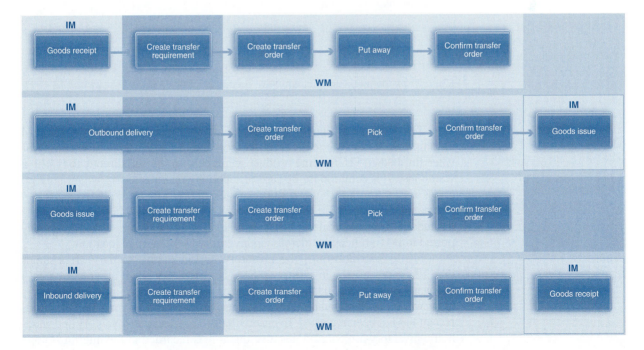

Figure 7-33: Scenarios for WM and IM activities

As the figure indicates, the order in which IM and WM activities are completed can vary from one scenario to another. Consider, for example, the scenarios diagrammed in the bottom two rows of Figure 7-33. The third row is a case in which the goods issue (for a sales order or production order) is posted before WM activities are recorded in the ERP system. This scenario can occur when either a customer or the production process needs materials urgently and the materials are removed from storage and shipped out to the customer or the production floor. In such cases, the materials are withdrawn from the warehouse and a goods issue is posted, but the WM activities of picking the materials and placing them in the interim storage area have not been *recorded*. Rather, they are recorded later as time permits.

Let's consider the impact of this type of movement on storage location and warehouse inventory. Figure 7-34 illustrates a scenario in which a company has 100 units in inventory prior to the process execution. It then ships 25 units to a customer. At the time of shipment, a goods issue is posted, and storage location inventory decreases by 25 units to 75. To keep storage location and warehouse inventory equal, the ERP system will post a negative quantity to the interim storage area (–25). As a result, warehouse inventory now becomes 75 (100 – 25). To reduce the warehouse bin inventory, a transfer order must be confirmed. When this occurs, a decrease of 25 units is recorded for warehouse bins, and an increase of 25 units is recorded for the interim storage area. As a result, the interim storage area shows a quantity of zero and warehouse bins indicate a quantity of 75, which matches the storage location inventory.

	Prior to process execution	IM activity (goods issue)	WM activity (confirm TO)
Storage location	100	75	75
Interim storage area	0	–25	0
Warehouse bins	100	100	75

Figure 7-34: Inventory impact when IM precedes WM

The last row in Figure 7-33 represents a case in which putaway in WM is completed before a goods receipt is recorded in IM. This situation can occur when finished goods from the production process are moved directly to bins in a warehouse. It is common in the case of repetitive manufacturing, where finished goods are continuously being produced (see Chapter 6 for an explanation). When the materials are brought to the warehouse for putaway, a transfer requirement or transfer order is created and confirmed. Goods issues are then periodically posted in IM to reflect the increase in inventory in the storage location.

Figure 7-35 illustrates the inventory impact of this scenario. It assumes that 100 bikes are in inventory initially and that 25 bikes are received into the warehouse. When the transfer order is confirmed, there will be 125 bikes in the warehouse bins, but only 100 in storage location inventory, because the goods receipt has not been recorded. To ensure that storage location inventory and warehouse inventory are equal, a negative quantity is recorded in the interim storage area. When the goods issue is posted, 25 bikes are added to both the storage location and interim storage areas, leaving a total of zero in the interim storage area.

	Prior to process execution	WM activity (confirm TO)	IM activity (GR)
Storage location	100	100	125
Interim storage area	0	−25	0
Warehouse bins	100	125	125

Figure 7-35: Inventory impact when WM precedes IM

Business Processes in Practice 7.3: The Virtual Truck Concept

Some of the office furniture products that Steelcase produces are too large to fit on racks or shelves and aren't appropriate for pallet storage. To accommodate these products, the warehouse operates on a "virtual truck" bin concept. Floor space in the warehouse is marked off into bins that represent the length and width of delivery trucks. As inbound goods are received, they are scanned with a bar code scanner that is connected to SAP ERP. In turn, the system confirms goods receipt automatically and then informs the workers which bin to store the goods in. When the bin (virtual truck) is filled and all of the goods for the outbound customer shipment are in place, the materials in the bin are "picked" and moved to a staging area near the truck dock. They are then "packed" for shipment and loaded onto the delivery truck. When a shipment is placed on the truck, a post goods issue is completed, which creates all of the paper shipping documents for the truck driver and triggers the printing of an invoice for the customer. Steelcase processes more than 1,000 outbound customer shipments per week in North America in this manner.

Source: Steelcase, Inc. Materials Planning Group

■ REPORTING

In this section we consider several examples of reports that contain information relevant to inventory and warehouse management. As in the case of other processes, a variety of reporting options are available in warehouse management, including status reports, work lists, online lists, and reports using the information system. A list of documents, such as transfer requirements and transfer orders, can be generated in a manner similar to the lists explained in previous chapters. Figure 7-36 illustrates a list of transfer orders.

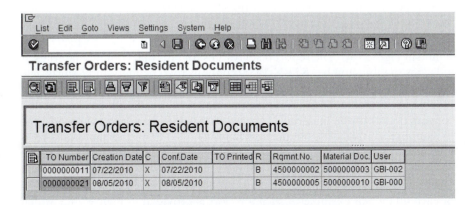

Figure 7-36: List of transfer orders. Copyright SAP AG 2011

Demo 7.9: List Report—list & transfer orders

Figure 7-37 is an example of an inventory status report. It displays inventory at the storage location level. Specifically, it indicates that there are 50 road helmets (RHMT1000) in the trading goods storage location (TG00) in the San Diego plant (SD00), in GBI's U.S. company (US00). It does not show inventory at the bin level.

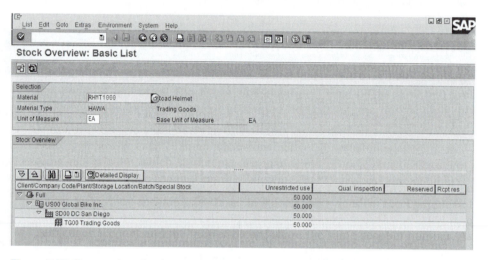

Figure 7-37: Storage location inventory report. Copyright SAP AG 2011

Figure 7-38 displays inventory at the San Diego warehouse. It indicates that there are 50 road helmets in the interim receiving storage area (GR Area External Receipts). This report was generated after a goods receipt against a purchase order was recorded, a process step that automatically generates a transfer requirement. Figure 7-39 is the same report after a transfer order has been created. Note that the 50 helmets in the interim receiving area now appear under the "Pick quantity" column, indicating that they need to be picked from the interim area. The 50 helmets also appear in the "Stock for put-away" column in the shelf storage area, where they are to be putaway. Finally, Figure 7-40 displays the same report after the transfer order has been confirmed. The status of the helmets in the shelf storage area has been changed from "Stock for putaway" to "Available stock."

Another useful report is the bin status report, an example of which is presented in Figure 7-41. The report displays a list of bins that contain materials. It indicates that bin number STBN-1-000 contains road helmets and t-shirts. The system can generate similar reports to display all bins or bins that are empty. Double-clicking on a bin that contains materials produces a drilldown report that conveys details of the materials. Figure 7-42 represents a drilldown report for bin number STBN-1-000. It indicates that the bin contains two materials (road helmets and t-shirts) and two quants. Recall that a quant is a quantity of materials with similar characteristics. In this example, there is one quant for each material. If necessary, the system can drill down further to display the details of each quant. An example of such a report is provided in Figure 7-43, which shows the quant for the road helmets in storage bin STBN-1-000.

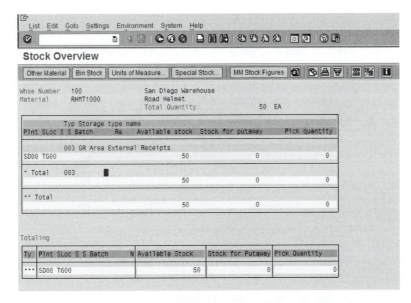

Figure 7-38: Warehouse inventory report—after goods receipt and TR are created. Copyright SAP AG 2011

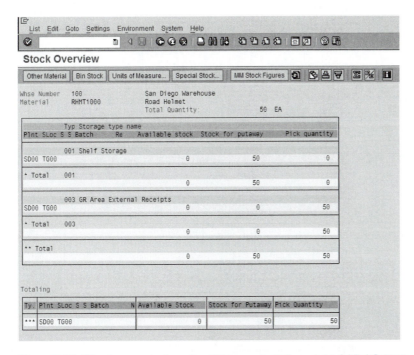

Figure 7-39: Warehouse stock—after TO is created. Copyright SAP AG 2011

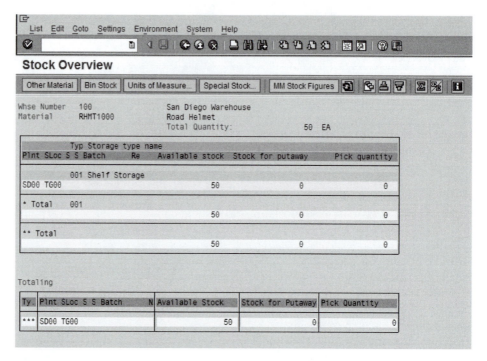

Figure 7-40: Warehouse stock—after TO is confirmed. Copyright SAP AG 2011

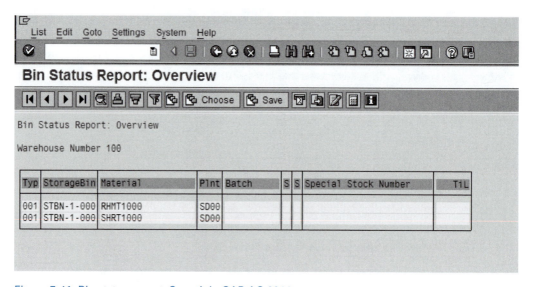

Figure 7-41: Bin status report. Copyright SAP AG 2011

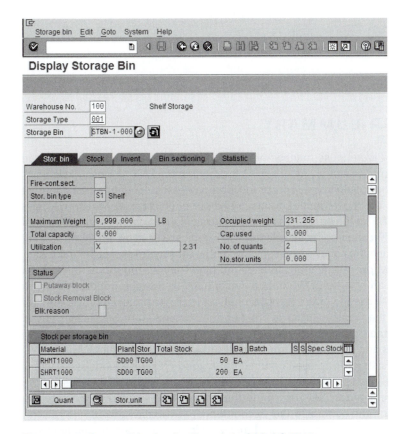

Figure 7-42: Storage bin details. Copyright SAP AG 2011

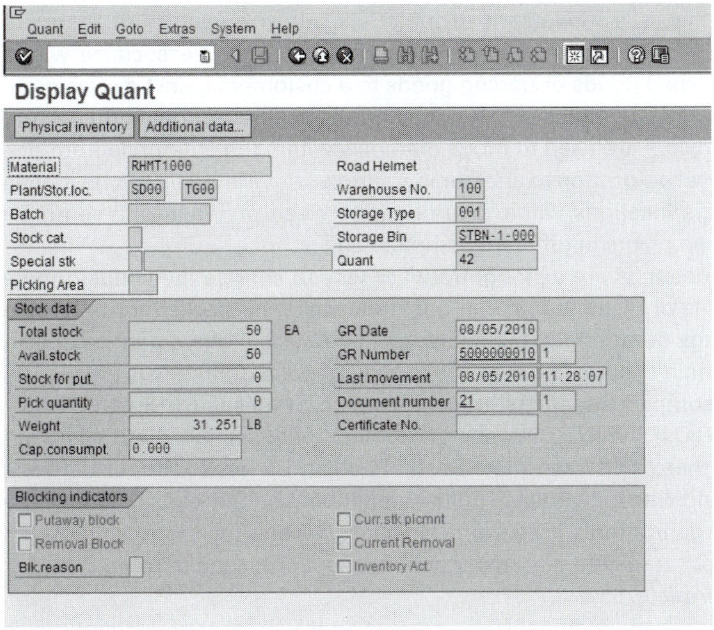

Figure 7-43: Quants in a bin. Copyright SAP AG 2011

Demo 7.10: Bin status report

CHAPTER SUMMARY

Inventory and warehouse management (IWM) processes are concerned with the storage and movement of materials in an organization. IWM is closely related to the procurement, fulfillment, and production processes. Inventory management (IM) involves the movement of goods in and out of plants, and warehouse management (WM) involves processes that permit sophisticated management of materials within and in-between plants. WM is typically used by organizations that have large quantities of expensive inventory that must be managed very closely.

The WM process is typically initiated by a transfer requirement, which is triggered by an activity in IM that creates a need to transfer goods. A transfer requirement is used to plan the movement, which is then executed by a transfer order. Once the transfer order is created, the materials are physically moved to and from the storage bins and then the transfer order is confirmed. Transfer requirements and interim storage areas are the key links between IM and WM.

IM consists of four goods movements: goods receipt, goods issue, stock transfer, and transfer posting. Goods movements are accomplished using specific movement types that determine the information needed to execute the movement and the general ledger accounts that are affected.

Goods receipt is a movement of materials into inventory; it therefore results in an increase in inventory. Typically raw materials and trading goods are received inventory from a vendor as part of the procurement process, and finished goods are received from the shop floor once the production process completes making them.

Goods issue is a movement of materials out of inventory; it therefore results in a decrease in inventory. Typically a goods issue is associated with a shipment of finished goods or trading goods to a customer against a sales order or an issue of raw materials or semifinished goods against a production order.

Stock transfers are used to move materials within the enterprise from one organization level or location to another in a simple way. Materials can be moved between storage locations within one plant, between plants in one company code, or between plants in different company codes.

Transfer postings are a straightforward way to change the status or type of stock, such as unrestricted use, in quality inspection, blocked, or in transit. Transfer postings do not necessarily involve the physical movement of goods, but they result in a change to the status or type of goods.

In more complex situations, transfers are accomplished with stock transport orders (STOs), which simulate one plant "purchasing" materials from another plant that "sells" the materials. STOs can be done without delivery, with delivery and with delivery and billing, depending on the level of complexity needed and organization's accounting policies. STOs offer many advantages over simple stock transfers or transfer postings, but also require more complex activities to complete.

Warehouse management (WM) operates on the concept of warehouses as logical units that manage and track the movement of goods in and out of storage locations. A warehouse must be associated with at least one storage location.

It is divided into one or more storage types. A storage type is a division of a warehouse based on the characteristics of the space, materials, or activity needed, such as shelf storage, pallet storage, or hazardous storage. Storage types can be further divided into storage sections, which are logical groupings of materials based on similar characteristics, such as weight, size, or activity. Within each storage section, materials are grouped into storage bins, which is where the actual materials are stored and are the smallest logical unit of storage that can be managed in WM. Each storage bin has a unique address which identifies it, typically based on a coordinate system.

Warehouse management is tightly integrated with the procurement, fulfillment, and production processes and can provide companies with a great deal of accuracy when managing large inventories of materials. There are multiple reporting options to view inventory status and activities across warehouses and plants from high-level activities to bin-level quantities.

KEY TERMS

Company code-to-company code transfer

End value

Inventory and warehouse management (IWM)

Inventory management (IM)

Increment

Interim storage areas

Picking area

Plant-to-plant transfer

Posting change notice

Quant

Stock transport order (STO)

Storage bins

Storage location-to-storage location transfer

Storage type

Transfer order (TO)

Transfer requirement (TR)

Warehouse

Warehouse management view

Warehouse management (WM)

REVIEW QUESTIONS

1. Identify and discuss the key organizational levels relevant to inventory management and warehouse management.

2. Discuss the key master data relevant to warehouse management.

3. Define the four types of goods movements in IM, and provide an example of each type.

4. Explain the material and financial accounting impacts of goods movements in IM.

5. Analyze the differences between one-step and two-step stock transfers.

6. Identify several possible scenarios for stock transfers, and explain the key differences between these scenarios.

7. What is a stock transport order used for? What are the advantages of using a stock transport order?

8. Explain the differences between using stock transport orders without delivery, with delivery, and with delivery and billing.

9. Describe the steps in the warehouse management process in terms of triggers, tasks, data, and outcomes.

10. Explain the role of the warehouse management process as it relates to (1) the procurement process, (2) the fulfillment process, and (3) the production process.

11. Explain the relationship between storage location inventory and bin inventory.

12. Describe the different options for the order of postings in WM and IM and the consequences of each option on IM and WM inventory status.

13. Identify the key reports available in warehouse management and the significant information found in these reports.

EXERCISES

Exercises for this chapter are available on *WileyPLUS.*

Creating Storage Bins Automatically

Storage bins can be created individually. However, a large warehouse will have a huge number of bins, often in the tens of thousands. In this case, creating each bin individually is extremely inefficient. Therefore, storage bins are generally created automatically by defining templates, structures, starting values, ending values, and an increment. Figure 7-44 illustrates three examples of how these elements are used in defining bins. The **template** defines the format to be used when creating bins automatically. It is 10 digits long and can include one alphabetic character (A), several numeric characters 0 through 9 (N), and several common characters (C), which can be either letters or numbers. In the first example, the template (first row) indicates that the bins

Template	A	N	N	C	C	C	C	C	C	C
Structure	A	B	C							
Start value	A	I	I							
End value	B	2	2							
Increment	I	I	I							

Example 1: 8 Bins created: A11, A12, A21, A22, B11, B12, B21, B22

Template	A	N	N	C	C	C	C	C	C	C
Structure	A	B	B							
Start value	A	I	I							
End value	B	2	2							
Increment	I	I	I							

Example 2: 4 Bins created: A11, A22, B11, B22

Template	A	N	N	C	C	C	C	C	C	C
Structure	A	B	B							
Start Value	A	I	I							
End Value	B	2	2							
Increment	I	0	I							

Example 3: 24 Bins created: A11, A12,....... A21, A22, B11, B12,....B21, B22

Figure 7-44: Automatic storage bin creation examples

will begin with an alphabetic character (A) followed by two numbers (NN). The seven remaining characters are common to all bins (C). Thus, a possible bin number is A12XXXXXXX, where "X" represents the common character.

The **structure** indicates how the noncommon digits will increase or increment. Essentially, digits with the same letter in the structure are incremented together, and digits represented by different numbers are incremented independently of one another. Thus, in the first example in Figure 7-44, each of the first three digits is incremented individually because each digit (column) has a different letter in the structure row (A, B, and C). Therefore, an increment in B will not automatically result in an increment in C. In contrast, in the second example the second and third digits are incremented together because they have the same character (B) in the structure row. Thus, if the second digit is incremented by 1, then the third digit also is incremented by 1.

The **start value** and **end value** indicate the starting and ending values of the noncommon digits in the bin numbers. In all three examples in Figure 7-44 the start values are A11 and the end values are B22.

Finally, the **increment** indicates how much each noncommon digit is to be increased by. In the first and second examples each digit is incremented by 1 unit (1 letter or 1 number). Thus, A is incremented to B, 1 is incremented to 2, and so on. In contrast, in the third example the second digit does not increase because the increment for that digit (column) is set to zero.

Let's turn to the first example. Bin numbers are determined from right to left. The first bin is A11, and each of the three noncommon digits (columns) is incremented separately. The rightmost digit will increment by 1—the increment identified in row 5—so the next bin will be A12. At this point, the rightmost digit has reached its ending value (row 4), so the digit immediately to the left will begin incrementing. Following the same rules, the next bins are A21 and A22. Finally, the first digit increments to "B," thus creating bins B11, B12, B21, and B22, for a total of 8 bins.

In the second example, the second and third digits are incremented together because they have the same value (B) in the structure. Consequently, bin values for these two digits will be 11 and 22. Combining these values with the value of first digit (A and B) will result in bins A11, A22, B11, and B22.

In the third example, the second and third digits increment together, but the increment value for the second digit is 0. Therefore the second digit will never increment. As a result, these two digits (second and third) will have 12 values ranging from 11 through 22. When these values are combined with the two values for the first digit (A and B), a total of 24 bins are created.

Figure 7-45 illustrates the bin creation data for GBI. GBI uses these two models to create bins in the shelf storage area and the pallet storage area, respectively. All bins begin with the common characters STBN- and end with the common characters 000. Thus, the sixth digit (column) is the only one that increments. For the shelf storage area the starting value is 1, the ending value is 3, and the increment value is 1. Similarly, for the pallet storage area, the start value is 7, the end value is 9, and the increment is 1. Consequently, three bins are created in each area.

Template	C	C	C	C	C	N	C	C	C	C
Structure						A				
Start value	S	T	B	N	-	I	-	0	0	0
End value	S	T	B	N	-	3	-	0	0	0
Increment					-	I	-	0	0	0

3 Bins created: STBN-1-1000, STBN-2-1000, STBN-3-1000

Template	C	C	C	C	C	N	C	C	C	C
Structure						A				
Start value	S	T	B	N	-	7	-	0	0	0
End value	S	T	B	N	-	9	-	0	0	0
Increment					-	I	-	0	0	0

3 Bins created: STBN-7-1000, STBN-8-1000, STBN-9-1000

Figure 7-45: Automatic bin creation—GBI

The Material Planning Process[1]

LEARNING OBJECTIVES

After completing this chapter you will be able to:

1. Explain the master data associated with the material planning process.

2. Analyze the key concepts associated with material planning.

3. Identify the basic steps in the material planning process and the data, documents, and information associated with them.

4. Effectively use SAP® ERP to execute the basic steps in the material planning process.

5. Extract and evaluate meaningful information about the material planning process using the SAP ERP system.

Material planning at GBI historically has been very informal. Planning for various types of materials has not been integrated with other processes. Instead, the company acquires or produces materials when it needs them. As GBI has expanded to include more facilities, materials, and customers, however, this informal planning has created myriad problems for the company. Inventory levels are rarely what they should be—too much in some cases, not enough in others. On several occasions, customers have expected products to be available sooner than GBI could provide them. The results of this lack of overall planning and coordination have been increased costs due to expedited procurement or production, unplanned expenses resulting from storing excess inventory, and lost sales. GBI's management fully understands that failing to plan adequately is equivalent to planning for failure. Their strategy for alleviating these problems is to implement an effective material planning process at GBI.

---

[1]The contents of this chapter were prepared with the expert assistance of Dr. Ross Hightower of the Mays Business School at Texas A&M University.

Material planning is concerned with answering three basic questions: (1) *What* materials are required, (2) *how many* are required, and (3) *when* are they required? The inability to answer any of these three questions accurately will result in inefficiencies, lost revenues, and customer dissatisfaction. The main objective of material planning is to balance the demand for materials with the supply of materials so that an appropriate quantity of materials is available when they are needed.

The first part of this equation—the demand for materials—is driven largely by other processes. For example, the fulfillment process uses trading goods and finished goods, and the production process uses raw materials and semifinished goods. If the materials are not available when they are needed, these processes will not function effectively. If raw materials are not available, for example, then the company cannot produce finished goods in a timely manner. Consequently, it will be unable to fulfill customer orders because it does not have the necessary materials in stock. This situation is known as a *stock-out*. A stock-out can result in lost sales if customers are not willing to accept late deliveries.

The supply side of the demand-supply equation is usually the domain of the procurement and production processes. That is, materials usually are either purchased or produced. Buying or producing more materials than what are needed will result in excess inventory, which ties up cash until the materials are eventually used. The money tied up in inventory represents an opportunity cost to the company. Additional costs are related to the cost of storage, insurance, and the risk of obsolescence. In addition, the value of some materials, such as computer components like memory and hard drives, can decrease rapidly. Thus, the longer the materials remain in storage, the more money the company loses. In some cases, materials may never be used at all and must be discarded, as illustrated in the example of Cisco Systems in Business Processes in Practice 8-1.

Business Processes in Practice 8.1: Cisco Systems

In 2001, Cisco Systems was selling huge amounts of their key networking products, driven largely by the dot-com boom. Cisco was having a difficult time keeping up with the demand for their products due to severe shortages of raw materials, so they had placed double and triple orders for some parts with their suppliers to "lock up" the parts. In addition, they had accumulated a "safety stock" of finished goods based on optimistic sales forecasts. When the Internet boom started to crash, however, orders began to taper off quickly. Even more damaging for Cisco, the company was unable to communicate the drop in demand through their organization so that they could reduce their production capacity to sell off their "safety stock" of finished goods and also reduce the amount of raw materials they were purchasing to reduce their supply buffer.

This mismatch between lower demand, substantial inventories of raw materials, and excessive production capacity ultimately forced Cisco to write off more than $2.5 billion of excess inventory from their books in 2001—the largest inventory write-off in history.

Source: Compiled from Cisco company reports; and "Cisco 'Fesses Up to Bad News," Infoworld, April 16, 2001.

The above discussion focused on fulfillment and production. Almost all processes, however, either use materials (e.g., plant maintenance, project system, warehouse management) or make them available when they are needed (e.g., project systems, inventory, and warehouse management). Therefore, material planning is one of the most complex processes within an organization. It uses data from many other processes, and it generates *procurement proposals*, that is, proposed methods of acquiring materials. These proposals are typically in the form of purchase requisitions or planned orders. Purchase requisitions, which we discussed in Chapter 4 (procurement), are requests to *purchase* materials. Planned orders, discussed in Chapter 6 (production), are requests to *produce* materials.

A simplified material planning process is depicted in Figure 8-1. The process begins with *sales and operations planning* (SOP), which uses strategic revenue and sales objectives established by senior management to create specific operations plans. The *demand management* step translates these plans into requirements for individual materials. *Requirements* specify how many of the materials are needed and when they are needed. These requirements are then used by the *materials requirements planning* (MRP) step to generate the final procurement proposals for all materials. These proposals trigger the production or procurement processes that make or buy the needed materials. Ultimately the company uses these materials to execute the fulfillment process.

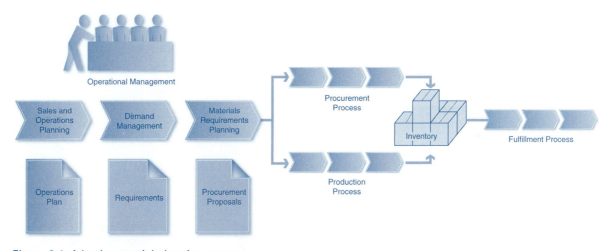

Figure 8-1: A basic material planning process

The organizational data relevant to the material planning process are client, company code, plant, and storage locations. Because we have considered all of these concepts in previous chapters, we will not discuss them in this chapter. The next section describes the master data related to the material planning process. This section is followed by a detailed discussion of process steps. We conclude the chapter with a discussion of reporting as it relates to material planning.

● MASTER DATA

The master data relevant to material planning are bill of material, product routing, material master, and product group. We discussed bills of material and product routings in detail in Chapter 6. Recall that materials are used in nearly all processes and that material master data are grouped by process, material type, and organizational level. We have also discussed various data (views) of the material master in previous chapters. In Chapter 5, we introduced MRP and work scheduling views, but we did not examine them in depth. In this section we will discuss these views at length because they are more directly relevant in material planning. In addition, we will discuss product groups as they relate to material planning.

MATERIAL MASTER

Data related to MRP and work scheduling are illustrated in Figure 8-2. MRP data can be quite extensive. Consequently, they are divided into four views or tabs—MRP 1, MRP 2, MRP 3, and MRP 4—to make the data more readable. These data are relevant to both discrete and repetitive manufacturing (explained in Chapter 6). Our discussion is limited to data relevant to discrete manufacturing. Both MRP and work scheduling data are defined at the plant level. That is, they are specific to each plant. These data determine which strategies and techniques the company will use when planning for the material. Each MRP view provides a specific set of data, as indicated in the following list.

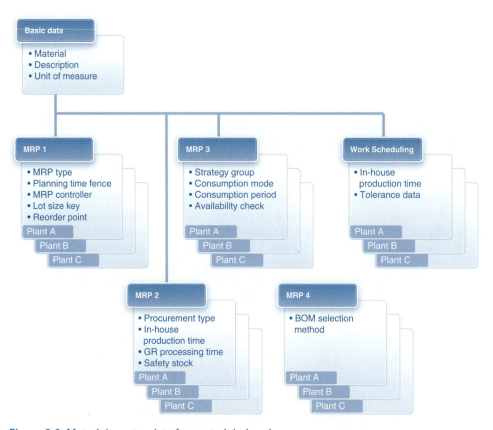

Figure 8-2: Material master data for material planning

- The MRP 1 view defines the overall planning strategy used for the material and determines how much material the company should procure.

- The MRP 2 view identifies the times the system can use for scheduling and conveys data that the system uses to determine how to procure materials (make vs. buy).

- The MRP 3 view identifies the strategy the system will use to calculate how much material is available, and it determines how the material will be produced.

- The MRP 4 view contains data that the system uses to select the correct BOM.

The work scheduling view contains data that determine production time such as setup, teardown, and processing time. We discussed these times in Chapter 6 in the context of work centers.

The next section provides a detailed discussion of the key data included in the MRP and work scheduling views of the material master.

Procurement Type

The outcome of the material planning process is one or more procurement proposals, which can trigger either the production or the procurement process. The **procurement type** indicates whether a material is produced *in-house or internally* (via the production process), obtained *externally* (via the procurement process), *both*, or *none*. Trading goods and raw materials are typically purchased from vendors. Consequently, the procurement type for such materials is specified as external. In contrast, finished goods and semifinished goods are typically produced in house. As a result, the procurement type for these types of materials is typically in-house production. Occasionally, however, when a company does not have the material or other resources to produce materials in house, it purchases them externally. In such cases, the procurement type is set to *both*. Procurement type none is appropriate for discontinued materials.

At GBI, the procurement type is defined as both for finished goods, as external for trading goods and raw materials, and as in-house for semifinished goods.

MRP Type

MRP type specifies the production control technique used in planning. Common production control techniques are *consumption-based planning*, *materials requirement planning*[2] (*MRP*), and *master production scheduling* (*MPS*). MRP type can also be set to "no planning," in which case the material is not included in the planning process.

Consumption-based planning calculates the requirements for a material based on historical consumption data. It manipulates these data to project

---

[2]The term *materials requirement planning* refers to both a planning technique and a step in the material planning process.

or forecast future consumption. The company then procures materials based on this projection. Figure 8-3 illustrates one type of consumption-based planning called *reorder point planning*. The vertical axis represents the *stock or inventory level*, and the horizontal axis indicates the relevant *time period*. Note that the stock level steadily decreases over time. The diagonal line that represents the changes in the stock level is the consumption line.

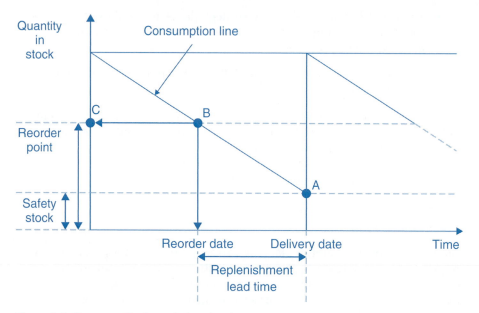

Figure 8-3: Consumption-based planning

Figure 8-3 also indicates a desired **safety stock,** which is the minimum desired level of inventory. The term *stock* is often used as a synonym for inventory. A stock-out will occur if a company has insufficient inventory to fill a customer order or to produce a finished good. As we discussed earlier in this chapter, a stock-out can lead to insufficient production and lost sales. Consequently, a company typically maintains a safety stock to avoid this situation. The material planning process monitors stock levels to prevent them from falling below the safety stock. The safety stock is specified in the material master.

To prevent stock levels from going below the safety stock level, the company must receive a supply of materials by the time the stock level reaches the safety stock level (point A in the figure). It takes some time for an order to be processed and for the shipment to be received. The time gap between placing an order—the *reorder date* in the figure—and receiving the materials—the *delivery date* in the figure—is called the *replenishment lead time*. To ensure that the company receives the materials by the desired delivery date, it must place an order early enough to give the supplier sufficient time to deliver the materials.

Most companies find it more valuable to determine when to place an order in terms of stock level than in terms of a point in time. Specifically, they order materials when the stock level reaches a predetermined level, known as the *reorder point*. The reorder point is calculated by drawing a vertical line from the order date to the consumption line (to point B) and then a horizontal line to the vertical axis (to point C).

The two other broad categories of consumption-based planning are *forecast-based planning* and *time-phased planning*. Forecast-based planning uses historical data to estimate or forecast future consumption. Organizations use the forecast to determine when to order materials. The advantage of this technique over reorder point planning is that it can consider consumption patterns that are more complex than a trend line. Time-phased planning is similar to forecast-based planning. It is used in cases where vendors deliver only on specific days of the week.

Regardless of the specific technique, consumption-based planning is relatively uncomplicated compared with materials requirements planning. It assumes that future consumption will follow the same patterns as past consumption. In addition, it does not take into account dependencies between different materials. For example, the need for wheels depends on the need to produce bicycles. In this case, consumption-based planning is not appropriate. This is because the need for wheels is not based on its past consumption; rather, it is based on the need to make bicycles. Companies generally reserve consumption-based planning for materials of low value or significance, such as nuts and bolts.

GBI uses consumption-based planning for materials classified as accessories, such as bike helmets (OHMT1000). Figure 8-4 illustrates the planning scenario for procuring helmets. In this example the replenishment lead time is 3 days, and the safety stock is 50 units. The consumption line, calculated from historical sales data, projects that inventory will fall to the safety stock level on day 7 (point A). To ensure that the helmets will arrive by that date, GBI must initiate the purchasing process on day 4 (7 minus the replenishment lead time), the reorder date. The reorder point is calculated by drawing a line from the reorder date to the consumption line (to point B) and then a horizontal line to the vertical axis (to point C). Thus, GBI must place an order for helmets when 125 or fewer helmets are left in stock.

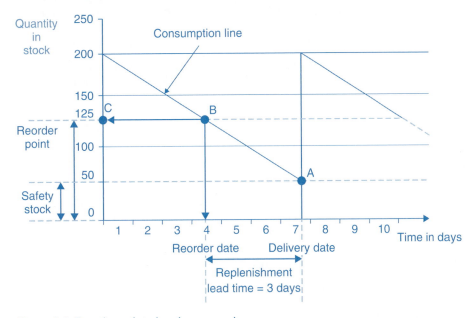

Figure 8-4: Reorder point planning example

In contrast to consumption-based planning, the MRP technique calculates requirements for a material based on its dependence on other materials. To understand the specifics of the MRP technique, we must first consider two related concepts—dependent and independent requirements. The terms *dependent* and *independent* refer to the source of the requirements. A material has a **dependent requirement** if its requirement is dependent on the requirements for another material. For example, a bicycle is made of several components such as wheel assemblies and a seat. The requirement for wheel assemblies and seats is dependent on the requirement for bicycles. Therefore, wheel assemblies and seats have a dependent requirement. Typically, semifinished goods (e.g., wheel assemblies) and raw materials (e.g., seats) have dependent requirements because they are used to make other materials (finished goods or other semifinished goods). In contrast, the requirement for bicycles, a finished good, is not dependent on any other material. Instead, it is based on customer demand. Thus, bicycles, and finished goods in general, have **independent requirements.**

The MRP technique is used to calculate and plan requirements for materials at all levels of the BOM. This procedure, known as *exploding* the BOM, is illustrated in Figure 8-5. The input to MRP is the independent requirement for the finished goods, which is calculated by the sales and operations planning step of the material planning process. We will examine this technique in greater detail in the process section of this chapter. For now, it is sufficient to understand that the independent requirements are determined based on actual and forecasted sales. These calculated requirements are called **planned independent requirements (PIRs)**. In contrast, actual sales orders are also known as **customer independent requirements (CIRs)**, or simply customer requirements. PIRs drive the requirements calculations for each successive level in the BOM. Going further, the requirements for each level are dependent on the requirement for higher-level materials. For example, if the PIR for bicycles is 100 and each bicycle uses 2 wheel assemblies and 1 seat, then the MRP calculation will create dependent requirements of 200 wheel assemblies and 100 seats.

A variation to MRP is **master production scheduling (MPS)**, which utilizes a process similar to MRP but focuses exclusively on the requirements

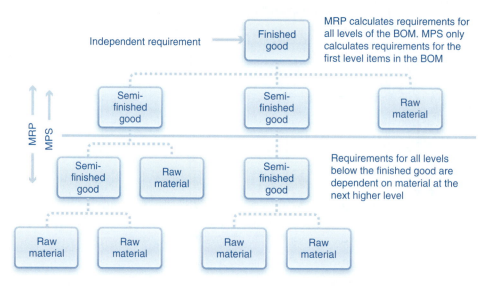

Figure 8-5: MRP vs. MPS

for the top-level items in the BOM. Companies use MPS for the most critical finished goods to ensure that resources and capacity are available for these materials before they plan for other materials. MPS is an optional step in the planning process and is usually followed by MRP, which completes the planning process for the remaining materials.

Lot Size Key

A lot size is the quantity of material that is specified in the procurement proposals generated by the material planning process. The lot size key specifies the procedure that is used to determine the lot size. A variety of procedures for determining lot size are available. The most basic procedures are *static lot-sizing* procedures, which specify a fixed quantity based on either a predetermined value (*fixed lot size*) or the exact quantity required (*lot-for-lot*). For example, when using the lot-for-lot procedure, if the calculated requirement for seats is 100, then the proposed order quantity is also 100. *Period lot-sizing* procedures combine the requirements from multiple time periods, such as days or weeks, into one lot. *Optimum lot-sizing* procedures take into account the costs of ordering and storing materials using techniques such as the *economic order quantity* and *economic production quantity* calculations. For example, if the calculated requirement for seats is 100, the proposed order quantity may be 500 if it is more economical to purchase the seats in larger quantities. GBI uses the lot-for-lot procedure to determine the lot size for all of its materials.

Scheduling Times

One task that must be performed by the planning process is to estimate the time needed to procure the necessary materials. This calculation is based on estimates of the time required to complete the various tasks that are included in the material master and the product routing. Common time estimates include:

- *In-house production time*, which is the time needed to produce the material in house.

- *Planned delivery time*, which is the time needed to obtain the material if it is externally procured.

- *GR (goods receipt) processing time*, which is the amount of time required to place the received materials in storage so that they are ready for use.

In-house production time and the GR processing time are used to determine procurement time for internally procured materials. For externally procured materials, the planned delivery time and the GR processing time are used.

In-house production time is further divided into three time elements: setup, processing, and interoperation. Recall the discussion of some of these elements from Chapter 6.

- *Setup time* is the time required to set up the work centers used in production.

- *Processing time* is the time required to complete operations in the work centers.

- *Interoperation time* is the time required to move materials from one work center to another.

Times can be lot size independent or lot size dependent. *Lot size independent* times remain the same regardless of the amount of material being procured. In contrast, *lot size dependent* times vary according to the lot size or quantity. Examples of lot size independent times are setup time, in-house production time, and the GR processing time. In contrast, processing time is typically lot size dependent.

The lot size independent in-house production time is an estimate of the total time required for production including the setup, processing, and interoperation times. Although the processing time normally depends on the number of units being produced, the lot size independent in-house production time is used when (1) the lot size is fixed, so that processing time is constant, or (2) the processing time is very short compared to the setup and interoperation times. When the processing time is large in comparison to the setup and interoperation times or when the quantity of material to be produced varies, a lot size dependent in-house production time is calculated using the three time elements (setup, processing, and interoperation).

Because companies utilize these various time estimates in the planning process to schedule procurement and production, inaccurate values will cause significant problems. Inaccurate schedules require manual intervention, and, if users find they can't trust the data in the system, they will learn to ignore them and create their own workarounds. Thus, it is imperative that an organization carefully analyze and monitor its processes for determining scheduling times.

Planning Time Fence

The material planning process often has to adjust the quantities and schedules it creates for procurement proposals. For example, the consumption of a raw material may be unexpectedly high because of higher-than-expected demand. In such cases the planning process may increase the quantities of existing planned procurements, or it may schedule them so the materials arrive earlier. Changes in procurement proposals far into the future normally are not a major concern, but changes to proposals in the near future can cause problems because other departments or processes in the organization may have incorporated the original proposals into their planning. For this reason, companies establish a period of time in which the ERP system is not allowed to automatically change procurement proposals. This time period is known as the planning time fence. If the planning time fence is 30 days, for example, then no purchase requisition that is dated 30 days or less from the current date can be changed automatically by the system. If changes are necessary, they must be made manually.

BOM Selection Method

Recall from Chapter 6 that a bill of materials (BOM) identifies the materials needed to produce a finished good. In some cases a single material can have multiple BOMs. For example, a company might use different BOMs for different plants or different lot sizes. Companies also generate multiple BOMs when they update their products. For example, if GBI plans to upgrade the touring bike model with a new tire beginning January 1, then it must create a new BOM for the bike in advance with a beginning validity date of January 1. At the same time, it must set the ending validity date of the current BOM to December 31.

Because several BOMs can exist for the same material, the ERP system must have a method to determine which BOM to use. The **BOM selection method** in the material master identifies the criteria the system should use to select the BOM. Examples of criteria are lot size and validity date.

Availability Check Group

The **availability check group** defines the strategy the system uses to determine whether a quantity of material will be available on a specific date. The most common method, called *available-to-promise* (ATP), considers a broad range of elements representing both the supply of and demands for the material. Supply elements include existing inventory, purchase requisitions, purchase orders, and production orders. Demand elements include material reservations, safety stock, and sales orders. The availability check group informs the system which supply and demand elements to take into account when determining availability. Because material availability is a concern in many parts of an organization, the availability check group is used by multiple processes. For example, the fulfillment process uses it to ensure that materials can be delivered to a customer on the requested delivery date, and the production process uses it to ensure that materials are available before production orders are released.

Strategy Group

Strategy group specifies the high-level planning strategy used in production. Production planning strategies fall into three broad categories: *make-to-stock*, *make-to-order*, and *assemble-to-order*. We introduced the first two strategies in Chapter 6, in the context of the production process. Business Processes in Practice 6-2 in that chapter presents examples of how Dell and Apple use make-to-order and make-to-stock strategies, respectively. In this section, we will extend the discussion of these planning strategies.

In the **make-to-stock (MTS)** strategy customer orders are fulfilled from an existing inventory of finished goods. The MTS strategy is usually employed by firms that produce a high volume of identical products. This strategy reduces the time required to fill customer orders because there is no need to wait until the materials are produced. In addition, it enables the company to produce goods at a constant rate and in optimum lot sizes, regardless of customer demand. In SAP ERP the simplest make-to-stock strategy is *net requirements planning* (**strategy 10**), in which the system generates procurement proposals based on calculated PIRs without regard to CIRs.

A common variation to the make-to-stock strategy is *planning with final assembly* (**strategy 40**). This strategy is also based on PIRs. Unlike the pure MTS strategy, however, this approach takes into account actual sales orders through a procedure called *consumption*. We discuss consumption modes in the next section.

In contrast to MTS, in **a make-to-order (MTO)** strategy the production of the finished goods and any needed semi-finished goods is triggered by a sales order. The company does not maintain an inventory of these materials. MTO is also referred to as *sales-order-based production*. In contrast to MTS, MTO is used when each product is unique. For example, if GBI introduced a line of high-end racing bikes designed specifically for individual riders, it would use MTO for these products. The bikes would not be produced until the order was received.

A variation of the MTO strategy is assemble-to-order (ATO), in which an inventory of components (semifinished goods) needed to make the finished good is procured or produced to stock. The production of the finished goods is triggered by a sales order and therefore uses an MTO strategy. ATO is commonly employed in an environment in which there are a large number of possible configurations of end items. For example, different computer configurations are possible using a number of different options for monitors, storage devices, and memory. A sales order for the finished product can usually be filled quickly because only the final assembly has to be executed. (The components are already in stock.) In SAP ERP, the ATO strategy is also referred to as *planning without final assembly* (strategy 50) or *subassembly planning*. Variations of both the pure MTO and MTS strategies offer more flexibility in meeting customer requirements.

Consumption Mode

A key point that emerges from the discussion of strategy groups is that the manner in which PIRs (planned independent requirements) and CIRs (actual customer orders) interact is determined by the planning strategy. On the one hand, in a MTS strategy such as net requirements planning, CIRs and PIRs are independent of each other, and procurement proposals generated by the material planning process are based *only* on PIRs. CIRs are fulfilled entirely from existing stock. On the other hand, under the planning with final assembly approach, procurement proposals take into account both PIRs and CIRs. However, procurement proposals are not created by simply adding the PIR and CIR quantities. This is because the PIRs are created in anticipation of customer orders, and CIRs are expected to consume the PIRs. In other words, sales orders are expected to be filled from the planned requirements. When a CIR consumes PIRs, it reduces the quantity of PIRs by the quantity of the CIR. This process is called *consumption*.

Table 8-1 illustrates consumption under the planning with final assembly strategy. In Example 1 a PIR of 50 exists when a CIR of 60 is created. Because the CIR is greater than the PIR, the entire PIR is consumed. Therefore, after consumption the PIR quantity is zero. The planning process will create a procurement proposal for the CIR quantity of 60 units. In Example 2 a PIR of 50 exists when a CIR of 40 is created. After consumption, 10 of the original 50 in the PIR remain. The planning process will create two procurement proposals: one for the PIR quantity of 10 units and one for the CIR quantity of 40 units.

	Before Consumption		After Consumption	
	PIR	CIR	PIR	CIR
Example 1	50	60	0	60
Example 2	50	40	10	40

Table 8-1: Consumption example

Thus, when PIRs are not consumed by CIRs (because there are not enough customer orders), the procurement proposals will result in an increase in the inventory of the material. In the opposite situation, when CIRs exceed available PIRs within the consumption period—that is, customer orders exceed the planned requirements—then the planning process generates additional procurement proposals to cover the difference.

The manner in which CIRs consume PIRs is determined by the *consumption mode*. Two commonly used consumption modes are *forward consumption* and *backward consumption*. A combination of forward and backward consumption is also possible. These alternatives are diagrammed in Figure 8-6. The top part of the figure illustrates backward consumption (mode 1); the middle part, forward consumption (mode 3); and the bottom part, backward and forward consumption (modes 2 and 4). In these illustrations the horizontal axis is the time line, the area above the time line represents the planned independent requirements, and the area below the time line indicates the customer requirements. The plan (PIR) is to produce or procure 40 bikes in each time period. In each case the company must fill a customer requirement of 60 bikes.

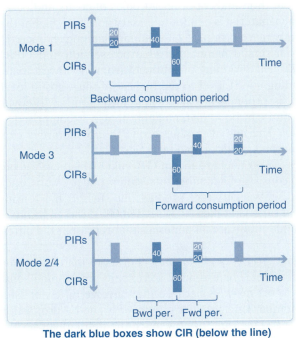

The dark blue boxes show CIR (below the line) and consumption of PIR (above the line). Light blue boxes are PIR.

Figure 8-6: Consumption modes

In *backward consumption*, customer requirements consume PIRs that are dated *prior to* the time of the customer requirements. Thus, to meet the CIR of 60 bikes, the immediately preceding PIR is consumed. Because this quantity (40) is not sufficient to satisfy the CIR (60), 20 bikes from the next preceding PIR are consumed. In *forward consumption*, customer requirements consume PIRs that occur *after* the date of the CIR. Thus, to meet the requirement of 60 bikes, the PIRs immediately *following* the CIR are consumed as needed—40 bikes from the first PIR and 20 from the next. Modes 2 and 4 use both forward and backward consumption. Mode 2 uses backward consumption first followed by forward consumption; mode 4 uses the reverse.

The *consumption period* indicates the number of days, before or after, from the CIR that PIRs can be consumed. PIRs outside the consumption period cannot be consumed by the CIR. The assumption is that, because of scheduling and capacity considerations, only PIRs in the same general timeframe as the sales order should be consumed by the CIR.

Demo 8.1: Review MRP and scheduling views for a material

PRODUCT GROUPS

When a company manufactures or sells many similar products, such as a furniture company with tens of thousands of different types of chairs and desks, planning separately for each material is neither necessary nor efficient. For this reason, companies generally place products with similar planning characteristics, such as similar types or similar manufacturing processes, into a **product group** or a *product family*. The grouping of products, from the lowest material (finished good or trading good) level to the highest product group level, is called *aggregation*. That is, products are aggregated into groups. Moreover, a higher-level product group can be *nested*, meaning that it is comprised of lower-level product groups. The lowest product group in *any* hierarchy consists of materials, either finished goods or trading goods.

Figure 8-7 illustrates the product groups for GBI bikes. The bicycle product group (PG-BIKE000) consists of a number of nested product groups. Each one of these groups represents a different product line such as the touring bikes (PG-TOUR000) and off-road bikes (PG-ORBK0000). The eight boxes at the bottom level of the hierarchy are all materials that represent the different bicycle models.

Materials and product groups can be members of more than one group for different planning scenarios. For example, a company might plan separately for domestic and export markets because they involve different sales patterns. Further, each member of a product group is assigned a proportion factor. A *proportion factor* is a measure of how much the item influences the product group. For example, in Figure 8-7, the product group for off-road bikes includes the Men's bikes and Women's bikes, with proportion factors of 65% and 35%, respectively. Thus, Men's bikes are more influential than Women's bikes in planning for the off-road bike group. Proportion factors are used in the material planning process to derive detailed plans from high-level forecasts. Forecasts and plans for the higher level product groups are *disaggregated* into plans for lower levels using the proportion factors. For example, if the plan calls for 1,000 off-road bikes, then the system automatically translates this information into a plan for 650 Men's and 350 Women's bikes. We address aggregation and disaggregation in greater detail in the process section of this chapter. Business Processes in Practice 8-2 describes product groups at Apple Inc.

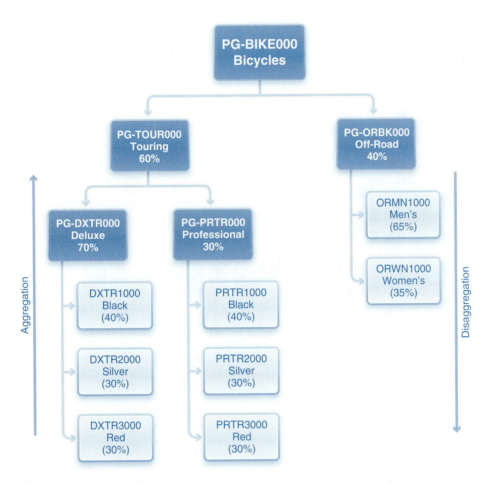

Figure 8-7: GBI product groups

Business Processes in Practice 8.2: Product Groups at Apple, Inc.

Apple provides an excellent example of how companies use product groups for material planning purposes. (Figure 8–8). Apple's product portfolio consists of several hardware, software, and service products, such as Macs, iPods, iPhones, iPads, and peripherals. If we look only at Apple's standard make-to-stock hardware products, we can begin to appreciate the complexity of the company's material planning process. Apple assigns each product to a product group, for example, Macs, iPads, and Peripherals and Accessories. Nested within the Macs product group are several product subgroups, for example, Desktops, Portables, and Servers. In turn, the product subgroups are subdivided into individual finished goods. Thus, for example, the product subgroup Portables is comprised of the MacBook, MacBook Pro, and MacBook Air. Significantly, many products within the same product group are manufactured from similar raw materials. For example, most of the products in the product groups for iPad, iPhone, and iPod contain the same processors and flash memory chips. However, only the iPod Touch and the iPhone share the same size touch screens. Thus, aggregation and disaggregation across product groups become increasingly complex when companies need to plan for shared raw material dependencies. For this reason, companies must employ accurate demand forecasting to ensure that material planning is executed properly.

Note: Apple changes its product offerings with great frequency. Figure 8-8 depicts the Apple mid-2010 product offering. Source: Apple company reports.

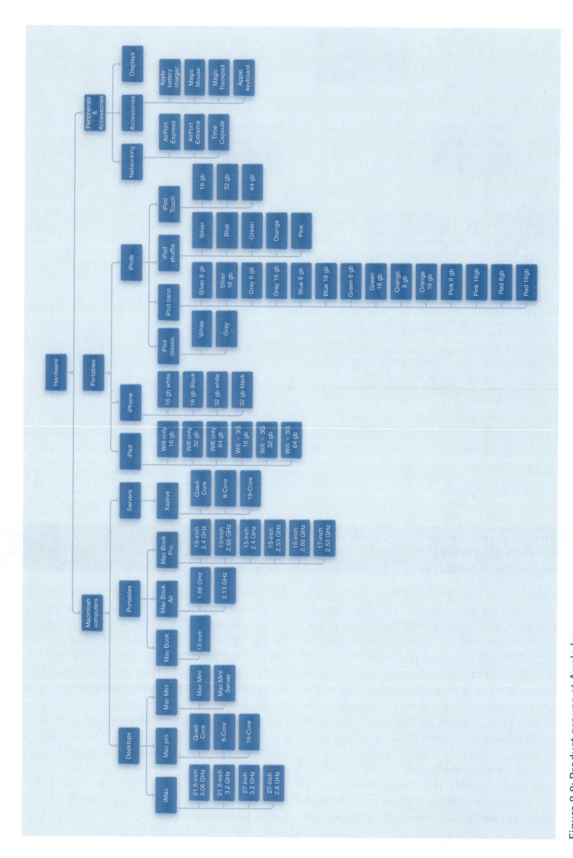

Figure 8-8: Product groups at Apple Inc

Demo 8.2: Review GBI product groups

■ PROCESS

In this section we will discuss the material planning process, which is presented in Figure 8-9. The first step in the process is often **sales and operations planning (SOP)**. SOP is a forecasting and planning tool that businesses use to enter or generate a sales forecast, specify inventory requirements, and then generate an operations plan. SOP typically involves finished goods. Therefore, the operations plan is, in effect, a production plan for these materials. The plan generated by SOP is called a *rough-cut plan* because the planning is usually at a highly aggregated level and is not very precise.

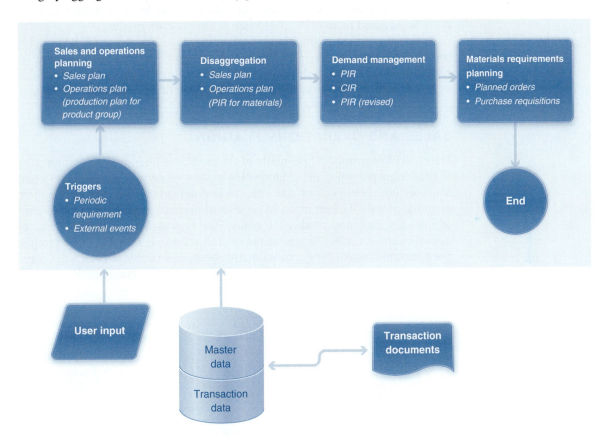

Figure 8-9: The material planning process

Whether SOP is required depends on the production planning strategy used for the material. MTO production does not require a production plan because production is triggered by sales orders. Therefore, SOP is not necessary. In contrast, MTS production requires a production plan based on a sales forecast because sales orders are filled from materials already in inventory. Consequently SOP is relevant for materials with the MTS strategy. For variations of MTO such as ATO, in which semifinished materials are produced ahead of time and placed in inventory, production plans must be created for the semifinished materials.

SOP creates a production plan at the product group level. In turn, these requirements must be translated into PIRs for the individual materials in the product group. This task is accomplished in the *disaggregation* step. The PIRs for the individual materials are then transferred to *demand management*, where they are revised and refined based on the specific planning strategies we discussed earlier. The final step, *MRP*, creates specific procurement proposals to ensure that sufficient materials will be available to cover each requirement.

The sales and operation step requires input from many parts of an organization and is often performed by the planning or forecasting group. After the production plan is transferred to demand management, it becomes the responsibility of the MRP controller. The *MRP controller* is the person or persons in an organization responsible for creating procurement proposals and monitoring material availability. All materials that are used in the planning process must be assigned to an MRP controller in the material master.

Our discussion of the material planning process will use GBI's bicycles product group (Figure 8-7) as an ongoing example. GBI initiates its material planning process when it develops its overall strategic plan. This plan includes expected sales for the bicycles product group (PG-BIKE000).

SALES AND OPERATIONS PLANNING

Figure 8-10 diagrams the elements of the sales and operations planning step. SOP is triggered when the organization wishes to revise its production plan. Most organizations perform this task at scheduled intervals depending on their planning process. For example, an organization may require quarterly reviews of sales forecasts and production plans. SOP may also be triggered by unexpected events such as changes in the overall economic outlook. For example, the financial crisis of 2008 caused many companies to revise their sales forecasts downward and reduce their production levels accordingly. SOP uses data from a variety of sources to produce a production plan.

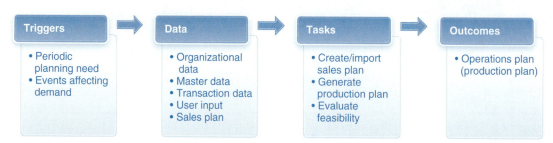

Triggers		Data		Tasks		Outcomes
• Periodic planning need • Events affecting demand		• Organizational data • Master data • Transaction data • User input • Sales plan		• Create/import sales plan • Generate production plan • Evaluate feasibility		• Operations plan (production plan)

Figure 8-10: Elements of the SOP step

SOP can generate several versions of a production plan based on different assumptions concerning the growth of the overall economy. Each plan incorporates different sales forecasts and desired inventory levels. The company then evaluates these plans to determine their feasibility in terms of production capacity. Generating multiple versions allows the organization to consider different planning scenarios. After evaluating the various plans, the company selects one scenario as the basis for further planning.

SOP can be either standard or flexible. With *standard planning* a company uses predefined planning models. These models are relatively simple, and they take into account total values for sales, production, and inventory levels for the entire organization. Therefore, standard planning can be employed only for highly aggregated planning. It is easy to use, however, and requires no preparation.

In contrast, with *flexible planning* a company uses tools to develop more complex planning models that contain far greater levels of detail. For example, an organization can create a model that breaks down sales to the distribution channel level and calculates production quantities for individual plants. However, flexible planning requires more-detailed data than does standard planning, and the desired planning models must first be created. Our discussion is limited to standard planning.

Data

Figure 8-11 illustrates the data utilized in the sales and operations step. The most critical data are a sales plan, existing inventory levels, and inventory requirements. Existing inventory levels can be transferred from inventory and warehouse management. Inventory requirements most frequently are determined based on economic and financial criteria such as storage costs, variations in expected customer demand, and production capacities. They can be calculated as a part of the overall strategic planning process.

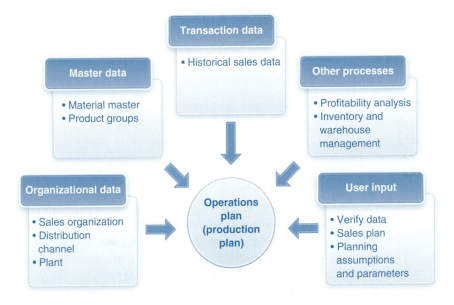

Figure 8-11: Data in the SOP step

Organizations execute planning for specific organizational levels and master data—for example, for specific product groups and specific plants.

Tasks

The tasks in the sales and operations planning step include creating the sales plan, specifying inventory requirements, and creating a production plan. The interface to complete the tasks in SOP is a simple-to-use spreadsheet-like tool called the *planning table*. Figure 8-12 illustrates a standard SOP planning table. The header area of the table indicates the product group and plant for which the plan is generated as well as the version number of the plan. (Recall that multiple versions of the same plan can be created for different planning scenarios.) The columns represent months by default, but users can specify other time periods. The table includes the following rows:

Product group	PG-BIKE000					
Plant	DL00					
Version	A00	Active version		Planning in multiple version possible		
	M01	M02	M03	M04	M05	
Sales	100	110	130	140	140	Forecasts can be transferred
Production	100	110	150	132	128	
Stock level			20	12		Production plan can be created sychronous to sales, according to target day's supply or target stock level
Target stock			20	12		
Day's supply			3	1		
Target day's supply						

Figure 8-12: Standard SOP planning table

- *Sales:* This row contains the sales plan.

- *Production:* This row contains the production plan, which is usually calculated by the system.

- *Stock level:* This row contains inventory levels, which are generated by the system when the production plan is calculated.

- *Target stock:* Desired stock (inventory) levels are entered in this row.

- *Day's supply:* Day's supply is the number of days the organization can expect to cover sales using only existing inventory. This number is calculated by dividing inventory by sales per workday in the period. The number of workdays is specified when the system is initially configured. This row is calculated by the system.

- *Target day's supply:* The desired day's supply is entered in this row.

The sales plan is entered first. Data for the sales plan can be obtained from a variety of sources:

- A sales plan based on desired levels of profitability can be imported from profitability analysis, which is one of the processes in management accounting.

- If the company anticipates that future sales will be the same as past sales, then it can transfer historical sales data from the sales information system (SIS), which we discussed in Chapter 5.

- Conversely, if the company expects future sales to differ from past sales but it believes it can predict them based on past sales, then it can create a forecast by inputting historical data from SIS into one of several forecasting models available in SOP.

- Employees can enter a sales plan manually based on either experience or a forecast from another program.

- A sales plan can be copied from the plan generated for another product group.

Regardless of which procedure the company uses, after it enters the sales plan the system generates a production plan based on one of the following options:

- *Synchronous to sales:* In this scenario, the system simply copies quantities from the sales plan row to the production plan row. Thus, the quantities in both rows are identical.

- *Target stock level:* In this scenario, the company specifies a desired stock level, and the system calculates the production quantities needed to meet the sales plan and achieve the target stock level.

- *Target day's supply:* This scenario is similar to the target stock level scenario. The difference is that the desired inventory levels are expressed in terms of day's supply instead of specific quantities. The target day's supply is specified by the user, and the system calculates the quantities in the production row required to achieve that target.

- *Stock level = 0:* In this scenario the desired stock level at the end of each period is zero. The system uses existing stock to cover sales until the stock level falls to zero. As long as there is any existing inventory, the company will not produce new material. When inventory reaches zero, the system calculates production quantities that will just cover sales quantities with no excess for inventory. Thus, the stock level row will be zero for every period.

Figure 8-13 illustrates a planning table for the bicycles product group for GBI's Dallas plant. The planning timeframe is 4 months. The planning scenario is one in which the system will calculate the needed production plan to meet the specified sales plan and the desired target stock levels. The top figure illustrates the planning table after the sales plan and target stock levels have been entered. The bottom table displays the results after the system has calculated the needed production plan. The production data are calculated by computing the total requirements (sales + target stock) and subtracting available stock (stock level from the previous month).

Figure 8-13 shows that the production plan for the bicycles product group for the 4 months is 1,100, 1,300, 900, and 850, respectively. Table 8-2 shows the calculation for the third month.

To calculate the day's supply, the system first determines the daily requirements by dividing the sales by the number of working days in the month. It then divides the target stock level by the daily requirements. The calculation for month 2 is shown in Table 8-3 (assuming 30 working days in month 2).

The target day's supply row in Figure 8-13 is empty because the values in this row would be entered by the user only if the method for calculating the production plan was based on the target day's supply.

	M01	M02	M03	M04
Sales	1000	1200	1000	900
Production				
Stock level				
Target stock	100	200	100	50
Day's supply				
Target day's supply				

	M01	M02	M03	M04
Sales	1000	1200	1000	900
Production	1100	1300	900	850
Stock level	100	200	100	50
Target stock	100	200	100	50
Day's supply	3	5	3	1
Target day's supply				

Figure 8-13: GBI SOP example

Sales		1,000 units
Target stock	+	100 units
Previous inventory	−	200 units
Production		900 units

Table 8-2: Production plan calculation example

$$\frac{\text{Target stock}}{\text{Daily requirements}} = \frac{200 \text{ units}}{(1{,}200 \text{ units} / 30 \text{ working days})} = 5 \text{ Day's supply}$$

Table 8-3: Day's supply calculation example

Outcomes

The outcome of SOP is one or more versions of the production plan. There are no financial implications and no material movements. Consequently, no FI, CO, or material documents are created.

Demo 8.3: Create an SOP for the bicycles product group

DISAGGREGATION

The SOP step creates sales and production plans at the product group level. After this step has been completed, the plans must be translated into plans for the finished goods in the product group hierarchy. This process step is called **disaggregation**. (We introduced disaggregation in our discussion of product groups.) The elements of the disaggregation step are diagrammed in Figure 8-14. Disaggregation is triggered when a new production plan is created. Organizational data (e.g., plant) and master data (e.g., product groups) from the production plan are used to calculate requirements for the materials in the product group. These requirements are then transferred to the demand management step for further planning.

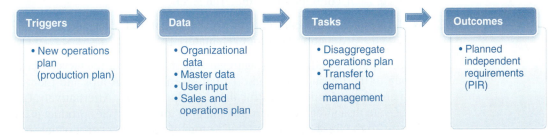

Triggers	Data	Tasks	Outcomes
• New operations plan (production plan)	• Organizational data • Master data • User input • Sales and operations plan	• Disaggregate operations plan • Transfer to demand management	• Planned independent requirements (PIR)

Figure 8-14: Elements of the disaggregation step

Data

The data used in the disaggregation step include product group data, the production plan from SOP, and user input (Figure 8-15). The system uses the proportion factors from the product group to compute the disaggregated values for each member of the product group. Recall that product group members are other product groups or, at the lowest level, materials. The user provides parameters that determine how the plan is disaggregated.

Tasks

The essential task in this step is to translate the plans generated in the SOP step for product groups into plans for the materials contained in those groups. Disaggregation can be completed for the entire product group hierarchy or for one or more levels of the hierarchy. Further, either the production plan or the sales plan can be disaggregated. Thus, a variety of options are available at this step.

- Disaggregate the production plan to one or more levels or down to the material level.

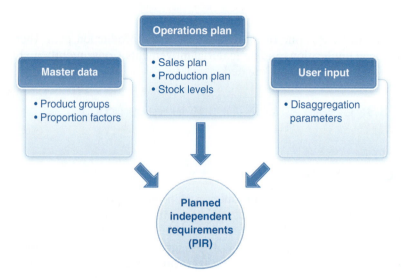

Figure 8-15: Data in the disaggregation step

- Disaggregate the sales plan down to the next level in the product group. The disaggregated plan is the sales plan for the next level and is used to calculate a production plan, as explained in the SOP step. Then, continue to the material level.

- Disaggregate the sales plan down to the material level, and calculate the production plan for each material.

One option for GBI is to disaggregate the sales plan for the bicycles product group to the touring bike and off-road bike product groups and then use SOP to create production plans for these product groups. Alternatively, GBI can choose to disaggregate the production plan for the bicycles product group all the way to the finished goods at the bottom of the product group hierarchy.

In our example GBI selects the second option. Recall from the example in the SOP step that the production plan for the first month is 1,100 units for the bicycles product group. The disaggregation step translates this value throughout the product group hierarchy, as illustrated in Figure 8-16.

The 1,100 bicycles are translated into 660 touring bikes and 440 off-road bikes using the proportion factors of 60% and 40%, respectively. The 660 touring bikes are further translated into 462 deluxe touring bikes and 198 professional touring bikes (70% and 30%). Finally, the deluxe touring bikes are translated into 184 black deluxe touring bikes and 139 each of the silver and red deluxe touring bikes. These production plan values are the PIRs for the three deluxe touring bikes for the first month. GBI completes a similar disaggregation for all members of the product group hierarchy and for all months.

Outcomes

The outcome of the disaggregation step is to calculate the PIRs for each planning period (e.g., week or month). These requirements are then transferred to demand management, as illustrated in Figure 8-17. The figure indicates that the plan for the product group deluxe touring bikes is disaggregated to the three materials in the group as material-plant specific PIRs. These data are then transferred to demand management.

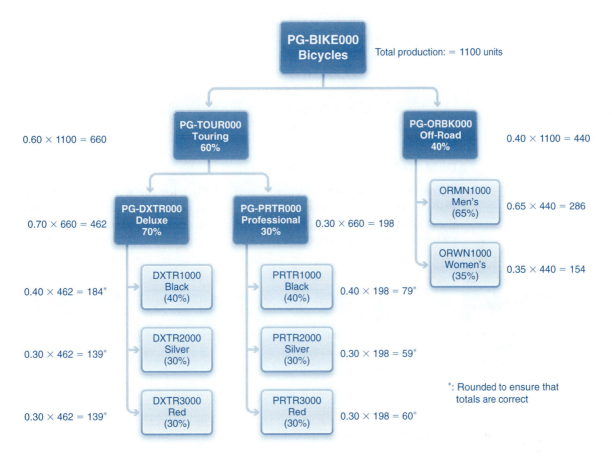

Figure 8-16: GBI disaggregation example

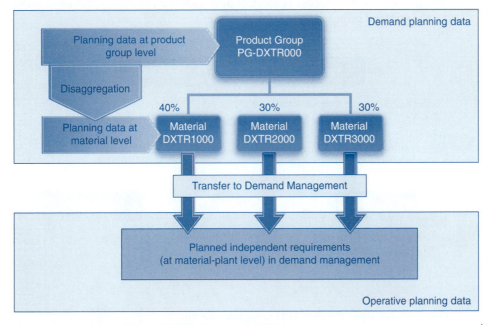

Figure 8-17: Transfer PIRs to demand management

As in the SOP step, no FI, CO, or material documents are created because disaggregation has no financial consequences and does not involve any material movements.

Demo 8.4: Disaggregate production plan and transfer to demand management

DEMAND MANAGEMENT

Demand management calculates revised PIRs for the materials using the PIRs from SOP (after disaggregation), actual customer orders (CIRs) from the fulfillment process, and data from the material master regarding planning strategies. Figure 8-18 illustrates the specific elements of the demand management step.

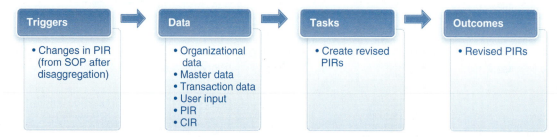

Figure 8-18: Elements of the demand management step

Data

Demand management (Figure 8-19) uses requirements data from SOP (PIRs) and the fulfillment process (CIRs). It also uses the planning strategy defined by the strategy group in the material master.

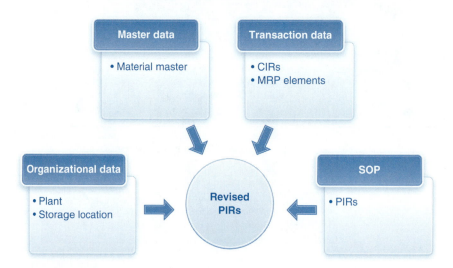

Figure 8-19: Data in the demand management step

Tasks

The primary task in demand management is to create revised PIRs for materials. Which procedure a company uses to calculate these requirements depends on the production planning strategy defined by the strategy group in the material master. As previously discussed, the production planning strategy determines whether production is triggered by planned independent requirements (MTS) or customer requirements (MTO), or if the interaction of these two types of requirements affects the planning process through consumption.

The demand management step is carried out automatically by the ERP system. However, the MRP controller monitors the results using a variety of reports and makes adjustments as needed. For example, if the process uses a planning strategy with consumption, then scheduling changes may be required when new customer requirements are created. With an MTO planning strategy, the MRP controller must monitor the inventories of subassemblies carefully because customer orders appear at unpredictable intervals.

Outcomes

The outcomes from demand management are PIRs for each material included in planning. These PIRs represent requirements for the materials for specific quantities and specific dates. They are then used by the MRP step. There are no financial implications and no material movements associated with demand management, so no FI, CO, or material documents are created.

MATERIALS REQUIREMENTS PLANNING

The final step in the material planning process is MRP, which calculates the net requirements for materials and creates procurement proposals—to make or buy the necessary materials—that ensure that the organization will have sufficient material available to cover its requirements. Figure 8-20 illustrates the elements of the MRP step.

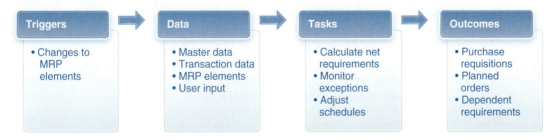

Figure 8-20: Elements of the MRP step

Recall that SOP generates plans at the product group level, and demand management generates plans at the material level. In contrast, MRP generates plans for materials as well as for the components and raw materials that are used to produce a material. That is, it plans for all levels of the BOM.

A variety of activities can affect material availability in the different processes as illustrated in the following list:

- Procurement: purchase requisitions, purchase orders, and goods receipts

- Fulfillment: sales orders, deliveries, and goods issues

- Production: planned orders, production orders, material reservations, and goods receipts and issues

These activities are called **MRP elements**, and they are used in the MRP step to calculate net requirements and to generate procurement proposals. Net requirements utilize all of the relevant MRP elements to calculate the quantities in the procurement proposals. We explain the net requirement calculation later in this section.

The MRP step can be executed manually. However, because numerous activities in other processes affect MRP, the planning situation is constantly changing. Therefore, companies frequently configure their ERP system to periodically execute the MRP step automatically. The MRP controller is typically responsible for monitoring the results of the planning process via a variety of reports that we discuss later in this chapter. He or she must then take appropriate actions to trigger necessary procedures. For example, planned orders must be converted to production orders or purchase requisitions. Production orders must be released so that production can begin. Planned orders might have to be rescheduled to resolve problems relating to scheduling or capacity. As you can imagine, in plants that use hundreds or even thousands of materials, the MRP controller can be very busy.

MRP can be executed for one plant, for multiple plants, or within MRP areas. An *MRP area* can include an entire plant or specific storage locations within a plant. Executing MRP for individual MRP areas enables a company to plan for one group of materials within a plant independent of other groups. For example, the company can plan for low-value materials separately from high-value ones.

Master production scheduling (MPS) is a specialized form of MRP that organizations use to plan for highly profitable materials or for materials that use critical resources. Materials planned by MPS are typically the finished goods at the top level of the BOM hierarchy. They are flagged as *master schedule items*, and they have priority for resources such as capacity and transportation. After planning the master schedule items, MPS creates dependent requirements for the components of those items. However, it does not plan them or any materials below them. After MPS is finished, MRP is used to plan the remaining materials. In many cases, only MRP is used.

Data

The data in the MRP step are illustrated in Figure 8-21. Master data used in the MRP step include material master, material BOM and—optionally—the routing. Material BOMs are used to determine dependent requirements. Recall that when multiple BOMs exist for a material, the method for determining which BOM will be used is defined in the material master. Normally, MRP uses the scheduling times in the material master to perform scheduling and to determine the order start date and the order finish date. These dates indicate

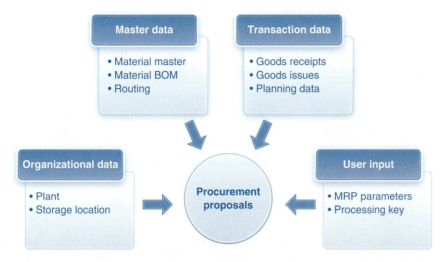

Figure 8-21: Data in the MRP step

when production must begin and when it will end. However, MRP cannot determine the details for individual production operations using times in the material master. If more detailed scheduling that includes operations-level data is required, MRP uses scheduling data in the product routing. The routing contains the operations and times required for production, so MRP can schedule each individual operation in detail. This type of scheduling, called *lead time scheduling*, is not normally performed until the planned order is converted into a production order.

Tasks

Figure 8-22 illustrates the tasks in the MRP step. These steps are performed automatically by MRP.

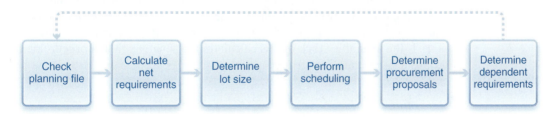

Figure 8-22: MRP procedure

Check Planning File

The first task in MRP is to determine which materials must be planned. Any change to an MRP-relevant material generates an entry in the *planning file*. Examples of relevant changes are changes to the scheduling times in the material master and changes to MRP elements such as inventory levels, purchase requisitions, and purchase orders. The materials in the planning file are coded so that finished goods are planned first, followed by components in the BOM for the finished goods, and so forth. Individual raw materials at the bottom of a BOM hierarchy are planned last.

Calculate Net Requirements

The next step is to determine whether there is a need to procure the material. This step is accomplished by performing a *net requirements calculation*, which takes into account all of the relevant MRP elements to determine whether a shortage of materials exists. If more materials are needed, then procurement proposals are generated to meet the shortfall.

The trigger for this calculation and the choice of the calculation method depends on the MRP type specified in the material master. If the MRP type is consumption-based planning, then the net requirements calculation determines the available stock according to the following formula:

$$\textbf{\textit{Available stock = Plant stock + Receipts}}$$

Receipts result from purchase orders, firmed purchase requisitions, firmed planned orders, and production orders. A purchase requisition or planned order is *firmed* if it is within the planning time fence. If available stock falls below the reorder point, then the material must be procured. Other consumption-based planning methods use similar calculations. Notice that neither independent nor dependent requirements are relevant for these materials.

If the MRP type is MRP or MPS, the net requirements calculation is triggered when an independent or dependent requirement exists. For each requirement, MRP performs the net requirements calculation to determine whether sufficient material exists to meet the requirement. The calculation is as follows:

$$\textbf{\textit{Available stock = Plant stock − Safety stock + Receipts − Issues}}$$

The calculation takes into account inventory by summing current plant stock and subtracting the safety stock. The system also takes into account all goods receipts and issues. Goods receipts result from purchase orders, firmed purchase requisitions, firmed planned orders, and production orders. Goods issues are the result of customer requirements, PIRs, and material reservations. If the available stock in this calculation is negative, then a procurement proposal is generated.

Determine Lot Size

If a procurement proposal is required, the system uses the lot size procedure to determine how much material to procure. The lot size procedure is defined by the lot size key in the material master.

Perform Scheduling

After MRP determines the lot size, it performs scheduling to determine whether the material can be acquired by the required date. MRP can utilize two types of scheduling: *backward scheduling* and *forward scheduling*. The system initially uses backward scheduling and employs forward scheduling only if backward scheduling is unsuccessful. Backward scheduling is illustrated in Figure 8-23.

Figure 8-23: Backward scheduling

In backward scheduling, the system starts at the requirement date and subtracts the procurement time to determine the date when the procurement process must begin. The times used are the scheduling times defined in the material master, depending on the procurement type. If the procurement type in the material is in house, then the *in-house production time* and *goods receipt times* are used. In contrast, if the procurement type is external, then the *purchasing department processing time*, *planned delivery time,* and *goods receipt times* are used. Unlike the other times, the purchasing department processing time is not included in the material master because it is not normally material dependent. These data are defined elsewhere in the system.

Ultimately, MRP will schedule all procurement proposals until it has scheduled the raw materials at the lowest level of the BOM. If the earliest start date falls prior to the current date, then the system will perform forward scheduling. Essentially, it shifts the material with the earliest start date to the first available future date and then schedules all of the other materials from that date working forward and using the same scheduling times. If the resulting schedule in not acceptable, then the MRP controller can manually adjust the schedule.

Determine Procurement Proposals

After the system has completed scheduling, the next step is to determine the type of procurement proposal to generate. Figure 8-24 illustrates the possibilities. For materials with the procurement type of in-house, MRP always generates planned orders. Planned orders must be converted to production orders by the MRP controller. This action triggers the production process described in Chapter 6.

For procuring materials externally there are three options. Which option is selected depends on the parameters defined in the MRP step. The first option is for the system to create purchase requisitions. The second is for the system to create planned orders, which are then converted manually to purchase requisitions. The advantage of creating planned orders is that it affords the MRP controller greater control over the planning process. When

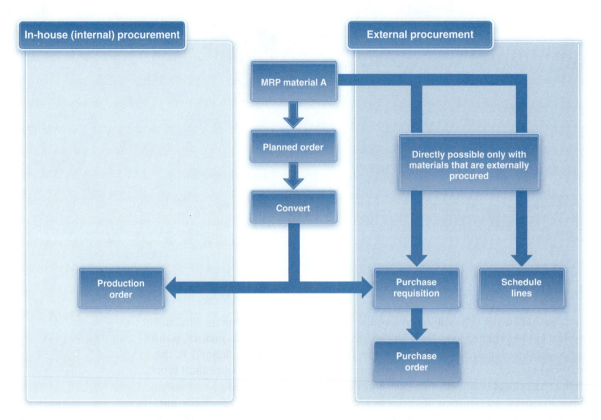

Figure 8-24: Procurement proposals

the system produces a purchase requisition, the purchasing department is responsible for acting on it to create a purchase order, and the MRP controller cannot modify the requisition. In contrast, when the system generates a planned order, then the MRP controller must make certain that it is converted into a purchase requisition in time for the purchasing department to process it and for the supplier to provide the materials by the scheduled date. A variation of this option is to create purchase requisitions in the opening period and then planned orders beyond the opening period. The *opening period* is the time during which the MRP controller can convert planned orders into production orders or requisitions. It is added in the scheduling process to give the MRP controller some flexibility on the exact date that planned orders are converted. The length of time of the opening period is defined in the system. This strategy expedites the procurement process in the near term while providing scheduling flexibility in the long term.

The last option is to create *schedule lines*. This option is relevant if the organization uses scheduling agreements. Recall from Chapter 5 that scheduling agreements are a type of contract in which the vendor agrees to deliver materials according to a specific schedule. The schedule line created by MRP is similar to the schedule lines in a sales order in that they both specify that a certain quantity of material will be delivered on a certain date. One major difference, however, is that the schedule lines generated during fulfillment indicate the customer's delivery requirements. In contrast, the schedule lines created by MRP identify the company's requirements to its vendor. Because deliveries follow predetermined schedules, the MRP controller cannot reschedule them.

Determine Dependent Requirements

For materials produced in-house, MRP generates dependent requirements for the components that are included in the material's BOM by exploding the BOM or calculating requirements for successive levels of the BOM. (Recall that we discussed BOM explosion earlier in this chapter.) Figure 8-25 illustrates options for the BOM explosion.

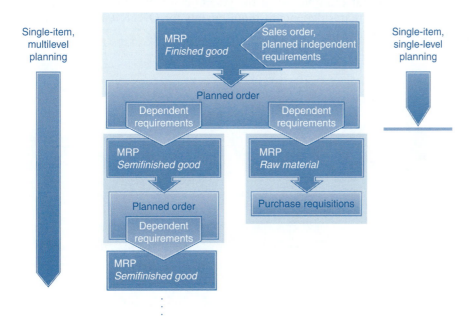

Figure 8-25: BOM explosion

If the company elects to use single-level MRP, then the process terminates after this initial step. If it selects the multilevel approach, then MRP performs the calculations for all levels. If any of the components that have dependent requirements are assemblies—that is, if they have their own BOMs—then MRP creates dependent requirements for the components in their BOMs. The process continues until the system has exploded all BOMs down to the level of individual raw materials.

After the planning is completed for all selected levels of the BOM for a material, MRP returns to the planning file and repeats the process for the next material that requires planning. Note that the actions MRP takes, such as creating dependent requirements, can also make entries in the planning file, which will cause further processing. The process continues until there are no more materials left to plan.

In our GBI example, the system created PIRs for eight materials when the production plan for the bicycles product group was disaggregated and transferred to demand management. The materials, represented by the boxes at the bottom of the hierarchy in Figure 8-16, include six types of touring bikes and two types of off-road bikes. Because these materials are finished goods, the system will first execute the MRP steps for each of these materials and create dependent requirements for the components in their BOMs. Figure 8-26 displays the BOM for the off-road bike. When the system has completed the

MRP steps for this bike, it creates dependent requirements for each of the materials in the first row of its BOM. After the system has completed the MRP steps for all eight finished goods, it executes the MRP steps for materials with dependent requirements—that is, the first-level components of the finished goods such as the off-road aluminum wheel assembly (ORWA1000) in Figure 8-26. When the ERP system has completed the MRP steps, for the first-level components, it creates additional dependent requirements for *their* components. Thus, in our example, when the system completes the MRP steps for ORWA1000, it creates dependent requirements for ORTR1000, ORTB1000, and ORWH1000.

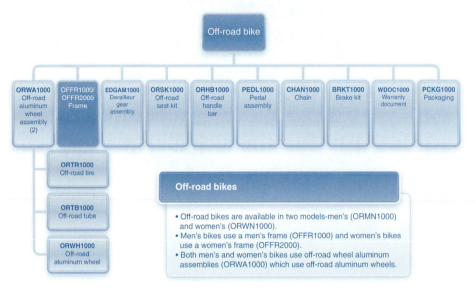

Figure 8-26: BOM for off-road bikes

A number of control parameters determine how the steps in the MRP procedure are completed. One of these control parameters, the **processing key**, determines how the materials in the planning file are processed. Three processing keys are available:

- **Regenerative planning (NEUPL):** Regenerative planning plans all MRP-relevant materials. All data from previous planning runs are discarded, and new data are generated. In this scenario every material is processed, not just the materials in the planning file. Therefore, when there are a large number of materials, this process can be very time consuming. For this reason it is rarely used.

- **Net change planning (NETCH):** In net change planning only the materials for which there has been an MRP-relevant change are planned. Recall from our discussion earlier in this chapter that an *MRP-relevant change* is any activity in the system that affects material availability, such as changes in the MRP elements for the material; and that these changes are identified by an entry in the planning file.

- **Net change planning in the planning horizon (NETPL).** Net change planning in the planning horizon plans only those materials for which there has been an MRP-relevant change within a specified period of time called the planning horizon. The *planning horizon* is defined during the configuration of the ERP system as a number of workdays. The planning horizon is usually specified to extend beyond the replenishment lead time for most materials.

The following additional control parameters determine the output of the MRP procedure:

- *Create purchase requisitions.* This parameter determines whether MRP (1) always creates purchase requisitions for externally procured materials, (2) creates planned orders, or (3) creates purchase requisitions only in the opening period and creates planned orders after the opening period.

- *Delivery Schedules.* Similar to the previous item, this parameter applies to scheduling agreements. The options are (1) not to create schedule lines, (2) to create them only during the opening period, or (3) to create them only within the planning horizon.

- *Create MRP list.* This parameter determines whether the system will create the MRP list, which we explain later in this chapter. Another option is to create the MRP list only for materials for which exception messages are generated. The ERP system generates an *exception message* when it encounters problems with scheduling. For example, if the system determines a start date that is in the past and can find no alternative, an exception message will be created.

- *Planning mode.* The planning mode parameter determines how previously created procurement proposals will be handled. The choices are to adjust the quantities and dates of existing proposals or to discard the proposals and create new ones.

- *Scheduling.* This parameter determines whether the system should calculate only basic dates using the scheduling times in the material master or whether it should perform lead time scheduling using the more detailed times in the routing.

Outcomes

The outcome of the MRP step is procurement proposals, usually in the form of purchase requisitions and planned orders, which trigger the procurement and production processes, respectively. This step has no financial implications, so no FI or CO documents are created. In addition, because no movement of materials has occurred, no material documents are created. Business Processes in Practice 8-3 describes planning at Steelcase, Inc.

Business Processes in Practice 8.3: Planning at Steelcase, Inc.

To ensure that the right materials are delivered to the manufacturing facilities at the right time in the right quantities, Steelcase must constantly monitor and manage the stock levels in the production warehouse and line storage while planning for constantly changing consumption levels from the manufacturing lines. Most Steelcase products are manufactured for a specific customer order (make-to-order), so there is a great deal of variability in what a plant must produce from one day to the next. Steelcase has also optimized each plant for the production of a specific type or set of products. For example, one plant might specialize in the production of office chairs while another focuses on manufacturing cubicles and filing cabinets. Although this strategy enables Steelcase to maximize its capital resources, it also introduces a great deal of complexity into the manufacturing planning process because customer orders must be split among multiple plants and then consolidated at a regional distribution center (RDC) for final customer delivery.

The standard lead time (from order placement until delivery) for a customer order is usually between 2 and 3 weeks. This schedule generates roughly 14 days of general visibility into manufacturing requirements from which raw material planning can be derived. However, each plant typically has visibility into what will be produced only 6 days before it needs to be shipped to the RDC. Thus, each manufacturing plant must usually procure, receive, and stage sufficient materials to complete the production of a customer order in less than a week. In addition, manufacturing plants can receive multiple deliveries of raw materials daily from suppliers. This arrangement reduces inventory carrying costs and optimizes the use of limited warehouse space. To manage this dynamic planning environment, Steelcase uses very advanced planning capabilities in its SAP system to constantly assess and plan material requirements. Every Steelcase manufacturing facility has around seven planning employees who constantly manage this process. Each manufacturing plant runs both MPS and MRP at least three times daily to assess the status and needs for all sales orders, materials, bills of materials, and inventory changes.

Source: Steelcase, Inc. Materials Planning Group.

Demo 8.5: Run MRP

● REPORTING

The reporting options in material planning are not as extensive as those in other functions. For example, there are no work lists that pertain to material planning. However, there are three very important tools that convey information about the planning situation: the *stock/requirements list*, the *MRP list*, and the *planning result report*.

STOCK/REQUIREMENTS LIST

The most important reporting tool in material planning is the stock/requirements list. We introduced this report in Chapter 6, where we explained that it displays all of the activities that could potentially impact material inventory. Earlier in this chapter we defined such activities as MRP elements. Thus, the stock/requirements list displays all MRP elements for a material. The MRP controller can use this report to determine whether any actions need to be taken. The data might indicate, for example, that planned orders should be converted to production orders. Figure 8-27 illustrates a stock requirements list for the black deluxe touring bike. The MRP elements visible in the Figure include planned independent requirements (**IndReq**), planned orders (**PldOrd**), and customer requirements (**CusOrd**).

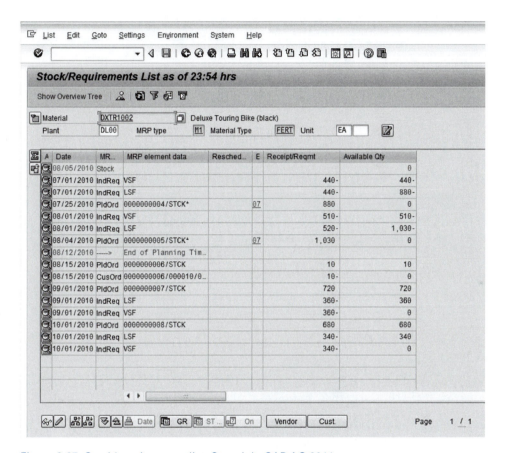

Figure 8-27: Stock/requirements list. Copyright SAP AG 2011

In addition to MRP elements, the stock/requirements list includes information such as existing stock level, safety stock, planning time fence, and exception messages. MRP generates **exception messages** when it encounters an issue such as a scheduling problem that it cannot resolve. The MRP controller is responsible for managing exception messages. Exception messages are indicated by a number in the column headed by the letter E (Exception). For example, in Figure 8-27 the 07 in the exception column indicates that planned orders 4 and 5 have at least one exception message. Figure 8-28, which displays the details of planned order number 4, shows that the order has two exception messages—number 06 and number 07. Different message numbers indicate different types of problems encountered by MRP. For example, message numbers 06 and 07 in Figure 8-28 indicate that the basic start and finish dates fall prior to the current date. In this case the MRP controller has to reschedule or cancel the planned order.

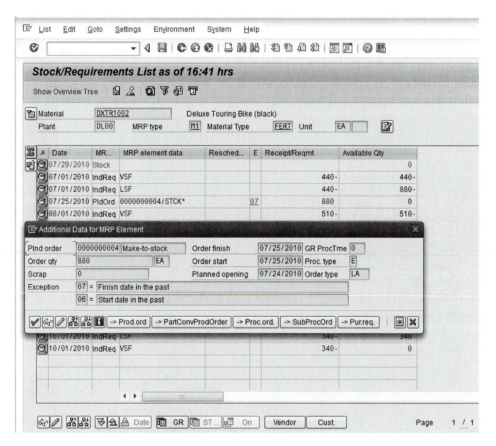

Figure 8-28: Exception message. Copyright SAP AG 2011

A report that can be obtained from the stock/requirements list is the *order report* (Figure 8-29), which shows the components required for sales orders, planned orders, and production orders. The report indicates the date when the materials are required, the quantity required, and whether sufficient materials are available to fill the order. The lightning bolt symbols to the left of the material numbers in the figure indicate that there is a problem with availability, and the exception messages on the right side describe the problems that the system has been unable to resolve automatically. Double-clicking on a material line in the order report retrieves the stock/requirements list for the material. The MRP controller can use this list to investigate and resolve the availability problem.

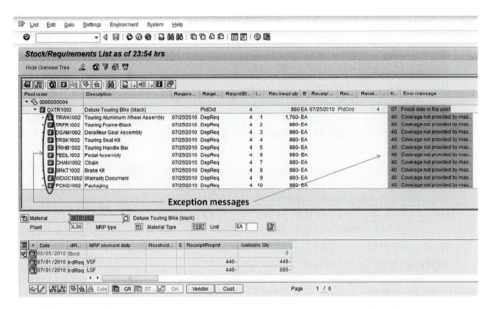

Figure 8-29: Material availability in the stock/requirements list. Copyright SAP AG 2011

Figure 8-30 displays the *stock statistics report*, which can also be accessed from the stock/requirements list. This report presents details of the inventory of the material as well as planned issues and receipts. The top of the figure lists warehouse stock, which is divided into stock that is available for planning (including unrestricted use stock, stock in quality inspection, stock in transfer, and consignment stock), and stock that is not available for planning (including blocked stock, restricted use stock, and stock returned to vendors). MRP will not

Stock Statistics

Warehouse stock

	Stk avail.for plg	Other stock
Unrestr.-use stock	0	
Blocked		0
Restricted-use stock		0
To qual. inspection	0	
Returns	0	0
In Transfer (Plant)		0
In transfer (SLoc)	0	
Unrestr. consignment	0	
Blocked consignment		0
Restr. consignment		0
Cnsgt in inspection	0	
SC Stock Unrestr.	0	
Qty insp.stck-vendor	0	

Total plant stock	0	Stock in Transit	0

In/outward movements

Fixed receipts	0	Planned receipts	3,320
Fixed issues	10	Planned issues	3,310

Sales Statistics   Stock Overview

Figure 8-30: Stock statistics. Copyright SAP AG 2011

consider the latter types of stock when it performs the net requirements calculation. The bottom of the figure shows issues and receipts. Fixed issues and receipts are those within the planning time fence, meaning they cannot be rescheduled or canceled automatically by the ERP system. The planned receipts and issues are outside the planning time fence, so they can be rescheduled or canceled.

The stock/requirements list is dynamic, and it displays the data for the material at the time the report was generated. For example, note the time stamp on the report title in Figure 8-27 (23:54 hours). This report should be refreshed periodically to retrieve the most current data.

> **Demo 8.6:** Review stock/requirements list and related reports

MRP LIST

Another useful report is the MRP list. The **MRP list** is similar to the stock/requirements list, but it displays static data as of the time the MRP step was executed. A comparison of the MRP list and stock/requirements list highlights changes to MRP elements that have occurred since MRP was executed. Figure 8-31 displays the stock/requirements list—MRP list comparison screen. The PIRs List 1 column is from the stock/requirements list, and the PIRs

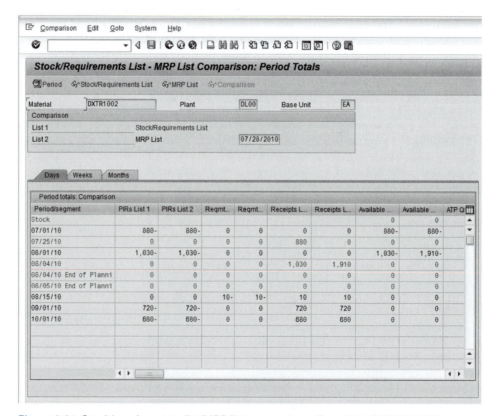

Figure 8-31: Stock/requirements list/MRP list comparison. Copyright SAP AG 2011

List 2 is from the MRP list. The two columns are identical, indicating that there have been no changes in the planning situation since MRP procedure was completed.

Demo 8.7: Review MRP list

PLANNING RESULT REPORT

Another report that shows the result of MRP is the **planning result report**, illustrated in Figure 8-32. Unlike the stock/requirements list, this report aggregates quantities for MRP elements to make it easier to view the overall picture. As with the stock/requirements list, individual MRP elements can be accessed and managed from this report. The report can be generated for both individual materials and product groups. Figure 8-32 illustrates the planning result report for the GBI bicycles product group. The report is divided into Receipts and Issues on the left of the screen. You can see from this report that planned receipts exist for three planned orders (for DXTR1000, DXTR2000, and DXTR3000) and one production order (DXTR3000). Going further, in the first month, planned receipts exist for 270 DXTR2000 and DXTR3000 (planned orders) and 113 DXTR3000 (production order). Thus, the total planned receipts for the first month equal 653 ([270 × 2] + 113).

The planned issues presented in the report include both PIRs and customer orders. A total receipt of 900 units is planned for the first month, all as a result of independent requirements for DXTR1000 (360), DXTR2000 (270), and DXTR3000 (270). Customer requirements are identified as orders under "Fixed external." The term *fixed* indicates that this order cannot be rescheduled because the customer is expecting it on a specific date. Although there are no customer requirements for the first month, there is a requirement of 100 DXTR1000 for the second month.

Time axis	M 09/2010	M 10/2010	M 11/2010	M 12/2010
▾ ☐ Receipts	653	1,137	950	850
▾ ☐ Planned	540	1,137	950	850
▾ ▦ Plnd order	540	1,137	950	850
• ▦ DXTR1000 DL00	0	500	380	340
• ▦ DXTR2000 DL00	270	375	285	255
• ▦ DXTR3000 DL00	270	262	285	255
▾ ☐ Produced in-hse	113	0	0	0
▾ ▦ ProdOrder	113	0	0	0
• ▦ DXTR3000 DL00	113	0	0	0
▾ ☐ Issues	900-	1,250-	950-	850-
▾ ☐ Planned	900-	1,150-	950-	850-
▾ ▦ IndReqmt	900-	1,150-	950-	850-
• ▦ DXTR1000 DL00	360-	400-	380-	340-
• ▦ DXTR2000 DL00	270-	375-	285-	255-
• ▦ DXTR3000 DL00	270-	375-	285-	255-
▾ ☐ Fixed external	0	100-	0	0
▾ ▦ Order	0	100-	0	0
• ▦ DXTR1000 DL00	0	100-	0	0

Figure 8-32: Planning result report. Copyright SAP AG 2011

Demo 8.8: Review planning result report

CHAPTER SUMMARY

Material planning is one of the most complex processes in an organization. The main objective of material planning is to balance the supply of materials with the demand so that a sufficient supply of materials are available when they are needed. Material planning is concerned with answering three basic questions: (1) What materials are required; (2) how many are required; and (3) when are they required? It uses data from several other processes, and generates procurement proposals in the form of purchase requisitions or planned orders.

The first step in the material planning process is sales and operations planning. SOP is a forecasting and planning tool that is used to enter or generate a sales forecast, specify inventory targets, and then generate a production plan at the product group level that satisfies the sales plan and inventory requirements. The production plan is disaggregated to the individual materials in the product group hierarchy and then transferred to demand management in the form of PIRs for materials.

The next step is demand management, which calculates revised PIRs for the materials using the disaggregated production plan from SOP, actual customer orders from the fulfillment process, and data from the material master regarding planning strategies.

The final step in the material planning process is materials requirement planning (MRP), which calculates the net requirements for materials and creates procurement proposals, usually in the form of purchase requisitions and planned orders. In turn, purchase requisitions and planned orders trigger the procurement and production processes to make or buy the necessary materials.

The master data that are critical to the material planning process are bills of material, product routings, material masters, and product groups. The material master includes several key data relevant to the material planning process. Procurement type indicates whether a material is produced in-house (via the production process), obtained externally (via the procurement process), either, or neither. MRP type specifies the production control technique used in planning. Common production control techniques are consumption-based planning, materials requirement planning (MRP), and master production scheduling (MPS).

Consumption-based planning calculates the requirements for a material based on historical data and a forecast that assumes that future consumption will follow the same patterns as indicated by the historical data. However, it does not take into account dependencies between different materials. Materials requirement planning (MRP) calculates requirements for a material based on its dependence on other materials. Independent requirements are determined using actual and forecasted sales. Dependent requirements are based on the requirements for another material. Master production scheduling (MPS) uses a process similar to MRP. However, it is employed only for the most critical finished goods, thus ensuring that resources and capacity are available for these materials before planning for other materials.

Production planning strategies are broadly categorized as make-to-stock, make-to-order, and assemble-to-order. They are specified in the strategy group category. Make-to-stock (MTS) is a planning strategy that fulfills customer orders from finished goods inventory. In contrast, in make-to-order (MTO), the production of the finished goods and any needed semifinished goods is triggered by a sales order, and no inventory of these materials is maintained. Assemble-to-order (ATO) is a planning strategy in which an inventory of components (semi-finished goods) needed to make the finished good is maintained in stock, and the final assembly of the finished goods is triggered by a sales order.

Products with similar planning characteristics, such as similar types, planning strategies, and manufacturing processes, are grouped into a product group or a product family. Product groups are used to disaggregate the demand for the higher-level groups to the materials in the lowest levels.

Reporting in material planning is limited to relatively few reports but includes three important tools to obtain information about the planning situation: the stock/requirements list, the MRP list, and the planning result report. The most important reporting tool in material planning is the stock/requirements list, which displays all MRP elements for a material and includes other information such as existing stock level, safety stock, and exception messages. The MRP list is similar to the stock/requirements list, but it displays static data as of the time MRP step was executed. A comparison of the MRP list and stock/requirements list highlights changes to MRP elements that have occurred since MRP was executed. Finally, the planning result report aggregates quantities for MRP elements to present an overall picture of receipts and issues. This report can be generated for individual materials or for product groups.

KEY TERMS

Assemble-to-order (ATO)

Availability check group

BOM selection method

Consumption-based planning

Customer independent
   requirements (CIR)

Demand management

Dependent requirement

Disaggregation

Exception messages

Independent requirements

Lot size

Lot size key

Make-to-order (MTO)

Make-to-stock (MTS)

Master production scheduling (MPS)

MRP elements

MRP list

MRP type

Net change planning (NETCH)

Net change planning in the planning
   horizon (NETPL)

Planned independent
   requirements (PIR)

Planning result report

Planning time fence

Processing key

Procurement type

Product group

Regenerative planning
(NEUPL)

Safety stock

Sales and operations
planning (SOP)

Stock/requirements list

Strategy group

REVIEW QUESTIONS

1. What is the main objective of material planning? What are the basic questions addressed by material planning?

2. List and describe the steps in the material planning process.

3. Which master data are relevant for material planning?

4. Define and explain the relevance to material planning of the following data in the material master:

    a. Procurement type

    b. MRP type

    c. Lot size key

    d. Scheduling times

    e. Planning time fence

    f. BOM selection method

    g. Availability check group

    h. Strategy group

    i. Consumption mode

5. Define and distinguish between consumption-based planning and materials requirements planning.

6. Explain how reorder point planning works.

7. Explain the differences between

    a. Dependent requirements and independent requirements

    b. Planned independent requirements (PIRs) and customer requirements (CIRs).

8. Explain the common time estimates included in the material master.

9. Identify and discuss the different types of in-house production times defined in the material master.

10. Compare and contrast the three production planning strategies discussed in this chapter.

11. Explain the process by which CIRs consume PIRs, and provide an example.

12. What are product groups? What is the role of product groups in material planning?

13. Compare and contrast aggregation and disaggregation.

14. What is the role of the MRP controller in material planning?

15. Briefly describe the steps in the material planning process in terms of the triggers, data, tasks, and outcomes.

16. Explain the functions and components of a planning table. Discuss the different methods of generating a production plan with a planning table.

17. What are the different options for disaggregating a sales plan or a production plan?

18. Explain the differences between MRP and MPS.

19. Describe the tasks completed in the MRP step of the material planning process.

20. Explain the different control parameters that determine the way the tasks in the MRP step are executed.

21. Discuss the different MRP processing keys.

22. Describe the net requirements calculation.

23. Explain the scheduling process in MRP.

24. Define and discuss the types of procurement proposals that can be created in MRP.

25. Assess the advantages and disadvantages of creating planned orders and purchase requisitions for externally procured materials.

26. Define MRP element.

27. Discuss the different reporting tools that are useful in material planning.

28. Distinguish between the stock/requirements list and the MRP list.

EXERCISES

Exercises for this chapter are available on *WileyPLUS*.

CHAPTER 9

Process Integration

LEARNING OBJECTIVES

After completing this chapter you will be able to:

1. Define process integration, and explain why this concept is fundamental to modern business operations.

2. Explain how the procurement, fulfillment, and IWM processes interact when a company fills a customer order for trading goods.

3. Identify and discuss the various integration points among the procurement, fulfillment, production, and warehouse management processes.

4. Analyze the financial and material impacts of the various steps in the integrated processes.

In Chapter 1 we introduced the key processes in organizations in simple terms. In Chapters 3–8 we examined six processes in detail:

- Financial accounting
- Procurement
- Fulfillment
- Production
- Inventory and warehouse management
- Material planning.

In addition, we briefly discussed management accounting concepts in several chapters. At this point, then, you should have a clear understanding of the triggers, data, tasks, and outcomes of these processes.

In Chapter 1 we also introduced the concept of process integration, which posits that the various processes are interdependent, so that steps in one process almost inevitably impact steps in other processes. For example, the material planning process generates planned orders and purchase requisitions, which in turn trigger the production and procurement processes, respectively. We illustrated process integration in Figure 1-3, which is reproduced in Figure 9-1.

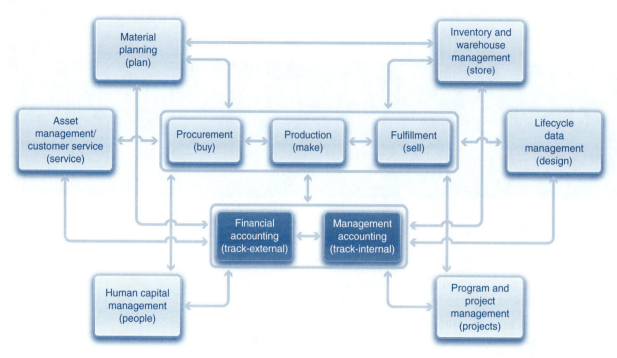

Figure 9-1: Integrated business processes

In Chapters 3–8 we also examined the numerous relationships between and among the various processes. For example, we explained that the procurement process can be triggered by a material need arising from production, fulfillment, or material planning. In turn, the procurement process frequently triggers warehouse management processes. In most cases, however, we did not elaborate on these integration points. Instead, we discussed each process independently of the other processes. We adopted this approach to keep the discussions of the processes relatively simple. To truly appreciate the complex operations of modern business organizations, however, it is essential to understand how the different processes interact.

In this chapter, we will approach the same processes that we covered in earlier chapters, but from a holistic, integrative perspective in order to highlight the deeper connections and key operational dependencies among them. To help you visualize these interdependencies, we will include two scenarios in which GBI needs to fulfill a customer order. In the first scenario, the order is for trading goods (t-shirts). This scenario will involve the procurement, fulfillment, and inventory and warehouse management (IWM) processes. Because it focuses on trading goods, however, it will not involve the production process. In contrast, the second scenario involves a customer order for a finished good (a bike) and thus will include the production process. Both scenarios will explore the flow of steps, documents, and data and will examine the outcomes across the multiple processes involved in fulfilling a customer order. In contrast to the earlier chapters, where we made many assumptions to simplify the explanation of the individual processes, these scenarios will introduce more complex and realistic decisions that the company must make as the steps cross process boundaries.

Because of the tightly integrated nature of business processes, enabling holistic process execution is one of the primary goals of an ERP system. By using a single, integrated ERP system, companies can provide "one version of the truth" to everyone involved in executing the various processes. An ERP system helps employees to understand how the different processes are interdependent while providing them with instant access to the data they need to make intelligent decisions.

We will begin by reviewing a few concepts from the different processes that are critical to understanding how these processes are integrated.

- In the material planning chapter we considered two fundamental production planning strategies: make-to-stock and make-to-order. Similar strategies are available for materials that are procured (purchased) from a vendor—procure-to-stock and procure-to-order. In the make-to-stock and procure-to-stock strategies, the inventory of materials serves as the buffer between the production and procurement processes on the one hand and the fulfillment process on the other. That is, the company executes the production and procurement processes to maintain a stock or an inventory of materials, from which it fills customer orders. In contrast, in the make-to-order and procure-to-order strategies, the company does not maintain an inventory of materials. Rather, customer orders received in the fulfillment process trigger the production and procurement processes as needed.

- In Chapter 4 we explained that the procurement process is triggered by a requirement that is generated by the fulfillment, production, or material planning process. Procurement is triggered by fulfillment when the company employs a procure-to-order strategy for trading goods. It is triggered by production when the company employs a procure-to-order strategy for raw materials. Finally, it is triggered by material planning when a company employs a procure-to-stock strategy for either raw materials or trading goods. We also included a scenario in which GBI purchased 500 t-shirts from Spy Gear because its inventory was low. This scenario presents a case in which the procurement process is triggered by a requirement from material planning. It also illustrates the strategy of procure-to-stock.

- In the chapter on fulfillment (Chapter 5), we described a process that employed a sell-from-stock strategy. For example, in the discussion of the availability check procedure we explained that the ERP system determines availability based on both current inventory and planned receipts from either procurement or production. Also, in the example in which GBI delivered deluxe touring bikes and t-shirts to Rocky Mountain Bikes, we assumed that the materials needed to fill the order were available in inventory. Consequently, GBI utilized the sell-from-stock strategy.

- Finally, the discussion of the production process in Chapter 6 focused on a make-to-stock scenario that assumed that the materials needed to make the finished goods were readily available. Thus, the scenario in which GBI manufactured men's off-road bikes was triggered by a need to increase inventory rather than by a customer order.

We can see, then, that the make-to-stock, procure-to-stock, and sell-from stock strategies use inventory as a buffer between processes, to de-couple them or make them less dependent on each other.

In this chapter, to illustrate the integration among processes, we will no longer assume that a sufficient inventory of raw materials (for production) and finished goods or trading goods (for fulfillment) exists. We will also examine the make-to-order and procure-to-order strategies. We will begin by considering the first scenario described above—filling a customer order for trading goods. This scenario will illustrate the integration among the procurement, fulfillment, and IWM processes.

■ PROCUREMENT, FULFILLMENT, AND IWM PROCESSES

We will use the following scenario in our discussion of integrated processes. Rocky Mountain Bikes (RMB), a GBI customer, has ordered 800 t-shirts (SHRT1000) from GBI. Because RMB is located in the Western U.S. sales organization, GBI will ship the t-shirts from its San Diego plant, which is warehouse management enabled. We will make the following assumptions:

1. The San Diego plant has 200 t-shirts in stock valued at a moving average price of $15.43 each.

2. The Miami plant has 1,500 t-shirts in stock valued at a moving average price of $15.25 each.

3. GBI can purchase t-shirts from Spy Gear at $14.95 each.

4. RMB has sent GBI a purchase order (PO) for 800 t-shirts.

5. GBI sells t-shirts for $30 each.

In this scenario the San Diego plant does not have a sufficient quantity of t-shirts in stock. Therefore, the customer order will trigger the procurement process. Recall that companies can procure materials from either an external source (a vendor) or an internal source (another plant). If the plant that is sending or receiving the materials is warehouse managed, then WM processes are triggered to pick or put away the materials. When the materials become available, then the fulfillment process can proceed to the shipping step.

Before we discuss this process in detail, let's review the financial accounting and material valuation data that exist at the start of the process. The balances in the relevant accounts are illustrated in Figure 9-2. Recall from the discussion of valuation class in the material master that the value of materials with similar characteristics is maintained in one general ledger account. In the case of GBI, the value of t-shirts (and all other trading goods) is maintained in one inventory account. As illustrated in Figure 9-2, this account has a balance of $25,961. (Table 9-1 provides an explanation of how this value is calculated.) To keep the discussion simple, we will not include the starting balances in any other accounts (e.g., bank, vendor, and customer accounts) or for other materials.

Although the total value of all trading goods is maintained in one general ledger account at the company code level, the valuation of the materials occurs at the plant level. That is, the materials can be valued differently in each plant. Further, the quantity and value of the materials are maintained in the material master for each material. Table 9-1 displays this arrangement for t-shirts in GBI's Miami and San Diego plants. The table shows the stock (status and quantity), the moving average price (MAP), and the value of the stock in each plant and for GBI as a whole. Note that the sum of the values at the plant level ($25,961) is the total value indicated in the inventory account in Figure 9-2.

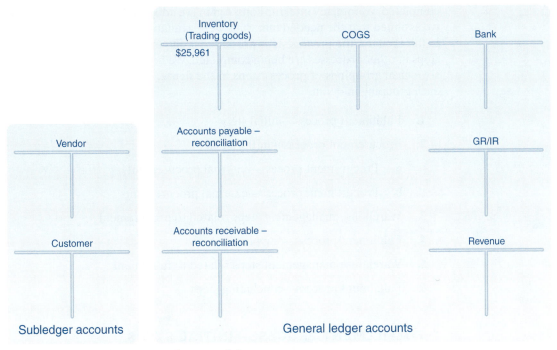

Figure 9-2: Account balances at the start of the process

Plant	Stock	MAP	Value
Miami	Unrestricted: 1,500	$15.25	$22,875
San Diego	Unrestricted: 200	$15.43	$3,086
Total GBI	Unrestricted: 1,700		$25,961

Inventory in San Diego: 200 * 15.43 = $3,086
Inventory in Miami: 1,500 * 15.25 = $22,875
Inventory in GBI: $3,086 + $22,875 = $25,961

Table 9-1: Plant stock valuation at the start of the process

Demo 9.1: Review financials and inventory (plant, storage location, and bin stock and value)

Figure 9-3 illustrates the integration among the fulfillment, procurement, and IWM processes. The integrated process is triggered by the receipt of a customer PO (indicated by "start" in the figure). Note that both the San Diego and Miami plants are included in this illustration. The steps that have a financial accounting impact are identified with an "FI" symbol, the steps with a controlling impact are identified with a "CO" symbol, and the steps with a material impact (i.e., goods movement) are identified with an "M" symbol. Recall that an FI document is created when a process step impacts the general ledger, and a material document is created when a process step involves a goods movement. When we discussed each process separately, all of the process steps were completed without any interruptions. Again, we adopted this approach because we assumed that the needed materials were available in inventory. In contrast, in this scenario the process steps presented in Figure 9-3 are interrupted while steps in other processes are being completed. We have identified the following six logical groupings of process steps in the figure. The next section examines each grouping in detail.

1. Fulfillment process—initial steps
2. Procurement process—initial steps
   a. Procurement process—internal procurement
   b. Procurement process—external procurement
3. Warehouse management steps related to procurement
4. Fulfillment process—shipping
5. Warehouse management steps related to fulfillment
6. Fulfillment process—concluding steps

1: FULFILLMENT PROCESS—INITIAL STEPS

The fulfillment process is triggered when GBI receives a purchase order from RMB for 800 t-shirts. The resulting steps are labeled "1" in Figure 9-3 and are reproduced in Figure 9-4.

To avoid making this discussion too complex, we did not include the presales steps (inquiry and quotation) discussed in the fulfillment chapter. After GBI receives the customer PO, the next step in the fulfillment process is sales order processing, in which GBI creates a sales order and executes an availability check for materials ordered. If GBI has sufficient materials in inventory to fill the order, then the fulfillment process proceeds directly to the shipping step. In Chapter 5 we assumed that the materials were available. In this scenario, as you can see from the previous discussion and Table 9-1, the San Diego plant does *not* have enough t-shirts in stock. Consequently, the fulfillment process is interrupted while San Diego procures the needed materials.

Demo 9.2: Create two customer orders

2: PROCUREMENT PROCESS—INITIAL STEPS

This shortage of materials creates a requirement for t-shirts in the San Diego plant. Consequently, it triggers the procurement process, labeled "2" in Figure 9-3 and reproduced in Figure 9-5. Specifically, the plant creates a purchase requisition in the requirements determination step of the procurement process. In our example, a requisition for 1,000 t-shirts is created. The requisition is then converted to a PO in the purchase order processing step. At this point, GBI has two options for acquiring the materials: internally from another plant and externally from a vendor (areas labeled 2A and 2B in Figure 9-3, respectively). If the Miami plant is able to supply the necessary quantity of t-shirts, then GBI

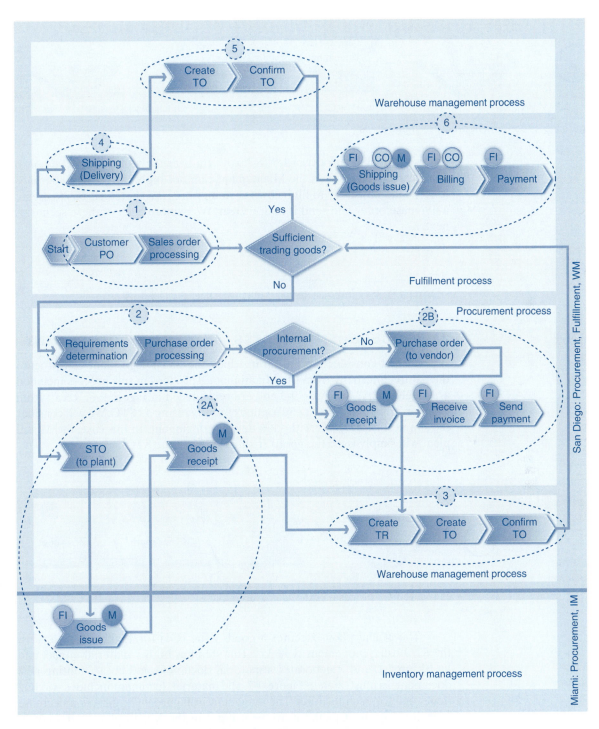

Figure 9-3: Procurement, fulfillment and warehouse management processes

Figure 9-4: Fulfillment process—initial steps

Figure 9-5: Procurement process—initial steps

can use a stock transport order (STO) to transfer the t-shirts from Miami to San Diego. Conversely, if the Miami plant cannot supply the t-shirts—perhaps it needs the inventory to fill its own customer orders—then GBI has to create a purchase order and send it to Spy Gear. We explore each of these scenarios next.

Demo 9.3: Create two requisitions and POs

2A: PROCUREMENT PROCESS—INTERNAL PROCUREMENT

We will first consider the option in which the San Diego plant can procure the t-shirts internally from the Miami plant. The steps in this process included are labeled "2A" in Figure 9-3 and are reproduced in Figure 9-6. Recall from Chapter 7 that there are several options for processing an STO. We will consider the simplest case—STO without a delivery document. In this case, the Miami plant will simply issue the goods (t-shirts) against the STO.

Figure 9-6: Procurement process—internal procurement

The Miami plant executes a goods issue (GI) for 1,000 t-shirts against the STO using movement type 351. This step has both a material impact and an FI impact, and it generates a material document and an accounting (FI) document, as illustrated in Figure 9-7. The material document includes two line items, one for each location. The document in Figure 9-7 indicates a decrease (negative sign next to the movement type) in the Miami plant and a corresponding increase in the San Diego plant. However, the status of the material being shipped is "stock in transit" in the San Diego plant, and a storage location is not included in the material document. The FI impact of this movement is captured in the accounting document in Figure 9-7. We explained in Chapter 7 that in a plant-to-plant movement, valuation occurs (1) at the time of the goods issue and (2) at the valuation price of the issuing plant. Thus, the FI document indicates a debit *and* a credit to the inventory account for trading goods. The

Figure 9-7: Material and FI documents at goods issue for STO

reason for this is that GBI maintains the t-shirt inventory in one general ledger account for all plants. The amount of the debit and the credit is based on the valuation price at the Miami plant (1,000 * $15.25). The entries in the general ledger accounts are illustrated in Figure 9-8.

Although there is no change in the value of the t-shirts in the general ledger, there is a change in value in the material master. This change is illustrated in Table 9-2. The quantity of materials in the unrestricted use status in Miami has decreased from 1,500 to 500, and there is no change in the moving average price. In contrast, the quantity of stock in transit in San Diego has increased

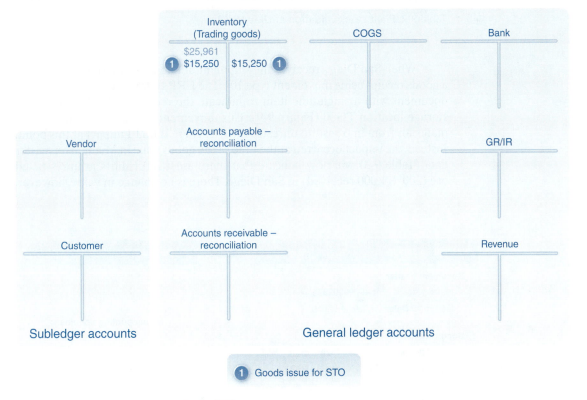

Figure 9-8: Account balances at GI for STO

by 1,000. In addition, a new moving average price has been calculated to take into account the difference between the old moving average price ($15.43) and the price at which the new materials are valued ($15.25). The new moving average price in San Diego is $15.28. (The calculation is included in Table 9-2.) It is important to note that although the valuation of materials has changed between the two plants, the total value of materials at GBI (Miami + San Diego) remains unchanged at $25,961.

Plant	Stock	MAP	Value
Miami	Unrestricted: 500	$15.25	$7,625
San Diego	Unrestricted: 200 Stock in transit: 1,000	$15.28	$18,336
Total GBI	Unrestricted: 700 Stock in transit: 1,000		$25,961

Calculation of MAP at SD00 after GI for STO

	Before GI	GI data	After GI
Quantity	200	1,000	1,200
Value	$3,086	1,000*$15.25 = 15,250	($15,250 + $3,086) = $18,336
MAP	$15.43		$18,336/1,200 = $15.28

Table 9-2: Plant stock valuation at GI for STO

When San Diego receives the shipment of t-shirts from Miami, it records a goods receipt using movement type 101. The ERP system creates one material document with a single line item to indicate the receipt of 1,000 t-shirts into storage location TG00 (Figure 9-9). This movement changes the status of the materials from in transit to unrestricted use. There is no FI impact at this point. Instead, the impact occurred at the time of the goods issue in Miami. The master data (Table 9-3) will now indicate that there are 1,200 t-shirts in unrestricted use (200 + 1,000 received) in San Diego. There is no change in value, however.

Figure 9-9: Material and FI documents at GR for STO

Plant	Stock	MAP	Value
Miami	Unrestricted: 500	$15.25	$7,625
San Diego	Unrestricted: 1,200	$15.28	$18,336
Total GBI	Unrestricted: 1,700		$25,961

Table 9-3: Plant stock valuation at GR for STO

Demo 9.4: Internal procurement for first PO

2B: PROCUREMENT PROCESS—EXTERNAL PROCUREMENT

In the event the Miami plant is unable to fill San Diego's requirement for t-shirts, then the San Diego plant dispatches a purchase order for 1,000 t-shirts to Spy Gear. The steps associated with this option are identified by the label "2B" in Figure 9-3 and are illustrated in Figure 9-10.

Figure 9-10: Procurement process—external procurement

When the San Diego plant receives the shipment from Spy Gear, it completes a goods receipt against the PO. Figure 9-11 illustrates the material impact and the FI impact of a goods receipt against a PO. In this scenario, one material document is created, with a single line item showing the receipt of 1,000 t-shirts in the San Diego plant via movement type 101. At the same time, an FI document is created to record the debit of $14,950 (1,000 t-shirts @ $14.95 each) to the trading goods inventory account and a credit for the same amount to the goods receipt/invoice receipt (GR/IR) account. The FI document reflects the entries in the general ledger illustrated in Figure 9-12—a debit to the inventory account with a corresponding credit to the GR/IR account. Thus, the value of inventory (trading goods) has increased to $40,911 ($25,961 + $14,950).

Finally, Table 9-4 displays the valuation of the materials at the plant level. The quantity, value, and moving average price for the t-shirts in the Miami plant are unchanged. The quantity of t-shirts in unrestricted use in San Diego has increased by the 1,000 received from Spy Gear. Because the price per unit for the t-shirts ($14.95) is different from the moving average price prior to the receipt ($15.43; see Table 9-1), the moving average price is recalculated to $15.03, as illustrated at the bottom of Table 9-4. Note again that the sum of the inventory in Miami ($22,875) and San Diego ($18,036) is equal to the value of inventory in the inventory account in the general ledger ($40,911).

Figure 9-11: Material and FI documents at GR for PO

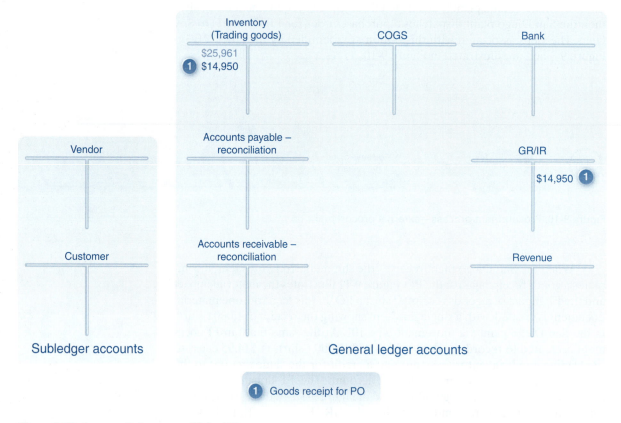

Figure 9-12: Account balances at GR for PO

Now that we have examined both the internal and the external procurement options, for the rest of the discussion we will assume that GBI has selected the external option. Under this scenario, the procurement process continues with the receipt of the vendor invoice followed by payment to the vendor. Figure 9-13 illustrates the general ledger impact of these two steps. When a vendor invoice is received and verified, the GR/IR account is cleared (debit posting), and the vendor subledger account is credited by the amount of the

Plant	Stock	MAP	Value
Miami	Unrestricted: 1,500	$15.25	$22,875
San Diego	Unrestricted: 1,200	$15.03	$18,036
Total GBI	Unrestricted: 2,700		$40,911

Calculation of MAP at SD00 after GR for PO

	Before GR	GR data	After GR
Quantity	200	1,000	1,200
Value	$3,086	1,000 ∗ $14.95 = $14,950	($14,950 + $3,086) = $18,036
MAP	$15.43		$18,036/1,200 = $15.03

Table 9-4: Plant stock valuation at GR for PO

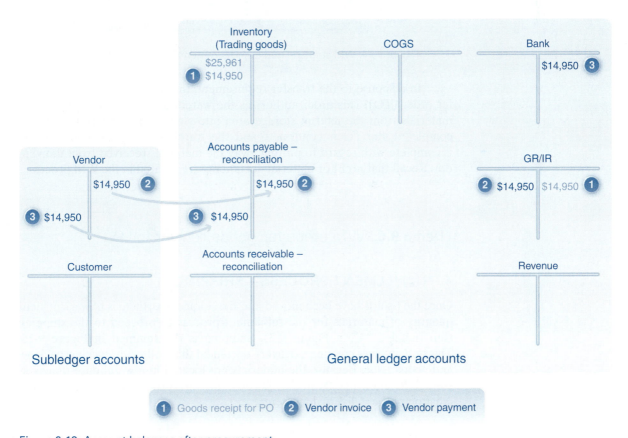

Figure 9-13: Account balances after procurement

invoice. In our example, the amount is $14,950 (1,000 t-shirts @ $14.95 each). When GBI makes a payment to the vendor, the bank account is credited by the payment amount, and the vendor subledger account and the accounts receivable reconciliation account are debited by the same amount. For both steps an FI document is created. Refer to Chapter 4 for an explanation of these steps.

Demo 9.5: External procurement for second PO

3: WAREHOUSE MANAGEMENT STEPS RELATED TO PROCUREMENT

Regardless of whether GBI procured the materials from internal or external sources, the goods receipt in the San Diego plant into storage location TG00 will trigger steps related to the warehouse management process (labeled "3" in Figure 9-3) because storage location TG00 is warehouse managed. These steps are illustrated in Figure 9-14. In this situation the goods received are placed in an interim storage area, and a transfer requirement (TR) is automatically created by the ERP system. The TR serves as a request to move them to an appropriate storage bin.

Figure 9-14: WM steps related to procurement

In response to the transfer requirement, the warehouse creates a transfer order (TO). This order authorizes the warehouse personnel to move the materials from the interim storage area into storage bins. When this step is completed, the TO is confirmed, and the warehouse management process is complete with regard to putting away the materials received from the vendor. Recall that no FI or material documents are created in the WM process.

Demo 9.6: WM steps for goods receipt for PO

4: FULFILLMENT PROCESS—SHIPPING

Once the t-shirts have been moved into the storage bins, there is now a sufficient quantity of materials for the fulfillment process to proceed to the shipping step (labeled "4" in Figure 9-3). Shipping is diagrammed in Figure 9-15. This step involves creating a delivery document that authorizes picking, packing, and goods issue. Because the materials are located in a warehouse-managed storage location (TG00 in San Diego), the WM process is triggered by the creation of the delivery document.

Figure 9-15: Fulfillment process—shipping

Demo 9.7: Create delivery for PO

5: WAREHOUSE MANAGEMENT STEPS RELATED TO FULFILLMENT

The trigger that initiates the WM steps is the delivery document. The delivery document serves as a request to move the needed materials (800 t-shirts) from the bins to the interim shipping storage area. The steps associated with this process are labeled "5" in Figure 9-3 and are reproduced in Figure 9-16. A transfer order is created based on the delivery document, the materials are moved from storage bins to the interim shipping storage area, and the transfer order is confirmed. This concludes the warehouse management steps associated with picking materials for shipment. No material or FI documents are generated.

Figure 9-16: WM steps related to fulfillment

Demo 9.8: WM steps for delivery

6: FULFILLMENT PROCESS—CONCLUDING STEPS

After the materials have been placed in the interim shipping storage area, the fulfillment process can be concluded. These steps (labeled "6" in Figure 9-3) are diagrammed in Figure 9-17.

Figure 9-17: Fulfillment process—concluding steps

The shipping step was partially completed when the delivery document was created. Now that the materials have been picked in the warehouse and moved into the shipping area, a goods issue is completed using movement type 601. This step generates a material document and an FI document, as illustrated in Figure 9-18, as well as postings to the general ledger accounts, illustrated in Figure 9-19. The material document records the removal of 800 t-shirts from inventory. The FI document indicates a credit of $12,024 to the inventory account and a corresponding debit to the cost of goods sold (COGS)

Figure 9-18: Material and FI documents at GI for delivery

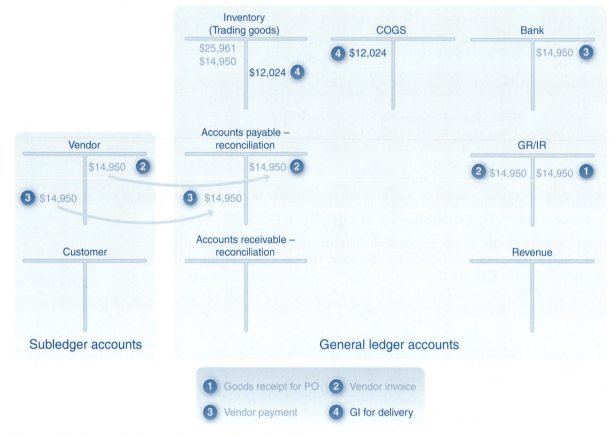

Figure 9-19: Account balances after goods issue for delivery

account. The amount of the debit and credit is the value of the 800 t-shirts at the current moving average price of $15.03. Finally, Table 9-5 illustrates the plant valuation of the materials after the goods issue is completed. Note again that the total valuation in the plants ($28,887) is equal to the value in the inventory account in the general ledger (the sum of the debits and credits). A controlling impact occurs if the profitability analysis process in management accounting is in use. The goods issue step provides the cost of goods sold data in determining profitability.

Plant	Stock	MAP	Value
Miami	Unrestricted: 1,500	$15.25	$22,875
San Diego	Unrestricted: 400	$15.03	$6,012
Total GBI	Unrestricted: 1,900		$28,887

Table 9-5: Plant stock valuation at GI for SO

The final steps in the fulfillment process are billing and receiving payment from the customer. In Chapter 5 we saw that when a customer invoice is generated, a credit is posted to the revenue account, and a debit is posted to the customer subledger account with an automatic posting to the accounts receivable reconciliation account. In Figure 9-20, the posting is for $24,000 (800 t-shirts @ $30.00 each). The entries for the payment step include a debit posting to the bank account and a credit posting to the customer account, with an accompanying automatic posting to the accounts receivable reconciliation account. Both steps result in FI documents. In addition, the billing step provides revenue data to the profitability analysis process in controlling. Please refer to Chapter 5 for an explanation of these steps.

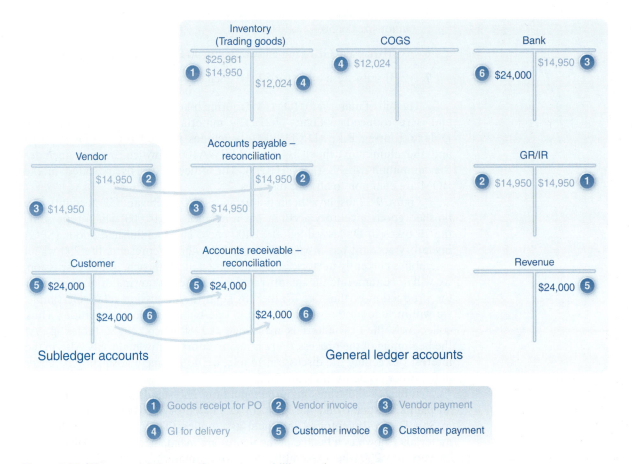

Figure 9-20: GL account balances after customer billing and payment

Demo 9.9: Complete fulfillment

● PROCUREMENT, FULFILLMENT, PRODUCTION, AND IWM PROCESSES

We now consider the scenario that includes production. In this scenario, Rocky Mountain Bikes (RMB) has ordered 40 Red Deluxe Touring Bikes (DXTR3000) from GBI. We will make the following assumptions:

1. The San Diego plant has 10 Red Deluxe Touring Bikes valued at a standard price of $1,400 each.

2. The Dallas plant currently does not have any touring bikes in inventory. When it does have these bikes, the standard price is also $1,400.

3. The Dallas plant has 200 aluminum wheel assemblies that are needed to produce touring bikes. The standard price for these wheel assemblies is $110.

4. GBI's vendor, Space Bike Composites, is able to supply all of the raw materials needed to make touring bikes.

5. GBI purchases raw materials in lot sizes of 200. It produces bikes in lot sizes of 50.

6. RMB has sent GBI a purchase order for 40 Red Deluxe Touring Bikes.

7. GBI sells these bikes for $2,800 each.

The bill of materials (BOM) for touring bikes was discussed in Chapter 6 and is reproduced in Figure 9-21. The material in our scenario—the Red Deluxe Touring Bike (DXTR3000)—includes the red frame (TRFR3000) and the aluminum wheel assembly (TRWA1000), which, in turn, includes the aluminum wheels (TRWH1000). The other materials indicated in the BOM are common to all touring bikes.

Figure 9-22 displays the initial balances in the relevant GL accounts. The finished goods inventory account has a balance of $14,000, which represents the 10 bikes in Dallas valued at $1,400 each. The semifinished goods (SFG) inventory account has a balance of $22,000, which represents the 200 wheel assemblies currently in stock in Dallas valued at $110 each. In our discussion, we will *not* enumerate the quantity and value of each raw material needed for the production of the bike. Rather, to keep the discussion relatively simple, we will include all the raw materials in one bundle in our calculations. Thus, collectively, the raw materials are valued at $480 per bike (see Table 9-6). At the beginning of the process, there is no inventory of raw materials. Also in the interest of keeping the discussion simple, we do not include starting balances in the other accounts in Figure 9-22.

Table 9-7 illustrates material valuation. The standard price for bikes in all plants is $1,400, and the only current inventory consists of the 10 bikes in San Diego. Inventories of wheel assemblies (TRWA1000) and the raw materials (shown as a bundle in the figure) are maintained only in Dallas. There are currently 200 wheel assemblies and no raw materials in stock.

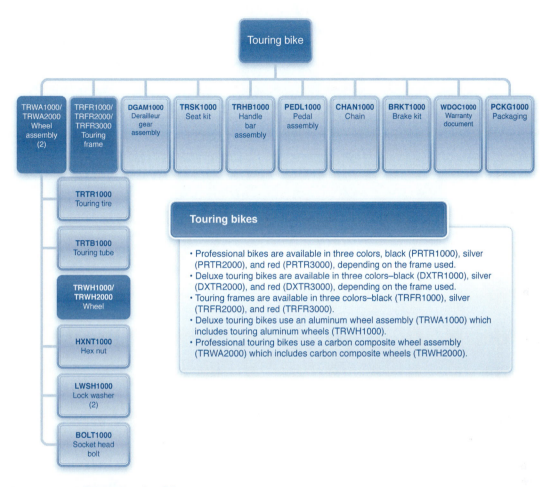

Figure 9-21: BOM for Touring Bikes

Material Number	Description	Cost
DGAM1000	Derailleur gear assembly	$75.00
TRSK1000	Seat kit	$50.00
TRHB1000	Handle bar assembly	$25.00
PEDL1000	Peddle assembly	$45.00
CHAN1000	Chain	$10.00
BRKT1000	Brake kit	$70.00
WDOC1000	Warranty document	$1.00
PCKG1000	Packaging material	$4.00
TRFR3000	Red touring frame	$200.00
	Total cost	$480.00

Table 9-6: Raw material cost per bike

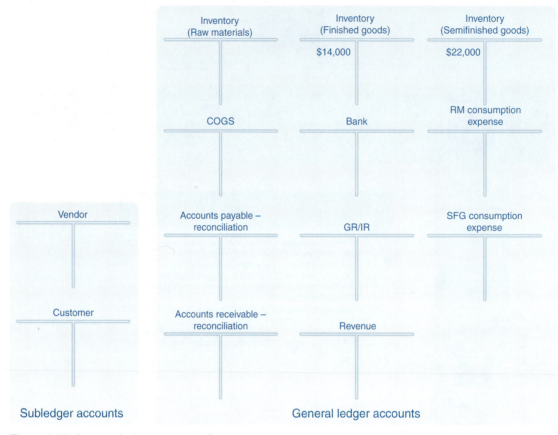

Figure 9-22: Account balances—start of process

Figure 9-23 illustrates the integration among the procurement, fulfillment, production, and IWM processes. When GBI receives RMB's purchase order for 40 Red Deluxe Touring Bikes, the fulfillment process is triggered. Because RMB is situated in the Western U.S. sales organization, the bikes will be shipped from the San Diego plant, which is warehouse management enabled. During the sales order processing step, the ERP system performs an availability check that indicates that only 10 bikes are available in inventory in San Diego. Consequently, the plant requests a stock transfer from Dallas via an STO. Because Dallas has no inventory of bikes, the STO is a requirement that will trigger the production process. Once production is completed in Dallas, the plant will complete a goods issue against the STO. This step reduces the inventory of bikes in Dallas and increases the inventory in San Diego, in the in-transit status. When the materials reach San Diego, the plant completes a goods receipt against the STO, which moves the bikes from in-transit to unrestricted use status. Because the storage locations in San Diego are warehouse managed, the goods receipt triggers the WM process to put away the bikes received from Dallas into storage bins. After this step has been completed, the fulfillment process can proceed to shipping. This step will again trigger the WM process, this time to pick the bikes needed to fill the order. After the bikes have been picked, the remaining task in the shipping step, goods issue, can be completed. Goods issue is followed by the last two steps in the fulfillment process—billing and payment.

Plant	Stock (DXTR3000)	Standard price	Value
Dallas	Unrestricted: 0	$1,400	$0
San Diego	Unrestricted: 10	$1,400	$14,000
Total GBI	Unrestricted: 10		$14,000

Plant	Stock (TRWA1000)	Standard price	Value
Dallas	Unrestricted: 200	$110	$22,000
Total GBI	Unrestricted: 200		$22,000

Plant	Stock (Raw materials)	Standard price	Value
Dallas	Unrestricted: 0	$480	$0
Total GBI	Unrestricted: 0		$0

FG inventory
San Diego: 10*$1,400 = $14,000
Dallas: 0*$1,400 = $0
GBI: $14,000 + $0 = $14,000

SFG inventory
Dallas: 200*$110.00 = $22,000

RM inventory
Dallas: 0*$480 = $0
Note: $480 is the total cost of all raw materials needed to make one Deluxe Touring bike. We have bundled the cost of all raw materials into one cost to keep the discussion simple. Refer to the BOM in Figure 9-21 and Table 9-6 for a list of raw materials needed.

Table 9-7: Material valuation at the start of process

The scenario described above represents the normal process established by GBI. However, let's consider two variations. In the first variation, if either the Miami plant or the Dallas plant has the needed quantity of bikes in its inventory, then GBI can make an exception to its normal process and authorize an alternate plant to ship the bikes directly to RMB. GBI will choose this option if it is necessary to ensure timely delivery to the customer. In another variation, RMB's order can trigger the Dallas plant to manufacture the bikes, as described above. Instead of sending the bikes to San Diego after production, however, Dallas can ship them directly to RMB.

As in our earlier discussion, steps with material and financial accounting impacts are indicated with "M" and "FI" symbols, respectively, in Figure 9-23. In addition, steps with a management accounting or controlling impact are identified with the "CO" symbol. Also as in the previous discussion, the process steps are interrupted while steps in other processes are being completed. We have identified the following 10 logical groupings of process steps in the figure.

1. Fulfillment process—initial steps

2. Inventory management (STO)—initial steps

3. Production process—initial steps

4. Procurement process (external)

5. Production process—continued

6. Inventory management (STO)—continued

7. Warehouse management process related to STO

8. Fulfillment process—continued

9. Warehouse management process related to fulfillment

10. Fulfillment process—concluding steps

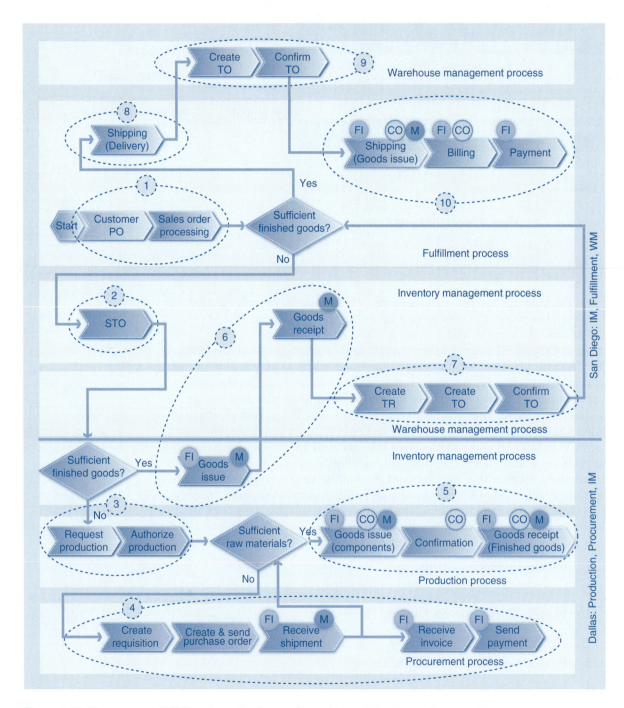

Figure 9-23: Procurement, fulfillment, production, and warehouse management processes

Demo 9.10: Review financials and inventory (plant, storage location, and bin stock and value)

1: FULFILLMENT PROCESS—INITIAL STEPS

RMB's purchase order triggers the integrated process and prompts GBI to create a sales order (Figure 9-24). The ERP system then executes an availability check, which concludes that the warehouse does not have the necessary number of bikes in stock.

Figure 9-24: Fulfillment process—initial steps

Demo 9.11: Create sales order

2: INVENTORY MANAGEMENT (STO)—INITIAL STEPS

Because the warehouse does not have a sufficient inventory to fulfill the customer PO, GBI follows its normal procedure and creates an STO requesting that the bikes be transferred from Dallas to San Diego (Figure 9-25).

Figure 9-25: Inventory management—initial step

Demo 9.12: Create STO

3: PRODUCTION PROCESS—INITIAL STEPS

When the Dallas plant reviews the STO, it checks its inventory and discovers that it does not have the number of bikes needed to meet the requirement in the STO. This calculation triggers the production process (Figure 9-26). The Dallas plant requests production by creating a planned order. Production is authorized, and the planned order is converted to a production order. Although GBI needs to produce only 30 bikes to meet RMB's order, it has decided to authorize a production lot size of 50 bikes. Recall that when the production order is created and released, the planned costs are included in the production order. Chapter 6 contained an extensive discussion of how the costing of materials produced is determined, including how variances are handled. In this section we will assume that the actual costs are the same as the planned costs and that there is no variance.

Figure 9-26: Production process—initial steps

The next step in the production process is to issue materials to the production order. A check of inventory (see Table 9-7) indicates that although the needed wheel assemblies (100; 2 per bike) are in stock, the needed raw materials are not.

Demo 9.13: Create planned order and production order

4: PROCUREMENT PROCESS (EXTERNAL)

The requirement for raw materials triggers the procurement process to acquire these materials (Figure 9-27). GBI issues a PO to Space Bike Composites for the quantity of raw materials it needs to produce 200 bikes because it is more economical to purchase these materials in larger quantities.

Figure 9-27: Procurement process (external)

Figure 9-28 illustrates the balances in the accounts payable (vendor) subledger account and the general ledger account at the conclusion of the procurement process. The FI impacts occur in the last three steps of the process—receive shipment (goods receipt), receive invoice from vendor, and make payment to vendor. The 200 units of raw materials are valued at $480 each for a total of $96,000.

Finally, Table 9-8 illustrates the material valuation after the procurement process is completed. The quantity and value of raw materials in Dallas have increased.

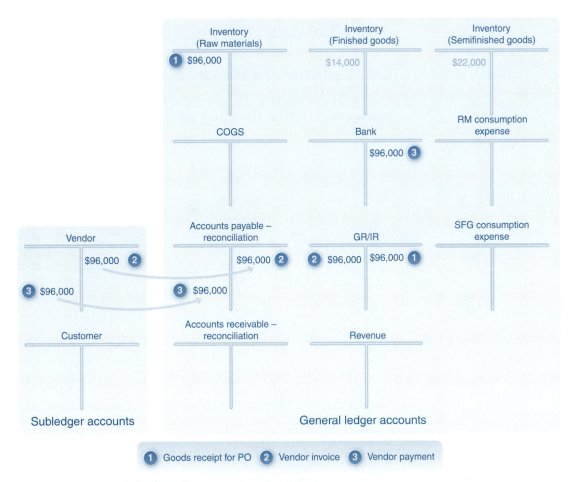

Figure 9-28: Account balances after external procurement

Plant	Stock (DXTR3000)	Standard price	Value
Dallas	Unrestricted: 0	$1,400	$0
San Diego	Unrestricted: 10	$1,400	$14,000
Total GBI	Unrestricted: 20		$14,000

Plant	Stock (TRWA1000)	Standard price	Value
Dallas	Unrestricted: 200	$110	$22,000
Total GBI	Unrestricted: 200		$22,000

Plant	Stock (Raw materials)	Standard price	Value
Dallas	Unrestricted: 200	$480	$96,000
Total GBI	Unrestricted: 200		$96,000

Table 9-8: Material valuation after procurement

Demo 9.14: Execute procurement process

5: PRODUCTION PROCESS—CONTINUED

Once GBI has received the raw materials from Space Bike Composites, the production process can continue (Figure 9-29).

Figure 9-29: Production process—continued

The account balances and material valuation after production has been completed are illustrated in Figure 9-30 and Table 9-9, respectively. The steps that have an FI impact are the goods issue and goods receipt. All three steps have a CO impact. During goods issue, the raw materials and semifinished goods needed to produce the 50 bikes are issued to the production order. This action results in a decrease in the quantity and value of the inventory of raw materials and semifinished goods.

The material accounts are credited, and the consumption accounts are debited. At this time, material and FI documents are created. These material costs are debited to the production order as actual costs (CO impact). After the bikes are produced and confirmed, they are received into finished goods inventory. Recall that the confirmation step has a CO impact in the form of a transfer of labor costs from the work centers to the production order. The goods receipt step increases the quantity and value of finished goods. At this point, the finished goods inventory account is debited, and the manufacturing output settlement account is credited (FI impact). In addition, the production order is credited by the value of the finished goods (CO impact). Since there is no variance between the planned and actual costs in our scenario, additional settlement steps discussed in Chapter 6 are not necessary.

Demo 9.15: Complete production

6: INVENTORY MANAGEMENT (STO)—CONTINUED

When the bikes have been received into inventory, the requirement in the STO can be addressed (Figure 9-31). A goods issue against the STO is executed in Dallas. This action results in a decrease in the inventory in Dallas and an increase

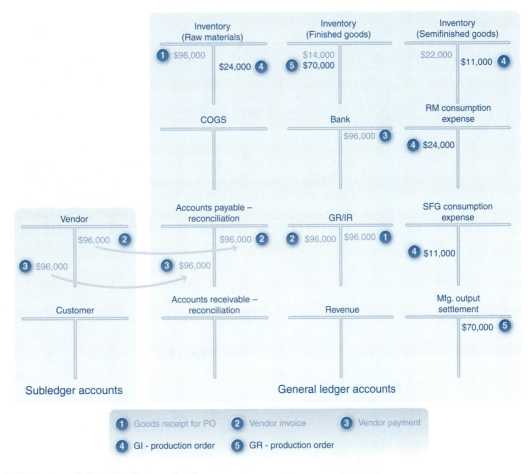

Figure 9-30: Account balances after production

Plant	Stock (DXTR3000)	Standard price	Value
Dallas	Unrestricted: 50	$1,400	$70,000
San Diego	Unrestricted: 10	$1,400	$14,000
Total GBI	Unrestricted: 60		$84,000

Plant	Stock (TRWA1000)	Standard price	Value
Dallas	Unrestricted: 100	$110	$11,000
Total GBI	Unrestricted: 100		$11,000

Plant	Stock (Raw materials)	Standard price	Value
Dallas	Unrestricted: 150	$480	$72,000
Total GBI	Unrestricted: 150		$72,000

Table 9-9: Material valuation after production

Figure 9-31: Inventory management—continued

in the inventory in San Diego. In addition, a debit and a credit are posted to the finished goods inventory account (Figure 9-32). Recall, however, that the quantity in San Diego has the status in transit (Table 9-10). When the bikes reach San Diego, the plant completes a goods receipt to change the status from in transit to unrestricted use (Table 9-11). There is no FI impact at the time of the goods receipt.

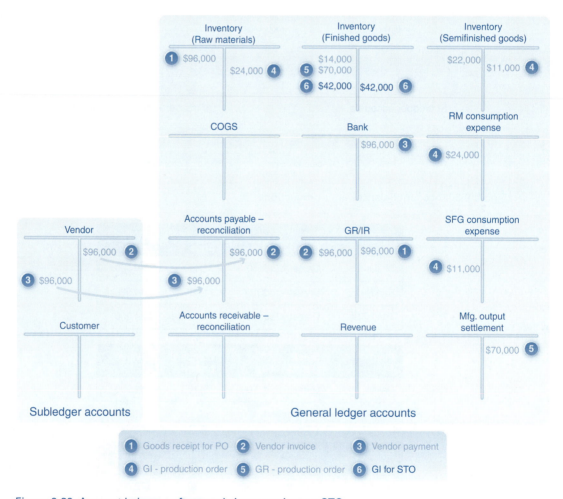

Figure 9-32: Account balances after goods issue against an STO

Plant	Stock (DXTR3000)	Standard price	Value
Dallas	Unrestricted: 20	$1,400	$28,000
San Diego	Unrestricted: 10 In transit: 30	$1,400	$56,000
Total GBI	Unrestricted: 30 In transit: 30		$84,000

Valuation for raw materials and semifinished goods is unchanged

Table 9-10: Material valuation after goods issue against STO

Plant	Stock (DXTR3000)	Standard price	Value
Dallas	Unrestricted: 20	$1,400	$28,000
San Diego	Unrestricted: 40	$1,400	$56,000
Total GBI	Unrestricted: 60		$84,000

Valuation for raw materials and semifinished goods is unchanged

Table 9-11: Material valuation after goods receipt against STO

Demo 9.16: Complete GI and GR for STO

7: WAREHOUSE MANAGEMENT PROCESS RELATED TO STO

When the bikes are received in San Diego, warehouse employees place them in the interim storage area and complete a goods receipt. The ERP system will automatically create a transfer requirement that triggers the WM process (Figure 9-33). In response, a transfer order is created that authorizes the warehouse employees to place the materials in bins. The bikes are moved into specific storage bins, and the transfer order is confirmed.

Figure 9-33: Warehouse management steps

Demo 9.17: Complete WM steps related to STO

8: FULFILLMENT PROCESS—CONTINUED

Once the bikes are in stock in San Diego, the fulfillment process, which was interrupted due to a shortage of inventory, can proceed to the shipping step (Figure 9-34). The first task in the shipping step is to create a delivery document, which authorizes warehouse personnel to pick, pack, and ship the order. There is no material or FI impact at this time. Recall that in the fulfillment process these impacts occur at the time of the goods issue.

Figure 9-34: Fulfillment process—continued

Demo 9.18: Create delivery for sales order

9: WAREHOUSE MANAGEMENT PROCESS RELATED TO FULFILLMENT

The storage locations in San Diego are warehouse managed. Therefore, a transfer order is created for the delivery document (Figure 9-35). The transfer order is used to move the bikes from the storage bins to the interim shipping storage area. Once this movement is completed, the transfer order is confirmed. Warehouse management steps do not have a material impact or an FI impact.

Figure 9-35: Warehouse management process

Demo 9.19: Complete WM steps related to sales order

10: FULFILLMENT PROCESS—CONCLUDING STEPS

Finally, when the bikes have been moved into the interim shipping area, the goods issue task in the shipping step can be completed (Figure 9-36). When GBI has completed the shipping steps, it then focuses on customer billing and payment.

Figure 9-36: Fulfillment process—concluding steps

The goods issue task has a material impact and an FI impact. It results in updates to the GL accounts and the creation of material and FI documents. Both billing and payment processing have an impact on the GL. In addition, the goods issue and billing steps provide data for profitability analysis in controlling. The FI and material consequences are illustrated in Figure 9-37 and Table 9-12, respectively.

The goods issue reduces the quantity and value of the finished goods. The finished goods inventory account is credited by the value of the shipment, and the cost of goods sold account is debited. Valuation occurs at the standard price of the material. At the time of billing, the customer account in the accounts receivable subledger is debited, and the revenue account is credited. The debit

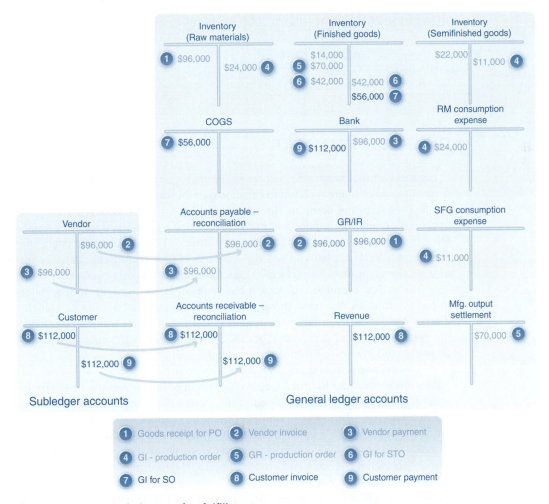

Figure 9-37: Account balances after fulfillment

Plant	Stock (DXTR3000)	Standard price	Value
Dallas	Unrestricted: 20	$1,400	$28,000
San Diego	Unrestricted: 0	$1,400	$0
Total GBI	Unrestricted: 20		$28,000

Valuation for raw materials and semifinished goods is unchanged

Table 9-12: Material valuation after fulfillment

to the customer account automatically results in a debit to the corresponding reconciliation account in the GL. These entries are based on the selling price of the bikes. Finally, when GBI receives RMB's payment, it credits RMB's customer account (and the reconciliation account), and it debits the bank account by the amount of the payment.

Demo 9.20: Complete fulfillment steps

CHAPTER SUMMARY

In the real world of business operations, processes are never as clean or as simple as they have been depicted in this book. In this chapter, we have attempted to illustrate both the complex interdependencies among processes across the organization and the impact that individual decisions can have for subsequent steps in the process or for related processes. Business must make their decisions, both large and small, with an acute awareness of these interdependencies and of the potential impact each decision can have across the organization.

In the first scenario GBI took a customer order for trading goods, determined whether to purchase those goods from an external vendor or transfer them from another warehouse, completed the purchase or transfer, managed the inventory of those received goods, and then completed the picking, packing, shipping, and invoicing for those goods to the customer.

The second scenario added the production process to address the need to fulfill a customer order for manufactured goods. In order to meet the needs of the production process, many additional steps were added that involved the sourcing and transfer of the raw materials needed to produce the finished goods. Throughout both processes, we kept track of the financial and material impacts of processes steps, and we illustrated the key role of data, decision making, and collaboration between and among functional departments in executing the processes efficiently. For example, some of these steps involved collaboration between GBI's Miami and Dallas warehouses. In addition, many decisions made throughout the process required real-time data from the ERP system.

This chapter also highlighted the central role of financial accounting in the execution of business processes by identifying the financial impact at each step of the process. Nearly every action that a company takes, from the smallest decisions on the shop floor to the most sweeping strategic decisions in the boardroom, has an impact on the company's financial status. Monitoring and managing the financial impact of process execution is fundamental to ensuring that a company is operating efficiently and that management always has a clear picture of the financial status of the enterprise.

By this point you should have a keen appreciation of the role of an integrated ERP system in the holistic execution of processes within an enterprise. Imagine if all of the steps in this chapter had to be executed in various disconnected departmental applications and employees in each group had no visibility into the activities of other groups. Going further, imagine the financial and managerial accounting nightmare involved in trying to track the impact of each activity simultaneously in each disparate system.

This textbook is the foundation for process awareness and knowledge. As you acquire more experience in the workplace, you will undoubtedly refer back to the concepts you have just learned. The information covered in this textbook represents the fundamental concepts that govern the operations of every large and medium-sized (and, increasingly, small) company on the planet. The knowledge you have gained from this textbook will provide you with a distinct advantage in the workplace. Appreciation for the role of business processes in the operations of companies coupled with hands-on exposure to the capabilities of the world's leading ERP system for executing and managing business processes will serve you well for the rest of your career.

REVIEW QUESTIONS

1. Explain the various strategies for the procurement, fulfillment, and production processes.

2. Explain the role of inventory in reducing the interdependence among processes.

3. Identify and discuss the steps in the integrated process that include the procurement, fulfillment, and IWM processes. Analyze the financial and material impacts of the various process steps.

4. Identify and discuss the steps in the integrated process that include the procurement, fulfillment, production, and IWM processes. Analyze the financial and material impacts of the various process steps.

5. Prepare a process diagram that displays the steps that GBI must execute in order to fill a customer order, based on the five assumptions listed below. Make certain to include the financial and material impacts of each step as illustrated in the chapter.

   a. Rocky Mountain Bikes has ordered 250 road helmets (RHMT 1000) from GBI.

   b. The San Diego plant has 50 road helmets valued at a moving average price of $25.13 each

    c. The Miami plant has 400 road helmets valued at a moving average price of $25.25.

    d. GBI has decided to move 100 road helmets from Miami to San Diego and purchase 300 helmets from Spy Gear at $25.54 each.

    e. GBI sells road helmets for $50 each.

EXERCISES

Exercises for this chapter are available on *WileyPLUS*.

Index